Contagious

CULTURES, CARRIERS, AND
THE OUTBREAK NARRATIVE

Priscilla Wald

Duke University Press   Durham and London   2008

© 2008 Duke University Press

9780822341536

Designed by C. H. Westmoreland
Typeset in Warnock Pro with Gotham display by
Keystone Typesetting, Inc.

Library of Congress Cataloging-in-Publication Data
and republication acknowledgments appear on the last
printed pages of this book.

In loving memory of Stanley I. Wald

Contents

Acknowledgments

It is with great pleasure that I acknowledge the people, communities, and organizations that have enabled me to write this book. I have been extremely fortunate in finding so many generous and passionate interlocutors who have challenged me to think ever more deeply about the questions that intrigued me and to push past my own assumptions to see those questions in new ways. I have learned more from them than I can put into words and could not have gotten this far without them. I regret that I do not have space to acknowledge everyone to whom I owe thanks, but please know how grateful I am to all of you.

I would like to thank the Cornell University Society for the Humanities for the fellowship support that gave me time and resources to work on this project as well as a wonderful community in which to do so. Special thanks to Mary Pat Brady, Laura Brown, Kate McCullough, and Shirley Samuels for the intellectual and social camaraderie during that year and beyond.

I have been especially lucky in having had assistance that went well beyond research from Monique Allewaert, Lauren Coats, Nihad Farooq, Erin Gentry, Meredith Goldsmith, Elizabeth Klimasmith, Gretchen Murphy, Eden Osucha, and Britt Rusert. Every aspect of the book is better because of their research skills, thoughtful commentary, and helpful insights. Thanks as well to Katherine Buse for patient and timely research assistance in the final days of copy editing.

For conversations that significantly improved this book and every other aspect of my work, I wish to thank Srinivas Aravamudan, Houston A. Baker Jr., David Brady, Rachael Brady, Sherryl Broverman, Ana Mari Cauce, Vincent Cheng, Robert Cook-Deegan, Kathryn Cook-Deegan, Lauren Dame, Wai Chee Dimock, Michael Elliott, Lisa Freeman, Susan Gillman, Gerald

Graff, Theresa Goddu, Sally Hicks, Karla F. C. Holloway, Howard Hor-
witz, Kelly Jarrett, Ranjana Khanna, Frances Kerr, Karen Krahulik, Mary
Layoun, Marilee Lindemann, Joshua Miller, Joycelyn Moody, Dana Nelson,
Marjorie Perloff, Charlotte Pierce-Baker, Janice Radway, Jennifer Reardon,
Augusta Rohrbach, Teemu Ruskola, Karen Sanchez-Eppler, Laurie Shan-
non, Maeera Shreiber, Nikhil Singh, Barbara Herrnstein Smith, Martha Nell
Smith, Shawn Michelle Smith, Maura Spiegel, Charlotte Sussman, Nancy
Tomes, Marianna Torgovnick, Maurice Wallace, Rebecca Wanzo, Lisa
Weasel, and Deborah Elise White, and to remember lovingly and gratefully
Gila Bercovitch, Charlotte Bonica, and Gillian Brown.

The members of my writing groups at Columbia University, the University of Washington, and Duke University made the process of writing richer
and much more fun than it would have been without them. For their commitment to the kind of collective vision and friendships that come out of
such groups, for their engaged responses to my work, and for sharing their
work in progress with me, I thank Linda Green, Zita Nunes, Maggie Sale,
Karen Van Dyck, Judith Weisenfeld, and Angela Zito; Christine DiStefano,
Susan Glenn, Angela Ginorio, Caroline Chung Simpson, Matthew Sparke,
and Shirley Yee; Ann Anagnost, Lucy Jarosz, Susan Jeffords, Victoria Law-
son, Lorna Rhodes, and Laurie Sears; Elena Glasberg, Cannon Schmitt, and
Dana Seitler; Anne Allison, Adrienne Davis, Laura Edwards, and Maureen
Quilligan.

For invaluable and generous advice, criticism, and much-needed encour-
agement on early drafts of the material in this book, I thank Dale Bauer, Jodi
Dean, and Gordon Hutner, and, at later stages, Nancy Armstrong, Thomas
Ferraro, Elaine Freedgood, Sean Metzger, David Palumbo-Liu, Julie Tetel,
and Gregory Tomso. I also thank Rita Charon and the anonymous reader
for Duke University Press for their careful and gracious reader's reports,
which improved the manuscript considerably, and Jan Boltman for her
excellent editorial eye. I am fortunate to have the opportunity to work with
the marvelous staff and editors at Duke University Press and have witnessed the care shown to every book that comes through the process.
Special thanks to Pam Morrison, Steve Cohn, Ken Wissoker, and the ever-
patient Reynolds Smith.

For cheerfully agreeing to read endless drafts and have one more conversation about minutiae, big ideas, and everything in between, for insights
and inspiration offered without my having to ask, and for kind words and
laughter when I most needed them, heartfelt thanks to Cathy N. David-
son, David Eng, Amy Kaplan, Robert Mitchell, Kathy Psomiades, Maureen
Quilligan, and Alys Eve Weinbaum.

Three people have been more than patient during the many years in which I was working on this project. Even when they were young and wondered if Mom were in the office or out of town, Evan and Nathaniel Donahue were generous, loving, and accepting. With Joseph Donahue, they have taught me to laugh, to care, to think and to learn in ways I could not have imagined, and to notice and celebrate the most important aspects of life. During the years of this project, Evan and Nathaniel have grown into insightful readers and thinkers as well and have contributed their considerable wit and wisdom to this project. To my most treasured companions and inspirations, Joseph, Evan, and Nathaniel, I express here in writing what I hope I convey to you daily: how grateful I am to you for who you are and how much you have inspired and taught me about everything.

Infection in the sentence breeds. . . .

—EMILY DICKINSON

Introduction

When the World Health Organization (WHO) issued a global alert on 12 March 2003, the especially virulent and "unexplained atypical pneumonia" soon to be known as severe acute respiratory syndrome (SARS) had already crossed a dozen national borders.[1] The disease had surfaced in China's Guangdong Province during the previous November, and a worldwide research effort soon identified "the first novel infectious disease epidemic of the 21st century, caused by a brand-new coronavirus."[2] Epidemiologists rushed to identify its source and the means and routes of its transmission; journalists scrambled to inform the public of the danger; and medical researchers labored to find a cure or at least produce a vaccine. Through their accounts of the outbreak, they quickly turned SARS into one of the "emerging infections" that had been identified as a phenomenon two decades earlier.[3]

While the coronavirus was new to medical science, the scenario of disease emergence was entirely familiar, and it facilitated the worldwide response to SARS. Accounts of prior disease outbreaks helped epidemiologists identify and respond to the problem. Such accounts also supplied points of reference for journalists seeking to inform the lay public about the spreading infection. Even medical researchers relied on their knowledge of similar microbes as they worked to understand the unfamiliar one. As these precedents allowed experts to make sense of a new situation, they also shaped what they saw and how they responded. The question simmering beneath even the most sedate accounts was whether this disease, with its unknown origins and alarming mortality rate, might be "the coming plague": the species-threatening event forecast by scientists and journalists and dramatized in fiction and film in the closing decades of the twentieth century.[4]

That possibility informs what I call "the outbreak narrative," an evolving story of disease emergence that I will chronicle herein.[5] Following the introduction of the human immunodeficiency virus (HIV) in the mid-1980s, accounts of newly surfacing diseases began to appear with increasing frequency in scientific publications and the mainstream media worldwide. These accounts put the vocabulary of disease outbreaks into circulation and introduced the concept of "emerging infections." The repetition of particular phrases, images, and story lines produced a formula that was amplified by the extended treatment of these themes in the popular novels and films that proliferated in the mid-1990s. Collectively, they drew out what was implicit in all of the accounts: a fascination not just with the novelty and danger of the microbes but also with the changing social formations of a shrinking world.[6]

Contagion is more than an epidemiological fact. It is also a foundational concept in the study of religion and of society, with a long history of explaining how beliefs circulate in social interactions. The concept of contagion evolved throughout the twentieth century through the commingling of theories about microbes and attitudes about social change. Communicable disease compels attention—for scientists and the lay public alike—not only because of the devastation it can cause but also because the circulation of microbes materializes the transmission of ideas. The interactions that make us sick also constitute us as a community. Disease emergence dramatizes the dilemma that inspires the most basic human narratives: the necessity and danger of human contact.

The outbreak narrative—in its scientific, journalistic, and fictional incarnations—follows a formulaic plot that begins with the identification of an emerging infection, includes discussion of the global networks throughout which it travels, and chronicles the epidemiological work that ends with its containment. As epidemiologists trace the routes of the microbes, they catalog the spaces and interactions of global modernity. Microbes, spaces, and interactions blend together as they animate the landscape and motivate the plot of the outbreak narrative: a contradictory but compelling story of the perils of human interdependence and the triumph of human connection and cooperation, scientific authority and the evolutionary advantages of the microbe, ecological balance and impending disaster. The conventions of the paradigmatic story about newly emerging infections have evolved out of earlier accounts of epidemiological efforts to address widespread threats of communicable disease. While I use "the outbreak narrative" to refer to that paradigmatic story, which followed the identification of

HIV, I use "outbreak narratives" broadly to designate those epidemiological stories. I return to the early years of bacteriology and public health in the United States to trace the impact of the discovery of the microbe on attitudes toward social interactions and collective identity that characterize the outbreak narrative of disease emergence.

Outbreak narratives and *the* outbreak narrative have consequences. As they disseminate information, they affect survival rates and contagion routes. They promote or mitigate the stigmatizing of individuals, groups, populations, locales (regional and global), behaviors, and lifestyles, and they change economies. They also influence how both scientists and the lay public understand the nature and consequences of infection, how they imagine the threat, and why they react so fearfully to some disease outbreaks and not others at least as dangerous and pressing. It is therefore important to understand the appeal and persistence of the outbreak narrative and to consider how it shapes accounts of disease emergence across genres and media. That is the project of this book. I am motivated in this work by my conviction that an analysis of how the conventions of the outbreak narrative shape attitudes toward disease emergence and social transformation can lead to more effective, just, and compassionate responses both to a changing world and to the problems of global health and human welfare.

WHEN MYTH MEETS MEDICINE

The terms of the familiar story surfaced in the earliest media accounts of "the first novel infectious disease epidemic of the 21st century."[7] A *New York Times* article promising to explain "How One Person Can Fuel an Epidemic" began, typically, with the dramatis personae of an unfolding tragedy: "A child in China so infectious that he is nicknamed 'the poison emperor.' A Chinese doctor who infects 12 fellow guests in his Hong Kong hotel, who then fly to Singapore, Vietnam and Canada. An elderly Canadian woman who infects three generations of her family."[8] Their unwitting role in the spread of the new virus turned these unfortunate sufferers into stock characters of a familiar tale. The epidemiological precedent of an "index case" responsible for subsequent outbreaks quickly transformed these figures from victims to agents—and embodiments—of the spreading infection. A twenty-six-year-old Singaporean flight attendant, for example, became infamous for "importing" the disease from China. It killed her parents and pastor, sickened other members of her family and community, and turned her into a national scapegoat when Singapore's minister of health announced at a press conference in early April that she "infected the whole lot of us."⁹

She was one among the SARS "superspreaders," as the media termed the "hyperinfective" individuals who ostensibly fostered infection by "spewing germs out like teakettles."¹⁰ The media treatment of superspreaders survived the scientific refutation of the concept, fueled by the regular appearance of their more notorious predecessors. The *Times* piece, for example, explained that "Gaetan Dugas, the gay airline attendant blamed for much of the early spread of AIDS in North America who was dubbed Patient Zero in Randy Shilts's book 'And the Band Played On,' would be considered a superspreader like Typhoid Mary because he willfully infected others" (A1). This description attributed intentionality to the superspreader, a term that was meant to refer only to someone who infects large numbers of people. The metamorphosis of infected people into superspreaders is a convention of the outbreak narrative, in which human carriers rhetorically (or, in some of the fiction, literally) bring the virus itself to life.

Yet even the most determined superspreaders could not do the work of infection without a conducive environment; SARS coverage dramatized the danger of human contact in an interconnected world. Photographs featured the fearful image of human interdependence in the masks sported by shoppers, store owners, flight attendants, and pilots, even by small children as they walked to school or pirouetted in ballet class. The masks depicted what SARS threw into relief: human beings' futile efforts to defend themselves against the threat of illness in the daily interactions made global by contemporary transportation and commerce. Human networks became the conduits of viral destruction. As one Singapore newspaper reported in early April 2003, it "took only a few dry coughs in Hongkong to spread the deadly Sars virus to seven people and kill the World Health Organisation (WHO) doctor who first identified it. And it took only a few air passengers for the illness to reach about 20 countries in Asia, North America and Europe" and for the WHO to declare the disease "'a worldwide health threat.'"¹¹ The Singaporean woman identified as a SARS superspreader was, like Gaetan Dugas, a flight attendant. The Chinese doctor traveled by bus from Guangzhou (in Guangdong Province), where he had been treating pneumonia patients, to Hong Kong, where he stayed in the Hotel Metropole. Other guests at the hotel who became infected included a businessman, who brought the disease to Vietnam, and the elderly Canadian woman mentioned in the *Times* piece, who brought it to Toronto.¹² The long incubation period was, according to one chronicler of the outbreak, "one of [the] most sinister aspects" of SARS, transforming infected individuals into "precisely [the] mechanism of contagion that caused panic in afflicted cities. That man next to you on the train, that lady coughing across the aisle—suddenly the means and modes of transit were rife with potential superspreaders."[13]

In these accounts superspreaders and worldwide interdependence turned the simplest interactions potentially fatal on a global scale. "A Shrinking World Raises the Risk for Global Epidemics," announced the *South China Morning Post* in the early days of SARS coverage; in the *New York Times* the author and physician Abraham Verghese blamed the threat of a pandemic on the interconnected "Way We Live Now."[14] A May 2003 article in *Newsweek*, "The Mystery of SARS," helped tell the story with photographs. A shared caption turned adjacent shots of a masked Lufthansa crew in an airport and a duck pen just outside of Guangzhou into an account of the changing spaces of globalization and their intrinsic dangers: "Fear of SARS prompts a Lufthansa crew to wear masks in the Hong Kong airport; the virus may have been born on a farm like the one above in Guangzhou, China, where animals and people live close together."[15] The conjoined images narrate the journey of SARS from its alleged origins on a "farm" in the midst of a metropolis to the routes of global commerce and transportation through which it spread. The juxtapositions supply the connections, plotting the routes of the disease from the duck pen, which suggests a lack of cleanliness and propriety—human beings living in close proximity to their animals, as in preindustrial times—to the airports and cities of the global village.[16]

Speculation shades into explanation, as the visual authority of the images obscures the caption's "may have." An accompanying article in the same issue of *Newsweek*, entitled "How Progress Makes Us Sick," reinforces the narrative of the photographs in its account of the new disease:

> The novel coronavirus that causes the syndrome emerged from Guangdong, the same Chinese province that delivers new flu viruses to the world most years. Pigs, ducks, chickens and people live cheek-by-jowl on the district's primitive farms, exchanging flu and cold germs so rapidly that a single pig can easily incubate human and avian viruses simultaneously. The dual infections can generate hybrids that escape antibodies aimed at the originals, setting off a whole new chain of human infection. The clincher is that these farms sit just a few miles from Guangzhou, a teeming city that mixes people, animals and microbes from the countryside with travelers from around the world. You could hardly design a better system for turning small outbreaks into big ones.[17]

sinister
Long
incubation

"Fear of SARS prompts a Lufthansa crew to wear masks in the Hong Kong airport . . .

The description locates the problem of SARS less in its novelty than in its familiarity as one among many "frightening new maladies" awaiting imminent release into the circuits of a global infrastructure. The piece offers HIV/AIDS as an important precedent of how "we placed ourselves in the path of the virus, we moved it around the world, and we're well poised to do it again" and explains that what turned a virus "into a holocaust was not just a new infectious agent but a proliferation of roads, cities and airports, a breakdown of social traditions, and the advent of blood banking and needle sharing."[18] Specific diseases blur together as emerging infections map the changing spaces, relationships, practices, and temporalities of a globalizing

. . . the virus may have been born on a farm like the one above in Guangzhou, China, where animals and people live close together." *Newsweek*, 5 May 2003, 28–29. © Peter Parks/Getty Images and Matthieu Paley/paleyphoto.com.

world. Guangdong exports disease as a commodity in the dangerously promiscuous spaces of a global economy conceived as an ecology.

The images and storyline of the *Newsweek* articles exemplify how social interactions, spaces, and practices as well as the public understanding of a communicable disease are all conceptually reconfigured by their association with one another. The "primitive farms" of Guangzhou, like the "primordial" spaces of African rainforests, temporalize the threat of emerging infections, proclaiming the danger of putting the past in (geographical) proximity to the present. The airport makes Hong Kong, New York, Toronto, and any other major city as much as Guangzhou the backdrop of the

photograph. The *Newsweek* pieces expressed concern about the stigmatizing of groups and spaces that characterized what some critics believed was
an exaggerated response to the threat of SARS; the admonition was in fact a
refrain in some of the media coverage worldwide that speculated about the
role of xenophobia in the tradition of "the Yellow Peril," in what one headline denounced as an "Epidemic of Fear."[19] Yet the depiction of Guangzhou
in *Newsweek* fueled those very biases.

The *Newsweek* accounts fostered "medicalized nativism," a term coined
by the historian Alan Kraut to describe how the stigmatizing of immigrant
groups is justified by their association with communicable disease; it implies the almost superstitious belief that national borders can afford protection against communicable disease.[20] As the *Newsweek* images show, medicalized nativism involves more than superimposing a disease threat on an
unfortunate group. Rather, the disease is associated with dangerous practices and behaviors that allegedly mark intrinsic cultural difference, and it
expresses the destructive transformative power of the group. Representing
the "primitive practices" on the Guangzhou farms as expressive of cultural
identity exemplifies medicalized nativism—in effect, the contagious nature
of those practices.

The temporal frame implicit in the description of certain practices as
"primitive" obscures the understanding of those practices as expressions of
poverty. While the social and spatial transformations of global modernity
exacerbate this poverty, the intrinsic temporality provided by the use of
"primitive" enables contradictory representations of global modernity in
media accounts of SARS: global networks as both threat and solution. It was
"thanks to technology and a spirit of global cooperation" that the virus was
rapidly identified and impeded, according to the first *Newsweek* article, and
the second reported the "good news . . . that the forces making microbes so
mobile are also making them easier to track."[21] SARS was "only the latest
reminder of how powerful [the new global] connections can be," and danger
was only one expression of that power.[22] Displacing the problem of poverty
onto the danger of "primitive practices" allowed these accounts to offer
modernization as a promised solution to, rather than part of the problem
of, emerging infections. In the process, they turned the duck farms of
Guangzhou into relics of an antiquated past rather than spaces of global
modernity.

The transformations, however, exert an insistent pressure partly through
the figure of the disease carrier, who embodies them. Superspreaders "aren't
just interesting because they're atypical," observes Nicholas Thompson of

the *Boston Globe*, "but because they serve as network hubs connecting everyone to everyone else, in a few short hops."[23] They are figures of fascination as well as of fear because of the connections they elucidate. The routes traveled by communicable disease light up the social interactions— the spaces and encounters, the practices and beliefs—of a changing world. That was as true at the beginning of the twentieth century, when healthy human carriers were first identified, as it is at the beginning of the twenty-first. Ideas about contagion register the intrigue and possibility as well as the anxiety generated by those changes.[24] The physiological metamorphosis of human carriers turns them into representational figures of the fact, the danger, and the possibilities of human interdependence in a shrinking world. Their lived experience of the impact of changing social interactions on individuals explains the hold they have had on the public imagination since the identification of the first healthy human carriers of disease in the early years of the twentieth century. An article about scapegoating and SARS in the *Irish Times* acknowledges the power of the figure in a description of the most notorious carrier, "Typhoid Mary," as a "mythic archetype of the pestilent immigrant infecting a healthy Western society."[25] "Typhoid Mary" was the first healthy human carrier of a communicable disease to be identified in the United States, and with "mythic archetype" the author conveys how her routine invocation as a point of reference has turned her into a stereotype, the paradigm of the superspreader. Critical of the stigmatizing, he uses "mythic" synonymously with false belief, but the more specialized meaning of the term aptly describes the representational potency of this paradigmatic figure and of the outbreak narrative to which the figure is central.

A myth is an explanatory story that is not specifically authored, but emerges from a group as an expression of the origins and terms of its collective identity. Its strong emotional appeal derives from and affirms the fundamental values, hierarchies, and taxonomies that are the preconditions of that identity. Mircea Eliade identifies myths by mood and plot: the sense of timelessness and renewal, of a connection to origins and sacredness, associated with "a periodic re-entry into Time primordial," where a primal struggle between destruction and endurance is repeatedly reenacted, and Claude Lévi-Strauss locates their appeal in their structure, which enables the coexistence of powerful social contradictions.[26] While "myth" is frequently a term associated with "primitive" cultures or used colloquially, as in the *Irish Times* article, to refer to a fictitious belief, myths remain a significant expression of theologically or supernaturally inflected collective identity in the contemporary moment. I follow Bruce Lincoln in defining myth as "a small class of stories that possess both credibility and *authority*," which they derive from their expression "of paradigmatic truth" and through which they "evoke the sentiments out of which society is actively constructed," and Joseph Mali in his use of the term to describe "the narratives that express and explain the beliefs in the common origins and destinies that alone turn the new 'imagined communities' into real, because very old, ones."[27] Especially prevalent during times of rapid social transformation, those stories articulate the "moral norms and social forms of life" as enduring truths.[28] Microbial invasions take a mythic turn when they are cast as the response of the Earth itself to human beings who have ventured into primordial places they should not disturb. Understood alternatively as defensive and vengeful, this primal reaction is a recurring feature of outbreak accounts not only in fiction and film but also in scientific and journalistic descriptions (where the term *primordial* appears frequently).

The carrier is the archetypal stranger, both embodying the danger of microbial invasion (most explicitly in the human-viral hybrids with whom I end this study) and transforming it into the possibility for rejuvenation and growth. "An ancient Muslim proverb has it that anyone who stays in a land where there is epidemic disease is a martyr and blessed," notes a writer in the *Boston Globe*.[29] Even more so the carrier, who both suffers and represents the sins of the modern world. This figure embodies not only the forbidden intrusions, the deep connections, and the most essential bonds of human communion but also the transformative power of communicable disease. Figures such as Typhoid Mary and Patient Zero become mythic in these accounts because of the simultaneous demonic and representative, even redemptive, but also distinctly social—one might even say, theosocial —functions that they perform.

Contemporary narratives of emerging infections register the influence of earlier accounts of plagues and theories of contagion, contemporary scientific explanations and social concerns. These narratives are critiques of socioeconomic inequities and titillating tales of apocalyptic struggles with primordial earth demons, hard-headed analyses of environmental exhaustion and hopeful stories of timeless renewal. As they simultaneously forecast the imminent destruction and affirm the enduring foundations of community, they offer myths for the contemporary moment, which explains the imaginative hold and the persistence of the story that I am calling "the outbreak narrative." The consequences in all of these realms when medicine meets myth is the subject of this book.

Across epochs and cultures, plagues have been formative in human existence and speculation. *The Iliad* and *Oedipus Rex* begin with plagues brought on by the transgressions of a king.[30] Plagues are the language of the gods' displeasure, and in learning to read that language, the kings come to understand themselves to be the unwitting source of their peoples' suffering. The plagues force them to assume responsibility for their actions, as they illustrate the relationship between the group and an anomalous individual.

The public-health historian George Rosen documents the development of "scientific" theories of epidemics as they suffused explanations of the sacred in Greece, culminating in a "great liberation of thought . . . during the fifth and fourth centuries B.C."[31] Observation suggested the transmissibility of certain diseases, but their source remained a mystery and was attributed to an imbalance between human beings and their environment.[32] Religious, social, and environmental explanations of communicable disease intermingled, and they were joined, gradually, by contagionist theories. Girolamo Fracastoro first articulated these theories in his 1546 book *De contagione, contagiosis morbis et eorum curatione* (*On Contagion, Contagious Diseases, and Their Treatment*), wherein he introduced the idea of seeds (*seminaria*) of disease.

For its earliest chroniclers—the physician Hippocrates, the historian Thucydides—plague ravaged the social order as much as it did individual bodies. The collapse of social relations, rituals, and institutions was the focus as well of later literary treatments, from Boccaccio's *The Decameron* (ca. 1350) to Daniel Defoe's *A Journal of the Plague Year* (1721), Charles Brockden Brown's *Arthur Mervyn* (1799), and Mary Shelley's *The Last Man* (1826). When communicable disease makes it dangerous to congregate and life threatening to minister to the sick, such collapses are not surprising. And the psychological numbing attendant on disasters of great magnitude compounds the dissolution of social organization. Boccaccio describes a lack of mourning and observes that "no more respect was accorded to dead people than would nowadays be shown towards dead goats. For it was quite apparent that the one thing which, in normal times, no wise man had ever learned to accept with patient resignation (even though it struck so seldom and unobtrusively), had now been brought home to the feeble-minded as well, but the scale of the calamity caused them to regard it with indifference."[33] And Defoe laments that the "Danger of immediate Death to ourselves, took away all Bowels of Love, all Concern for one another."[34]

Yet these same depictions also suggest that the experience of a communicable-disease epidemic could evoke a profound sense of social interconnection: communicability configuring community. In *The Decameron* the plague insists on the connections from which people hope to flee: "Whenever those suffering from it mixed with people who were still unaffected, it would rush upon these with the speed of a fire racing through dry or oily substances that happened to be placed within its reach." Before concrete evidence of microbes, the spread of disease appeared to be a mystical force as "it also seemed to transfer the sickness to anyone touching the clothes or other objects which had been handled or used by its victims" (51). These bonds cannot be refused, and recognition of their indissolubility motivates the youthful protagonists of *The Decameron* to affirm basic social principles both in the ritualized society that they design and in the stories that they tell.

An epidemic was a shared experience on multiple levels. The narrator of Mary Shelley's *The Last Man* describes how the disasters of the plague "came home to so many bosoms, and, through the various channels of commerce, were carried so entirely into every class and division of community."[35] Contagion was the color of belonging, social as well as biological. The common susceptibility of all people attested to the common bonds of humanity, and the idea of a plague as a great equalizer, affecting rich and poor, worldly and devout, was a regular theme in the literature. Grief itself could mark those bonds, as in Shelley's description of how a young mother's response to her child's slight illness "proved to her that she was still bound to humanity by an indestructible tie" (388).

Literary depictions of plague-ridden societies evince the complex vocabulary through which members of a ravaged population both respond to epidemics and experience the social connections that make them a community. The word *contagion* means literally "to touch together," and one of its earliest usages in the fourteenth century referred to the circulation of ideas and attitudes. It frequently connoted danger or corruption. Revolutionary ideas were contagious, as were heretical beliefs and practices. Folly and immorality were more often labeled contagious than were wisdom or virtue. The medical usage of the term was no more and no less metaphorical than its ideational counterpart. The circulation of disease and the circulation of ideas were material and experiential, even if not visible. Both displayed the power and danger of bodies in contact and demonstrated the simultaneous fragility and tenacity of social bonds.

Theories of communicability and ideas about the social implications of epidemics circulated together through the many stories told about plagues in history, science, and fiction. In different places and at different times, one or another of the theories would dominate, but they remained more or less in flux until bacteriology, which emerged in the late nineteenth century, demonstrated how specific microbes caused communicable diseases and documented routes of transmission that had hitherto only been suspected. Calling it "the most radical revolution in the history of medicine," Mary Douglas laments that the rise of bacteriology not only altered theories of contagion, but also subsequently affected theories about the earliest religious rituals and social organization. As an anthropologist, she is troubled that the lessons of bacteriology have made it "difficult to think of dirt except in the context of pathogenicity."[36] And she complains that the study of comparative religion, with disciplinary roots in the same moment, has "always been bedeviled by medical materialism" (29), a term that she adapts from William James to name the fallacy of attributing a primarily hygienic explanation to the earliest religious rituals. Analyses performed through the bacteriological lens, she argues, miss the point of prohibitions, which are designed not to forestall disease, but to mark dangerous transgressions—"a symbolic breaking of that which should be joined or joining of that which should be separate" (113)—that result in disease and other forms of divine retribution. Prohibitions light up the margins, where categories get murky; they make social organization both visible and appealing. Hygienic explanations occlude the fact that prohibitions offer symbolic expressions of social organization. Such explanations also obscure how much the social meaning of prohibitions affects the representation and experience of disease and the idea of contagion. "Even if some of Moses's dietary rules were hygienically beneficial," Douglas quips, "it is a pity to treat him as an enlightened public health administrator, rather than as a spiritual leader" (29).

The new science supplied a vocabulary that shaped contemporary ideas not only about the distant past but also about interactions and practices in the current moment. Yet, as Douglas suggests, attitudes toward communicable disease and contagion continued to register their dense history, and dirt and disease remained (and remain) symbolically powerful. Hygienic motivations not only failed to tell the story of ancient religious rituals, but they were also not the full story of more contemporary public-health theories and practices. Public-health administrators in the early twentieth century were not quite the heirs of Moses, but, especially in the midst of an epidemic (or threat of one), they were in their fashion high priests of contagion and community, dispensing the principles of social cohesion through the practices of disease prevention.

For public-health officials, communicable disease was both a medical and a social problem, and they promoted the mutual influence of scientific and social theories of contagion as they drew on the two fields of inquiry. The growth of cities gave rise to what they saw as "promiscuous" social spaces: people literally and figuratively bumping up against each other in smaller spaces and larger numbers than ever before. Microbes thrived in such environments, producing widespread infections that, in turn, provided researchers with the opportunity to study them. At the same time, new cultural encounters inspired social theorists to study group interactions and social ties. Scientists and social theorists often read each other's work, but, more important, they were motivated in their work by related phenomena: the social and medical consequences of the changing spaces and interactions of an increasingly interconnected world. Conceptual exchange between them was inevitable.

Two especially influential theories of the source of social bonds register the conceptual impact of contemporary scientific research. Émile Durkheim and Sigmund Freud both wrote their studies of totemic religion and the origins of social organization—*Elementary Forms of Religious Experience* (1912) and *Totem and Taboo* (1913), respectively—at the height of the bacteriological revolution when microbes were making headlines, and in the two countries, France and Germany, that pioneered work in the field.[37] An interest in the power of contemporary prohibitions and social organization sent both in search of the origins of that organization, and both found in the concept of contagion the principle through which to describe how the mystical force of the sacred inexorably spills into the profane through physical contact or through symbolic association. With *contagion*, they named a sacred force so powerful, Durkheim explained, that even the most "superficial similarity" between objects or ideas was enough to initiate the process.[38] Contagion was a principle of classification that displayed the rationale of social organization and was, therefore, the force that bound people to the relationships that constituted the terms of their existence. It supplied the logic of totemic belonging and allowed the theorists to explain social cohesion. With these accounts, they sought to make the routes of cultural transmission as visible as bacteriologists of their own moment had made pathways of disease transmission. Durkheim believed that with its elucidation of categories, the concept of contagion laid the groundwork "for the scientific explanations of the future" (365). Categories of belonging and theories of microbial infection came together in that most mythic— and most scientific—figure, the human carrier, who formed a link in Freud's study between his patients and "primitive" culture.

Freud wrote *Totem and Taboo* to explain the prevalence of the incest taboo across cultures in social and psychoanalytic rather than medical terms. The story of Oedipus gives his account its narrative frame. Freud begins this story of social origins with the premise that the "two crimes of Oedipus"— incest and patricide—are the source of what "forms the nucleus of perhaps every psychoneurosis."[39] Asserting that these crimes find open expression in "primitive" cultures and early childhood, he fashions his analysis into a myth about social belonging and organization for the modern age. The connection he makes between neuroses and human history begins with what he calls Charles Darwin's "historical" explanation of the incest taboo: his hypothesis, based on observation of animals, of a primitive horde in which the sons' sexual jealousy prompts the father to expel the sons, who eventually band together to kill the father and take his women, their mothers and sisters (125). But Darwin, he explains, did not offer sufficient proof of his hypothesis to establish its authority over other theories. For that proof, Freud turns to psychoanalytic observations of children and analysands and to the story of Oedipus, which is foundational to his theories of both childhood development and psychoneuroses. Attributing to the sons the ambivalence that he had identified in his analysands, Freud slips from his account of Darwin's speculation into past-tense narration to create a scenario in which the sons alleviated their remorse for their deed by animating the father in a totem that they were then forbidden to kill. They also denied themselves their prize by prohibiting sexual relationships with the women of the horde. The hypothesized "primitive horde" becomes the posited "primal horde" (142 n. 1) as Freud transforms Darwin's musings into a story of the origins of religion and society in which the "totem meal" becomes "a repetition and a commemoration of this memorable and criminal deed, which was the beginning of so many things—of social organization, of moral restrictions and of religion" (142).[40]

The story of the primal horde is, of course, the Oedipal drama writ large. Freud's patients' neuroses are the keys to his transformation of the myths— of human origins and of Oedipus—into a theory of civilization. The influence of bacteriology on Freud's thinking surfaces in a figure that recurs in his obsessive patients' fantasies. Describing the resemblance between taboos and the contagious (associational) thinking characteristic of neurosis, Freud notes that certain people or things become "impossible" for his "obsessional patients [who] behave as though the 'impossible' persons and things were carriers of dangerous infection liable to be spread by contact on to everything in their neighborhood" (27). He explains that these persons are "impossible" because of their association (often accidental) for the obsessive patients with forbidden ideas, desires, and even spaces, but he does not address why this impossibility takes the form of communicable disease.

The idea of a healthy human carrier of disease was one of the most publicized and transformative discoveries of bacteriology. It was widely discussed in both the medical literature and the mainstream press in Europe and North America in the early decades of the twentieth century. The identification of such people clarified the routes of disease transmission and revolutionized epidemiology and the practice of public health. Carriers were the dangerous strangers one encountered with alarming frequency in an increasingly interdependent world, and they were the most precious intimates dangerously estranged by the discovery of their carrier state. They made visible the contact that people did not necessarily know they had had—items shared, spaces frequented—as well as those they may not have wished to make known. Carriers were also at the center of the public debates about social responsibility. They put on display, and even helped to foster, changing ideas about the relationship of the individual to the group and to the state as the lessons of bacteriology animated the tension between the right to privacy and the responsibility of the state in the maintenance of public health.[41] When carriers unwittingly caused an outbreak of a communicable disease, the nature of the violation was as uncertain as the locus of blame. They represented the question of culpability in the absence not only of intention but more fundamentally of self-knowledge. It is no wonder, then, that such figures would be available for symbolic appropriation to mark the transgressive associations of Freud's patients.

The question of culpability leads Freud back to Oedipus, who makes his earliest direct appearance in the text in a footnote in which Freud explains that unwitting transgression of a taboo does not mitigate guilt: "The guilt of Oedipus was not palliated by the fact that he incurred it without his knowledge and even against his intention" (68). In Sophocles' play, despite Oedipus' ignorance of his crimes, the plague caused by his transgression necessitates his punishment. In that sense, he anticipates the superspreader: the Singaporean flight attendant who infected a nation, or Typhoid Mary, who made her epidemiological debut just several years prior to the publication of *Totem and Taboo*. Human carriers teach the shared lesson of psycho-analysis and bacteriology: that human beings lack self-knowledge. Like Oedipus, we do not know who—or what—we are. It is what makes us dangerous, and it mandates new codes of conduct.

The nature of the transgression of Freud's Oedipus is at the heart of his punishment; he enacts primal fantasies that are so socially destructive that he must be transformed into a figure of pity and disgust before he can be redeemed. His crimes place him at the portals of civilization, where vio-lence and sexuality must be carefully ritualized. The earliest identified hu-man carriers analogously dramatized the need for new ways of being in a world of newly identified microbes and increasing human contact. The spread of infection required rituals of cleanliness that were implicitly sex-ualized as well. Human carriers readily became scapegoats: examples of the transgressions of the group for which they symbolically suffered.[42] But they were even more important and exemplary for what they displayed. As they became reintegrated (through punishment, treatment, or both), the human carriers, like Oedipus, bore witness to the workings of a transformative social and epidemiological power. Freud's retelling of the Oedipus story mythologizes the lessons of the bacteriological revolution, and it illumi-nates the mythic features of healthy human carriers as they cast the drama of disease outbreaks in terms of a continuing struggle for human survival against the destructive forces of nature and hubris. Nancy Tomes sees in "the tones of awe and apprehension so frequently apparent in early ac-counts of the microbial world . . . the lingering influence of religious and magical views of disease."[43] These views sound more than just the echo of past beliefs. They are the pitch of contagion as it constitutes mythic social bonds that hum with the exquisitely tenacious fragility of an ever-present threat.

Those social bonds are reinforced by the institutional legacy of commu-nicable disease: the policies and practices set in place to prevent or manage devastating outbreaks. Epidemics dramatize the need for regulation with, as George Rosen puts it, "terrifying urgency," and they set in motion what he calls "the administrative machinery for disease prevention, sanitary super-vision, and, in general, protection of community health."[44] They paint the pathways of interdependence with the brush of mortality and can help to overturn or reinforce governing authority. The memory of epidemics, how-ever, is typically harnessed in the service of reinforcement. Rosen shows how epidemics, among other health concerns, fostered the parallel growth of the state and the idea of public health by helping to fashion the concept of a population. A cohesive collection of people offered a way to represent, measure, and enact the increasing centralization of power in the state.

Rosen chronicles the gradual sense, beginning in the sixteenth century, that the supervision and regulation of the health of that population should be the responsibility of the state, and the corresponding alignment of the welfare of the population with the welfare of the state. Different state forms produced a variety of regulatory bodies. Especially influential was the German idea of "the medical police" (*Medizinischepolizei*), a term coined in the mid-eighteenth century, which registered the responsibility—and authority—of the government to create and implement health policy.[45] The slightly later French term *hygiene publique* further developed the idea, firmly establishing, in Michel Foucault's words, "the politico-scientific control of [the] environment."[46] Foucault extends Rosen's analysis into a theory of power that he calls "biopolitics" and describes as "the endeavor . . . to rationalize the problems presented to government practice by the phenomena characteristic of a group of living human beings constituted as a population: health, sanitation, birthrate, longevity, race. . . ."[47] He argues that the concept of public health was formative for modern society, and epidemics were important because they manifested the need for protection in the form of regimented social behavior. Only war could inflict devastation on such a scale, but the violence of war could not rival the inescapability or level of destruction of the worst epidemics that history had recorded. Late-eighteenth-century sanitary practices and public-health policies, which had emerged from the quarantine procedures in Europe of the late Middle Ages, left a spatial legacy as well in the physical organization of cities during this period.[48]

Biopolitics concerns the emergence of institutions, policies, and practices that shaped the contours of a "population." While the language of "social welfare" suggests how and why members of a population might identify with the state, Foucault does not offer a sustained account of the affective experience of a sense of belonging that turns people into "a people." As narratives such as *The Decameron* demonstrate, the social experience of disease, the image of communicability, and the materialization of interdependence that characterize depictions of epidemics suggest an epidemiology of belonging through which people might experience their emergence as "a population." The idea of contagion was demonstrably formative for the experience of "community" in the early years of bacteriology, when Freud and Durkheim were writing.

The discoveries of bacteriology did not emerge through the pure culture of a laboratory. They were, rather, filtered through these complex, even perverse and contradictory, ideas about contagion as they circulated in communicable-disease narratives. Although they found expression in a variety of genres and fields, the narratives were formulated in the terms of epidemiology.[49] Arising originally from the observation of outbreaks of disease, epidemiology supplies the methodology and the story of public health, incorporating data collection and statistical analysis into a narrative that makes sense of the calculations. "As epidemics occur across time and in different places," explains the epidemiologist Thomas C. Timmreck, "each case must be described exactly the same way each time in order to standardize disease investigations. As cases occur in each separate epidemic, they must be described and diagnosed consistently from case to case, using the same diagnostic criteria."[50] Epidemiologists build on precedents from previous outbreaks that they hope will make future outbreaks comprehensible, and ultimately preventable, or at least containable. When epidemiology turns an outbreak of communicable disease into a narrative, it makes the routes of transmission visible and helps epidemiologists anticipate and manage the course of the outbreak. In that transformational capacity, the epidemiological narrative is, like the microscope, a technology, and it is among the epistemological technologies that delineate the membership and scale of a population.

From precedents and standardization a recognizable story begins to surface. Epidemiologists look for patterns. For Timmreck, the job of epidemiologists is to characterize "the distribution of health status, diseases, or other health problems in terms of age, sex, race, geography, religion, education, occupation, behaviors, time, place, person, etc." (2). The scale of their investigation is the group, or population, rather than the individual, and they tell a story about that group in the language of disease and health. "'An outbreak,'" observes the virologist Philip Mortimer, "'like a story, should have a coherent plot.'"[51] In their investigations epidemiologists rely on and reproduce assumptions about what constitutes a group or population, about the definition of pathology and well-being, and about the connections between disease and "the lifestyle and behaviors of different groups" (21). These classifications inform the epidemiological narratives, and they can thereby import cultural assumptions that are substantiated by the authority of medical science and the urgency of a public health threat.

Heather Schell notes that the "statistical techniques for descrying a pattern in seemingly disparate incidents" that epidemiology offers make it "an extremely powerful tool for creating master narratives about the world."[52] When done with attention to narrative detail and to the rhythms by which stories unfold, epidemiological accounts can harness the appeal of detective stories. Such accounts were conspicuously fashioned with that appeal in mind by journalists and scientists in the years following World War II. Both groups saw in epidemiology the chance to tell a good story, and in those stories, the opportunity to promote an important field of inquiry. Paul de Kruif had demonstrated the market for tales of scientific discovery in his bestselling 1926 book, *Microbe Hunters*. Although their work took many of his heroic scientists into the field, de Kruif, a bacteriologist, glorified laboratory research.

It was not a scientist, but a graduate of the first class of Columbia University's school of journalism who first explained the storytelling appeal of epidemiology for a broad audience. Geddes Smith, like de Kruif, had been born in the 1890s, during the early years of bacteriology, and had come of age with the unfolding of the promises of the new science. He saw in epidemiology "the biological drama that lies behind the Black Death—and Mary Lou's sniffle."[53] His instinct for the drama of epidemiology sent his book, *Plague On Us*, into three printings within a decade. In this book Smith exploited the narrative structure and logic of epidemiology, anticipating by nearly half a century the formula that would turn the epidemiological account into an outbreak narrative of disease emergence. *Plague On Us* demonstrates how formulaic—and formative—that story is.

"OF BACTERIA, MOSQUITOES, MICE AND MEN"

Smith is first of all a storyteller, and the brief prologue to his book displays his craft as it establishes the theme of the book: communicable disease is at once (and paradoxically) a foe to be conquered and a fact of life to be accepted. On one hand, Smith lionizes the contemporary scientist and chronicles the victories of modern medicine; on the other hand, he punctuates his account with reminders of the fields still unconquered. Of the "men in search of knowledge," he notes that "nothing is too small for them, nothing (save influenza, perhaps) too large" (1). The ability to track microbes around the globe has conquered at least the superstition that viewed "pestilence" as "something visited on sinners by the angry gods" (1). With the clear-sightedness of science comes the catalog of victories, the epidemics of history that seem consigned to the past. But if the superstitions woven into the formative myths of the Western tradition by Homer, Sopho-cles, Boccaccio, and others have passed, the lessons of classical tragedy emerge in the reminder framed in the question that follows the catalog: "Are we then so wise that we have beaten our parasites?" (1). Hubris, as is well known to most historians and tragedians—especially when, as so often, they are one and the same—always precedes a fall.[54] In the end, writes Smith, "to seek sustenance, multiply, and die is the common lot of bacteria, mosquitoes, mice and men" (156).

Epidemiology dramatizes human beings' mortal struggle with their en-vironment, social and biological. The qualification in the parenthetical "save influenza, perhaps" resurfaces more forcefully in the concluding para-graph of Smith's prologue, the seed of defeat in the flower of victory: "Influ-enza kept step with the last war. If it came tomorrow we could not stop it. The lords of Europe are fighting again. Masses of men are bombed out of their homes and cities, hounded into exile, driven hither and thither in a greater dislocation of ordered living than any rational man would have thought possible. Such a world is in peril of pestilence. It is early to boast" (2). The heroic account of epidemiology is inflected by the shadow of the tragic and familiar tale of hubris and human ambition. It is the shadow tale that comprises the drama of the spread and containment of communicable disease.

No figure better embodied the tension between scientific achievement and the uncontrollable human factor than the healthy human carrier, who was the linchpin of the bacteriological theory of contagion.[55] "It was hard to believe unreservedly in contagion," writes Smith, "when A was sick while B, at his elbow, stayed well, but C, at B's elbow, fell sick of A's disease; men turned naturally enough to the air and stars to explain how infection fell upon both A and C" (130). So the discoveries of bacteriology that allowed scientists to identify and explain the healthy carrier turned superstition to science. Smith equivocates, however, when he observes that "like God in Voltaire's epigram the carrier or missed case would have had to be invented if he had not existed, and now we postulate B—as in the spread of polio-myelitis—even before we prove him" (130).[56] A discovery of the science and an invention of the (narrative) art of epidemiology, the carrier lives Smith's observation that the "chief source of infection for mankind . . . is mankind itself. Most of the communicable diseases from which men suffer are kept in circulation, *like original sin,* by the human race" (129, emphasis added). The metaphor is revealing; communicable disease retains its religious asso-ciations despite the discovery of the microbe. As communicability personified, carriers are its (human) figures, its agents, running the gamut of human agency from unwitting germ disseminators to intentional dispensers of contagion. Human recalcitrance is animated for Smith in the figure of "Typhoid Mary, of dismal fame" (180). As the solution to the puzzle of contagion, carriers also promise a salvation that they finally cannot deliver.

Communicable disease is a function of social interactions, and Smith emphasizes the potential for epidemics that attend the commercialization of air travel. The unprecedented mobile carrier makes especially apparent the intricate networks of human existence and human interdependence. But the carrier does not need literally to travel in a world that has come to rely on the circulation of all kinds of goods. A story of tainted oysters leads Smith to meditate on how "the elaborate system by which" the appetites of fifteen hundred people "were titillated might become the means of broadcasting infection. Some of them inherited the ills of strangers a thousand miles away. It's a complicated world, and only endless vigilance on the part of people we never see makes it tolerably safe to live in" (228). The networks of daily existence have transformed the herd into an amorphous entity constituted through airwaves as well as air travel. Communicable disease marks the increasing connections of the inhabitants of the global village as both biological and social, the communicability of germs and ideas "broadcast" together in an ever more elaborate network of human existence. The explosion of a disease outbreak into an epidemic or pandemic marks, in this formulation, the tragic consequences of human behavior amplified by the web.

Communicable disease illustrates the logic of social responsibility: the mandate to live with a consciousness of the effects of one's actions on others. The idea of a healthy human carrier means that it is possible to constitute a threat without knowing it, making the mandate especially urgent. In the earliest accounts the carrier is frequently a stranger, a figure conventionally marked as an object of desire and fear. But the carrier might also be the uncanny figure of the familiar estranged. Like Oedipus, unaware of who and what he is, and therefore the unwitting source of plague, the carrier confounds categories. In an especially surprising illustration of such confounding, Smith defines children as "immigrants into the human herd— immigrants whose susceptibility dilutes herd resistance and so helps to keep certain diseases in circulation" (141). The observation captures the chaotic and recombinatory nature of communicable disease, as the ultimate familiars become the ultimate strangers. Ironically, they are threatening because of their own susceptibility—because, that is, they are threatened—and the future agents of the community's reproduction carry the threat of its annihilation. By casting children as immigrants, Smith identifies the fundamental instability of community. Communicable disease marks both the potential destruction of the community and the consequences of its survival. It is the figure of a necessary and even generative disequilibrium.

It is also the alibi for the governance mechanisms of the community, which must safeguard its charges against disease. For Smith, anticipating Rosen and Foucault, those efforts are best exemplified by quarantine, particularly at seaports and airports, which marks the "effort to put a fence around an entire nation" (192). With such a barrier, the state imagines the disease as a foreign threat and in fact, in a strategy I explain in chapter 1, uses the disease to imagine the nation as a discrete ecosystem with its own biological as well as social connections. To the model it provides for spatial organization, quarantine imparts the imperative of public health. Healthy carriers pose a particular challenge to quarantine efforts, and therefore to the nation thus conceived (as I discuss in more detail in chapter 2). Bacteriology fashioned a biological explanation of a mythic figure, but the science could not fully shake the mythic inflection.

The unpredictability led epidemiologists, in Smith's account, to look for "a formula for epidemics" (158) or to unravel "the plot of an epidemic" (206). These formulations projected a narrative logic onto epidemics, and the role of epidemiology was at once to read and to write the epidemic as a story of detection with predictive value. Narrative was thus central to epidemiology, which marked the conjunction of art and science, where it epitomized the most profound faith in human achievement. The disease detective stories that Smith places in the middle of *Plague On Us*, although rudimentary, manifest his insight into the assumptions of an emerging field and his prescience about its entertainment value.

DISEASE DETECTIVES

The contours of these epidemiological detective stories began to fill out in the 1950s with the appearance in the popular media of accounts that featured the work of the newly formed and provocatively named Epidemiological Investigation Service (EIS) of the Communicable Disease Center (CDC). *Time* and *Newsweek* published brief articles with the same title, "Disease Detectives," on the same day, 19 January 1953. Both described the formation of the EIS (in 1951) under the leadership of an ambitious public-health officer, Alexander D. Langmuir, who had joined the CDC two years earlier, in 1949. The creation of the EIS was fueled by the anxieties surrounding biological warfare that had intensified with the beginning of the Korean War in 1950. Langmuir, a key player in the politics of institutionalized public health, used those anxieties to argue for the importance of epidemiology and contributed significantly to the building of the CDC.[57] With his flair for public relations, Langmuir may well have initiated stories such as the ones that appeared in *Time* and *Newsweek,* which he viewed as excellent publicity for the EIS and for epidemiology generally. With titles designed to evoke Arthur Conan Doyle's most celebrated detective—"The Case of the Camp Sewage" or "The Case of the Carrot Salad"—they offered brief accounts of mysterious outbreaks solved by Langmuir's disease sleuths.

Similar accounts appeared over the next two decades in such journals as *Reader's Digest* and *Parents' Magazine,* but no one did more to popularize and develop the genre than an enterprising *New Yorker* writer named Berton Roueché.[58] The author of a column entitled "The Annals of Medicine," Roueché had been drawing material from the New York City Health Department when the EIS caught his attention. He approached Langmuir, who quickly recognized the opportunity that Roueché's columns provided to recruit and even train officers for the EIS, as he noted in his introduction to a 1967 collection of Roueché's essays, *The Annals of Epidemiology.*

Both Roueché (in his preface) and Langmuir call attention to the significance of the narrative form of Roueché's stories. Roueché specifically invokes Conan Doyle as his model, but he is quick to point out that his progenitor "derived the Holmesian method from that of the great Edinburgh diagnostician Dr. Joseph Bell." Langmuir also locates "the origins of the science . . . in the narrative descriptions and historical accounts of epidemics."[59] The narrative springs naturally, as he explains it, from the systematic thinking of scientific observers; it represents the discovery and expression of the epidemic's own logic. Langmuir identifies "an attention-winning pattern" that makes Roueché's stories so useful as well as engaging, and, in doing so, he articulates the formula of an outbreak narrative from "a single patient placed in an exact time and location, and with vividly described symptoms" to "the main epidemiological question" of the source, means, and routes of transmission "until all of the pieces of the puzzle fall into logical place and the problem is solved" (xvii). Thus is the epidemiological narrative of the outbreak written. Asserting the derivation of this "pattern" in scientific observation, Langmuir establishes it as intrinsically scientific (hence authoritative): science inherent in the narrative act. The stories derive their authority from their predictability and, in turn, establish the scientific validity of the approach they describe.

They also establish a national context for the disease detectives. *Parents' Magazine* calls them "our national 'disease detectives'" and compares the CDC to the FBI, as does *Reader's Digest* with its article "Medicine's FBI."[60] Microbes are dubbed "public enemies far more dangerous" than the criminals on the FBI's Most Wanted lists.[61] The EIS is the CDC's "surveillance unit" that "keeps watchful eyes on disease outbreaks throughout the world" (21). Global surveillance is here configured as a national public-health necessity born of increasingly global interdependence: because of plane travel, "cholera in Bombay can be an immediate threat to San Francisco, yellow fever in West Africa a potential danger to New Orleans" (21). Thus were the conventions set for the narrative of disease emergence that would surface three decades later.

In the intervening years, as communicable diseases had become increasingly less of a threat, as the widely publicized polio vaccine brought one of the most devastating of them under control, and as epidemics of life-threatening communicable diseases began to fade from historical memory in North America and Europe, epidemiologists increasingly turned their attention to noncommunicable diseases such as cancer and autoimmune conditions, to detrimental collective behavior such as smoking and violence, and to environmental hazards. The global eradication of smallpox led by Donald A. Henderson of the CDC (now named Centers for Disease Control) during the 1970s ushered in a general sanguinity about the threat of communicable-disease outbreaks. It was a short-lived sanguinity, however, and the Cassandras among the tropical- and infectious-disease specialists, who had never ceased their warnings, were proved all too right as the earliest of the so-called emerging diseases burned through entire villages, scarcely noticed until they began to appear in the world's metropolises.

With that appearance came accounts of emerging infections that generated the concept of disease emergence. Globalization was indeed the source of the spread. As foretold, microbes circulated through air travel, commerce, and the circuits of capital, and they materially expressed the predictable contact anxieties. But, as I have suggested, the experience of communicable disease and the idea of contagion evident in these accounts was not new. I offer in chapter 1 an anatomy of emerging-infection accounts in the late twentieth century in the United States. While the United States lagged behind Western Europe both in public-health initiatives in the nineteenth century and in scientific developments in bacteriology in that field's earliest years, the twentieth century witnessed increasing U.S. economic and political dominance in the institutionalization of ideas about global health worldwide. By the end of the century, cultural production would reinforce the importation of these ideas. The "outbreak narrative," while not exclusively a U.S. phenomenon, is part of that production.[62] Its circulation across genres and media makes it at once the reflection and the structuring principle of scientific and journalistic accounts, of novelistic and cinematic depictions of communicable-disease outbreaks, and even of contemporary historical studies of the central role of communicable disease in human history.

I have described the importance of the identification of the healthy human carrier to the stories and history of epidemiology. None is more summoned than Typhoid Mary, and I chronicle in chapter 2 the story of this notorious figure as it was written in the scientific literature and journalism of the early twentieth century. The transformation of Mary Mallon into "Typhoid Mary" was a public-health story that fashioned a vocabulary of social responsibility from the lessons of bacteriology. It reflected a new way of thinking about social relationships and individual responsibilities in the United States in an increasingly interconnected world. And it has become a signature example of the dilemma of public health. In chapter 2 I consider its narrative legacy.

The city was the location of most such public-health stories, and changing ideas about social interactions and urban environments formed their backdrop. Those changes were the subject of the nascent field of urban sociology. I describe in chapter 3 the mutual evolution of theories of cultural and microbial transmission in the work of the sociologist Robert Park and his colleagues in the early years of the Department of Sociology and Anthropology at the University of Chicago. Central to what they called their "science of society" was the concept of "social contagion," which described how the circulation of ideas and attitudes turned individuals into social groups and eventually into cultures. Their explanatory principles of social formations included an ecological vision of interdependence and the figure of the stranger as an agent of dangerous and productive change. With their ideas about social contagion, urban ecologies, and assimilation cycles, Park and his colleagues imagined the transformation of local into national communities in a global context as they formulated what I call a "Communicable Americanism." I show in chapter 3 how the intermingling of social and scientific theories of contagion led to the articulation of a form of collective identity and a principle of belonging that is at the heart of the outbreak narrative.

The image of a cultural "invasion" that Park borrowed from botany and zoology for his study of human ecology would take on a more sinister cast in the paranoid climate that followed World War II. The language of both internal threat ("public enemies") and imminent threat from abroad, as well as the need for surveillance, featured in the *Reader's Digest* article "Medicine's FBI," exemplifies the vocabulary of 1950s virology as it fused with the politics of the Cold War. In chapter 4 I document the impact of both the science and the politics on the idea of contagion and the evolution of the outbreak narrative. Surfacing routinely in outbreak accounts, this language established disease outbreaks as "foreign" or "alien" agents that posed a national threat. In the mainstream media as well as in policy documents the threat found literal expression in invocations of germ warfare; it is evident in the assurance at the conclusion of *Time's* "Disease Detectives" that "public health officers who have had a year's duty in the E.I.S. would be the best-equipped disease detectives if biological warfare should come."[63]

The carrier gained renewed attention in these case studies, embodying both the importance of social responsibility and the need for disease detectives trained to identify such people. These ideas as well as the narrative form were fleshed out in the popular fiction and film of the period, in which the animated virus took a variety of shapes, among them, as Kirsten Ostherr argues, the invading alien of 1950s science fiction.[64] The pod people of Jack Finney's oft-told tale, *The Body Snatchers,* had an especially strong hold on the public imagination and, as I will show, exemplified the epidemiological horror story that would come to endow the outbreak narrative with the conventions of horror. The many retellings of Finney's story demonstrate how it evolved with the changing scientific theories and social concerns, from its novelistic and cinematic incarnations in the 1950s culture of paranoia to its animation in the 1978 film that uncannily forecast the early years of the HIV/AIDS epidemic, which would come to public attention just a few years after its release.

The tempering of the Cold War and the precipitous eulogies for the global threat of communicable disease had made the viral pod people somewhat anachronistic and campy by 1978, but their heirs would resurface with a vengeance, literally, with the identification of HIV and the failure of containment efforts worldwide. HIV/AIDS brought the idea of emerging infections to public consciousness. The devastating epidemic had all the makings of an outbreak narrative, except one: it could not be contained. It is surely the most documented epidemic of all time, but, as I argue in chapter 5, it cannot be directly incorporated into the mythic dimensions of communicable-disease outbreak narratives. Indirectly, however, the HIV/

AIDS epidemic is an informing presence in those narratives in their many manifestations, and the sinister viruses incarnated in the scientific, journalistic, and fictional Patients Zero are among its legacies. These figures look back to the pod people of the 1950s as they herald the bioterrorists of contemporary fiction and film. Tracing the evolution of these characters and the narratives that feature them is central to my aim in this project, which is to understand the appeal and consequences of stories about disease outbreaks and disease emergence generally. The outbreak narrative is conventional and formulaic, but it is also always evolving. Stories of disease emergence in all their incarnations are so powerful because they are as dynamic as the populations and communities that they affect.

Imagined Immunities

1 The image of the desolate African camp decimated by an unknown hemorrhagic virus was already a stock scene of journalism and fiction when Wolfgang Petersen's film *Outbreak* opened with it in 1995. Journalistic photographs and accounts and novelistic depictions had begun to burn it into the American collective consciousness, as they marketed and managed the scientific concern about emerging infections. Petersen's film combined that with many other stock images to dramatize the outbreak story and facilitate its emergence in popular culture. It offered the audience the visceral experience of the graphic description—and the particular horror—of a person's being liquefied by a hemorrhagic virus. And it rehearsed a scenario in which the outbreak of a horrific disease could travel the routes of a global economy to make a small California town almost (but not quite) as expendable to the U.S. military as an African camp—its inhabitants *almost* becoming, in the icy words of Donald Sutherland's marvelously sinister character, General McClintock, acceptable "casualties of war."

The credits open with a quotation from Joshua Lederberg calling viruses "the single biggest threat to man's continued dominance on the planet."[1] The epigraph from Lederberg, a geneticist and Nobel Laureate, conferred the sanction of science on the formulaic story about how an Ebola-like hemorrhagic virus might chart a course through the global village from Zaire to Boston and California, and it helped to make the film part of the alarm that Lederberg and his colleagues sought to sound at the waning of the twentieth century. In the early years of the Cold War the U.S. military had treated anticipated epidemics, which they feared would follow a germ-warfare attack, as a national priority, but subsequent decades had dulled that threat. The miracle of antibiotics and other medical victories (such as the eradication of naturally occurring smallpox in 1977) seemed to have made infectious disease a relatively minor inconvenience in the global North. In the early 1990s Donald A. (D. A.) Henderson, who had spearheaded the smallpox-eradication program for the World Health Organization, somberly recalled that in 1969 the Surgeon General had called the problem of infectious disease in the United States "marginal" in a speech he delivered at the Johns Hopkins University.[2] But by the 1990s, HIV and other untreatable communicable diseases had shown the optimism to be premature.

Richard M. Krause of the National Institutes of Health (NIH) had heralded the problem of these infections in his 1981 book, *The Restless Tide: The Persistent Challenge of the Microbial World.* But the threat posed by viral epidemics was not widely acknowledged until a 1989 conference, held at the end of the decade in which HIV had compelled international attention. The conference assembled prominent infectious- and tropical-disease specialists (and one medical historian) to address the outbreak of numerous newly identified or resurfacing communicable diseases.[3] With the term *emerging infections,* they connected those outbreaks, defining a phenomenon for which they then sought a comprehensive explanation. Co-sponsored by the National Institute of Allergy and Infectious Disease, Rockefeller University, and the Fogarty International Center, the conference spawned committees and publications that addressed the topic, including the Institute of Medicine's 1992 report *Emerging Infections* (of which Lederberg was a coeditor) and a 1993 collection of essays from the conference, *Emerging Viruses.* Emerging infections, the participants concluded, were the consequence of globalization. An expanding human population worldwide meant that human beings were living and working in previously uninhabited places and coming into contact with unfamiliar or dormant microbes, which in turn globe-trotted by hitching rides in hosts—human, animal, and insect—using the variety of transportation networks that constitute the global village.

Those networks also helped to produce social and political transformations that were of particular interest to social scientists. Studies of political affiliation, especially of the nation, proliferated, turning critical attention to the forms of belonging that had dominated the modern world and speculating about their fate.[4] Belonging took a biological turn in a cluster of studies penned in the 1990s by scientists who addressed the role of communicable disease in shaping human migrations, populations, and communities. Such works as the biologist Christopher Wills's *Yellow Fever, Black Goddess: The Coevolution of People and Plagues* (1996), the immunobiologist Michael B. A. Oldstone's *Viruses, Plagues, and History* (1998), and the physiologist Jared Diamond's bestselling *Guns, Germs and Steel: The Fates of Human Societies* (1997) put the relationship between disease emergence and demographic change in historical context.

Meanwhile, the mainstream media, fiction, and film were bringing the epidemiological sensation of disease emergence to a broad public. *Outbreak* was but one of many fictional and nonfictional accounts of emerging-disease outbreaks that dramatized the scenarios that infectious- and tropical-disease specialists were debating in their meetings and publications. Nonfiction bestsellers—such as Richard Preston's 1994 *The Hot Zone*, which first appeared as a *New Yorker* article entitled "Crisis in the Hot Zone" in 1992, and Laurie Garrett's 1994 *The Coming Plague*—heralded the danger of these species-threatening events, and they were quickly supplemented by novels and films, including *Carriers* (Patrick Lynch, 1995), *Contagion* (Robin Cook, 1995), *The Blood Artists* (Chuck Hogan, 1998), *Twelve Monkeys* (dir. Terry Gilliam, 1995), *The Stand* (dir. Mike Garris, 1994), and *Outbreak*.[5] D. A. Henderson believed that the outbreaks themselves served "usefully to disturb our ill-founded complacency about infectious diseases," and it is no surprise that Lederberg lent his words to Petersen's film.[6] Lederberg and his colleagues welcomed almost any means of calling attention to what they saw as an impending disaster; Lederberg had in fact leaked the story that inspired Preston to write *The Hot Zone*.[7] Scientists and science writers who had seen the effects of hemorrhagic viruses were especially eager to convey the magnitude of the problem. Even at their most sensational, fiction and film provided a way to educate the public about the threat and the science of these deadly infections.

Fictional accounts of outbreaks did more than reflect and convey the lessons of science; they also supplied some of the most common points of reference, which influenced social transformation and disease emergence in their own right. One of the most commonly evoked and formative images of disease emergence is in fact drawn from a novel that preceded the Washington conference by two decades. Michael Crichton's 1969 novel, *The Andromeda Strain*, which was made into a film in 1971, tells the story of mysterious microbes that are brought back to Earth on a space probe and wipe out most of a town in the Arizona desert, killing either instantly or indirectly (through madness) and leaving only two survivors. The unfamiliar microbes turn out to be common terrestrial organisms mutated by extraterrestrial exposure: the lethal and mysterious effect of space exploration.[8] The microbes dissipate on their own, and, in fact, the incorrect assumptions and dangerous fail-safes nearly lead the scientists to create the apocalypse they had been trying to prevent.

The term "Andromeda strain" has become shorthand for sudden devastation caused by mysterious microbes and mismanagement: a clash of ecosystems with cataclysmic consequences on a global scale. It invokes the terror of a species-threatening event and transforms the dangerous terrain of space exploration into the perilous landscape of global development. Laurie Garrett reaches for this common referent in *The Coming Plague* to describe the foreboding articulated at the 1989 conference: "The Andromeda strain nearly surfaced in Africa in the form of Ebola virus; megacities were arising in the developing world, creating niches from which 'virtually anything might arise'; rain forests were being destroyed, forcing disease-carrying animals and insects into areas of human habitation and raising the very real possibility that lethal, mysterious microbes would, for the first time, infect humanity on a large scale and imperil the survival of the human race."[9] Garrett is an important presence in my study not only because her bestselling book was one of the first and most responsible journalistic sources to bring the problem of disease emergence to a mainstream audience, but also because *The Coming Plague* exemplifies how a conscientious, informed, compassionate account of disease emergence can be complicated by language and images that tell competing stories. Garrett uses the Andromeda strain, for example, to dramatize the threat of rapid and careless development and the failure to consider the consequences of human encroachment on "primordial" ecosystems that harbor unfamiliar and deadly microbes. She offers as the only "wonderful news in the emerging disease story" the observation that "nearly all outbreaks and epidemics are the fault of our own species—of human beings—not of the microbes."[10] Human behavior can change the circumstances that "imperil the survival of the human race."

Yet Garrett's rhetoric undermines her analysis. Throughout *The Coming Plague,* animated, "primordial" microbes wage war on a besieged humanity. They turn the "African" landscape primitive, recasting the effects of poverty as a temporal lag (as in the SARS photos that juxtaposed the Hong Kong airport with a Guangzhou duck pen). Garrett's use of the passive construction ("megacities were arising"; "rain forests were being destroyed") suggests mysterious, transformative forces beyond the reach of human agency. The developing outbreak narrative that she helped to produce casts "Africa" as an epidemiological ground zero, otherworldly (literally *alien*), a primordial stew out of which "virtually anything might arise." Although Lyme disease could be equally subject to Garrett's analysis, and appears in the litany of emerging infections in the scientific literature, Lyme, Connecticut, is not, for Garrett or her audience, a place in which virtually anything might arise. Even accounts of the Four Corners outbreak of the hantavirus, which can be as lethal as Ebola (and which Garrett treats in *The Coming Plague*), did not evoke the Andromeda strain despite its geographical proximity to Crichton's setting (in the Arizona desert). Garrett unwittingly infuses her socioeconomic analysis of disease emergence with the distorting conventions of a horror story.

The analyses in science journalism such as Garrett's were neither false nor deliberately slanted. They were often epidemiologically useful, facilitating rapid identification of and response to public health threats. But the embellishments accrued, circulating (like microbes) until they became conventions. As fictional outbreak accounts dramatized the scenarios of disease emergence, they consolidated the conventions of the familiar story. In this chapter, I will chronicle the circulation of the language, images, and story lines through scientific and medical publications, journalism, fiction, and film to document how they became conventional and to introduce the narrative they produced in the process. That narrative links the idea of disease emergence to worldwide transformations; it interweaves ecological and socioeconomic analysis with a mythic tale of microbial battle over the fate of humanity. The outbreak narrative fuses the transformative force of myth with the authority of science. It animates the figures and maps the spaces of global modernity. It also accrues contradictions: the obsolescence and tenacity of borders, the attraction and threat of strangers, and especially the destructive and formative power of contagion. It both acknowledges and obscures the interactions and global formations that challenge national belonging in particular. By invoking Benedict Anderson's *Imagined Communities* in my chapter title, I mean to designate how the outbreak narrative articulates community on a national scale, as it depicts the health and well-being of those legally within the borders of the state as a mark of their belonging. The outbreak narrative is a powerful story of ecological danger and epidemiological belonging, and as it entangles analyses of disease emergence and changing social and political formations, it affects the experience of both.

DISEASES WITHOUT BORDERS AND THE OUTBREAK NARRATIVE

Microbial indifference to boundaries is a refrain in both scientific and popular writing about emerging infections. "Like science," Krause explains at the beginning of his foreword to *Emerging Viruses*, "emerging viruses know no country. There are no barriers to prevent their migration across international boundaries or around the 24 time zones."[11] Emerging infections offer proof that the industrialized and technologized North cannot afford—economically, socially, politically, and medically—*not* to think about health globally. The 1992 report issued by the Institute of Medicine's Committee on Emerging Microbial Threats to Health begins with the observation that the HIV "disease pandemic surely should have taught us, in the context of infectious diseases, there is nowhere in the world from which we are remote and no one from whom we are disconnected."[12] Preston dramatizes the point in *The Hot Zone* when a man suffering from an especially devastating hemorrhagic fever, Marburg, boards a plane. "A hot virus in the rain forest lives within a twenty-four-hour plane flight from every city on earth," Preston writes. "All of the earth's cities are connected by a web of airline routes. The web is a network. Once a virus hits the net, it can shoot anywhere in a day—Paris, Tokyo, NY, LA, wherever planes fly."[13]

Like Garrett, Preston follows much of the scientific literature on the topic when, despite evidence to the contrary, he depicts this "microbial traffic" as one-way: *from* the primordial rainforests of the impoverished developing world *to* the metropolitan centers of commerce and capital.[14] This convention is part of the vocabulary and geography of disease emergence. An infection may be endemic to an impoverished area, but it *emerges* when it appears—or threatens to appear—in a metropolitan center of the North. That is why microbes can be simultaneously "primordial" and "emerging."

Although scientists and science writers widely credit HIV with the renewed attention (in the North) to the global threat of infectious disease, hemorrhagic fevers, such as Ebola, Lassa, and Marburg, typically dominate these accounts.[15] Like HIV, they cause gruesome illnesses and death, but they are more infectious and have significantly shorter incubation periods and duration. Victims generally fall ill within two weeks of infection (usually more quickly), and the progression of the outbreak is easy to track. While the HIV/AIDS epidemic had spread beyond containment by the time of the 1989 conference, teams of epidemiologists and researchers from such agencies as the Centers for Disease Control and Prevention (CDC), the WHO, and the United States Army Medical Research Institute of Infectious Diseases (USAMRIID) had been able to stem the recent outbreaks of hemorrhagic fevers that did not burn out on their own.[16] To those who had witnessed the effects of these fevers, however, the nightmare scenario would be a fusion of the two: a virus with the traits of the hemorrhagic fevers and the scope of HIV.

Such a virus, in fact, would offer new perspective on the HIV/AIDS epidemic, which Preston makes clear in his depiction of the victim of the Marburg virus, whom he calls Charles Monet. In *The Hot Zone* Preston tracks the dying man's journey from the rainforest to a crowded urban hospital in Nairobi, Kenya, in vivid detail, introducing HIV as an incidental time frame and implicitly a harbinger of even worse things to come: Monet "came into the country [Kenya] in the summer of 1979, around the time that the human immunodeficiency virus, or HIV, which causes AIDS, made a final breakout from the rain forests of central Africa and began its long burn through the human race."[17] After a quick chronicle of the (hypothetical) routes of HIV along the Kinshasa Highway, he brings the virus to the foot of the mountain, Mount Elgon, where Monet is presumed to have contracted Marburg, as though Marburg were a stepped-up version of HIV: "HIV is a highly lethal but not very infective Biosafety Level 2 agent. It does not travel easily from person to person, and it does not travel through the air. You don't need to wear a biohazard suit while handling blood infected with HIV" (4–5).[18] By contrast, Marburg is volatile and rapid. Preston's depiction of its effects reads like a description of the ravages of HIV on fast forward.

Monet's doctors in rural Kenya put him on a plane for Nairobi, and Preston slides into the language of the horror story. Shifting into the present tense and second-person address, he turns the reader into a passenger witnessing a monstrous transformation: "The seats are narrow and jammed together on these commuter airplanes, and you notice everything that is happening inside the cabin. . . . You would not have been able to ignore the man who was getting sick" (17). Preston lingers on the details of Monet's metamorphosis: "Perhaps he glances around, and then you see that his lips are smeared with something slippery and red, mixed with black specks, as if he has been chewing coffee grounds. His eyes are the color of rubies, and his face is an expressionless mass of bruises" (17). We watch his head turn black and blue as the "muscles of his face droop. The connective tissue in his face is dissolving, and his face appears to hang from the underlying bone, as if the face is detaching itself from the skull" (17–18). Charles Monet literally liquefies as he loses his personality to a damaged brain. The process, Preston explains, is called "depersonalization . . . the liveliness and details of character seem to vanish" as he becomes a "zombie" (15), "an automaton" (19), and, later, a "human virus bomb" (21). Preston establishes the horror of the virus in the dehumanizing effects of infection; it is a gruesome death.

Preston is a science writer, and he wrote *The Hot Zone* for a general audience, but his book was hailed by many of the scientists involved in work on emerging infections because they believed that it could get the attention of a dangerously complacent medical establishment, government, and public. A frequent complaint that echoed through the 1989 conference and the work it generated addressed the insufficient and ever-dwindling support that scientific research in the area had received in the 1960s and 1970s. Karl M. Johnson, who had himself contracted Bolivian hemorrhagic fever in the early 1960s while serving in the field as a "virus hunter" for the NIH, ended his contribution to the conference volume, *Emerging Viruses*, with the hope both that "zoonotic medical virology" would not join "the growing list of the earth's extinct species" and "that this book would stimulate a growing awareness of this danger."[19] Consequently, the report ended with a call for more research, more resources, better detection, surveillance, and communication systems, and a change in human behavior. The problem, according to the Institute of Medicine report, was that the threats had to be perceived, detected, and understood before an effective response could be mounted.[20] Fear is a great motivator, so the scientists welcomed even sensationalistic accounts such as Preston's and their fictional counterparts, like *Outbreak*, which augmented the horror and immediacy of a threat that seemed remote in the North.

Even in their more sedate incarnations, such as Garrett's, accounts of disease emergence used sensationalism—"the coming plague"—to convey the urgency of the threats enumerated by the scientists, including ignorance, sanguinity, and resource shortage. The intended audience could recognize itself in the unsuspecting populace represented in this work. But every horror story has its heroes, and the science journalism also featured the figure of the heroic disease detective from the CDC, USAMRIID, or other government organization risking his or her life in the field to solve the deadly mystery of an outbreak. This figure was a comforting one, especially in view of the HIV/AIDS epidemic's challenge to the complacency of the medical establishment with regard to the imminent conquest of communicable disease. The expert was on the job in the field, or, for that matter, in the biocontainment laboratory, a stock set in journalism, fiction, and film. Preston begins *The Hot Zone* by reproducing the stages that Lt. Col. Nancy Jaax has to pass through as she enters Biosafety Level 4 (Biohazard) of her laboratory at USAMRIID. Film critics consistently remarked on *Outbreak*'s state-of-the-art replica of such a lab, through which a rolling camera travels, moving through the corridors at eye level, pausing to introduce each successive biosafety level. A blue filter casts an otherworldly haze on this world of scientific expertise. Bright red and yellow liquids in each room, which suggest the danger of bodily fluids, supply a vocabulary of contagion. Those colors (not always in liquid form) serve as visual refrains in subse-

quent scenes throughout the film, reminders of danger and scientific expertise in the field and in the laboratory. Everything is connected in *Outbreak*.

Typically, outbreak stories convey that expertise as the ability to make the
unseen world appear. Visual technologies, from electron microscopes to
epidemiological maps and charts, are an important part of the outbreak
narrative. Maps of geographical areas, often dotted with pins or, in films,
with colored lights, represent epidemiological work in progress, associating
even maps that were not so marked with expertise and with the global surveillance the infectious disease accounts called for—and, of course, with
infection. These maps evoke both fear and reassurance. Dots or lines signal a
spreading infection, often following the routes of trains, planes, buses, cars,
and trucks as they transport carriers and their viruses rapidly around the
globe. But the maps also help the epidemiologists solve the puzzle of the
disease and thus represent evidence of experts on the case, a materialization
of the epidemiological work that generally gets the threat under control.
Appearing in key scenes in *Outbreak* from hospitals and military bases to the
situation rooms of the highest echelons of government, for example, they
serve as technological counterpoints. For General McClintock they are
instruments of fear, designed to persuade reluctant legislators of the need to
contain the epidemic at all costs, while for Sam Daniels (Dustin Hoffman)
and his USAMRIID team they offer clues to a more humane solution.[21] In
Patrick Lynch's *Carriers,* maps convey the helpless desperation of Brigadier
Sutami, who keeps a record of new outbreaks of the epidemic burning
through Sumatra by placing small black pins on the map each time a new
case is reported. In a two-week period, Sutami charts the dramatic progress of
the disease, as the pins move from "a line, shadowing a fifty-mile section of the
Hari River," to a network reaching "out in every direction: north and south to
villages on the Trans-Sumatran Highway, west toward Minang Highlands and
now east as far as Jambi."[22] The map expresses the ambiguous geography of an
interconnected world, through a disease that insists on the limits of his power
and efficacy and his dependence on U.S. technological know-how, which (as
he will never know) caused the problem in the first place.

While the experts are busy tracking the microbes, the disease does its
own work of revelation, making visible the social interactions of the imagined community. Microbes tell the often hidden story of who has been
where and when, and of what they did there. Contagion, that is, charts
social interactions that are often not otherwise visible, and the manifestation of those contacts and connections is another important feature of
outbreak narratives. "Rapid globalization of human niches requires that
human beings everywhere on the planet go beyond viewing their neighbor-

hoods, provinces, countries, or hemispheres as the sum total of their personal ecospheres," writes Garrett. "Microbes, and their vectors, recognize none of the artificial boundaries erected by human beings."[23] The human contact materialized by the spread of a communicable disease reveals an interactive and interconnected world. It makes visible the nature of those exchanges that are often concealed; communicable disease offers records of desire, of violence, of sexual commerce, all of which are especially apparent in sexually transmitted diseases. The outbreak narrative incorporates those records as it fashions the story of disease emergence.

The opening scene of *Outbreak* features the geography of disease emergence and the visual expression of scientific expertise. The film begins with a bird's-eye view of treetops and, in what would quickly become a characteristic establishing shot of outbreak films, sweeps down into a localizing site of infection.[24] The landscape depicted in this shot was already disturbingly familiar from the science and science journalism. An explosion is followed by a close-up of a colobus monkey and soldiers fighting in a jungle; the film cuts to a shot of a primitive village identified as a mercenary camp in the Motaba River Valley of Zaire in 1967. Violence and disease are linked in this landscape: generic African social unrest with a subtext (for the historically informed) of destabilization caused by an unpopular, CIA-backed president. The descent of a helicopter and the USAMRIID team that disembarks in biocontainment suits indicate an illness dangerous enough to catch the attention of U.S. military scientists. A low-angle shot enhances the authority of these disturbingly faceless professionals as they survey the horror that is not, they learn, the worst of it. That epithet is reserved for the pile of dead bodies that depict the full ravages of the illness. The indirection of the shot of the bodies augments the suspense: the camera zooms in for a close-up of an image in the plastic visor of General McClintock's biocontainment suit, which comes gradually into focus as a hazy reflection of the distorted and bloody face of a corpse. The shot depicts the spectator's view *visibly* mediated through McClintock's. We depend on him to deflect "the worst of it" for us and to act on his expertise. We are not privy to the reasoning behind his decision to bomb the camp after he has promised to send help, but his response attests to the seriousness of the illness and the apparent need for containment and sacrifice. His authority is evident in his command to his associate, Billy Ford (Morgan Freeman), who is silenced when he tries to question McClintock's decision.

Outbreak constructs expertise from the outset as the public's dependence on experts' ability to see and respond to what the public cannot. The film depicts magnified images of viruses—through an electron microscope—in addition to epidemiologists' charts and maps. These complementary ways

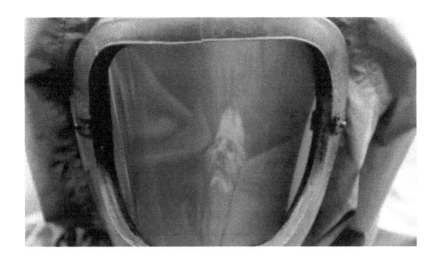

General McClintock (Donald Sutherland) sees "the worst of it" in *Outbreak* (dir. Wolfgang Petersen, 1995).

of viewing the microbe, however, are only the first step in addressing the problem. With their expertise thus established, the epidemiologists must work against time to identify the source of the outbreak and the means of transmission, and then to determine how to resolve it. That effort constitutes the plot and storyline of the film: the outbreak narrative.

The outbreak narrative is itself like the epidemiological map and the electron microscope, a tool for making the invisible appear; it borrows, attests to, and helps to construct expertise. The points on the epidemiologist's map and the organism under the researcher's microscope make little sense without the story that is told about transmission. And that story cannot account for the spread of the disease without registering the interactions that bear witness to the connections of human communities, which are conceived simultaneously on local, national, and global scales. The outbreak narrative manages the consequences, as it makes sense of, what the communicable disease makes visible.

THE MYTHIC STRUGGLE OF VIRAL INFECTION

The outbreak narrative pits human being against microbe. For Lederberg, the challenge for the public, and even for scientists, was "to accommodate to the reality that Nature is far from benign; at least it has no special sentiment for the welfare of the human versus other species."[25] This perspective was disturbing, Lederberg believed, because it required human beings not only to accept a decentered view of their place in the universe but also to imagine the possibility of their own extinction. An ecological view of disease emergence held that newly surfacing infections marked human beings' coming into contact with new microbes—microbes into whose environments an expanding population ventures (as they clear forests, for example), microbes whose animal-host populations suddenly grow because of environmental changes (such as an increase in the numbers of deer mice, which carry hantavirus), and microbes that mutate for a variety of reasons, including the proximity of pigs and ducks in some agricultural practices. The medical historian invited to present at the 1989 conference, William H. McNeill, explained that outbreaks and epidemics of new diseases signaled "ecological disequilibrium" and represented the inevitable condition of human progress.[26] The lesson of history was that epidemics burning through populations always left survivors, but Lederberg and others argued that history could not offer a definitive lesson for the future. The most difficult thing for people to accept, they knew, was that, as Lederberg ominously intoned, the "survival of the human species is not a preordained evolutionary program."[27]

Lederberg intended his insight to highlight the seriousness of the problem and the need for, and possibility of, microbe management. Most discussions of emerging infections took up the challenge in some form and stressed the "wonderful news" of human responsibility. The emphasis on human agency put the survival of the species in the hands of human beings, who would presumably be more invested in human survival than Lederberg's indifferent Nature.[28] "When faced with the horror of microbial epidemics," Garrett observed, "it is tempting to throw up one's hands in fear and resign one's self to fate, as one might do for such natural disasters as earthquakes and tidal waves. So it is with relief that we realize that microbes generally spread by exploiting human behaviors—behaviors that may be changed or avoided, thus reducing or eliminating the opportunities for transmission of bacteria, viruses, fungi, and parasites."[29] Tony McMichael hopefully advocated the gradual acquisition of "an ecological perspective on humankind within the world at large" for its palliative possibilities, and Krause, in *The Restless Tide*, answered his own question, "Is mankind helpless to prevent the unexpected in human history—or if not to prevent at least to blunt the consequences?" with an affirmation of "omens for optimism" and an insistence that "we do, indeed, have sovereignty over our destiny."[30] Even Lederberg ended his contribution to *Emerging Viruses* by asking "whether people will continue unwittingly to precipitate emerging diseases and suffer the consequences, as has happened throughout history, or will begin to take responsibility for these human actions."[31] The survival of the species may not be preordained, but human beings could nonetheless ensure it (contrary, perhaps, to the dictates of evolution). The threat of apocalypse hovered as a reminder. "Humanity," Garrett warned, "will have to change its perspective on its place in Earth's ecology if the species hopes to stave off or survive the next plague."[32]

The earliest wave of fictional outbreak scenarios in the 1990s did not embrace a change in worldview. Although they often espoused an ecological perspective, they dramatized the human irresponsibility that caused outbreaks in a series of violations that ranged from the theft of an imported monkey from a primate-quarantine facility and its illicit sale to a California pet store (*Outbreak*) to biowarfare. The cast of characters in these works included indifferent bureaucrats and unscrupulous, profit-motivated corporate executives, arrogant scientists, and well-meaning humanitarians. The plots underscored the logic of regulations and the importance of obedience to avoid the outbreak or to contain its spread. *Outbreak* even affirmed the difficult decision military personnel must make to shoot their countrymen who attempt to violate the quarantine established to contain the outbreak in an infected California town. Neither the analysis of the problem nor the imagined solutions entailed a radical shift in perspective.

Fictional and nonfictional accounts alike harnessed the apocalyptic energy of a possible species-threatening event, often distorting science in the process. In his novel *Carriers*, for example, Patrick Lynch distinguishes between the expected illnesses resulting from new contacts and what he calls an "unnatural" die off in a primate holding facility in Maryland that signals the onset of a dangerous hemorrhagic virus in *Carriers:* "When you moved an animal from one part of the world to another, you inevitably exposed it to new microbiological environments to which its immune system was not adapted. When Europeans and Native Americans first started coming into contact with each other, epidemics were often the result; a bacterium or virus that gave a Mayan laryngitis could kill a Spaniard, and vice versa. That was what ecosystems were all about. Yet there was something about . . . the way all eight monkeys had fallen sick at the same time, within hours of each other, and just the look of the dead animal, that felt— it wasn't easy to find a word for it—unnatural."[33] The ferocity of the disease distinguishes it from the expected—or "natural"—disequilibrium.

The death of the monkeys signals a threat that is more serious than a temporary imbalance, the Andromeda strain hovering in the interstices of the imagination. By calling the deaths unnatural, however, Lynch manifests the difficulty of accepting the implacability of Lederberg's nature.

Nothing better illustrates the reluctance to accept Nature's indifference toward human beings and the turn from the ecological analysis in accounts of emerging infections of all varieties than the seemingly irresistible tendency to animate a microbial foe. Most nonfiction accounts of infectious disease begin by stressing the accidental nature of infection: the collision of human beings and microbes resulting from social or biological changes that bring them newly into contact. Scientists emphasize the microbes' lack of conscious agency. But the animation of the microbe invariably surfaces during the course of these accounts. It begins with a reminder that microbes are living parts of an ecosystem and that the primary objective of organisms is to survive. That objective quickly becomes the manifestation of a "will to survive," and the organism commences its emergence into agency. Microbes, Krause observes in a 1992 article in *Science,* "are not idle bystanders, waiting for new opportunities offered by human mobility, ignorance, or neglect. Microbes possess remarkable genetic versatility that enables them to develop new pathogenic vigor, to escape population immunity by acquiring new antigens, and to develop antibiotic resistance."[34] They are "more than simple opportunists. They have also been great innovators."[35] They are "predators . . . adapting, changing, evolving," and they are canny, having, as Garrett puts it, "the ability to outwit or manipulate the one microbial sensing system *Homo sapiens* possess: our immune systems."[36] In discussions of infectious disease, microbial agency thus slides imperceptibly into enmity, especially in descriptions of specific outbreaks. Preston calls viruses "molecular sharks, a motive without a mind."[37] The motive is survival, but it is distinctly intentional: "Compact, hard, logical, totally selfish, the virus is dedicated to making copies of itself—which it can do on occasion with radiant speed. The prime directive is to replicate."[38] And his language here is not considerably more dramatic than that of the researchers and epidemiologists about whom he writes.

Among microbes, viruses come in for especially sinister attribution in these accounts, perhaps in part because they cause most hemorrhagic fevers and because antiviral drugs are typically less effective than antibiotics, which makes it harder to stem their progression. It is not unusual for a virus to be described as a foreigner or even an immigrant, as in Barbara Culliton's reference to "another unwelcome immigrant, . . . Seoul virus, a cousin of

Asian Hantaan virus, which causes hemorrhagic fever."[39] The metaphor reinforces the association of strangers, particularly immigrants, with disease outbreaks; in this case, the importation of a deadly virus shades into an image of Korean immigration. Bioterrorist scenarios grow logically out of this formulation, especially following the bombing of the World Trade Center and the Pentagon on 11 September 2001.[40]

The microbes are not only sinister; outbreak accounts manifest researchers' respect for and even awe of their foe. " 'Isn't it true that if you stare into the eyes of a cobra, the fear has another side to it?' " Karl Johnson asks Richard Preston. "The fear is lessened as you begin to see the essence of the beauty. Looking at Ebola under an electron microscope is like looking at a gorgeously wrought ice castle. The thing is so cold. So totally pure.' "[41] Tom Geisbert, who first identified the Reston virus as Ebola, sees "white cobras tangled among themselves, like the hair of Medusa. They were the face of Nature herself, the obscene goddess revealed naked. This life form thing was breathtakingly beautiful. As he stared at it, he found himself being pulled out of the human world into a world where moral boundaries blur and finally dissolve completely. He was lost in wonder and admiration, even though he knew that he was the prey."[42] And when Sam Daniels gets his first glimpse of the virus in *Outbreak,* he exclaims, "You have to love its simplicity. It's one billionth our size, and it's beating us."

The regard is even more than the appreciation of a brilliant general for a worthy foe. It is closer to the mystical bond hunters often describe with the animals they stalk, and Geisbert, an avid hunter, moves from hunted to hunter when he regrets that "he couldn't bring [the virus] down with a clean shot from a rifle."[43] The mystical response is evident in descriptions of the earliest visualizations of viruses, which introduced scientists to a new life form—to something, in fact, that challenged their very conception of life, since viruses could only sustain themselves and reproduce inside of a host cell. They existed in a liminal state, a kind of suspended animation, when outside the host cell. The awe of being in the presence of a new life form, or perhaps of a life form that could alter the way science conceptualized life, characterized many early descriptions of viruses and survives in how they are depicted in the outbreak narrative.

The antiquity of the microbes imparts a mythical cast to their battle with human beings. In *The Hot Zone* Preston posits the genesis of Ebola in the "earth's primordial ocean, which came into existence not long after the earth was formed, about four and a half billion years ago. . . . This suggests that Ebola is an ancient kind of life, perhaps nearly as old as the earth itself.

Another hint that Ebola is extremely ancient is the way in which it can seem neither quite alive nor quite unalive" (85), a feature of viruses generally. One researcher, in disposing of the Ebola-infected corpse of a monkey, considers that he is "in the presence of another life form, which was older and more powerful than either of them, and was a dweller in blood" (81). And the Ebola Zaire strain seems "to emerge out of the stillness of an implacable force brooding on an inscrutable intention" (100). It is a timeless struggle that takes its combatants back to a prehistoric past, explaining the identification of a virus with "Nature herself." They have the quality of forbidden knowledge, "the obscene goddess revealed naked."

Emerging infections in these accounts are paradoxically a product of global modernity and an indication of a return to a primitive past, a world not only without antibiotics (within the memory of people who are still alive today), but one in which medicine offered treatments that were often no more effective than prayer and witchcraft. Describing the contemporary millennial world "from the microbes' point of view," Garrett remarks in *The Coming Plague* that "it seems . . . as if the entire planet, occupied by nearly 6 billion mostly impoverished *Homo sapiens,* is like the city of Rome in 5 BC."[44] The global village, the result of human progress, has ironically thrown the North back in (medical) time.

That temporality also characterizes representations of the geographical places that are typically associated with these diseases and that seem to spread with them: timeless, brooding Africa or Asia, the birthplace of humanity, civilization, and deadly microbes. Culliton, for example, documents Morse's observation that "most of these 'threatening' viruses have an African or Asian heritage, quite likely because they evolved along with humans. . . . Many have existed undetected and, apparently relatively harmlessly, in remote areas."[45] When such scientific observations reach the mainstream media and mingle with the other conventions of the outbreak narrative, they infuse a geography of disease. Maps work similarly. Although the outbreak that Preston describes occurs in Reston, Virginia, and arrives in primates imported from the Philippines, a map of central Africa, prominently featuring the rain forest and the Kinshasa Highway, precedes the seven-page reproduction of the stages through which Nancy Jaax must pass to enter her lab. The map and the opening discussion of Charles Monet depict the African continent as the source of emerging infections. Garrett's book features six maps, including one of Amazonia and three of regions in Africa.[46]

With its "African or Asian heritage," the ancient microbe incarnates the place of its ostensible origin, which spreads, with the disease, to the site of its outbreaks. Outbreaks of infectious disease in impoverished areas in the North are characteristically seen as the indication and result of "third-worldification." The term is disturbing in its suggestion that the conditions of poverty and disease originate in developing regions, and it exemplifies the "biologizing" of social forces and global inequities against which Paul Farmer repeatedly cautions in his work.[47] Such formulations implicitly constitute disease outbreaks as the incarnation of a timeless and diseased "Third World" leaking, through the microbes, into the metropolises of the "First World." Cultural analysts have noted the anxieties about globalization expressed in these accounts in which diseases almost invariably emerge from Africa, occasionally from Asia or South America. Charting the one-way course of such diseases, accounts of emerging infections turn space into time, threatening to transform a contemporary "us" into a primitive "them."[48] This rhetoric stigmatizes impoverished places as it obscures the sources of poverty and of the "uneven development" that characterizes globalization.[49]

Emerging infections become, in these accounts, phantasms of consequences and, with the attribution of motive, revenge, but where one might expect the vengeance of the impoverished and oppressed, it is instead displaced onto the obscene goddess, Nature herself. Emerging infections foretell, in the words of Karl Johnson, "that our earth is, in fact, a progressively immunocompromised ecosystem."[50] For Preston, writing in *The Hot Zone*, the response is deliberate: "The earth is mounting an immune response against the human species. It is beginning to react to the human parasite, the flooding infection of people, the dead spots of concrete all over the planet, the cancerous rot-outs in Europe, Japan, and the United States, thick with replicating primates, the colonies enlarging and spreading and threatening to shock the biosphere with mass extinctions" (406–7). Preston speculates that "the biosphere [may] not 'like' the idea of five billion humans" or perhaps human beings are just so much "meat" that cannot "defend itself against a life form that might want to consume it." In either case, the "earth's immune system, so to speak, has recognized the presence of the human species and is starting to kick in." Although he marks his awareness of the metaphoric nature of his remarks with devices such as the scare quotes around "like" and the phrase "so to speak," Preston seems to find the concept irresistible, and he concludes by wondering if "AIDS is the first step in a natural process of clearance" (407).

The immune response in Preston's depiction is a cleansing that stops just short of an act of vengeance. In other accounts—especially fictional ones—

the microbes are more conspicuously vengeful. In *Outbreak* the USAMRIID personnel who are sent to Zaire to investigate the outbreak learn from a local doctor that the sole survivor of the afflicted village, "a local ju-ju man, witch doctor" who remained in a cave during the course of the outbreak, believes that the gods have been angered by the building of a road through the forest (to Kinshasa). And one of the characters in Lynch's *Carriers* offers a similar interpretation of a devastating infection that is burning its way through the Indonesian rainforest. " 'We don't belong here,' " she laments. " 'We're the disease here. We're the virus. The forest knows that. And it wants to destroy us.' "[51] The formulation turns the ecological perspective for which Lederberg calls into an apocalyptic battle between humanity and microbial spirits of animus. Yet, the battle is consistently staged in the "primordial" landscapes of various developing nations where new roads are being built and new markets defined (and mined). These locales, and the history of exploitation that has produced the conditions in which disease flourishes, suggest that the microbial vengeance expresses the return of a colonial repressed.

Outbreak accounts give microbes a natural history in the primordial landscape of the developing world; they offer a contemporary analysis in their depiction of a careless human intrusion on a discrete, prehistoric ecosystem combined with the poverty and violence that appear endemic to these regions. Omitted in their distant histories and contemporary analyses, however, is the history of colonialism and decolonization. The politics of the Cold War, which strongly influenced the conventions of viral representation, also produced the idea of the "Third World" as well as the patterns and conditions of development that have become synonymous with the term.[52] During the Cold War, "health" was a conspicuously invoked index of "civilization" and of the distinction between "developed" and "developing" as well as a justification for intervention by the First or Second Worlds in the designated Third World. Summoned as a threat posed to and by particular regions, communicable disease was used to generate the geographical idea of the Third World. The history of decolonization surfaces in occasional allusions in contemporary discussions of global health. In *Betrayal of Trust: The Collapse of Global Health* Laurie Garrett begins her discussion of the 1995 Ebola outbreak in Kikwit, Zaire, with the decolonization of the region, and *Outbreak* similarly sets the scene of the first Motaba outbreak in the bloody rebellion against CIA-backed President Mobutu.[53] But without an analysis of how communicable disease, along with poverty and violence, contributed to the construction of the geographical idea of the Third World, even accounts that acknowledge how the politics of colonialism and decolonization produced contemporary conditions can reproduce the geography of disease that is such a consistent feature of the outbreak narrative. The anthropomorphized microbe manifests the difficulty of accepting the indifference of Lederberg's "Nature," and it offers an important means by which global politics—the obscured power relationships and other Cold War legacies named by the term "Third World"—finds expression in outbreak narratives.

The outbreak narrative is haunted by the unacknowledged legacy of decolonization and its expression in disease emergence; it promotes instead an understanding of communicable disease as a cause rather than an expression of social formations throughout history. That understanding also characterizes a cluster of studies that addressed the role of epidemics in the history of human conquest and migration. Writing in 1976, William McNeill, in *Plagues and Peoples,* argued that infectious disease was part of the natural balance of a global ecosystem and therefore offered "a fuller comprehension of humanity's everchanging place" in that balance, which "ought to be part of our understanding of history."[54] While historians had previously documented the impact of disease outbreaks on particular social formations and political events—Hans Zinsser's popular *Rats, Lice and History* (1934) is a notable example—McNeill's goal in *Plagues and Peoples* was to integrate infectious disease more fully into human history by demonstrating its formative role in the shaping of populations and communities. The book circulated widely, earning McNeill both a general audience and credibility among scientists, as his presence as the sole historian (and nonscientist) presenting at the 1989 emerging-infections conference attests. It also articulated an idea of communal belonging in epidemiological terms that has become central to the outbreak narrative.

The 1990s witnessed a trend in such histories, and Christopher Wills, Michael Oldstone, and Jared Diamond, among other scientist-historians, followed McNeill in locating the origin of large-scale infectious disease outbreaks in the earliest agricultural settlements, where people lived in close proximity to each other, to their domesticated animals, and to their waste products. Central to their analyses was an important epidemiological distinction between Eurasia, where such communities were not only common but also in frequent communication with others (trade routes, military campaigns), and the Americas, where more scattered communities, fewer herd animals, and significantly greater isolation created more immunologically naïve populations that were devastatingly susceptible to the germs of their would-be (and ultimately successful) European conquerors.

With her pithy epithet "the germ theory of history," Heather Schell characterizes this historiographic trend, and she is critical of the totalizing tendencies of their grand narratives, which she believes "remove the politics from history, both the making and the telling of it" by "reading human events as a lesson in epidemiology."[55] The germ theorists indeed risked offering biological explanations of history that subordinate human power struggles to chance ecological events, although their intention—and often their achievement—was to complicate rather than to replace traditional human-centered historical analyses. For Diamond, an environmental explanation of successful conquest and development challenged the more troubling claims that such victories resulted from the conquerors' intrinsic cultural or technological superiority. And McNeill, in *Plagues and Peoples*, pointed to the "very potent biological weapon" that populations "acquired" when "they learned to live with the 'childhood diseases' that can only persist among large human populations" (69). In his analysis, as in Diamond's, victory is not necessarily evidence of military or cultural superiority; immunologically stable populations needed neither aggression nor technological sophistication to *digest* the collection of "culturally disoriented individuals" (71) who remained after an epidemic had burned through a small, isolated population, leaving them vulnerable to absorption by the epidemiologically more stable population.

Stability, of course, lasts only as long as the population is not exposed to new microbes, and outbreaks and epidemics throughout history signal increased human interconnection. With more routine contact, the disease incidents appeared most frequently in the smaller, isolated populations, resulting in their incorporation into ever more interdependent and far-reaching social and commercial networks, which McNeill labels a new, or "modern," disease regime.[56] These histories underscore the selective advantages that are conferred by herd immunity, a term coined in 1923 by W. W. C. Topley and G. S. Wilson to explain how a reduction of susceptible individuals in a population stems the spread of infectious diseases.[57] Herd immunity is an epidemiological concept that focuses on the biology of a population rather than of an individual or disease. The epidemiological explanation of human events offered in these germ theories do not necessarily preclude human agency, but they offer an epidemiologically based conception of community, which is further developed in the outbreak narratives.

Communicable diseases, in these accounts, shaped populations and civilizations. Infections sailed along trade routes, marched with soldiers, and migrated with refugees from oppression or with farmers in search of fertile land, and they blazed through populations with devastating effects. But gradually these diseases burned out. Populations, like individuals, adjust to disease. "When a given disease returned at intervals of a decade or so," McNeill explains, following a Darwinian logic, "only those who had survived exposure to that particular infection could have children. This quickly created human populations with heightened resistances": plagues sweeping through populations etched communal affiliations in the genetic resistances of their survivors (an alternative to Geddes Smith's children-as-immigrants).[58] Through such adjustments, communities formed that could effectively be defined by their shared immunities. For the germ theorists, in other words, these diseases offer material evidence of routinized human interactions as well as of established settlements (evidence, that is, of civilization), and their spread constitutes populations with herd immunity. Those who do not perish in the epidemic might have a genetic predisposition to resist the disease, which they pass on to their offspring. Or they develop immunities from having survived it that prevent its recurrence. A significant number of immune individuals will serve as buffers, keeping the disease from spreading widely if it is again introduced. The germ theorists use the term *population* interchangeably with *community*. Epidemics, in their analyses, leave in their wake communities with a biological as well as social basis: individuals connected biologically, in something other than a kinship relationship (although it might suggest a shared genetic predisposition to disease resistance).

These communities are populations conceived, in effect, as immunological ecosystems, interdependent organisms interacting within a closed environment marked by their adjustment to each other's germs. Impending disequilibrium is fundamental to this depiction of community, since each new contact might upset the balance. Germ theories of history depict communicable disease as fundamentally transformative. From an ecological perspective, such transformations are not apocalyptic. While catastrophic infections can result in the annihilation of an existing community, the devastation will in turn precipitate new communal affiliations. Germ theories of history stress both the certainty of transformative infections and the ultimate survival of the species. McNeill ends *Plagues and Peoples* with the observation that "ingenuity, knowledge, and organization alter but cannot cancel humanity's vulnerability to invasion by parasitic forms of life. Infectious disease which antedated the emergence of humankind will last as long as humanity itself, and will surely remain, as it has been hitherto, one of the fundamental parameters and determinants of human history" (291). Yet Wills has "no doubt that if a new virus emerged that killed rapidly and spread easily, it would soon be halted by the frenzied marshalling of the entire armamentarium of modern epidemiology and medicine. . . . [E]ven such diseases are surprisingly vulnerable if we keep our wits about us and attack them where and when they exhibit their greatest weakness."[59]

Infection almost exclusively favors the powerful in germ theories of history. The germ theorists offer intrinsically Darwinian explanations of how contemporary power relations evolved, and the implication is that infections that will perpetually reconfigure these communities will not ultimately interfere with the continuing (and linear) progress of civilization. That narrative might explain the lack of attention to the bidirectionality of infection in these accounts. While the epidemics that facilitated the conquest of the Americas did not generally affect the conquerors, infectious disease significantly impeded colonizing projects throughout history. Germ theorists typically do not consider the latter events, although those events gave rise to the field of tropical medicine, which had important roots in colonial history.[60] Implicit in the history of tropical medicine is the image of tropical places as dangerous and diseased and of disease as resistant to the civilizing project. Disease is not on the side of the colonizer in this case; the colonizer, in fact, is an intruder. Medicine, by contrast, is part of the civilizing process, an expression at once of colonial power and the benefits of colonization.

A cultural preoccupation with contagion, evinced in increased scientific attention as well as journalistic and fictional treatments, typically coincides with a similar attention to the idea of interdependence, among people and among species. Nancy Tomes documents such a coincidence in the United States at the close of the nineteenth century, when the earliest discoveries of bacteriology gave rise to what she calls the "gospel of germs," and the unprecedented levels of immigration, innovations in travel, and transformation of the economy produced "a growing sense of interdependence and interconnectedness among people, objects, and events far separated in space and time."[61] A century later, the interdependence of a global village and the microbial exposure that it engenders have become widely discussed topics in the United States, as Diamond exemplifies when he notes that the contemporary "explosive increase in world travel by Americans, and in immigration to the United States, is turning us into another melting pot— this time, of microbes that we previously dismissed as just causing exotic diseases in far-off countries."[62] In these cases, as well as in the 1950s, when the nascent science of virology similarly became intertwined with fears about germ warfare and Communist infiltration, the nation has been (and is) the primary scale on which, medically and politically, a response to the threat is most immediately imagined.

Geddes Smith offers quarantine as the most apparent assertion of the nation on the epidemiological landscape, and indeed typically in outbreak narratives, the effort to contain the spread of a disease may involve international cooperation, but is cast in distinctly national terms, especially in the United States. The global threat has a national solution. In an imaginary global outbreak that several scientists staged at the 1989 conference Llewellyn J. Legters, acting as chair of an Emergency Interagency Working Group, noted the obvious self-interest for U.S.-run disease-surveillance systems in other countries, and he asserted that "technologically speaking, we have world leadership responsibilities."[63] And Lederberg calls "improved local health . . . a beneficial side product"—as opposed to the intention—of such systems.[64] Health is first, foremost, and unquestionably a national responsibility. There are, of course, global health agencies, such as the WHO, and there are local agencies that serve specific regions, but the story told by the designation of political responsibility and funding structures is that the responsibility for collective health is understood to be primarily national (CDC, NIH, USAMRIID).

The outbreak narrative reinforces national belonging through more than the identification of the health of the population with state institutions. The depiction of contagion offers a visceral way to imagine communal affiliations in national terms. Writing near the end of the twentieth century, as familiar models of political belonging were increasingly eroded by new global formations, Benedict Anderson penned his study of how community was imagined on a national scale. His influential work, *Imagined Communities,* was one of the proliferation of academic and popular studies of nations and nationalisms in the last decades of the twentieth century. Those studies along with the germ theories of history that followed in the mid-1990s suggest a pervasive interest in the formation and experience of community as the millennium approached. The outbreak narrative manifests that fascination as well, and it reveals points of intersection between those genres: the nationalist implications of the germ theories and the incorporation of communicable disease into the imagining of the nation.

The nation is imagined, argues Anderson, because most of its members will remain strangers, "yet in the minds of each lives the image of their communion."[65] His challenge is to show how and why that communion takes the form of the nation. Conceding that "all communities larger than primordial villages of face-to-face contact (and perhaps even these) are imagined," he distinguishes communities "not by their falsity/genuineness, but by the style in which they are imagined" (6–7). Novels and newspapers, and the rise of print culture generally, are central to his analysis, and his theory is significant in part for his assertion of the materiality of the imagination and the importance of stories and images in the production of political identity: the replacement of kinship networks by the experience of communion with strangers in a shared political space.

Imagined Communities helped to create a vocabulary that brought political and literary theorists into dialogue about the lived experience of a national culture. Narrative in particular became central to subsequent theorists as they sought to understand how the imagined community structures the experience of personhood as well as peoplehood. *"Every social community reproduced by the functioning of institutions is imaginary,"* notes the political theorist Etienne Balibar, by which he means that "it is based on the projection of individual existence into the weft of a collective narrative, on the recognition of a common name and on traditions lived as the trace of an immemorial past."[66] The historically specific imaginary of the national formation is marked by "a people" that finds its reflection in the "immemorial past," the myth, of the state. The "fundamental problem" in his view "is to make the people produce itself continually as national community" (93). But how, he asks, can this "fictive ethnicity . . . be produced in such a way that it does not appear as fiction, but as the most natural of origins?" (96). The germ theorists of history offer such origins in their biological inscription of the social forged by a communicable disease. If the past in these accounts was not quite primordial, it was close enough to "immemorial" to feel mythic: horizontal comradeship that approached a bodily communion through the vividly depicted sharing of germs. Amid the pressures of an insistently globalizing political and cultural economy, the nation was being theorized and reimagined.

If germ theories of history offer a model of community conceived as the ("natural") reproduction of a people, the outbreak narrative fashions it as a nation, speaking to Balibar's "fundamental problem" of how that people continues to reproduce itself in national terms, despite, or because of, its registering the anxieties of globalization. Communicable diseases know no borders, and the global village is the biological scale on which all people and populations are connected. While emerging infections are inextricable from global interdependence in all versions of these accounts, however, the threat they pose requires a national response. The community to be protected is thereby configured in cultural and political as well as biological terms: the nation as immunological ecosystem. The logic of those terms runs much deeper than state mechanisms and inflects the conception of community articulated in the narratives. Outbreak narratives actually make the act of imagining the community a central (rather than obscured) feature of its preservation. As communicable diseases depict global connections, and the ecological perspective of the germ theories stresses communal transformation, the *conspicuously imagined* community is certainly in danger of dissolution. Yet, from its fragility—its tenuousness—it also derives power, reminding its citizens that the community, and all of the benefits it confers on them, is contingent on their acts of imagining, just as the literal health of the nation depends on their obeying the regulations set in place by medical authorities.

THE THEOLOGY OF THE IMAGINED COMMUNITY

The biological aspect of community articulated in the idea of herd immunity makes any catastrophic illness a communally transformative event at the deeply conceptual (and psychological) level as well as, more explicitly, in social terms. Outbreak narratives manifest an ontological tremor, which the canny Preston turns into an out-and-out earthquake when he describes the earth's immune system's kicking in to fight off the human infection. Dramatic outbreaks return to a kind of prehistory, a moment that resonates with the biologically transformative power of a deadly communicable disease. This ostensible connection to the past combined with the uncertainty of the future promoted by the hovering threat of apocalypse inflects communal transformation with preternatural, often religious, significance in these accounts.

These features are subtle and unacknowledged in most nonfiction accounts, but they are dramatized in the fiction. While outbreak narratives proliferate in periods of major demographic shifts and increased social contact, their mappings do more than register the related anxieties surrounding contagion and assimilation. They address even as they express those anxieties, materializing the microbial communions that mark the theology of the imagined community as communicable disease transforms a social group into a mystically connected biological entity. They are at the same time stories of tragedy and triumph, horror and salvation. Even in secular narratives by science writers, the epidemiologist emerges as the victorious storyteller and priestly guardian of those who dwell (legally) within the borders of the state.

Networks of contagion are vividly depicted in the fiction. Stephen King devotes a full chapter of *The Stand* to detailing the casual contacts and ready transmission of the lethal superflu that ends the world as we know it. An insurance salesman, Harry Trent, contracts the virus from a highway patrolman who stops him for speeding. "Harry, a gregarious man who liked his job, passed the sickness to more than forty people during that day and the next. How many those forty passed it to is impossible to say—you might as well ask how many angels can dance on the head of a pin."[67] Such catalogs attest to communities linked by more than our imaginations— linked rather by the experience of being human in and moving bodily through the same shrinking world.[68] We may sit with our morning coffee, reading our newspapers and imagining (implicitly) our connections with the strangers engaged in the same acts, as Benedict Anderson suggests, but those connections become much more palpable and revealing on the epidemiologist's map. The maps and chronicles of contact offer biological evidence of social interactions, and they implicitly envision the biological underpinnings of an imagined community.[69]

The networks in the fiction represent the protagonists' common humanity through their common susceptibility. The strange virus in Robin Cook's 1997 novel, *Invasion*, has been activated by aliens who had planted it in the primordial DNA out of which all living creatures, including human beings, evolved. As a fundamental component of all living organisms—with an emphasis, in the novel, on human beings—it reinforces a sense of relatedness. "'Knowing it is happening and that all humans are at risk'" makes Cassy Winthrope, one of the book's uninfected protagonists and the fiancé of the index case, "'feel connected in a way [she has] never felt before. I mean,'" she proclaims, "'we're all related. I've never felt like all humans are a big family until now. And to think of what we have done to each other.'"[70]

The transformative and potentially catastrophic effects of the spreading contagion gives it a power that borders on the mystical in the outbreak narrative. Harold Lauder, the lovesick poet in *The Stand*, tries to read the devastating epidemic of a deadly superflu in conformity with the longings of his heart. To the object of his long unrequited love, Frannie Goldsmith, the only other survivor in their small Maine town, Harold gushes, " 'For two people from the same town—two people who know each other—to both be immune to something this big—it's like winning the megabucks lottery. It has to mean something.' "[71] To Frannie, it does mean a common bond, but she protests that there must be others, as indeed there are. Harold may be wrong about what the flu means, but King turns the escaped microbe of bioweapons research gone wrong into a mystical agent, as the noble-hearted among the survivors are drawn in their dreams to the brave new world founded by Mother Abagail (played beatifically in the film by Ruby Dee) in the name of God, and the sinners to Satan's henchman, Randall Flag (Jamey Sheridan).

While few outbreak narratives are as explicitly religious as *The Stand*, King captures the aura of the transformations that are subtly evident in the rhetoric and imagery of these accounts as the events take narrative shape. The mysticism emerges not only in the communal metamorphoses but also in the act of scientific transformation itself: when scientists, that is, begin to understand and harness the power of the virus. In *The Hot Zone*, for example, Preston describes the "classic Ebola face" of monkeys that had been injected with the virus in a research laboratory as looking "as if they had seen something beyond comprehension. It was not a vision of heaven" (79). The virus had come from the blood of a young nurse, Mayinga N, and Preston animates it when he describes how the "strain of viruses that had once lived in Nurse Mayinga's blood now lived in small glass vials kept in superfreezers at the Institute" (78). Nurse Mayinga surfaces periodically not only in *The Hot Zone* but also in other accounts of emerging-infection research, and the description of the glass vials often invokes some brief version of the story of her infection.

She is a tragic figure in *The Hot Zone*, a young student from an impoverished family who had just received a scholarship to go to college in Europe. Preston describes her as "a pleasant, quiet, beautiful young African woman, about twenty years old, in the prime of her life, with a future and dreams," dearly loved by her parents, "the apple of their eye" (111). Her infection was sacrificial, the result of her caring for a dying nun in a hospital in Zaire, and Preston recounts her denial of her encroaching illness compassionately, refusing to condemn her for having thereby exposed the population of Kinshasa to a deadly infection when, ignoring her symptoms, she ran errands in the city and even shared a bottle of soda with someone. The WHO feared "that Nurse Mayinga would become the vector for a worldwide plague . . . a species-threatening event" (113), but no one became sick, and, with her vials of blood living on in laboratories worldwide, she came to embody the transformative power of science and the promise of an antidote. While Nurse Mayinga died a terrible death, her blood, like her story, has followed the circuit of a scientific community from Africa to Maryland. In both lies the promise of a cure, the triumph of (U.S.) medical science. Her disease and death facilitated her entrance into the sacred space of the imagined community of the United States, and her consistent invocation in the literature constructs her as a kind of patron saint of the virus who died somehow for our sins and ultimately for our salvation. Preston's language suggests communion: Nurse Mayinga living on through the sacrament of the virus.

Nurse Mayinga is sanctified following a gruesome death from a disease that she did not transmit to others. The stranger/carrier has a more complicated role in the outbreak narrative. Such figures—for example, the protagonists of Holden Scott's *Carrier* (2000) or Chuck Hogan's *Blood Artists*, whose infections turn them into deadly disseminators—embody both the uncertainty of disease transmission and the urgency of scientific expertise. Long before the sources or routes of transmission could be identified, of course, communicable diseases were blamed on foreigners, strangers, and travelers as well as other internally marginalized groups. Yet the discovery—or, as Bruno Latour argues, the invention—of microbes made it possible to document the routes of transmission and the existence of healthy human vectors of disease, turning the stranger/carrier into the scientific fact of a medical threat and the embodiment of the fundamental paradox in the principle of community.[72]

Travelers indeed introduce new microbes into a community. But strangers are also essential to the health and growth of a community, both culturally and biologically. A population that is too self-enclosed suffers from inbreeding and is therefore more susceptible to outbreaks (and stagnation) with serious consequences for the population. According to Christopher Wills, diseases as well as strangers are "generators of diversity"; they help to promote human genetic variation, which is beneficial to the survival of a population.[73] As the carrier of both unfamiliar microbes and genes, then, the stranger is at once dangerous and necessary. As the potential distributor of those microbes, even the non-alien carrier functions as a kind of stranger, the figure who must be identified, contained, and reintegrated.

The community articulated through disease is balanced precariously between its fear and exclusion of strangers and its need for them, poised anxiously between desired stasis and necessary flux.

The outbreak narrative demonstrates the incorporation of the stranger/carrier in some form into the community. That incorporation is often conceived as a communal sacrifice; it shows the power of the agents of transformation, and it can be performed in different ways. Carriers can be identified, documented, and literally contained by public-health officials representing the power of the state, as in the case of Mary Mallon ("Typhoid Mary"); they can be domesticated through the practices of social responsibility (manners, ethics, rituals) that register the internalization of state mechanisms of surveillance and discipline. The typhoid carriers who, unlike Mallon, agreed to refrain from occupations that involved handling food or submitted to the removal of their gall bladders, a common treatment of the carrier state with insignificant success rates, were offered as examples of socially responsible citizens. These figures can also be contained symbolically, transformed by a narrative that turns them, like Nurse Mayinga, into a blessing. These are rituals of assimilation, versions of all such practices that perform and display the incorporation of outsiders into the community. In the outbreak narrative the stranger/carrier materializes, and amplifies, the disequilibrium that strangers characteristically represent. The process through which the stranger is incorporated into the community converts the threatening disequilibrium into a principle of renewal. The threat of instability or imbalance, that is, becomes an attribute of the biologically based community conceived increasingly as a discrete ecosystem.

The imagined community of the nation, argues Benedict Anderson, should be treated "as if it belonged with 'kinship' and 'religion,' rather than with 'liberalism' or 'fascism.'"[74] In germ theories of history and emerging-infection accounts, immunity replaces genetic kinship, offering a bodily connection through which to imagine a distinction between the communion of connected strangers and the threat of invasive or undesirable ones. The transformation happens through the epidemiological stories that configure the outbreak narratives. The balance of the community marked by immunity is always precarious, with the requisite number of strangers—those required to ensure a healthy and diverse gene pool—weighing constantly against the threat of too many strangers, hence social breakdown or anarchy in politics and germs. It is also a central feature of these stories to depict the community as an immunological ecosystem in a distinctly national and medical frame. Most explicitly, the health and safety of the citizens is linked to national borders, as in Smith's quarantine model, but those borders are powerfully reinforced by the fashioning of the theology of the imagined community in national terms.

Michel Foucault defines *population* as a biologically imagined community when he describes how medical and public-health practices served as "biopolitical strategies" that conjured the concept of a population into existence in the eighteenth century to justify a new form of government: the liberal state. Biopolitical strategies, however, are neither self-evident nor static; they must be made meaningful and continually reproduced. And they evolve as they help to transform political and social formations. Constituted by and circulating through media, narratives produce that meaning, which is never stable. The narratives depict networks and affiliations on varying scales: local, regional, national, global. The relationships that comprise "populations" or "ecosystems" or "networks" are always in flux; even if they are imagined biologically, they can be variously defined.

The impending catastrophic epidemic is a dramatic way of representing the (false) promise of the nation as a balanced ecosystem. One need not dispute the epidemiological histories of McNeill and the others to note that demographic movement and disease mutation, among other factors, certainly complicate the idea of a stable community configured through shared immunities. The epidemiological maps demonstrate the porousness of borders and the impossibility of total regulation. The sites of regulation—the censuses, maps, museums, and, more broadly, national narratives that Anderson calls the "institutions of power"—promote national self-definition, as Anderson claims, but they attest equally to an ongoing metamorphosis, to the permeability of boundaries and flux of populations.[75] The ever-present health threat, in other words, signals at once the (presumed) need for the power of the state to regulate its borders and protect its citizens and the limits of that power. Outbreak narratives derive their subtle and complex power less by sustaining the language of crisis than by invoking the precariousness of the imagined community; that precariousness empowers the individual and elicits what I see as a consensual act of imagining. What, after all, keeps citizens believing in the authority of Anderson's "institutions of power" even when they have recognized them as the source and products of their own imagining? Knowing that the community is tenuous and vulnerable, it seems, puts the burden of upholding it—through actions or through acts of the imagination—on the ordinary citizen. The community needs its imaginers.

This act of will (or of imagination) is what constitutes the imagined community: individuals' awareness, however tenuous, that they participate in the act of imagining community, that they must commit themselves to its articulation. But they have to be persuaded that the national community should be maintained. Experts who safeguard their health and well-being represent the need for that community and embody its values. Part of the struggle between Sam Daniels and General McClintock in *Outbreak*, for example, is over their representative Americanness. McClintock is higher up in the chain of command, but Daniels's principled defiance of (bad) orders is characteristic of the American hero, as reinforced in the wake of the very public trial of Lieutenant William Calley, in 1971, for the infamous 1969 massacre at My Lai during the Vietnam War. During the trial, Calley notoriously offered in defense of his actions the claim that he was following orders as he had been trained to do since the time he had joined the army.[76] The physical safety that rests in the hands of the representative American epidemiologist subtly and mystically evokes, in these stories, an ontological register. The link between national identity and physical existence is materialized in the common susceptibility—the vulnerability—that is the inverse of herd immunity.

In *Invasion* Cook dramatizes the precariousness of the community and the common susceptibility of humanity in the literal metamorphosis of the infected individuals into reptilian creatures who function as a collective. The transformation begins—humorously, although significantly—with the conversion of the infected into environmentalists with strong feelings for their fellow creatures. "'It's like they're different people,'" complains one uninfected teenager about her infected parents. "'A few days ago they had like zero friends. Now all the sudden they're having people over . . . at all hours of the day and night to talk about the rainforests and pollution and things like that. People I swear they've never even met before who wander around the house. I've got to lock my bedroom door'" (117). On the surface, the aliens seem to offer the imagined community par excellence, but they take the image of their connections to an extreme. Cassy and her co-survivalists realize that they are free to use the Internet to communicate because the infected "'don't seem to need it since they appear to know what each other are thinking'" (290). Cook's grammatical infelicity ("each other are") reflects the melting of individual identities into an indistinct collective, a hive mentality, that is characteristic of fictional outbreak narratives and complements the "depersonalization" (liquification) performed, as in Preston's description, by the virus.

In contrast to the aliens, the uninfected emerge as spokespersons for a humanity that is synonymous with individualism and that looks remarkably American in its articulation. Cassy's last name, Winthrope, even summons the first governor of Massachusetts, John Winthrop. The virus steals people's identities, taking away their imaginations and the possibility and will for individual action: depersonalization writ large. As Beau explains to Cassy, " 'The alien consciousness increases with every person changed. The alien consciousness is a composite of all the infected humans just like a human brain is a composite of its individual cells' " (263). The imagined community, by contrast, requires the act of imagination: the strangers must constitute the community by actively imagining, not just passively accepting, their connections.

Cassy is especially horrified to discover that Beau cannot draw on the collective information available to him to learn the location of his home planet or even his original physical form. The imagined community requires the act of remembering, even if, as in Anderson's formulation, it is the deliberate act of remembering, collectively, what to forget. The aliens are the ultimate viral colonizers, living entirely in the present and parasitically. The alien community is, in effect, too assimilative; strangers become absorbed too fully and literally lose their identities. This assimilation is extended past the experience of the individual to the group; the aliens have arrived to assimilate the Earth into a larger cosmic community. Cassy is speechless when Beau explains that Earth's isolation is over; he is building a transportation mechanism that will bring Earth out of its isolation and into the galaxy, a cosmic analog of globalization, but with the United States/Earth as colonized space.

The less fantastical *Outbreak* stages the dangerous moment of transformation in a crowded movie theater in a small California town. The scene opens with the convergence of clusters of people on the movie theater on what is evidently a warm autumn evening. At the end of the twentieth century, film represented one of the most important media of cultural transmission that, as Arjun Appadurai notes, was globalizing the imagination.[77] In this movie theater, the global circuits in which the quiet seaside town of Cedar Creek is inscribed have a deadly analog in the circulation of the Motaba virus. A high-angle shot of the unsuspecting moviegoers ominously suggests the ineluctable fate into which they are walking; a cut displays the magnified microbes released by the cough of an infected man as they enter the mouths and season the popcorn of the laughing crowd. The extreme close up of microbes circulating in the movie theater transforms the blurred individuals of Cedar Creek into "casualties of war," which the film depicts as a challenge to their rights as American citizens. The decision of General McClintock to treat the citizens of a northern California town no differently from mercenaries in Zaire—to order their annihilation just as he had ordered the bombing of the camp—constitutes the dramatic denouement (and the jolt) of the film: the unsettling feeling of (mis)recognition captured in the shocked refrain "But these people are Americans, sir." The virus, like an "unwelcome immigrant," has altered the citizens of the town, literally in the sense of turning them into something *other:* they have been "thirdworldized." The film casts the problem as a violation of their rights and claims not as human beings, but as Americans.

General McClintock demonstrates the consequences of the label "casualties of war" at a cabinet meeting when he dispassionately pushes Operation Clean Sweep. The president is absent from this meeting. He is attending an East Asian economic summit and performing his duties as a world leader, but leaving a leadership void at home, which initiates a struggle over the terms of Americanism. Backed by the familiar map of the United States on which he dramatizes a scenario of national saturation within forty-eight hours if the virus spreads beyond Cedar Creek, McClintock enjoins the assembled government and military officials to "be compassionate, but be compassionate globally." Global compassion in his usage means thinking beyond the individual, but not beyond the nation, which tacitly becomes the scale on which the debate is staged. McClintock's disturbing lack of passion contrasts with the emotion of the vice president, who is chairing the meeting in the absence of the president. Wielding a copy of the U.S. Constitution, he vehemently reminds the room of its provision that "no person shall be deprived of life, liberty or property without due process." If they advise the president to go through with Operation Clean Sweep, he admonishes, every person in the room—government officials and the medical experts they have assembled—must stand with the president and assure the American public that there was no other way to contain the (national) threat. The decision must involve personal responsibility and an attention to the rights and lives of individuals. To illustrate the point, he throws onto the table photographs of infected individuals from the California town, proclaiming, "Those are the citizens of Cedar Creek. These are not statistics, ladies and gentlemen. They're flesh and blood. And I want you to burn those into your memories. Because those images should haunt us till the day we die." McClintock's recommendation, made in the interest of national health, risks sacrificing the benevolent concern for the individual that is the watchword of American ideology, what allegedly distinguishes the U.S. democracy, in the language of the Cold War, from the exchangeable collectivities: hazy socialisms, communisms, fundamentalisms—and viruses. His own status as an American is increasingly eroded throughout the film, as Americanism becomes aligned with more than a national identity, with, rather, a point of view and set of values that he lacks.

The image of a young infected mother supplies the face of suffering and sacrifice as an animated, if implausible, "casualty of war" and affirms the vice president's perspective. The shot freezes on her picture, which is at the top of the pile of the photographs on the table, and the viewer recognizes her as the case that the narrative of the film has followed through several scenes. We see her first as a devoted mother obediently and tearfully leaving her husband and two daughters to go to an army center for testing. Broken-hearted, she refuses to let her young daughter hug her, thereby protecting the child and embodying, in her obedience to the army's mandate, the principle of social responsibility. We cut to a vial of blood labeled with the number she has been assigned, 612, and follow it into the laboratory where Sam Daniels's colleague, Casey, is examining blood samples. With each positive result, he becomes more upset, nearly exploding when he examines the vial labeled with the young mother's number; like Daniels, Casey has retained his compassion and his deep concern not "globally," as McClintock uses the term, but for the individuals behind the numbers. He is, in other words, an *American* as much as a scientist as he labors heroically to stop a virus to which he eventually succumbs. The camera itself seems to manifest compassion: as fleeting shots reveal dead bodies as they are being sealed in body bags, the camera allows only a glimpse of one that is barely recognizable as the young mother.

In the logic of the film, the American mercenaries in Zaire have given up their rights as Americans, which are functions of both geography and behavior.[78] But the citizens in the California town have not. The film makes the distinction through visual images that equate Americanism with the state's *benevolent* concern for the individuals as well as the individual's sense of responsibility to the collective. The army's Americanism is troubled by the image of their entering the town stealthily at night while the frightened citizens of Cedar Creek watch anxiously from behind closed curtains. The scene references war movies, commonly from the Cold War era, in which an invading army of Nazis or Communists enters a village. It was a stock scene used as well in propaganda films, such as *Red Nightmare* (produced by the Department of Defense in 1962), which depicts a scenario —literally, a nightmare—in which (Soviet) Communists infiltrate and take over a generic American small town. *Outbreak* gradually shifts the terms until the apparent perpetrators of the townspeople's unfortunate transformation—the virus itself, those deemed responsible for its spread, and especially those who make the unpopular decision to sacrifice these individuals for the good of the group—replace the victims of the virus in their exclusion from Americanism.

In some of the less subtle outbreak narratives, the germs overtly challenge Americanism rather than humanity—or, humanity conceived through the terms of Americanism. Cold War points of reference are common in such narratives. The uninfected renegades in Cook's *Invasion*, for example, find a maverick scientist who is working in Paswell, Arizona (invoking Roswell, New Mexico, the site of a legendary U F O crash), in an underground laboratory originally designed for research motivated by the fear of possible Russian germ warfare. One of the group finds it "ironic" that a facility "built to help thwart a germ-warfare attack by the Russians . . . instead is to be used to do the same thing for aliens."[79] The novel is itself a reworking of Jack Finney's 1955 *The Body Snatchers,* and the protagonists' solution to the invasion—the release of an engineered rhinovirus that kills the alien virus, leaving human beings unharmed—summons *War of the Worlds,* H. G. Wells's 1898 novel, which eventually became a popular 1953 film.[80]

The explicit politics of outbreak narratives vary. Patrick Lynch, for example, who is English, ends *Carriers* with a critical commentary on the U.S. military's handling of an epidemiological crisis that cutting-edge science had inadvertently perpetrated on Sumatra. The character Carmen Travis, an epidemiologist, justifies her efforts to repatriate the unwitting carriers of the virus by assuring the Indonesian general, " 'If there's one thing this outbreak has taught us, it's that Muaratebo [the virus] does not respect national boundaries. Neither should science, or medicine for that matter.' " But Carmen is also an officer in the military. As the narrator ominously remarks, "The fact that they [the U.S. government and the military] would never share" their information about the source of the virus "with the Indonesians was something Iskandar [the general] could not suspect."[81] Yet outbreak narratives, including *Carriers,* consistently register anxieties about the global village that reflexively imagine the containment of disease in national terms against its actual and threatened border crossings.[82]

Equally at fault in *Carriers* are Euroamericans who intrude on the rainforest. Jonathan Rhodes is a botanist and environmentalist, who, when the novel begins, is living in Sumatra, where he is "mapping out the huge variety of plant species in environments perpetually under threat of destruction by settlers, ranchers, or logging companies" (12). His name, redolent of colonialism, colors his presence in Sumatra. His ex-wife Holly's insistence that she and her family do not belong in the rainforest, that they are the "virus" that the forest "wants" to destroy, is only the most explicit articulation of the novel's overwhelming sense that Euroamerican people and objects are out of place in the Indonesian rainforest. Rhodes is partly and inadvertently responsible for the virus, which is the result of ethically questionable top-secret scientific research conducted on human embryos in an underground laboratory in New Mexico that has its counterparts in both *The Hot Zone* and *Invasion*. Corporate greed and scientific hubris motivated the violations of protocol that caused the problem, which began when research conducted on a rare genetic mutation called the Methuselah syndrome turned to gene therapy. When scientists replaced the gene, they simultaneously removed the mechanism for suppressing a deadly hemorrhagic virus that was embedded in the DNA. The virus killed all of the scientists in the laboratory, but not before they had implanted genetically altered ova in a carrier of a deadly mutation, Holly Becker, who had received the experimental procedure at the insistence of her (then) husband, Jonathan.

Although the unholy marriage of scientific research and capitalism (the corporation doing the research has a profit rather than a primarily humanitarian motive) turns one of Jonathan's daughter's into the carrier of the virus, it is her foray into the jungle that results in her exposure to the triggering agent, a plant native to the Indonesian rainforest. Speculating before the fact (before, that is, he has knowledge that an altered egg has been implanted), the scientist who has posited a link between the disease and genetic experimentation imagines the possibility of such an event: "'The kid wouldn't necessarily know anything was wrong. In fact, things would be great—no hereditary defect. The child might be short a few million of this protein kinase that has no particular function in the normal run of things. Maybe he'd suffer some obscure side effect. A small deformation of the cuticles, who knows? Or nothing. Then along comes the antigen. Florists in Chicago start stocking a new South American cactus, whatever. It flowers once a year. Kid walks by the florist, catches a whiff of cactus pollen. A chemical signal on the pollen surface is recognized. Suddenly the genes coding for the virus light up, and half the population of Chicago dies of a viral hemmorhagic [sic] fever'" (346). The significant detail is the importation of the cactus—in Jonathan's daughter's case, the contact with the plant in the rainforest. The carrier is inadvertently exposed because of the networks of a global economy. While *Carriers* demonstrates the impact on the developing world of corporate and policy decisions across the ocean, the novel strongly endorses a vision of globalization as a dangerous mixing of cultures.

Science and viruses may well know no boundaries, but national borders reassert themselves in the monitoring and treatment of epidemics and in the political economy of disease. The nation's job is to safeguard its citizens, reclaiming its own as it reestablishes the stability of the community. Epidemiologists, often with military affiliations, like Daniels and his colleague Major Salt (Cuba Gooding Jr.), are the standard heroes of these accounts, and they have their nonfictional counterparts in such legendary figures as Karl Johnson and Don Francis. Daniels's epidemiological detective work in *Outbreak* leads to more than his understanding of the disease and how it is spreading. It also helps to establish him as the arbiter of Americanism, when, during the course of his investigation, he discovers that McClintock and Ford are engaged in the development of illegal biological weapons for the protection of which McClintock refuses to use the antidote they have produced in Cedar Creek. "It's our little secret, Billy," he tells Ford, as they stand, backs to the camera, looking at the slides that show the source of the outbreak to be, as he puts it, "our old friend." McClintock's description of the citizens as casualties of war becomes more literal and more sinister in light of that information.[83]

The film sets Daniels up as a foil for McClintock from the moment Ford sends Daniels's team to the Motaba River Valley to investigate the outbreak of the virus. Their approach and landing mirrors the earlier landing of Ford's and McClintock's team, but the film quickly establishes the distinction. While the biocontainment suits in the opening scene eerily obscure the faces of the epidemiologists, the visors of Daniels's team are transparent, and compassion and anguish are evident in their expressions. They walk slowly through the town, clearly shaken when they discover men, women, and children horribly disfigured and tormented by the disease. They are more respectful of the local doctor than their earlier counterparts had been. The doctor is well informed about the nature and course of the disease and guides them through the village, where he has already taken measures to ensure its containment. This recasting of the opening scene troubles the authority conferred on McClintock, whose unilateral decision to bomb the camp—against Ford's protest—comes into question.

Daniels's ultimate showdown with McClintock puts heroic obedience to conscience in conflict with obedience to orders as it establishes the terms of—and the general's exclusion from—Americanism. McClintock will not rescind his order to bomb Cedar Creek even when he learns that Major Salt has successfully developed an antidote. Daniels and Salt valiantly commandeer a helicopter to try to stop the bombing, and the pilots of the bomber are caught in a verbal battle between Daniels and McClintock, as Daniels tries to unmask McClintock's real motivation. "If you think I'm lying," he pleads, "drop the bomb. If you think I'm crazy, drop the bomb. But don't drop the bomb just because you're following orders." And then to McClintock: "If you manipulate the truth, the president, the country, the Constitution, then it's not just the town you're killing, it's a big piece of the American soul, sir." A plea for human life slides into a contest over national values; the transformation of the sick people of Cedar Creek into representative Americans turns the bombing of the town into a violation of Americanism rather than—or conceived as—humanitarianism. The epidemiologist-statesman prevails, and a chastened Ford relieves McClintock of his command.

Daniels and Salt are full-service medical professionals whose Americanism consists in substituting a medical cure for a military solution. They implausibly find the tiny primate host and manufacture a sufficient amount of serum to save the town, while pausing long enough to confront the fighter plane in their helicopter and prevent the pilots from dropping the bomb. This Americanism needs a multiracial face in order to counteract the identification of that cure with national identity rather than humanity. The multiracial face of this Americanism obscures the racism of outbreak narratives as it presumably countermands the callous disregard of African life manifested in the opening scene of the film. (For no reason involving the plot, the television movie version of *Carriers*, which was made in the United States, moves the site of the outbreak from Indonesia, the novel's setting, to Africa.) The task of this multiracial American team is to protect American borders from corporate greed, from social irresponsibility (the seemingly harmless theft of the infected monkey from the primate holding facility), and, implicitly, from the native African virus that poses a threat, in the film's terms, to innocent Americans. The threat of Motaba naturalizes the boundaries of the medically imagined community: the American ecosystem.

Scenarios as different as those in *Carriers* and *Outbreak* dramatize the logic of emerging-infection accounts in which the virus emerges as the result of an ill-informed mixing of cultures. Daniels and his team learn that the index case of the contemporary outbreak in Zaire had been working on building a road through the jungle to Kinshasa (often mentioned, as in *The Hot Zone*, in discussions of the origins of HIV and other emerging diseases). He had spread the disease to the rest of the members of the town when he had drunk from a public well. The local doctor does not dispute the belief of the only uninfected inhabitant of the village—the juju man who won't communicate with foreigners—that the virus is a punishment for the intrusion on the jungle that the road represents. Despite the exoticism with which the film undermines him, the ju-ju man's perspective is familiar as he expresses an isolationism that is an extension of the analyses in emerging-infection accounts such as Garrett's and Preston's, or even the more scientific versions of Lederberg, Morse, and Krause. Scientific implausibility and ideological flourish notwithstanding, Daniels and Salt display their own shamanism as high priests of scientific Americanism, experts who preserve the sacred space of the nation from its overly literal defenders who took the virus from the jungle without its antidotal wisdom.[84]

If epidemiologists map the imagined community of the global village, charting infectious diseases as they cross national borders, the depiction, as much as the management, of those diseases reinforces the boundaries. The use of disease to imagine as well as regulate communities powerfully enacts the most anxious dimensions of national relatedness. The inextricability of disease and national belonging shapes the experiences of both; disease assumes a political significance, while national belonging becomes nothing less than a matter of health. With their powerfully defining ambivalence, those terms mandate the dangerous necessity of the stranger and the representational technologies by which that stranger is brought into the community. As a cleansed Oedipus blesses the Athenian democracy, a contaminated but contained Nurse Mayinga blesses the land that stores her blood. For her story, like so many others, at once implies U.S. medical (and military) supremacy and inspires the imaginings at the heart of that community.

The Healthy Carrier

2 In 1907 the discovery of the first known "chronic typhoid germ distributor"—or *healthy carrier*—was announced to the members of the Biological Society of Washington, D.C.[1] The theory that an apparently healthy person could transmit a communicable disease was already under investigation in Europe and the United States, but the research was new and controversial.[2] No one had persuasively documented such an individual in the United States until an engineer in the U.S. Army Sanitary Corps known for his work on typhoid was called in to investigate a typhoid outbreak in a house on Long Island. He was Dr. George A. Soper, and the "carrier" he discovered was Mary Mallon, an Irish immigrant who worked as a cook for the family vacationing in the Long Island house and who would become infamous as "Typhoid Mary." She would become the most invoked symbol of the dangerous carrier of communicable disease from that time into the present, as a result of the stories fashioned about her in the years following her identification.

Soper was a masterful storyteller, and the early accounts of his discovery conspicuously present his epidemiological investigations as narratives of detection.[3] The details are convincing and conform to the expectations of the narrative. Having ruled out all other possibilities of transmission in the house and grounds, to which the disease had been confined, he became suspicious of a missing cook and set out to find Mary Mallon. Enlisting the help of the somewhat shady owner of the employment agency through which Mallon had found work, he discovered a trail of typhoid epidemics that tracked her through her domestic engagements. Here, he concluded, was the "fact" that could substantiate the hypothesis of the healthy carrier of typhoid. And he proceeded to locate and contact Mallon to inform her of her status as a "living culture tube and chronic typhoid germ producer."[4]

According to these accounts, Mallon dismayed the medical and public-health communities by her unwillingness to believe Soper's hypothesis and submit to be tested for evidence of the typhoid bacillus. The child-hygiene pioneer Sara Josephine Baker, sent in her capacity as a public-health official to collect blood and urine specimens from Mallon, described her as "maniacal in her integrity," and Soper reported being stunned that he could not "count upon her cooperation in clearing up some of the mystery which surrounded her past. I hoped," he explained, "that we might work out together the complete history of the case and make suitable plans for the protection of her associates in the future."[5] Public-health officials responded to Mallon's recalcitrance by forcibly removing her to a contagious hospital, where they ordered the collection and evaluation of her bodily excretions. "It was her own bad behavior that inevitably led to her doom," remarked Baker. "The hospital authorities treated her as kindly as possible, but she never learned to listen to reason."[6]

Mallon's 1909 legal appeal brought her plight to public attention, and she elicited a significant amount of public sympathy, but the court declared her a threat to public health and ordered her return to the Riverside Hospital on North Brother Island, off the east coast of Manhattan. A change in the administration of the department of public health resulted in her liberation the following year; she was ordered to give up her profession and to report regularly to the department of public health. But within two years of her release, Mary Mallon assumed an alias and disappeared. In the story Soper tells about his nemesis, this willful disobedience proved beyond doubt that she was the threat he had avowed her to be from the start. His version of her story dominated the newspaper accounts of her rediscovery in 1915, which depicted her as a public menace and ensured her enduring notoriety as "Typhoid Mary."

The story derives its power from its role in demonstrating an important scientific theory: the existence of a healthy human carrier of a communicable disease. The idea of the healthy carrier was based on the assumptions of the germ theory of disease—that specific microbes caused particular diseases—as well as on epidemiological observation. The identification of such individuals in turn supported that theory, which was still contested in the early twentieth century and shaped the direction of medical research and public health policies. For public-health workers, the healthy carrier was "not merely a passive transmitter of infection" but "also a breeding-ground and storehouse of these specific organisms" that offered "the best explanation for the maintenance of the infection in communities."[7] Healthy carriers mandated the role of experts, both in the laboratory and in the field, who could make visible what most people could not see but which constituted a threat to their health and well-being: microbes and the means of their transmission.

In the laboratory, ever-improving microscopes and staining techniques made it possible to identify and classify microbes. The identification of a healthy carrier, however, relied primarily on narrative evidence: the creation of a compelling story about the etiology of a disease outbreak. The story had to turn theories—in this case, the discoveries of bacteriological research—into plausible explanations, and technical terms and concepts into the "truths" of lived experience. Turning the identification of a healthy carrier into a story was central to the development of epidemiology. The story explained how epidemiological investigation worked, as well as why it was so important. It transformed the threat of Mary Mallon, the healthy carrier, into "Typhoid Mary," the symbol of epidemiological efficacy.

The story of that transformation was the U.S. archetype, as well as the most sensationalist manifestation, of the healthy-carrier narrative. The story demonstrated, first, that she was a human vector of typhoid (that is, she was capable of transmitting without falling victim to the disease); second, that she posed a danger to the community; and, finally, that her isolation was justified. In so doing, it established the social as well as medical importance of epidemiology. The healthy human being turned pathogen called attention to the bodily interconnectedness of people living in and moving through the shared spaces of cities and of the nation. The story of Typhoid Mary helped to fashion the experience of those spaces, showing how the realization of those connections required new models of being in the world. It offered a medical basis for emergent ideas of social and political belonging, including a renovated sense of social responsibility in a time of growing individualism.[8] The impossibility of identifying all healthy carriers meant that all individuals had to change their behaviors and social interactions. Cleanliness became not only a solution but a measure of citizenship, for, as one writer intoned, "modern science has shown us that the environment which man makes for himself, the habit of life which he practices, determines his liability to the disease."[9] Conversely, the unfortunate metamorphosis represented by the carrier state raised a political dilemma that the story also addressed: the conflict arising from the state's obligation to safeguard both civil liberties and public health and well-being. Weaving ideas about contagion into the fabric of social being, these public-health accounts introduced experts, such as the epidemiologist, who would serve a mediating role between citizens and the state. In so doing, they helped to facilitate a shift in scale of public-health initiatives from the local to the national.

The story of Typhoid Mary was actually a composite of accounts penned not only by Soper but also by lawyers, journalists, and members of the medical and public-health establishments. Despite its prototypical status, her story was not entirely unfamiliar. At the time Soper charged the cook with her carrier status, typhoid was endemic, prevalent to the point of national crisis, according to the medical and popular press of the time (which may partly account for the public fascination with this case), and each of the outbreaks had been investigated and evidently explained in some other way. Soper and his colleagues therefore had to demonstrate that Mallon's connection to those outbreaks was causal rather than coinciden-tal. Soper had to create a persuasive narrative, and he did so not only through laboratory work and the epidemiological narrative of detection but also by borrowing the features of another, more familiar, story of contagion: the conventional melodramatic tale of venereal disease.

Hints of venereal contagion permeated the accounts of the carrier cook, and they registered the power of that imagery at the turn of the twentieth century. Venereal disease evoked social as well as medical anxieties. From the medical to the popular press, religious treatises to popular fiction, dis-cussions of venereal disease addressed the transformations in the structure and function of families and the gender roles they reproduced that resulted from the pressures of urbanization and industrialization. These discussions typically worked to negotiate changes in familial and social structure by linking changing gender roles and sexual mores to the fate of the white race and therefore to the security of the nation. And they inflected the emergent story of "Typhoid Mary."

In turn, the story of the first known healthy carrier of typhoid did more than influence public-health policies. It harnessed the authority of science to depict the medical implications of the changing spaces, interactions, and relationships attendant on urbanization and industrialization. And it en-trusted the fate of the white race and the health and welfare of the nation to social engineers such as George Soper.

SOCIAL BEING: INTERDEPENDENCE, RESPONSIBILITY AND SOCIAL CONTROL

The vision of social organization that emerged in public-health writings found theoretical expression in the work of the nation's earliest sociologists. Where the former called attention to the new responsibilities that came with increasing interdependence, the latter sought to discover principles that governed social interactions. Writing at the turn of the century, the sociologist E. A. Ross popularized the term *social control* to describe "the goodness and conscientiousness by which a social group is enabled to hold together."[10] The concept was part of the early sociologists' efforts to develop a science of society that would help them understand the laws and conventions that promoted such cohesion.

In his 1901 book-length study of social control, Ross locates his contemporaries' interest in the vicissitudes of social control in the great transformations of their moment: the political upheavals and economic developments that put people in unprecedented social contact. It is a time, he writes, of consolidation, in which "powerful forces are more and more transforming into *society*, that is, replacing living tissue with structures held together by rivets and screws" (432). Increased mobility and the growth of cities were replacing the "living tissue" of extended kinship groups and small communities with the "rivets and screws" of more anonymous and transient affiliations. The more abstract connections did not breed isolation or alienation, but rather a new model of affiliation that intrigues Ross: "As the means of communication improve," he writes, "as the school and the press grow mighty, and as man dares to look up from his engrossing daily task, the ease of comprehending distant persons and situations enables fellowship to overleap the limits of personal contact" (435). Anticipating late-twentieth-century theorists of nation, such as Benedict Anderson, Ross explains that he is witnessing, in these imaginings of fellowship, "the rise of the *nation*" (435).

If the technologies of modern life amplify a sense of interdependence, its rhythms afford increased opportunity for expressions of individuality and, with it, a "more searching and pervasive means of control" (432). The weakening of familial and communal ties loosened the bonds of moral codes, and sociology would replace them with social explanations and criteria for evaluation. A more scientific penology, for example, would evaluate and punish crimes not chiefly on the basis of the depravity of the individual criminal act but "primarily *according to the harmfulness of the offence to society*" (110). By these standards, a crime of negligence might meet with a more severe penalty than a crime of passion. Ross explains that the law "will be hard," for instance, "on the careless train despatcher, because mistakes *must not* occur in despatching trains" (110). Social welfare was the responsibility of individuals.

The public-health campaign against the spread of communicable disease was one among a variety of projects that demonstrated the need, and enlisted individuals in the quest, for a more rationalized social control. If sociology sought to document the intimate connections of individuals in the modern world, the identification of healthy human carriers of communicable disease dramatized those connections through the routes of contagion that it enabled epidemiologists to chart. A proliferation of hygiene manuals in this period cast the drama in militaristic terms, incriminating anthropomorphized germs and, by extension, sick individuals. "Disease germs are the greatest enemies of mankind," a biology professor explained to the young audience intended for his 1910 *Primer of Sanitation*.[11] "Between these germs and the body there is never-ceasing war" (11). With this rhetoric, the author put distance between the bodies of his young readers and disease, but he also enlisted them in the fight through images of their susceptibility. An illness attributed to an infectious agent implicitly represents a moral defeat: "After all," he concludes, "most families suffer from germ diseases more because of their own carelessness than because of the faults of others" (191). Carelessness was the ultimate social sin.

These manuals urged individuals to take responsibility for their own health in language that at once advanced the premises of social responsibility and registered an accompanying change in the understanding and treatment of disease. As historians of medicine have noted, the change followed the advent and wide-scale acceptance of bacteriology. The social and environmental focus of the nineteenth-century sanitarians, which was compatible with the theory that filth (and miasma) generated disease, gave way to the more individualistic strategies of health management that emerged from the germ theory of disease. Social responsibility and bacteriological individualism came together in the focus on individuals as agents responsible for their own health as well as for the health of those with whom they may come in contact.

Charles V. Chapin, a leader in the field of public-health policy in the early years of the twentieth century, argued for the new directions in health policy in his 1910 field-defining book, *The Sources and Modes of Infection*. Chapin called for immediate modification in the "prevailing notions as to the sanitary functions of the state" and in the common belief among "the laity and the lay press . . . that most of the infectious diseases have their origin outside of the body, in filth" or at best "attach equal importance to external sources of infection."[12] Chapin conceded that specific sanitation initiatives, such as improvements in the disposal of human excrement and in water purification, had resulted in the diminution of particular diseases and that hygienic municipal habits promote hygienic personal habits, which are "doubtless an important factor in the prevention of contagion" (28). Yet he insisted that "except for one or two diseases, and except for very indirect effects, the cleansing of streets, alleys, and back yards, of dwellings and stables, the regulation of offensive trades, and the prevention of nuisances generally, have, so far as we can see, no relation to the general health, nor any value in the prevention of specific diseases. While municipal improvements such as the above are desirable, there is little more real reason why health officials should work for them, than there is that they should work for free transfers, cheaper commutation tickets, lower prices for coal, less shoddy in clothing or more rubber in rubbers,—all good things in their way and tending towards comfort and health" (28). Chapin advocated individual activism in the prevention of disease—the minimizing of "contact infection" by proper behavior, such as "keeping our fingers out of our mouths, and also everything else except what belongs there" (164). Like the author of the *Primer of Sanitation,* he urged individual responsibility and personal habits as the greatest weapons in the war against the microbes, and individuals as the most important units for medical focus. The shift not only enlisted individuals in their own care-taking but also emphasized their social responsibility to the ever-widening circles with whom they were directly or indirectly in contact: personal susceptibility transformed into an image of community.

The medical individualism fostered by bacteriology entailed a new articulation rather than a rejection of environmentalism, and it took shape as preventive medicine, which many viewed as the cornerstone of public health. By the time Chapin penned his influential remarks, Sara Josephine Baker had already begun to implement preventive medicine reforms as chief of the New York City Department of Health's Division of Child Hygiene. Baker used the most current scientific techniques to design and justify the social reforms that stemmed from what "at that time . . . really was a startling idea": that "the way to keep people from dying from disease . . . was to keep them from falling ill. Healthy people didn't die."[13] The task was not possible, Baker argued throughout her career, without a fusion of perspectives. Attention to germs and individuals was a part of, not an alternative to, social reform. Even in the highest echelons of bacteriology, scientists cautioned against what the German medical researcher Ferdinand Hueppe called "the ontological contemplation of diseased cells and disease-producing bacteria," referring to the tendency to think of microbes as exclusive agents of disease and to ignore the environments in which they flourish.[14] Railing against the animistic and superstitious thinking that characterized much medical research in his day, Hueppe found even such prominent figures as

Robert Koch and Louis Pasteur, widely hailed as the founders of modern bacteriology, guilty of the ontological fallacy that he labeled "a mere remnant of priest medicine" that "can have no place in any scientific conception of biology, pathology or hygiene" (vi). By contrast, he insisted on a more dynamic (and environmentalist) conception of disease, one that understands it as "a process resulting from the action of a series of factors of unequal value" (275), as a chain of interlinking events, including microbes and environments receptive to their proliferation.

Advocates of public health made considerable use of the discovery of the healthy carrier to promote that conception of disease.[15] Neither personal vigilance nor laboratory science was sufficient to safeguard against healthy carriers, who, often unbeknown to themselves as well as others, literally embodied communicable disease. The medical establishment struggled to imagine the implications of, and thereby conceptualize, an outwardly healthy individual whose body had become the site of infectivity.

With the earliest identification of microbes had come a litany of hitherto unseen dangers. From specialty journals such as *Science* and the *American Journal of Public Health* to popular periodicals including *Harper's, Good Housekeeping, Literary Digest,* and *Scientific American,* the press regaled the public with theories of contagion spread by books, telephones, postage stamps, and especially railroads. The publicity surrounding the discovery of healthy human carriers and the epidemics they generated—beginning with Typhoid Mary—made those figures increasingly the focus of the danger. "The nightmare of disease germs everywhere, in books and brooks, and through all the ambient air, need plague us no more," readers of *Harper's* learned in 1912. "It is our fellow-man and our pets, and the disease-spreading vermin, that we should learn to fear."[16] That same year, F. M. Meader began his *New York State Journal of Medicine* article, "Treatment of the Typhoid Carrier," with a medical observation illustrated by a literary allusion.

> Man is the great reservoir from which most human ailments are derived. This conception has arisen only during recent years when it was discovered that many pathogenic organisms might live a parasitic existence in one man, only to produce the disease in the next when suitable conditions occurred. As it were, a man may become a Trojan horse and his unsuspecting neighbors, like the ancient Greeks, welcome him to their midst, and if their defenses are impaired, welcome him to their sorrow. This great fact of human carriers of disease germs, about whom no quarantine signs are evident, makes this subject of first importance. It is difficult to detect these individuals, and it is even more difficult to treat them when discovered.[17]

While one may hope that Dr. Meader's knowledge of medicine exceeded that of classical literature (the Greeks were inside the horse and were unwittingly admitted inside the walls by the unsuspecting Trojans), his example nonetheless makes the point that the apparently healthy carrier represents a serious and pernicious public-health threat. It also illustrates the shift in how bacteriology was presented to the general public: as pathogenic microbes produced and transmitted through social interactions. Human carriers embodied the unknown and unseen dangers of all human contact.

Those working in the medical specialty of phorology (the study of carriers) knew that they had to make social as well as scientific sense of the carrier state. One phorology textbook offers a particularly lively example. Writing in 1922, when carrier work was well into its second decade, Major Henry J. Nichols of the U.S. Army Medical Corps stepped up the militaristic language as he cast the struggle in ontological terms. "The parasitology of Pasteur and Koch," he explains, has become "linked up with Darwin's grand conceptions and has taken its place in the scheme of the struggle for existence. . . . It pointed to a new possibility in the outcome of the fight of man against his parasites. The patient may recover with complete destruction of the parasite. The parasite may win with death or disability of the patient. But there may also be a draw with the production of a carrier."[18] The high stakes evoked by the Darwinian model find expression in the language of demonization. "While we accredit nature with marvelous adaptations for the welfare of mankind," remarks Nichols, "it should not be forgotten that a typhoid gall bladder or a diphtheria tonsil represent [sic] a diabolical mechanism for the perpetuation of some of man's real enemies. It is the aim of preventive medicine to break up this balance in favour of man" (18). Nichols carefully posits a diseased organ on the border between "man" and "his parasites," between civilization and nature. That diseased organ becomes a paradigm for an environment gone awry, one that ultimately constitutes a threat to civilization itself. The definition and perpetuation of humanity are equally at stake in the battle that Nichols describes, and medical personnel and carriers alike must be prepared to sacrifice the carriers' organs in the greater cause of the preservation of mankind.

Phorology called for the application of scientific medicine to the project of public health, and it entailed an understanding of the individual as embedded in social contexts. Nichols concluded the introduction to his book with an impassioned polemic: "As physicians and citizens we need to realize, once for all, that while in some respects the individual is an ultimate unit, in others, he is only a part of higher units, the family, the community, and the nation, and he cannot exist without them. Hence, medically as well as biologically, the interests of the whole, that is, of the race, are greater than those of the individual parts. On the other hand, it is the individual who, in the long run, profits from the welfare of the group" (18). Hovering on the border between sickness and health, the carrier turns the focus on other borders as well: the porous and permeable borders of the body and the equally permeable borders between social units—among classes, neighborhoods, municipalities, and even nations. Constituting a threat to those borders, the carrier, one of "the individual parts," comes dangerously close to being equated with the dissociable diseased organ.

Such are the implications of social being for Nichols, who contends that "if we . . . view the individual as a social being, it is also indicated to determine whether he is a carrier" (115). The sentence can be read in two ways: first, if we understand that individuals are social beings, then we must acknowledge their susceptibility to contagion; second, if we acknowledge that they are social beings, then we must also ask them to subordinate their individual rights to the greater good of the community. Nichols argued for a kind of supervision that was practicable in the military, with its clearly delineated structures of authority, and during epidemics when the danger was apparent and immediate, but which was much more controversial in the daily workings of society. Such measures were nonetheless widely advocated, as in the numerous calls in the mainstream as well as medical press to require all food workers to carry certificates from the Board of Health. The healthy carrier dramatized the biological underpinnings of all social interactions and their potential danger in an increasingly interconnected social world. The responsible belonging that was the ideal of citizenship stemmed from a recognition of susceptibility that required the curtailment of personal liberties, some of which were newly articulated in the last decades of the nineteenth century. The carrier state marked and negotiated a mutually defining transformation in both scientific and sociological thinking. As a demonstrable fact of medical science, and a being empirically determined to be a threat to public health, the healthy carrier displayed the complex and even contradictory consequences of those changes.

For the medical historians Judith Walzer Leavitt and J. Andrew Mendelsohn, accounts of the first identified healthy human carrier of typhoid manifest an individualism that is consistent with the medical perspective that Nichols criticizes and attest to the triumph of the language of laboratory science over the language of rights and justice. While Leavitt concedes that the social dimension of public-health policies ultimately tempered the bacteriological perspective, Mendelsohn demurs.[19] Labeling typhoid policy in this period "humane but not social," he attributes specifically to phorology the erosion of social explanations and factors and their conspicuous replacement with scientific ones (and with increased attention to the individual) in the etiology of disease and in the articulation of public-health policy more generally.[20] Since bacteriologists and their advocates worked to locate, record, and track carriers, rather than to alleviate the conditions in which diseases like typhoid flourished, he argues, the carrier state they theorized maintained, as it exemplified, the bifurcation between the scientific and the social.

Their arguments rest largely on the ultimate fate of Typhoid Mary, specifically on the scientific justification of her incarceration. Consideration of the broader features of the narrative of Typhoid Mary, however, suggests that the medical individualism of the period did not so much replace as renovate an earlier conception of the socially embedded individual. The principle that emerges from the narrative is "social being," to borrow Nichols's term: the sense of personal responsibility to the group generated by the powerful dramatization of human interconnectedness. The concepts of personhood that circulated in accounts of Mary Mallon were articulated through the terms and according to the assumptions of social being. Her fate included more than her incarceration. Soper had promised to tell her story, and her narrativization entailed an important transformation. When the media and the medical establishment conspired to turn Mary Mallon into "Typhoid Mary," they publicly enacted the metamorphosis of an individual into "a social being." And when Mary Mallon refused to accede to the authority of public-health officials and medical personnel, when she would not join in the battle by dissociating her organs from her self and surrendering her body to science, she constituted a threat to the idea of personal responsibility in an age of interdependence. Designating her "Typhoid Mary," the public-health officers reclaimed her body and reestablished order. As "Typhoid Mary," she embodied the premises, justification, and ultimate victory of their model of personhood. In the stories they told about her, they used medical expediency to justify and authorize that model, but the stories manifest less the distinction between scientific individualism and environmentalism than the power of their conjunction.

Mary Mallon was not representative. At the time of her discovery, her dilemma was unique in the United States, and, as both Leavitt and Mendelsohn note, the 1909 decision authorizing her confinement set no legal precedent for the treatment of carriers. But "Typhoid Mary" has served as an archetype of the carrier (as her story has of the carrier narrative) from the scientific, sociological, and journalistic literature of her own period into the present. In the story of Mary Mallon's transformation into "Typhoid Mary," disease-producing microbes commingled with the implications of interdependence to produce an experience of connectedness that interfused biological, social, and political belonging.

A NATIONAL DISEASE

In the early years of phorology, studies of typhoid dominated the literature. The chance occurrence of Soper's discovery partly explains that early emphasis, but the disease had its own national profile, which it brought to the story of Typhoid Mary. Among the communicable diseases commonly understood to pose the greatest threat in the United States at the turn of the century, only typhoid spread more widely through contamination of the food and water supply than through intimate contact. More than most other diseases, then, typhoid required a combination of social and scientific solutions. Even the most outspoken "individualists" acknowledged the importance of municipal reforms that addressed the storage and distribution of food and water for the control of typhoid. "Among the common infectious diseases," Chapin told his readership, "typhoid fever is practically the only one at present of any great importance to the people of Western Europe and North America which is often disseminated by means of drinking water." Therefore he finds it "worth while to make large expenditures for its prevention."[21]

Probably because of typhoid's mode of transmission, outbreaks carried with them the particular onus of personal, familial, and national failure. As the title of one article proclaimed, typhoid was a "national disgrace," a disease of "dirt, poverty, and national carelessness."[22] It was, announced another, "a disease of defective civilization."[23] And a third noted the lesson taught "by sad experience that the measure of typhoid fever in any community is the measure of the distribution of human filth in that community, and that the dissemination of human excrement will inevitably result in the spread of typhoid fever."[24] Typhoid marked the failure of industrialization, of social responsibility and control, and of modernity. Prior to the discovery of Mary Mallon and other carriers in the United States and in Europe, typhoid had largely been associated with contaminated fluids (water supply and milk) as well as with certain foods, such as oysters, that were tainted by their contact with those fluids. The earliest suspected "carrier" was the ordinary housefly; with the advent and wide-scale acceptance of bacteriology, housewives and screens were repeatedly enlisted in the campaign against what one report called the "simplest" health problem and the "least excusable" disease. In that report, "Typhoid: An Unnecessary Evil," Samuel Hopkins Adams told his *McClure's* readership that "all typhoid is traceable to polluted water. If, for a year, the world were to stop drinking dilute sewage, typhoid fever would vanish from our vital statistics."[25] Typhoid resulted from the ingestion of fecal matter, as many authors of this period liked to explain: a result of an industrializing nation's inability to reabsorb its waste.

The routes of its communicability highlighted the infrastructures that constituted interdependence both locally and nationally. Typhoid vividly depicted the social networks of the modern nation, bringing the problem spots into focus, and it helped to justify national, as well as local, public-health initiatives. It was one among a number of communicable diseases with an etiology and infectivity that were clarified by the discoveries of bacteriology. It therefore helped to bring the science into the service of the state. The discovery of microorganisms that could be identified as causing diseases such as typhoid, tuberculosis, anthrax, diphtheria, and puerperal fever involved a changing understanding not only of disease and the body but also of the nation. Most notably, the discovery of microorganisms allowed scientists to chart contacts that would otherwise have been invisible to all participants. When people became ill with typhoid, it meant that they had ingested someone else's bodily excretions. The source of an epidemic in Lawrence, Massachusetts, could be traced to the effluvia of a sick mill worker in Lowell; those whose illness led Soper to Mary Mallon could be assured that at some time they had ingested the cook's bodily waste.

The connections were more than imagined; typhoid made gruesomely literal the material relations of, and the intimate contact with, strangers in the industrial, immigrant city. The discovery of human vectors of disease fleshed out the contours of contact phobias, explaining the easy enlistment of typhoid (among other diseases) in the discourse of "race suicide," the sociological and political laments that the white race was facilitating its own demise. Typhoid epidemics typically struck the affluent as often as the destitute. They thereby served as a convenient analog for the extinction of the white race that was to attend the competition offered by the cheap labor of migrants and immigrants. Physically and economically, in other words, white middle-class America was apparently under siege. Epidemics, moreover, were the disruptive result of increased global commerce and contact with other cultures, races, and places in which dangerous microbes flourished. They spurred many in the medical community to join politicians in linking health reform to increased nationalism. The English psychiatrist Havelock Ellis expressed a typical sentiment when he observed that since disease (like capital) does not maintain borders, a health-reform program required "a strong national sentiment and some degree of realised national progress." Medical threats brought cultural biases to life in those arguments. Ellis's warnings distinctly betray not only bias but fear of a colonial repressed returning as a catastrophic communicable disease: "Before we have continued long on the path [to health reform] we may at any moment be confronted by the westerly movements of some monstrous epidemic coming out of its Asiatic lair and breathing forth death and misery."[26] Bacterial microbes gave new expression to medicalized nativism, typically animating the vague menace that lurked abroad.

Communicable diseases, such as typhoid, also confounded the chauvinism that invoked epidemics in nonindustrialized nations and regions to mark modern progress and superiority. A medical doctor writing about typhoid for the *American Review of Reviews* vividly expressed the national disgrace conferred by typhoid in his piece "Fighting American Typhoid." He begins with a lushly written depiction of sanguine Americans:

> Asiatic cholera, for many weeks last year and up to the coming of the present winter, visited the European peoples, especially in Russia; and morning after morning the American citizen, educated, sovereign, eminently practical, not to be put upon, free as the upward-soaring lark—and all that sort of thing— has, in glancing over his newspaper, pitied those poor folk for the sufferings they had to endure by reason of their ignorance and their supineness. And as regularly, along with his breakfast cup of coffee, has the American citizen been blessing himself that he is not as those blind, bludgeoned, superstitious moujiks, who so submissively endure and die of cholera. Pending such unctuous reflection he has held in abeyance, somewhere among the subliminal strata of his consciousness, any consideration of American typhoid.[27]

The excessive prose captures the American reader's presumed smugness and illusion of safety. Clause upon clause conveys the reader's dissociated perusal of the report of an epidemic elsewhere, until the intrusion of *American* typhoid confounds the distinction between an American "us" and a Russian "them": the disease metamorphoses Americans, making them as "foreign," as unrecognizable to themselves, as the Russian moujik is to them. Dr. Huber enjoins his readers to look at "them" and see "us." And he calls for the mobilization of citizens against the disease as a patriotic measure: "The better citizens we are, the more surely, the more satisfactorily our laws will be enforced. And what can the citizen better work for than the conservation, through the government, of the home" (348). Typhoid threatens the American's recognizable self: the sovereignty, the home, and, by extension, the larger community, the nation, by which that "self" is defined.

Compounding that menace is the representation of typhoid as a military disaster—literally, a threat to the security of the nation. The title of a *National Geographic* piece, "Our Army Versus a Bacillus," drives home the point, which surfaces throughout typhoid literature, that hygiene is a military issue. The disease "exacted a toll in the northern army during the Civil War of 80,000 cases, and was the cause of not less than *86 per cent of the total mortality* of the American Army in the Spanish War of 1898."[28] The author lauds the Japanese army, by contrast, for its successful preventive measures and depicts military success as contingent on attention to hygiene.

Immigrants and tenements became a focal point of the threat, even though the medical literature regularly established the inassociability of typhoid with a particular class or group of people. Nevertheless, the connection was more than an analogy. Contagion in general was a fact of, as well as a metaphor for, life in the crowded conditions of urban spaces. Tenements of immigrants and migrants offered the most visible representation of the excesses of industrialization and of the limits of assimilation. Nationally, industrial prosperity produced insufficiently absorbed waste as it produced insufficiently absorbed foreigners (migrants and immigrants). The denizens of the tenement were readily identified with the waste, and that tendency was reinforced when epidemics accompanied immigrants or when they spread to the tenement where conditions favored their growth. Diseases associated with bodily excretions, like cholera and typhoid, evoked particular fear and disgust, which were displaced easily onto that same population, especially the most recent immigrants. The ingestion of waste made people ill; that waste could not, therefore, be assimilated. Making that inassimilability visceral, typhoid lit up the inassimilability of the products of industrialization with which waste was associated, including immigrants and other residents of the tenement viewed as a national burden. The polluted fluids of the immigrant, nonwhite, or generally impoverished body became the polluted fluids of the body politic. The threat of national disaster, articulated in the language of nativism, was a consistent refrain in the typhoid literature of the period, which in turn facilitated the changing scale of public-health initiatives.

Writings about typhoid in the popular and medical press registered the nation's ambivalence toward its own rapid industrialization, which found particular expression, following the identification of Mary Mallon, in the impossibility of identifying and documenting healthy carriers. Officially tracking individuals, especially immigrants, was the object as well of the reforms of the census in the late nineteenth century and early twentieth, initiated by the statistician and outspoken nativist Francis Amasa Walker. The 1906 Naturalization Act, with its emphasis on documenting immigrants, came out of the spirit of those reforms, and in that spirit, public-health officials like Soper and Nichols mused about how the identification and control of healthy carriers could eliminate or at least significantly contain the threat of many communicable diseases. A healthy public marked the power of both the state and the nation (the body politic). Communicable-disease outbreaks could be appropriated as a perverse beacon of national success, as in Adams's observation that "the disease . . . runs parallel to industrial prosperity. . . . When business is good, typhoid rates boom," but only when recast as a call to public action and a reaffirmation of national potential.[29]

The bacteriological identification and classification of disease-causing microbes animated the "great enemy of mankind" and reinforced a militaristic understanding of disease as it offered the promise of humanity's ultimate victory over this foe. The meaning of those microbes, and the diseases they represented, was, of course, never stable. Lurking in the festering swamps of a tropical jungle or the filthy corners of a New York tenement, they embodied a foreign menace; felling a Roosevelt scion or the sturdy troops of a U.S. battalion, they marked a national failure. Disease could signal personal shortcomings or confer the status of innocent victim. The symbolic fluidity of diseases and their microbes derived their meaning from the stories among which they circulated. The stories of the scientific and epidemiological identifications of the healthy human vector of disease, which helped to recast public health as national security, enlisted bacteriologists and public-health officials as well as microbes in the project of representing the importance of social measures that reinforced national borders and documented individuals. These stories derived their authority not only from the language of science but also from the narrative precedents of communicable-disease accounts on which they invariably built. The frequently long latency periods of venereal diseases, their transmission by apparently (although not actually) healthy people, and the means of that transmission made carriers of venereal disease an especially vivid prototype for other kinds of disease carriers. The familiar narratives of venereal disease had also already associated communicable disease both with the changing dimension of social control and with threats to the nation. The story of Typhoid Mary imported those features, but it also transformed them as it recast both the challenge of carriers and the solutions they mandated.

"TYPHOID MARY" AND HER ANTECEDENTS

Mary Mallon's recalcitrance, her reluctance to believe she was spreading typhoid, and her unwillingness to meet with public-health officials became more central and elaborately recounted each time Soper told the story. With each version, Soper fleshed out the details of her life, shifting his emphasis from the detection of the carrier to a more comprehensive portrait of the woman. In his 1919 version, from an article titled "Typhoid Mary," Soper described the help that he had had in arranging a surprise interview with the reluctant cook from "a friend whom she often visited at night in the top of a Third Avenue tenement."[30] Twenty years later, he would elaborate on their relationship, noting that at the end of her workday, Mallon retired "to a rooming house on Third Avenue below Thirty-third Street, where she was spending the evenings with a disreputable-looking man . . . [whose] headquarters during the day was in a saloon on the corner. I got to be well acquainted with him," Soper admits. "He took me to see the room. I should not care to see another like it. It was a place of dirt and disorder. It was not improved by the presence of a large dog of which Mary was said to be very fond."[31] The dirt and disorder mark social margins and the hint of categorical breakdown, which Soper casts in sexual terms. Typhoid is not a sexually transmitted disease, but with his attention to the evident sexual activity of this unmarried Irish woman, whose affection for her lover's dog adds to Soper's disgust, he summoned the conventions of a venereal-disease narrative. Mallon inhabited the spaces and indulged in the behavior of a fallen woman, and Soper's depiction implicitly coded her disease as a result of her illicit behavior.

Although identified through specific outbreaks, venereal disease was certainly rampant in this period, and cautionary tales abounded in a variety of media.[32] Types, rather than individuals, surfaced as the central figures of danger in these accounts. Typically, either the female prostitute or the man who frequented her was the targeted source of social campaigns, but the fallen woman—the young girl gone to ruin—was the stock figure of the cautionary tales. Venereal disease posed a threat in these accounts to the future of the family, the nation, and the white race. Historians of the period have documented a preoccupation with female sexuality, which they attribute to generalized anxiety about rapid social change.[33] Joanne Meyerowitz persuasively argues that the preoccupation overlapped with broader concerns about the implications of female mobility, triggered by the rapidly expanding population of single women in the cities in the early decades of the twentieth century, whom she calls "women adrift." These women called attention to changing mores and social organization—so much so, in fact, that they were often the subject of sociological study in its formative years. Prostitution certainly existed in the city, but it was not a new threat, and urgent denunciations of the oldest profession responded more to the perceived dangers of a new social organization than to an upsurge in the trade. Ruth Rosen describes the "uneasy truce between society and prostitution," which is periodically "broken by outbursts of social indignation" marked by a preponderance of literature about prostitution.[34]

Fallen-woman narratives accompanied these outbursts. They encompassed a variety of stories and genres unified by their condemnation of female sexuality that was not sanctioned by the state through marriage. The stories conflated prostitution with premarital sexual activity, the latter often depicted as leading to the former, and offered a variety of reasons for the fall. Some women, according to one medical journal, were "born prostitutes," but most fit the same writer's description of "the innocent girl of normal physiologic attributes who is always in danger of becoming a social outcast through ignorance of those laws which it is our [society's and especially the medical establishment's] duty to see that she thoroughly understands before it is too late."[35] The fallen woman characteristically lacked proper supervision because she had immigrated or migrated to the city and lived among temptations and without benefit of friends or relatives. As the story goes, she was often lonely and therefore easily persuaded to follow her heart. She could be led to her fall by her desire for luxuries she could not afford. While historically the women most likely to choose prostitution had exhausted other options for subsistence or found them less desirable, the fallen woman of literature (and melodrama) occupied one of the two former categories. Her "illicit" sexuality consigned her to the margins of society, where, at least in her literary manifestations, she generally did not survive.

Discussions in popular and specialty journals about the social dangers posed not only by prostitutes and fallen women but also by women whose unconventionality subjected them to the charge increased steadily throughout the first two decades of the twentieth century. From the pages of medical journals, health professionals decried the threats that extramarital sexuality posed to the family, the institution of marriage, and the nation. They medicalized the threats by casting them in the terms of venereal disease, which interfered with the reproduction of white middle-class citizens. In 1906, while Soper was tracking down Mary Mallon, the Section on Hygiene and Sanitary Science of the American Medical Association sponsored a series of papers on marriage and health, which were presented at the meeting of the association and reprinted that year in its main publication, the *Journal of the American Medical Association (JAMA)*. Two Chicago doctors, Bayard Holmes and Albert H. Burr, evoked "the physical and evolutionary basis of marriage" to depict the profound social danger of venereal disease.[36] Evolutionary arguments about marriage, advanced as well by sociologists such as Ross, naturalized the institution by establishing its roots in "family" groupings that evolved because they presumably facilitated the survival of the members of these groups. Assuming that "the most important function of the human body, biologically, is reproduction," Burr characterized "the supreme importance of woman in these relations" as "apparent when we consider her office in prenatal existence; her role as the nourishing mother; her place as the very foundation stone of every hearth and home, and her life as the vital center about which cluster families and tribes and nations. . . . The welfare of society depends far more on the physical, moral and intellectual excellence of woman than on that of 'mere man' "[37] Neither these views nor their expression in a medical journal was unusual. It was commonly argued that the nation had a biological as well as social basis in the family, and the institution of marriage safeguarded the reproduction of both. Marriage was therefore a medical as well as a social and political concern, and any threat to the socially sanctioned sexuality expressed by the institution of marriage was a threat to the nation. Venereal disease marked the violation of the marriage contract by at least one of the members of the marriage, typically the husband, even if it occurred before the marriage. According to Burr, that transgression "outrival[ed] the criminal interference with the products of conception as a cause of race suicide" (1887–88). Burr's nation was distinctly white and at least middle class.

The enormous representational power of venereal disease derived from its confounding of the distinction between the social and the medical. The "supreme importance" of the woman to the reproduction of that nation similarly superimposed her biological onto her social role, turning what one widely read treatise on the subject called the *"vinculum matrimonii"* into "a chain which binds and fetters the woman completely."[38] The volume, *Social Diseases and Marriage*, was penned by Prince Albert Morrow, a dermatologist who studied syphilis in Europe in the late 1870s, early in his medical career, and went on to become one of the foremost publicists of the disease and its consequences. The founder of the American Society for Sanitary and Moral Prophylaxis in 1905, he also translated and authored numerous books and articles, the best known of which was his 1904 *Social Diseases and Marriage*. Morrow christened venereal disease the "social disease," and he posited prostitutes and husbands as the perpetrators and "the idolized daughters, the very flower of womanhood," as the victims. The binding chain of marriage makes the daughter-turned-wife "the passive recipient of the germs of any sexual disease her husband may harbor." The social transformation turns dangerously physical when, "on her wedding night she may, and often does, receive unsuspectingly the poison of a disease which may seriously affect her health and kill her children, or, by extinguishing her capacity of conception, may sweep away all the most cherished hopes and aspirations of married life. . . . [A]n 'innocent' in every sense of the word—she is incapable of foreseeing, powerless to prevent this injury. She often pays with her life for her blind confidence in the man who ignorantly or carelessly, passes over to her a disease he has received from a prostitute" (22).

In his role as husband, the infected man disrupts the natural (biological) metamorphosis of social roles, preventing the daughter from becoming a mother and thereby corrupting the institution of marriage, when, having failed to respect the sanctity of his role, he carries a disease into his family. Venereal disease exposes the transgression of those social roles and manifests the biological and social consequences of that transgression. In an essay in the *American Journal of Sociology*, Morrow specifically vilified the "evil" of a disease passed through marriage for its corruption of an institution that emerged "for the purpose of regularizing sexual relations between men and women, and the creation, care, and maintenance of children . . .—not offspring merely, but children born in conditions of vitality, health, and physical vigor, and capable of becoming useful citizens to the state."[39] The potential to become "useful citizens"—a category that Morrow, following the prescriptions of his day, reserved for the white middle and upper classes—turns *biological* offspring into *social* children. The white man who deviates from the prescribed (and anticipated) social role of husband risks subjecting his future family to a disease that challenges the reproduction of the white race.

Morrow spent his career advocating for a social response, including publicity, education, and public-health regulations, to the conditions favoring the spread of the "social disease." His work attests to the lack of distinction between the social and the medical that characterized discussions not only of venereal disease but also of other social and medical afflictions. Social problems were as "contagious" as diseases. Typical of this usage is a response to Morrow that immediately followed his piece in the *American Journal of Sociology*. The author, A. B. Wolfe, a professor of economics and sociology at Oberlin College with a specialty in population and economic theory, joins Morrow in his advocacy of public education about venereal disease, noting that "when we talk about publicity and education we mean that the social consciousness should be opened to these social dangers of contagious vice and disease."[40] Representing both vice and disease as *social dangers* and as *contagious*, Wolfe follows a sociological usage of the term *contagious*. The usage was more than metaphorical; it registered sociologists' efforts to understand scientifically the communicability of ideas and sensations. They believed that communication involved unwitting physiological responses that made ideas and sensations as communicable as microbes.[41] Vice was as communicable for them as venereal disease, and both fell under the auspices of sociology as well as public health. The idea of social being embodied especially by the healthy carrier reinforced, and helped to develop, the concept of social contagion.

While Wolfe shared Morrow's formulation of the problem, he departed radically from his diagnosis and solution. "The problem of the family is in more ways than one the problem of women," he conceded. But "so long as woman was regarded mainly as a vehicle for sex gratification and a cheap housekeeper combined, so long as it is thought that 'the noblest thing *any* woman can do is to be a good wife and mother,' so long as women are not gladly and consciously recognized by man to be a part of the human race as well as bearers of it, that long will the ideal of the family leave much to be desired and the actual family remain a heavily sociological problem."[42] Appearing in 1909, the year of Mary Mallon's publicized court case, Wolfe's analysis offers insight into the anxiety that she elicited. The challenge to woman's primary role as bearer (or carrier) of the human race raised the question not only of who would do the bearing in her place if she turned to competing pursuits but also of what she might carry instead. Typhoid Mary may have offered an answer; unmarried, sexually active women (and their nonmonogamous married counterparts) certainly did. The trend toward the general direction that Wolfe advocated, the move toward greater female agency and mobility, prompted renewed attention to the problem of female sexuality and its consequences.[43] Wolfe was not entirely alone in offering female mobility as a partial antidote to the contagion of vice and disease, but the overwhelming trend was to reincorporate it as part of the problem. Social and medical contagion mutually reinforced each other, as social transgression carried the threat of communicable disease, which in turn portended social dissolution.

More typical than Wolfe's proposal were the calls for greater moral standardization of women that issued from the pages of academic and medical journals as well as the pulpit and the popular press. The implicit threat of venereal disease often colored these discussions of female mobility, giving form to the unnamed danger associated with social change. One of the foremost students of the changing roles of women in society was the University of Chicago sociologist W. I. Thomas, who first spelled out the transformation in "The Adventitious Character of Woman," published in the *American Journal of Sociology* in 1906, the year of the American Medical Association (AMA) symposium and of Soper's first encounter with Mary Mallon. Arguing for the evolutionary basis of marriage and gender roles, Thomas observed that women had originally been dominant but gradually, in response to social change, had "dropped back into a somewhat unstable and adventitious relation to the social process," and modern women—especially American women—had become dependent instead on communities for regulation.[44] The problem with that dependency, he explains, is that "an unattached woman has a tendency to become an adventuress—not so much on economic as on psychological grounds" (41), for when "the ordinary girl . . . becomes detached from home and group, and is removed not only from surveillance, but from the ordinary stimulation and interest afforded by social life and acquaintanceship, her inhibitions are likely to be relaxed" (41–42). With the words *unattached* and *detached,* Thomas gives spatial expression to a relationship to community that he characterizes as superficial. He finds the outcome of women's detachment sufficiently predictable to offer as a narrative:

> The girl coming from the country to the city affords one of the clearest cases of detachment. Assuming that she comes to the city to earn her living, her work is not only irksome, but so unremunerative that she finds it impossible to

obtain those accessories to her personality in the way of finery which would be sufficient to hold her attention and satisfy her if they were to be had in plenty. She is lost from the sight of everyone whose opinion has any meaning for her, while the separation from her home community renders her condition peculiarly flat and lonely; and she is prepared to accept any opportunity for stimulation offered her, unless she has been morally standardized before leaving home. To be completely lost sight of may, indeed, become an object under these circumstances—the only means by which she can without confusion accept unapproved stimulations—and to pass from a regular to an irregular life and back again before the fact has been noted is not an unusual course. (42)

The passage reads like a plot summary of Theodore Dreiser's *Sister Carrie,* a novel published and reviewed (although not widely) in 1900. Thomas may have read—or perhaps read about—the book, although Doubleday, Page, Dreiser's original publisher, had distributed it without publicity, and it had sold fewer than five hundred copies before being allowed to go out of print.[45] Whether or not Thomas had read it, the similarity between his description and the plot of the novel attests to a familiar story, a cultural narrative that was circulating in a variety of forms.

Despite the allusions to their sexual activity—explicit in the case of the character Carrie Meeber—neither Thomas's "unattached girl" nor Dreiser's eponymous heroine suffers the conventional fate of the fallen woman. Unlike that stock figure, Carrie does not only survive, she prospers. And she does not repent. Many of Dreiser's readers were troubled by his failure to punish her in his novel. The anonymity afforded by the city allows Carrie to move from poverty to comfort as she assumes the fictive role first of the wife of an ambitious salesman, and then of the already married manager of a prominent saloon, with whom she flees to New York City from Chicago. Remaining undetected in her deceptions, she eventually leaves the manager for a successful and respected stage career, although the end of the novel finds her yearning and discontented. She is Thomas's unattached woman, a newly articulated type whose salient feature, it seems, was the ability to disappear in plain view, to *pass from a regular to an irregular life and back again before the fact has been noted.*[46] The narrative of this type shifts the focus from the unwitting girl as victim, as in the fallen-woman narrative, to the unattached woman as threat in need of detection and supervision. While the conventional fallen woman is recognizable as such to her contemporaries, the unattached woman is visible, as a type if not as an individual, only to experts such as sociologists—and to novelists.

Implicit in her ability to disappear is the threat of her circulation and of what she might bring back. When she returns from wherever she has been, the community that had lost sight of her will not know what she might be *carrying;* a communicable disease and a fatherless baby can both introduce the threat of race suicide. Sexuality is not the only problem. Her ability to disappear and reappear also represents the community's lack of control of its spaces. Thomas's and Dreiser's narratives register the effort to make sense not only of apparently new female types and behavior but also of a changing conception and experience of space. Sociologists materialized the changes that intrigued them in their description of the "promiscuous spaces" of the city, where people mingled with strangers, where boundaries were fluid, and where traditional spatial segregation according to class, race, religion, sexuality, gender, nationality held no purchase. These spaces offered the opportunity for both anonymity and dangerous attractions, at once tempting and allowing the unattached woman to disappear. She inhabited those spaces and came to embody the breakdown of familiar classifications and other social codes in which the sociologists saw both possibilities and danger. Even more than the recognizably fallen woman, she represented the reorganization of the familiar social relations that constitute recognizable communities.

Ruth Rosen describes the irony of the spatial transformation effected by Progressive reformers at the turn of the century: as identifiable vice areas ("red-light districts") were closed down, they were "replaced by the riskier, but less visible, act of streetwalking."[47] While the protagonists in the fallen-woman narratives become physically identifiable as prostitutes, the unattached woman such as Carrie Meeber, like a streetwalker, might turn up anywhere. She is even more dangerous, however, because her signature characteristic is her unrecognizability; her spatial liberties leave her unmarked by her behavior.

The pressing threat of the unattached woman was that, even more than her middle-class counterpart, for whom invisibility was not so easy an option, she embodied the breakdown of the codes of social control that accompanied social, economic, and spatial transformations on both local and national levels; her ability to become undetectable highlighted the uncertainty and instability of social roles. Able to "pass" as respectable, the unattached woman inspired anxious discussion about the reproduction (in all senses) of economic and racial hierarchies and the sociopolitical identities they subtended.

Since the sexuality and reproduction that were centrally in question found expression for most cultural commentators as the threat of prostitution, the instability and uncertainty that accompanied socioeconomic and spatial reorganization were deflected onto heightened concern about that particular social issue. The idea, for instance, that the entrance of women into the more anonymous (and less supervised) spaces of the professional world led to prostitution was circulated not only in popular media but, again, in medical journals, where the danger of female mobility was thereby medicalized. While the stage had been frequently thus assailed, the beginning of the twentieth century witnessed a broadening of professions that posed a threat to white women's virtue. The readership of the *JAMA*, for example, learned that "another source of prostitution is the entrance of women into industrial life. For centuries she was surrounded by home life and home industries. Then the spinning wheel gave way to the loom in factories, the needle yielded to the sewing machine, the individual worker changed into a 'hand,' producing in the factory a certain part of the whole. Women have entered the professions, arts and literature with success. She has gained independence, but is lost to family life and its beneficial influences."[48] The definition of the prostitute was clearly expanding to encompass women who ventured into anonymous spaces and who abjured the marriage bond.

Throughout this passage, the writer, Ludwig Weiss, signals his implicit concern with the woman's evident detachment. Using the alienating metonymy of industrialization (the production of "a certain part of the whole"), he depicts her corresponding transformation into "a 'hand.'" In the context of the severed bonds of her home life and the alienating world of the factory, the unattached woman becomes herself not only "a certain part of the whole," but specifically a *hand*. Explicitly, the writer calls attention to the dehumanization inscribed in common slang, such as "factory hand" or "farm hand." But hands were also singled out in medical journals and the popular press during this period in commonly featured warnings about the particular danger they posed in the transmission of disease. Assertions about Mary Mallon's notorious lack of cleanliness were based on the assumption that her unwashed hands were the means through which she spread typhoid. The entrance of women into the social spaces of industrial life resulted not only in their contamination but also in their transformation into contaminants.

Mary Mallon was the unattached woman par excellence, and her mobility, her sexuality, and her ability to disappear were a significant part of the story. A fallen woman was Soper's ideal protagonist. He had come to the house in Oyster Bay at the behest of the owner who was worried that the outbreak of typhoid among the family who had rented his house (and for whom Mallon had served as a cook) would make it impossible to find future renters. In the case of the missing cook, responsibility for the outbreak devolved on a person rather than a space, and, even better, a person whose behavior called for the special skills of an epidemiologist and the implementation of public-health measures. But Mary Mallon was neither a prostitute nor ill, and she carried typhoid rather than venereal disease. Her unwitting spread of disease through the daily activities of her life made her culpability hard to assess.

The distinction between the story of Mary Mallon and the conventional fallen-woman tale clarifies how communicable disease and the figure of the healthy carrier influenced changing ideas about space and social interactions. Although the line may blur, the fallen-woman narrative typically preserves some distinction between spatial and sexual promiscuity. Not so the narrative of the healthy human carrier. When typhoid replaces venereal disease, that distinction collapses, since the disease spreads through contact often sustained unknowingly in the course of a daily routine. In a paper delivered at the annual AMA meeting one year after Soper introduced the idea of a healthy human carrier, William H. Park, a pioneer in the study of healthy carriers and the physician who treated Mary Mallon during her first medical incarceration, acknowledged the impossibility of discovering and isolating all such people. Instead, he explained, "we must . . . turn to the more general methods of preventing infection, such as safeguarding our food and water, not only chiefly when typhoid is present, but at all times, for we now know that in every community, whether it be large or small, unsuspected typhoid bacilli carriers may always be present."[49]

While fallen-woman narratives cast suspicion on unsupervised women and certain sexualized spaces, the ominous threat of unsuspected carriers turned everyone and every place into a potential public-health threat. In the former, spatial promiscuity allowed for meetings that were both unsupervised and that enabled anonymous strangers to mingle, which entailed the possibility of liaisons across racial, class, even sexual boundaries. In accounts of carriers, however, spatial promiscuity entailed unwitting bodily exchange, such as the ingestion of the carrier's bodily discharges (characteristically urine or feces). Because typhoid was the result of unknowing bodily contact, all spaces became ambiguous: almost sexual, but not quite; something new and unfamiliar. There was a further breakdown of familiar classifications and categories. Carrier stories turned strangers into people in intimate though unacknowledged contact, but strangers were not the only healthy carriers. The carrier status could turn the nearest of kin into dangerous figures. Park specifically remarked on "the predominance of women who are carriers over men, and especially married women who have borne children"—in other words, *mothers*.[50] As far as potential infection from a healthy carrier was concerned, there was no distinction between the home and the red-light district, except, perhaps, that the visible dirt of the latter inspired greater precaution, making the former (the home) a site of greater personal danger from infection. While Soper and other medical and public-health officials offered hygienic practices, especially hand washing, as the most important safeguard against the danger, the message of the healthy-carrier account was that those actions were finally insufficient. The danger of spatial promiscuity in the fallen-woman narrative was that it might lead to sexual promiscuity; the carrier narrative, by contrast, located the danger of infection directly in spatial promiscuity itself.

METAMORPHOSES

Ludwig Weiss oscillates, in his *JAMA* piece, between the plural subject *women* and the singular pronoun *she*. The grammatical infelicity suggests an inexpert stylist, but it also appears with striking regularity in such discussions, registering a way of thinking about the problem of the disappearing woman that has an analog in the sociologists' strategic use of types. The pronominal use of *she* for *women* turns the range of working women in factories, the arts, and professions into a single type whose story can be predicted and whose experiences can be categorized, like Thomas's unattached girl coming from the country to the city. Weiss's grammar prevents the disappearance of these women from view as he incorporates them into a narrative that is so legible, it seems, that he does not even have to make the actual connection to prostitution. Recognizable types and narratives effectively compensate for the disappearance of the familiar spaces, making unattached women visible, comprehensible, and apprehensible.

The "typing" performed implicitly through Weiss's faulty grammar was, for sociologists, an important part of their emerging methodology. Sociology sought to make social dynamics visible, and identifying types was central to that process. Soper's transformation of Mary Mallon into "Typhoid Mary," which he conspicuously performed in the stories he told about her, similarly fashioned her as a type—the healthy human carrier—which turned the unattached woman into a medical threat. Those stories became fundamental to how he represented his work as a public health officer as they fleshed out the bacteriological theory of the healthy human carrier.

Despite numerous frustrating attempts, Soper was finally unable to discover familial connections or personal motivations for Mary Mallon. The
narrative of Typhoid Mary serves in their stead, charting the movements of
the peripatetic cook as it "places" her in social, and ultimately historical,
terms. Her recalcitrance is an important part of that story. In the last of
many essays he wrote about his discovery of and encounters with her, Soper
recalled visiting her at the hospital where he tried to enlist her as a col-
laborator in the telling of her story, with her liberation and more as a
promised reward. "I will do more than you think," he promises. "I will write
a book about your case. I will not mention your real name: I will carefully
hide your identity. I will guarantee that you will get all the profits."[51] But
Mary Mallon remained inexplicably silent—inexplicably, that is, for Soper.
To a friend, she wrote plaintively about her incarceration, her fears and
suspicions, and her refusal to cooperate: "Im a little afraid of the people—I
have a good right—for when I came to the Department the said they were in
my track later another said they were in the muscels of my bowels + laterly
the thought of the gall Bladder I have been in fact a peep show for Evrey
body even the Internes had to come to see me + ask about the facts alredy
known to the whole wide world the Tubrculosis men would say there she is
the kidnapped woman Dr. Parks has had me illustrated in Chicago I wonder
how the said Dr. Wm. H Park would like to be insulted and put in the
journal + call him or his wife Typhoid William Park."[52] With these words,
she manifests a lack of faith in the medical personnel who, despite urging her to have her gallbladder removed, repeatedly tell her contradictory
things about the source of the typhoid bacilli she has been excreting. Particularly striking is the final lament in which she expresses her dismay
at being put on public display as a specimen, demonstrable proof of the
hypothesized healthy carrier state. Soper, that is, had asked Mallon to make
visible what the organisms under the microscope could only suggest: that
an apparently uninfected person could transmit the typhoid bacilli to other
(unsuspecting) people and make them sick. And when she would not comply, he turned her into a "peep show," first for the medical and public-
health communities, and subsequently, through his narratives, for the general public.

The responsibility of human vectors, especially healthy carriers, for typhoid outbreaks was at least a controversial subject in the medical establishment when "Typhoid Mary" came into existence, one that would
continue to be debated within the scientific community for several years
following the initial discovery of healthy carriers. As late as 1911, W. H.

Hamer urged his Royal Society of Medicine audience to be cautious in the deployment of any new theory, especially one with such consequences. "It is, indeed, a very debatable point," he argued, "whether there is, in fact, any conclusive epidemiological evidence to show that typhoid bacillus carriers (or paratyphoid bacillus carriers) are a source of danger."[53] Responses to his paper ranged from pointed disagreement to cautious concurrence: challenges, such as Hamer's, to the human-vector thesis were increasingly rare by 1911. Yet it is certainly not surprising that, five years earlier, Mary Mallon would have been dubious about what the medical establishment was telling her. Nonetheless, with her refusal to believe, Mallon struck at the nerve center of the new scientific authority that Progressives like Soper sought to claim for themselves. With her refusal to accept the role he fashioned for her, she also confounded his demonstration of the power and importance of epidemiology.

Soper responded to Mallon's refusal to cooperate by telling a different story, by his own admission, from the one he had initially offered to tell. The first offer was of a case study from which, as he saw it, both would profit. She would receive financial benefits (in addition to the assurance of anonymity), and he would presumably enhance his professional reputation as he advanced science. All she had to do, again from his point of view, was to submit to being the proof that substantiates the hypothesis. When she declined his offer—ironically, by (silently) retreating into her toilet—Mary Mallon challenged the authority of both medical personnel and empirical data. In turn, Soper told a story that focused on her recalcitrant behavior, which became, particularly in his numerous retellings, the sign of her criminality. In response to Mary Mallon's refusal to collaborate with him, he reconstituted his authority in his moralistic tale, the outcome of which was her life sentence. He turned her into "Typhoid Mary," whose behavior called for, and whose story exemplified, the importance of developing better measures of public health and social control. It is impossible to know whether or not the unfortunate cook really would have been, as Baker suggests, "a free woman all her life" if she had behaved differently, but transgressiveness inheres in Soper's and others' very descriptions of her, which suggests that cultural biases and miscommunication influenced perceptions of her behavior.[54]

Accounts of Mallon suggest that ethnicity, class, and occupation, combined with her condition, ensured her transformation into an object of disgust and reprobation in the public-health and medical literature of the period. The generally enlightened Sara Josephine Baker, for example, described the Irish as "incredibly shiftless, altogether charming in their abject helplessness, wholly lacking in any ambition and dirty to an unbelievable degree" and noted as a matter of fact that "the Irish and the Russian Jews vied for the distinction of living in the most lurid squalor. The Irish did it . . . out of a mixture of discouragement and apparently shiftlessness."[55] And E. A. Ross speculated, in a discussion of race suicide, "that it is probably the visible narrowing of the circle of opportunity through the infiltration of Irish and French Canadians that has brought so low the native birth-rate in New England."[56]

With Irish immigrants and their descendants constituting more than one-third of New York City's population at the beginning of the last decade of the nineteenth century, the Irish were certainly a visible presence.[57] Unlike many other immigrant groups, Irish immigration was heavily female and unmarried; women comprised more than one-half of the immigrants from Ireland in this period. Hasia R. Diner documents the tendency of single Irish women, especially immigrants, to gravitate to the occupation of domestic servant, which, although advocated by Progressive social reformers, was stigmatized among the working classes and the general population.[58] The stigma as well as the dependence on and "fear of their social inferiors" (88) that Diner also chronicles gave rise to the stereotypes, perpetuated in all forms of media from the period, of lazy, slovenly, dirty, unskilled (especially at cooking) Irish women servants to which descriptions of Mary Mallon consistently and strikingly conform. She seems startlingly typecast for her role in the narrative.

The leading lady of Soper's stories is "an Irish woman about forty years of age, intelligent, tall, heavy, single and non-communicative."[59] As Leavitt and Alan M. Kraut remark, Soper's description of her consistently underscores her departure from conventional norms of white femininity, as, again, is consistent with depictions of Irish women servants generally.[60] She is tall and excessive, "a little too heavy," as Soper's 1939 account explains, and "those who knew her best in the long years of her custody said Mary walked more like a man than a woman and that her mind had a distinctly masculine character, also."[61] His portrait, however, corresponds neither to that of Baker, who describes her—in contrast to her general depictions of the Irish—as "a clean, neat, obviously self-respecting Irishwoman with a firm mouth and her hair done in a tight knot at the back of her head," nor, as Leavitt notes, to the photographs of Mary Mallon from this period, which depict a slender, attractive woman.[62] Soper's protagonist looks as she behaves: according to what is expected of Irish immigrants, domestic servants, and unattached women. And most of the subsequent depictions of her build on his accounts. In his descriptions of a sexually transgressive, generally recalcitrant, masculine woman, Soper marked her as socially deviant. When he added "chronic germ distributor" to the list of her other traits, he cast her as a threat to public health, and the metamorphosis into "Typhoid Mary" was complete; she became recognizable, that is, within the specific terms of the narrative that he fashioned.

For Kraut, Mallon was a victim of medicalized nativism. "In American legend and lore," he writes, "Mary Mallon has become synonymous with the health menace posed by the foreign-born."[63] The combination of her medical condition and her social status constituted her danger to an *American* public. But contagion did not simply stand in for the immigrant threat; the concept of a healthy carrier of a communicable disease was, in turn, shaped by the association. The story of Typhoid Mary contributed to the formation of new medical and social categories and to their mutual influence. Each retelling of the story brought out more details of Mallon's background and behavior, developing the associations between them and communicable disease. The evolving story shows the medical and legal establishments in the process of determining not just the treatment but the representation and larger implications of healthy carriers. The particularities of Mary Mallon affected the public understanding of the concept of the healthy carrier and the response that such an entity required. Her story, and the concept of the healthy carrier that it made available, helped to fashion a distinctly medicalized understanding of social being and social control.

"Typhoid Mary" was produced through a series of events and accounts that document the evolution of those concepts. Mallon was christened "Typhoid Mary" not by Soper, but by Milton J. Rosenau, a prominent public-health official, in response to William Park's paper, which was discussed in Park's absence at the annual meeting of the AMA in June 1908. Park used Mallon as a case study to demonstrate the existence of chronic and healthy carriers, but the main thrust of his paper was the epidemiological question of what to do about this new category of healthy carrier, in a sense a new category of person. Observing that "the case of this woman brings up many interesting problems," he asked, "has the city a right to deprive her of her liberty for perhaps her whole life? The alternative is to turn loose on the public a woman who is known to have infected at least twenty-eight persons."[64] In the end, although he argued that the presence of typhoid-bacilli carriers typically called for preventive measures rather than the less practicable solution of lifetime isolation, he made an exception "in the case of the cook already described [Mary Mallon], where conditions increase the danger to such a point that an attempt at some direct prevention becomes an essential."[65] Park never mentions Mallon's recalcitrance, but refers instead to dangerous "conditions," her occupation and social position, that make her confinement "essential." There is a larger principle at work in the passive construction of the sentence: state intervention (never articulated as such) "becomes an essential," and the individual is implicitly but fundamentally conceived as a person with non-negotiable responsibilities to the community. Park authorizes himself, and, by extension, other unspecified officials, to determine when conditions mandate such intervention.

In the ensuing discussion, reprinted with the original paper in the *JAMA*, Rosenau responds to another discussant's suggestion that surgical removal of the gallbladder might cure this condition by stating his conviction that if Park were present "he would say that 'typhoid Mary' refuses to submit to surgical interference." She is named into her notorious public identity in the act of a refusal of medical authority. Yet Rosenau acknowledges her possible justification in this challenge when he concedes that "the gall bladder is not the only source of the typhoid bacilli that appear in the feces."[66] Exonerating her of precisely the kind of unreasonable recalcitrance consistently emphasized by Soper, he leaves only the ominous, unspecified "conditions" as justification for Mallon's incarceration. She is detained because the department of public health, as well as Mallon herself, has a responsibility to the community. She is not a criminal, but her condition—the nature of her occupation and social position combined with her production and dissemination of typhoid bacilli—requires ongoing isolation and treatment. In this context, Rosenau replaces Mallon with her alter ego, named by the dehumanizing epithet "typhoid Mary." Identified with and by the disease that she carries, "Typhoid Mary," a social being, is justifiably taken out of circulation, despite the possible violation of her rights, and despite the fact that her actual responsibility for the cases of typhoid charged to her still remained to be incontrovertibly demonstrated. If the documentation of human vectors as causal agents illustrated and justified the concepts of social responsibility and medicalized social control, these concepts, in turn, provided an especially fertile environment for the thesis of human vectors as causal agents of communicable disease. The concepts emerged together.

Debates about the fate of healthy carriers crossed noticeably from medical societies and journals to public fora and tabloids when Mallon brought her situation before the courts. In June 1909 she hired a lawyer and filed a writ of habeas corpus, requiring the Board of Health to justify her detention before a court of law. Filing for dismissal of the writ, the Board of Health cited as the reason for her confinement her infection "with the bacilli of typhoid" and her current "treatment under the care of physicians" of the Riverside Hospital. Even the most detailed statement, offered by the Riverside physician Fred S. Westmoreland, based the conclusion "that the patient would be a dangerous person and a constant menace to the public health at large" only on "the large quantities of typhoid bacilli existing in the alimentary tract, or gall bladder of the patient and her occupation as a cook *or* the fact that she may at any time come in contact with people wherein they would be likely to be infected with the typhoid bacilli."[67] While Soper particularized Mallon's case by insisting that her lack of cooperation explained her detention, the legal documents demonstrate that more was at stake in the trial: scientific discoveries had introduced unforeseen dangers of social interaction.

In her reading of the central issues of the trial, Leavitt demonstrates that the case had three distinct components.[68] Since Mallon's attorney had submitted the reports of a private laboratory that contradicted the findings of the Riverside laboratory by discovering no typhoid bacilli in her bodily excretions, the court had first to decide which laboratory reports were valid. Once it tacitly favored the Board of Health reports, the court still had to decide whether or not the presence of typhoid bacilli meant that Mallon was responsible for typhoid outbreaks, and, finally, whether or not such responsibility justified her confinement. Mallon used the image of a damsel in distress to counter the portrait of a "chronic typhoid germ distributor," calling her treatment "unjust, outrageous, uncivilized" and noting her astonishment "that in a Christian community a defenseless woman can be treated in this manner."[69] Against her opponents' efforts to depict her through the disease she carried, she sought to emphasize her humanity and her womanliness: her humanity as demonstrated by her conformity to gender expectations. But the court ruled in favor of the Board of Health, finding, according to a *New York Times* article, that "her release would be dangerous to the health of the community. The court therefore, said the Justice, did not care to assume the responsibility of releasing her."[70]

The trial, as the *New York American* forecast, was "expected to demonstrate just how far the Board of Health powers go." And so it did, in this individual case. But, as Leavitt notes, it failed to establish a precedent, confirming only Mallon's exceptional status. For Leavitt, the decision was important because it established a new acceptance of scientific authority in the legal measurement of truth. She remarks on "the ease with which the health department lawyer assumed that laws written about people sick with infectious disease could be applied to this new category of healthy people who harbored bacilli (especially when faced with evidence upon which two laboratories disagreed) even while they wrote of their uncertainty elsewhere."[71] But where Leavitt sees an easy assumption, I see a conspicuously unresolved legal contest. Lawyers for the Board of Health argued for the extension of those laws, while Mallon's counsel argued against it. The court in this case had to resolve the clash of rights that the new category of a healthy human carrier introduced. The court's decision registered deferral: Mallon's petition was denied, but no strong statement was forthcoming from the bench. Mary Mallon was sent back to Riverside Hospital because the court did not want to accept responsibility, as the *New York American* reported it, for the possible threat she posed. The case certainly raised the question of the place of scientific authority in the courtroom, but the court demurred. The more immediate cultural impact of the trial was to bring Mallon and her alter ego, and the perplexity that they represented, into the public arena and to demonstrate that scientific discoveries required the rethinking of accepted wisdom not only in the sciences but also in the social realm. In court, the carrier pointed to the interconnectedness of spheres of knowledge as well as of human beings.

Mallon was not a stranger to media coverage in 1909, but her court case brought the complex social and political issues of her situation more pressingly to the attention of the media both within and beyond the borders of the United States. Public opinion divided in response to her. A cartoon in the British magazine *Punch* showed her frying sausages comprised of distinctive typhoid bacilli; a letter to the *New York Times* asked, why not "start a colony on some unpleasant island, call it 'Uncle Sam's suspects,' . . . request the sterilized prayers of all religionized germ fanatics, and then leave the United States to enjoy the glorious freedom of the American flag under a medical monarchy."[72] Mallon was sometimes cast as a dangerous "living culture tube" passing among an unsuspecting populace, but more often as a member of that populace deprived of the full and equal rights to which she was entitled by a frighteningly unresponsive government; she either carried or embodied a threat to citizens of a government that was supposed, either way, to protect them. A *New York Times* editorial that appeared in July 1909 described Mallon's case as extraordinary since "it is unusual that a healthy individual should carry enough dangerous bacteria to be a source of infection to others who are healthy" and wondered if somebody had "blundered in diagnosing it."[73] Her case made apparent the ambiguities entailed in the growing expectations and authority of state-regulated public health. And the frequency with which the topic occurred in the popular press beginning the same year suggests that it helped to initiate public debate about the category.

The change in the administration of the Department of Health in 1910 that brought Mallon's long-awaited release nonetheless did not leave her entirely at liberty. She was forbidden to practice her trade and was required to report regularly to the Department of Health, but, after three captive years, she was finally otherwise free to pursue her life. Health Commissioner Ernst J. Lederle, who ordered the release, manifested the same uncertainty about how to conceptualize and legislate healthy carriers that the 1909 court case had failed to resolve. According to the *New York Times* article that reported Mallon's return to public circulation, "Dr. Lederle admitted that there might be other persons quite as dangerous to their neighbors as 'Typhoid Mary' from their peculiar harboring of germs. This, he said, was one reason why he did not think that she should be any longer singled out for confinement."[74] And nearly a year later, in December 1911, the *New York Times* placed Mallon at the center of another suit with the headline, "'Typhoid Mary' Asks $50,000 from City."[75] Reporting Mallon and her lawyer's intention to file suit, the writer confirmed that "the physicians of the Health Department have never been able to discover that Mary herself ever had typhoid." The continuing struggle over both the issues of the case and the representation of Mary Mallon registers the efforts of the medical and scientific communities, the media, and the public to come to terms with the status of a healthy carrier and its conceptual implications.

Other healthy carriers met with more understanding, compassion, and leniency than did Mary Mallon, even under similar circumstances. Surely Mallon had the misfortune to be the first publicized case in the United States, a metaphorical oldest child who suffers from the inexperience of those in charge. Her story reflects a concept (the healthy carrier) in transition and in need of definition. Yet it registers other changes as well. In her many identities—including Irish immigrant, domestic servant, sexually active unmarried woman, and typhoid carrier—"Typhoid Mary" embodied the conjunction of challenges to the concept of Americanism represented by the demographic and social changes of an industrializing and expanding nation. In all of the versions of her story, her disease and in particular her status as a typhoid carrier are coded as gendered, racial, sexual, and class-based challenges to the family and to the nation, and, consequently, to the reproduction of white America. But neither the stories nor the challenges

WORKED AS A COOK AND WAS SUPPOSED TO HAVE SPREAD TYPHOID GERMS

GAVE DETENTION WARD MEN A HARD TUSTLE.

Media response to Mary Mallon was mixed. This composite of cartoons appeared in the *New York American*, 30 June 1909, 3. Reproduced from the Collections of the Library of Congress.

they register were static. The retelling of her story over the years features changing ideas about the environment in which bacteriological theories of contagion were deeply embedded.

WHAT MARY KNEW: MEDICALIZING
THE GENDER MENACE

The "Typhoid Mary" who has become a fixture in popular culture emerges less from her initial identification than from her reappearance in 1915, the year Soper published his second account of her. Mary Mallon's release from Riverside in 1910 had not been unconditional; she had to agree not to work as a cook and to keep the Board of Health apprised of her whereabouts. Eventually, she stopped reporting to the Board, and this failure for many put her criminality beyond dispute. She was rediscovered in 1915 during a typhoid outbreak at the prestigious Sloane Hospital for Women, where she was employed as a cook. This time, the media foregrounded her behavior rather than her condition to justify her confinement, and surely her violation of the conditions of her release was not likely to gain sympathy for her plight. This time, public-health authorities argued, she knew better. This time she could have prevented the outbreak.

So ran public opinion as well, and accounts of Mary Mallon following her rediscovery were markedly less sympathetic to the cook. *Outlook*, for example, coupled "Typhoid Mary" and the unfortunate immigrant Nathan Cohen (dubbed in the headline "A Man without a Country") as "two strange cases, both illustrating how hardship is often unavoidably inflicted upon individuals by society in its efforts to protect itself."[76] The Russian Cohen, who had immigrated to the United States via Brazil and been diagnosed as insane within three years of his arrival, found himself in perpetual transit between the United States and Brazil, neither of which would accept him. Caught literally between cultures, Cohen was forced to play out a physical analog to intracultural existence: a man without a country is a man without cultural identity, a man excluded from personhood. Cohen's misfortune in fact elucidated that of Mary Mallon's. The healthy carrier in her way confounded familiar categories; the nature of her disease made her hard to categorize and harder still to identify. But, argued *Outlook*, "Nathan Cohen's affliction is dangerous to no one but himself, although it may render him dependent upon society. It is different with the woman known as 'Typhoid Mary.'" According to this reporter, Mallon's behavior had made her incarceration necessary. Unwilling to take the "precautions, which require some intelligence and consideration for others, 'Typhoid Mary' . . . will probably be cut off from society or allowed to go at large only under surveillance for the rest of her days." And when the *New York Times* announced that " 'Typhoid Mary' Has Reappeared," the subheadline ran "Human Culture Tube, Herself Immune, Spreads the Disease Wherever She Goes." Her culpability is not in question in this piece: "When Mary Mallon first swam into the public" as "one of the most celebrated bacillus carriers in the world, a cartoon appeared in one of the daily newspapers [the *New York American*] representing Mary before a large frying pan tossing a typhoid germ in the air like a flapjack. She has returned to justify her reputation."[77] *Swimming* into the public, Mallon is herself a bacillus, "dispensing germs daily" with an intentionality that melts her condition into her behavior.

The fact that she should now have known about her condition and therefore have taken precautions only partly explains this characterization. It also signaled the wider acceptance of the concept of the healthy carrier. Such acceptance established the responsibility of the individual, conceived through the terms of social being, to the group and meant that the healthy carrier could be disciplined by the appropriate authorities. Soper declared " 'the problem of eliminating typhoid [to be] more than one of general city sanitation; it is a problem of individual cleanliness, and until that side of the problem is attacked typhoid will remain with us a remnant and reminder of those dark ages of ignorance and filth before science showed how wasteful and needless was disease.' "[78] Human beings are social beings, and communicable disease manifests both their transgressions against that concept and the consequent breakdown of social control in an urban, industrial—spatially promiscuous—environment.

The *New York Times* article registers another important change that the previous half decade had wrought on the story of "Typhoid Mary." Soper rather than Mallon dominates the piece in terms of coverage and of voice. His picture rather than hers appears in the center of the page. At this point, the story broadens into a tale of bad management and improper housekeeping. The case of Mary Mallon, notes Soper in a subsequent retelling of her tale, "shows how carefully we should select our cooks, and it calls attention in a startling manner to the fact that we ordinarily know very little about them. It confirms the truth of the adage that the more we pay the less we know about our servants."[79] The responsibility for that knowledge devolves exclusively on the lady of the house: " 'Who is your cook?' " he asks in the 1915 *New York Times* account. " 'Has she ever had typhoid? Has she ever nursed a typhoid patient? It should be of special interest to housewives to know that for some mysterious reason a large proportion of all bacillus carriers are women'"—more specifically, according to one medical study, *housewives.*[80] That information was a staple in both medical and popular discussions of carriers.

For Leavitt, "being a carrier was a gendered condition, one in part defined by sex-role expectations. As cooks, all women food handlers were potentially dangerous to the public health, whether they were employed outside the home or within it."[81] Women did not have to be carriers to be dangerous. All women were potential carriers. Their gender roles actually made them more susceptible to the carrier state, since, as Soper explained, women, especially mothers, were the most likely nurses of the family. It is not surprising, then, as the popular and specialty media reported, that female carriers significantly outnumbered males. Causality was often lost in these discussions, as the carrier state itself became gendered: the healthy carrier emblematically perverting the reproductive role of the good mother, the bearer of the human race, as A. B. Wolfe had observed.

In the emerging story of "Typhoid Mary," however, the homemaker introduced the threat of contagion less as a potential carrier than by poorly executing her duties. In the *Times* piece, Soper follows his observation about female susceptibility to the carrier state with a description of domestic irresponsibility in how "'a lady engage[s] a cook.'" She goes to an employment office to interview a number of candidates who, she is told, "'have good references as to character and ability, and she employs the one who makes the best personal impression. In five minutes she has satisfied herself concerning the person who is to perform the most important functions in the household: the preparation of food for the family. That food can, quite innocently, be polluted by the cook and made the vehicle of sickness and death. And the cook's part in the epidemic will never be suspected.'"[82] He plays to the fear of bringing the foreigner into the house—the immigrant, the lower class, the nonwhite stranger. Disease comes with her, and death: one family even loses its only child ("'a beautiful and talented girl'") to the carelessness of the absent or nonvigilant mother, the white middle-class woman who shirks her responsibility. Discussions abounded at this time, in both popular and medical journals, about whether municipal governments should document healthy carriers and whether there should be widespread testing to determine who might be in that category. For Soper, it fell to the homemaker to get a complete medical history of the servants. It was her duty as a citizen, a public responsibility to support the "'machinery of the city'" as it worked to eliminate the communicable diseases that unnecessarily threatened the health of the nation. The housewife, like the public-health officer, had to become more adept at surveillance. And they had to work together.

The professionalizing of homemaking was already under way when Mallon resurfaced. In 1909 founders of the Home Economics Movement began to introduce college and university curricula designed to turn housework into a science and to represent it more accurately as a profession. Their curriculum included bacteriology, and they trained their graduates to run a disease-free as well as an efficient house. The leaders of the movement did not expect their graduates, in most cases, to spend their time actually performing housework. Rather, they were expected to know how to run a household, and they were to understand that household as their responsibility, if not always as their sole domain. This widespread and successful movement articulated the terms of social responsibility for white middle-class American women.[83] The Home Economics Movement made clear that the lady of the house was exclusively responsible for the efficiency and health of her home, especially in light of the discoveries made by bacteriology with which every "scientific" homemaker should be familiar. Adjacent to the *New York Times* piece that reported the apprehension of "Typhoid Mary" was a story with a headline that concisely expressed the sentiment of the Home Economics Movement: "Business Woman Most Domestic: Can Keep House More Scientifically and Successfully than One Who Has No Outside Interests, Says Edna Ferber." The mother's responsibility for the health and reproduction of the family was beyond dispute for Ferber, an author known for her depictions of strong, independent professional women.

The presumably chance juxtaposition of these articles fleshed out an implication of Soper's story. Mary Mallon shared the blame with another character—or character in absentia. The complement of the leading lady was none other than the missing mother. The story is a cautionary tale of bad domestic management, at once implicating the bad homemaker and illustrating the need for new models of intervention and supervision. The families in each epidemic are identified (if at all) by the father's name, including details of his occupation and social status, while no mention is made of a mother. Yet the domestic servant, an Irish immigrant, is in the house precisely because the mother did not adequately do her job, and she therefore provided the enabling environment for the disease carrier. The mother's negligence introduced into the house a disease explicitly coded as both a national and a domestic threat, and she made the home, and the white middle-class American family, susceptible to dangerous foreigners and their native confederates.

The negligent white middle-class mother was the subject of considerable debate during these years, in which she had a variety of incarnations, including "the New Woman," "the Modern Woman," and, in the United States, "the American Woman." The negligence was not limited to actual mothers, but extended to women who refused to marry or bear children as well, since the white middle-class woman's role in producing "good citizens" made that refusal a manifestation of her maternal negligence. The New Woman married late if at all, had few, if any, children, and was preoccupied with concerns that many social commentators considered frivolous. Carroll Smith-Rosenberg calls her "a revolutionary demographic and political phenomenon."[84] Although her fictional prototypes frequently concerned themselves with leisure activities, her real-life manifestations had more substantive ambitions and were interested, as Smith-Rosenberg shows, in "professional visibility" as they worked for "innovative, often radical, economic and social reforms" (245). The terms on which they most characteristically staked their claims were educational, professional, and political. The New Woman was not a prostitute and may or may not have been sexually active, but her refusal of marriage or conventional gender roles put her sexuality at the forefront of public debate and framed the terms of her condemnation.[85]

In that sense, she resembled the unattached woman, but while the unattached woman was troubling because of her disappearing act, social critiques of the New Woman lamented the visibility with which she flaunted conventions and embraced her freedom. The distinction between them is evident in the different natures of the threats posed by Mary Mallon and the missing mother, a function of their different classes. The spectral presence of the New Woman in the story of "Typhoid Mary" shows how the changing demographics and social relations—conceived especially through destabilizing gender roles and the (feared) impact of that instability on the white American family—were medicalized.

An especially vivid (and humorous) example of a metaphoric medicalizing of the gender menace appeared in a letter published in the *Spectator,* a London periodical that served as the model for the *Nation,* a year after Mallon's "discovery." The writer was Andrew Macphail, a prominent Canadian medical and military historian, as well as medical doctor. With his medical interests and training—he was the founding editor of the *Canadian Medical Association Journal*—Macphail could plausibly have heard of Mallon's case by 1908, since Soper had introduced her to the medical community in April 1907, and his address had been published in the June issue of *JAMA*. But whether or not Macphail had the story of Mary Mallon in mind when he described the "American Woman," nemesis of the dedicated homemaker, as a communicable disease, his commentary (which was reprinted in the *Living Age*, an eclectic, Boston-based periodical that collected and ran a number of letters and essays on "the American Woman") reproduced important features of her story.

Noting "her" precedents in history, legend, and especially fiction, Macphail explains that the "American Woman" proliferated in an industrialized society. She is not "confined to, or even especially characteristic of, the United States" and to understand her in those terms would be similar to assuming "that the common scale which destroys apple-trees is found nowhere else than in San José, or that the potato-bug confines its ravages to Colorado. . . . It is a familiar fact, however, that a disease which occurs sporadically in one *milieu* will burst into an epidemic of unexampled fury when it is transformed to a new environment."[86] An epidemic does not necessarily imply contagion, although he forecasts the principle of herd immunity in his description, and this "epidemic of unexampled fury" certainly appears poised to spread across borders, carried by women.

Macphail carefully (and typically) distinguishes the American Woman as a type from "the mothers, wives and daughters of the average American man," and, in the 1910 essay in which he expands on his original letter, he diagnoses "her" as the victim of industrialization, a woman whose "natural occupations" vanished "when the family life was swallowed up in the industrial life."[87] The unhappy survivor of the effects of industralization becomes the American Woman when she fails (or refuses) to find a worthy substitute for the domestic duties she has relinquished and when she refuses to reproduce the numbers of offspring that her preindustrial forerunner bestowed on a growing nation. In her refusal of domesticity and reproduction, she promotes and embodies social, political, and cultural disruption, and her behavior is communicable.

Like typhoid, she represents the perils of prosperity. One piece from the *Nation*—reprinted in the *Living Age* a year and a half prior to Macphail's letter—described the frivolousness of "the American woman" as "the 'show' in successful America, somewhat overdone and too exacting to the eyes of a European audience, but clever and very creditable to the management."[88] The author invokes the influential theorist of American life Thorstein Veblen in his analysis of the corruption that gives rise to her: "the industrial male conqueror . . . display[s] his financial power through the ostentatious waste and conspicuous leisure" embodied by his wife and daughters. If, argues the author, a woman's social work is to display her husband's power, then *woman's* cultural work is to attest to the industrial might of the emerging world power. She is like the "ostentatious waste" of the feudal state. And, like typhoid, she also marks the danger posed by the failure of reabsorption, which turns waste into pollution.

The "American" in "American Woman" describes character traits and behavior, cultural rather than political belonging. The communicable danger she poses suggests a culture in uneasy relation to national frontiers, which it is precisely the job of the bearer of "useful citizens" to reinforce. This task of national reproduction, like the term "New Woman," was in no way particular to the United States, although the national epithet in the term "American Woman," used by both U.S. and non-U.S. writers, was significantly less common elsewhere. The epidemic that Macphail described—the communicability of female behavior—was actually more than metaphorical in his view. Like Wolfe's contagious vice, it was evidence of the communicability of culture that sociologists were beginning to call *social contagion.* Women were the primary bearers of culture, and they had to be encouraged in their work of containing, if not preventing, infection as they set about their task of reproducing national subjects and a salubrious national culture. In his letter Macphail suggested as a "cure" for the disease of the "American Woman" that "all women becom[e] nurses and cooks" (ironically, the very occupations that made them so susceptible to the carrier status and therefore dangerous to the home they were supposed to protect).

In response, the editor of the *Spectator* issued his one corrective: the important work of reproducing the nation was more a function of attitude than of occupation. The properly motivated woman of leisure "can find plenty to do if she has the will and is inspired by a sound tradition of domestic and social duty."[89] But parenting and homemaking had to be her primary professional focus. The fate of the nation was in the hands of parents; the sentiment was echoed widely, from the political pulpit to the medical journal. The editor made that point by invoking Theodore Roosevelt's frequent and often public proclamations of the danger to any nation— he made lavish use of the term *race suicide*—when "the men of the nation are not anxious . . . to be fathers of families, and . . . the women do not recognize that the greatest thing for any woman is to be a good wife and mother," precisely the sentiment that troubled Wolfe.[90] A medical doctor from Philadelphia expressed prevailing medical wisdom when from the pages of the *Pennsylvania Medical Journal* he enjoined, "Mothers, teach your boys patriotism and citizenship and your girls to be womanly women, to the uplifting of the home and motherhood."[91] And Albert Burr, in his 1906 AMA speech, viewed "late marriage" as one of the "principal causes" of the imminent threat to the white American family. It represented an unnatural suppression of "the sexual passion [which] is strong, as nature intends it to be," and it leads many to "fall."[92]

Reinforcing the understanding that parenting as well as bearing Americans was a medical as well as social issue, the Home Economics Movement made familial and national health a central occupation of the professional housewife. Race suicide, like typhoid, was a health concern, a manifestation of the physiology of ontology and citizenship, indirectly linked to prosperity. The language of professionalized homemaking and motherhood as patriotic duties could be extended even to some women who did not become mothers or homemakers if they participated properly in the reproduction of gender roles so central to the making of Americans. Social reformers such as Jane Addams and Lillian Wald adopted the language of professionalized motherhood to describe the "social work" they did in the settlement houses, which entailed turning immigrant (and even wayward native-born) girls into American women (as opposed to "the American Woman") and immigrant mothers into American mothers.

Soper's invocation of that language in the *New York Times* account of Mallon's rediscovery enlisted housewives in the project of epidemiology. Described in the piece as a "doctor to sick cities, rather than to sick individuals,"[93] he offered the women he addressed strategies that would safeguard their families against the invisible, pervasive threat of the healthy human carrier. His terrain was the city, but he could not enter all of their homes, so he deputized them in the language of scientific homemaking. "'The problem of eliminating typhoid is more than one of general city sanitation'" (4), he explained. Discovered in "of all places, a maternity hospital" (3), Mary Mallon represented a danger that, together, the sanitary engineer and the scientific homemaker could contain. Among the epidemiological tools he offered the homemaker was the story of "Typhoid Mary."

THE ENDS OF THE STORY: SURVEILLANCE AND CONTAINMENT

The original story was, ironically, an important feature of Mallon's recapture. She was identified because her "fellow-servants" jokingly and unwittingly nicknamed the incognito Mallon "Typhoid Mary." The epithet called attention to the hospital's cook during an outbreak of typhoid and led Soper to his nemesis. If the identification of a healthy human carrier underscored the need for epidemiology, the story of "Typhoid Mary" conspicuously displayed the triumph of public managers. After all, the public-health officials turned her into "Typhoid Mary," and as "Typhoid Mary," she was rediscovered, marked, and ultimately contained. In that incarnation, Mary Mallon could not disappear, and she could not endanger her fellow citizens. It also made her comprehensible. As Mary Mallon, her motives were, as described by Soper, inscrutable. As "Typhoid Mary," she was a recalcitrant criminal, and a repeat offender at that, an undeniable "menace to the community," according to Soper's 1939 account.[94] In that way, he made sense of her resistance to his story and her refusal to accede to his narrative, his requests, and his recommendations.

Undocumented women, immigrants, and carriers, all in their fashion, posed a distinct danger to the reproduction of white America. The concept of a socially responsible individual, as articulated in the carrier narratives, presumed general acknowledgment of the need for documentation and state surveillance. The narrative that put "Typhoid Mary" into circulation represented, and effected, that documentation. "Typhoid Mary" embodied the reassuring fantasy that surveillance works, that the subject was eventually apprehensible, comprehensible, and manageable.

Soper ended his 1919 account with Mallon's recapture and offered as the lesson of the "story of Typhoid Mary . . . how difficult it is to teach infected people to guard against infecting others."[95] In 1939, however, he followed her back to North Brother Island, from which, he noted, she never again sought to escape. Contrary to some, who "think she had come to recognize her condition as inevitable and had become reconciled to a life of imprisonment," Soper explained his own belief "that a change had come over her" that "was both mental and physical," a conversion of sorts in which even if she could not accept the explanation of public-health officials, she came to accept their literal authority and conformed to the life they had chosen for her.[96] If Mary Mallon evoked the fallen woman in Soper's narratives, "Typhoid Mary" corresponded to the well-disciplined citizen: the citizen subject, that is, disciplined by the epidemiologist's mechanisms of visibility, specifically, in this case, naming, narrating, and mapping. Soper's narratives thereby transformed Mary Mallon the threat into "Typhoid Mary" the archetypal, because comprehensible and apprehensible, citizen. Describing her in 1919 as "a mysterious, non-communicative, self-reliant, abundantly courageous person; a character apart, by nature and by circumstance," he believed that she was "strangely chosen to bear the burden of a great lesson to the world."[97] He assimilated her in a story that was as much a reassuring national fantasy as a cautionary tale. Making her visible and replacing her unknowable personal history with a documented public history, he displayed the power of state apparatuses to naturalize strangers and, by implication, constitute subjects.

As such, "Typhoid Mary" embodies the contained danger of spatial promiscuity. The incarceration of Mary Mallon is in that context less important than the narrativization of "Typhoid Mary." While the former removes the threat of one woman, the latter describes the threat of the healthy carrier and locates it as a constitutive principle of a community conceived in the terms of social being. Emerging from the depictions of the healthy carrier is not only the threat posed by the carrier to every individual (common susceptibility), but the potential of every individual to be a healthy carrier and hence to pose that threat to others. It is in that sense that "Typhoid Mary" is archetypal and that her story approaches a national myth. The lesson of her story is that all individuals must strive to know themselves even as, like Oedipus, they recognize themselves as fundamentally unknowable to themselves. Identification of the healthy carrier (knowability) becomes a shared responsibility: experts can count on—in fact rely on—the cooperation of the general public, which entails routine behaviors, such as practices of cleanliness, especially hand washing, as well as adherence to conventional (gender and class specific) social roles.

The story of Mary Mallon is not just about the behavior of a recalcitrant carrier, but about a whole environment conducive to the spread of communicable disease. When individuals inevitably—as Ross argued—jealous of their liberty chafed under the perceived constraints of a more intense and deliberate social control, the carrier narrative not only enjoined their informed acquiescence in its strategies but also renovated their sense of agency through the concept of social responsibility.

Carrier narratives helped to transform the spatial and social relationships of a community imagined according to the precepts of turn-of-the-century U.S. nationalism: strangers in the simultaneously generative and dangerous contact of affiliative bonds. On the surface, medicalized nativism seemed to register the desire to exclude strangers. But it also served an important socializing function as it made visible the mechanisms of assimilation by showing how the contagious immigrant needed to and could be transformed into a productive American.[98] In the carrier narrative, the implications of (a new kind of) intimacy—materialized in nonsexual bodily contact—changed the meaning of that contact as they recast the nature of individuals' relation to the community as well as the experiences of the spaces in which they inevitably interacted.

Communicable Americanism

SOCIAL CONTAGION AND URBAN SPACES

3 The social reformer and journalist Jacob Riis listened to the reports of the investigators for the Tenement House Commission in the mid-1880s with a mixture of satisfaction and rage. His own angry accounts of the conditions of New York tenements had helped bring the commission into existence, and their studies confirmed his worst charges. "I wanted to jump in my seat at that time and shout Amen," Riis recalled many years later. "But I remembered that I was a reporter and kept still. It was that same winter, however, that I wrote the title of my book, *How the Other Half Lives*, and copyrighted it."[1] What he felt he could not say as a reporter, he would proclaim as the author of his crusading book. Moral outrage and condemnation permeate his analysis and his tone. "If it shall appear that the sufferings and the sins of the 'other half,' and the evil they breed, are but as a just punishment upon the community that gave it no other choice," he wrote, "it will be because that is the truth. . . . In the tenements all the influences make for evil; because they are the hot-beds of epidemics that carry death to rich and poor alike; the nurseries of pauperism and crime that fill our jails and police courts; . . . that maintain a standing army of ten thousand tramps with all that that implies; because, above all, they touch the family life with deadly moral contagion. This is their worst crime, inseparable from the system. That we have to own it the child of our own wrong does not excuse it, even though it gives it claim upon our utmost patience and tenderest charity."[2]

The tenement was both repository and mirror; there, Riis believed, the cultural detritus collected, and there the burgeoning metropolis could see reflected the dark side of its glories. Riis was not alone in his fear. In fiction and journalism, social reformers consistently reminded readers that the tenements were not a world apart, that they were not effective spaces of quarantine and did not contain the disease and crime that they fostered. Communicable disease in particular vividly depicted the connections between impoverished urban spaces and the larger metropolises. Such warnings had been issued throughout the nineteenth century. One influential pamphlet penned in the 1830s by a prominent English medical doctor and social reformer, James Phillips Kay, shows, as Mary Poovey notes, how "cholera provides the metaphor that draws all of society's problems into a single conceptual cluster."[3] Kay used the disease to dramatize the common membership of rich and poor in what Poovey calls the "social body" and to further the reformist goal of state aid to the poor. While a standing army of ten thousand tramps would erupt into apocalyptic conflagration only in fiction (as in Joaquin Miller's 1886 novel, *The Destruction of Gotham*), communicable disease had long been a feature of everyone's lived experience.

The public-health movement gained momentum as the century progressed; epidemics of communicable disease fueled the movement and called attention to the dangerous conditions of the spaces of urban poverty. The particular association of those spaces with immigrants in the United States intensified nativism by materializing and amplifying the fear of communicable-disease epidemics imported by immigrants and bred by the squalor of the tenements. Nayan Shah documents the spike in anti-Chinese bias following outbreaks of smallpox in the 1860s, 1870s, and 1880s in San Francisco's Chinatown, and Howard Markel shows how the 1892 typhus and cholera quarantines exemplified and justified anti-Semitism as they disproportionately and inequitably targeted Eastern European Jews. The interweaving of public-health concerns with nativist sentiment intensified the stigmatizing of already despised populations and the spaces where they lived. The fear of infection legitimated legal and spatial responses to social biases.[4] It transformed as it marked group identities and inflected ideas about cultural and political belonging.

A tenuous line separates reasonable concern from anxious displacement. Riis's armies and germs cross that line, as they animate the more pernicious threat of the tenements: the "moral contagion" that erodes the very basis of society. Created by the excesses and indifference of capital, the tenements breed dangerous germs (literal and metaphorical). The rich share susceptibility, as they share space—in the same social body—with the impoverished. Yet "moral contagion" is distinctly metaphorical, and it represents the transformation, in Riis's passage, of the literal conditions of the tenement into "a just punishment upon the community."

Even as Riis penned the words "moral contagion," the bacteriological discoveries that brought disease-causing microbes before the public in the late nineteenth century were breathing new life into the term *contagion.* Bacteriological discoveries enabled scientists and public-health officials to map the routes of contagion with increasing accuracy. The spread of disease materialized social interactions generally and broadened interest in the mechanisms of contagion. Reanimated, the term circulated among reformers and fiction writers, journalists and sociologists, who capitalized on its currency by applying it to a range of cultural phenomena. The pages of the *American Journal of Sociology,* founded in 1895 to help define the field, illustrate the popularity of the term and its increasingly medical inflection.[5] Researchers and theorists used contagious disease both literally and metaphorically in the studies of urban space and national affiliation, of assimilation and ghettos, to explore the phenomenon of cultural contact. Associates caught culture from one another; generations, from their predecessors. Or they shared immunities. In an installment on social control, E. A. Ross defined social influence as "the contagion of emotions, ambitions, desires" that "results from the contact and intercourse of men as individuals."[6] This understanding of the "contagion" of social influence does not represent an obvious departure from Riis or, in fact, from much earlier social observers. But with its circulation in the sociological literature, *contagion* gradually evolved from a metaphor to a carefully articulated sociological concept. Formalized as *social contagion,* it named the primary mechanism of social cohesion in the emerging science of society.[7]

Social contagion registered the inflection of bacteriology in the changing understanding of social interactions and community formation, as is evident in a widely influential essay that helped to inaugurate urban studies in the United States.[8] Robert E. Park's "The City: Suggestions for the Investigation of Human Behavior in the Urban Environment" appeared in 1915, more than two and a half decades after Riis's book, and his use of *social contagion* in the essay illustrates the difference between sociology and social reform. It also demonstrates the commingling of biological and sociological theories about contagion that would become foundational for the outbreak narrative.

Like Riis, Park began as a journalist and social reformer. Along with other journalistic luminaries, including Lincoln Steffens and Stephen Crane, he had worked as a police reporter on the infamous Mulberry Street beat, where Riis was an éminence grise.[9] But by the time Park wrote "The City," he had been recruited to the University of Chicago by the relatively new, but influential, department of sociology and anthropology, where he quickly became a leading architect of the emerging discipline of sociology. Among Park's earliest sociological publications, "The City" heralded what would become his lifelong interest in urban spaces and neighborhoods, especially tenements, where he believed he could best isolate and describe the principles of group formation. In the essay, Park locates the "special importance" of "the segregation of the poor, the vicious, the criminal, and exceptional persons generally, which is so characteristic a feature of city life" in "the fact that social contagion tends to stimulate in divergent types the common temperamental differences, and to suppress characters which unite them with the normal types about them."[10] Like Riis, he marks the social influences of the tenement as contagious. Where Riis's *contagion* refers to the effect of the tenement on society as a whole, evidence of cohabitation in a shared environment (Poovey's "social body"), however, Park's names the mechanisms that constitute social bonds. Riis's *moral contagion* signals a threat to a cohesive entity, in other words, while *social contagion* identifies a process of social transformation.

Although the term *social contagion* does not appear frequently in the 1915 essay or its several revisions and reprintings, it is key to the theory Park was beginning to work out. With a background in literature and philology, Park knew the power of words, and he surely chose this term carefully as he sought to explain the nuances of his distinctions. When Park moves away from the tenements in the essay to articulate general principles, the term *social contagion* becomes *communication*. "The mechanism of communication is very subtle," he writes, "so subtle, in fact, that it is often difficult to conceive how suggestions are conveyed from one mind to another. . . . Individuals . . . inevitably communicate their sentiments, attitudes, and organic excitements, and in doing so they necessarily react, not merely to what each individual actually does, but to what he intends, desires, or hopes to do" (598–99). The subtlety of the influence that he describes pushes past metaphor: the material of culture is transmissible and transformative.

While the different contexts in which he uses the terms *contagion* and *communication* in the essay seem to tease them apart, their mutual inflection emerges from this work. For Park, understanding how groups form and cohere was a central task for the nascent discipline of sociology. He would spend most of his career as a sociologist refining the idea that communication "is, if not identical with, at least indispensable to, the cultural process" and that "communication creates, or makes possible at least, that concensus [*sic*] and understanding among the individual components of a social group which eventually gives it and them the character not merely of society but of a cultural unit."[11] Communicating individuals were mutually, although not equally, transformed, and that process attested to the communicability—and materiality—of culture. The tenement interested Park as an illustration of basic social principles rather than as an expression of social ills, and it offered an excellent case study for the sociologist. Where social reformers like Riis went into the spaces of poverty looking for social breakdown, Park and his colleagues went searching for principles of association.

Bacteriological theories of contagion and the lessons of epidemiology informed Park's approach to the study of communication and social spaces. When the sociologist Luther L. Bernard asked him to write an account of the evolution of his methodology, Park underscored the importance of a diphtheria epidemic that he had covered as a journalist. During his investigation, he had "plotted the cases on a map of the city and in this way called attention to what seemed the source of the infection, an open sewer." This strategy, in turn, led to his belief that "with what [he] called 'scientific reporting' the newspaper might do systematically what it was then doing casually."[12] But the commercial pressures of newspaper publishing complicated that goal. Sociology afforded a better means to develop a system of social analysis than journalism. Park believed that if epidemiologists could chart the routes of transmission of a communicable disease, and laboratory scientists could identify the disease-producing microbe, the scientist of society, using the city as a laboratory, could chronicle and ultimately influence the transmission of the material of culture.

Where the science of bacteriology could now document microbial exchange, the science of society attempted likewise to explain its cultural analog. The connection did not remain at the level of analogy. Communicable disease attested to an underlying biotic community, an ecosystem comprised of interdependent human bodies, animals, and plants. Epidemics were the natural expression of contact among individuals and groups, as was the social contagion that transformed them into social communities. The sociologists' mappings made the metamorphosis visible; they displayed the process of community formation and the creation of social spaces out of the ecologies that represented the chance encounters of human beings. In "The City" and related work, and in the many students Park and his colleagues trained in their years at the University of Chicago, sociologists helped to define the terms through which subsequent cultural theorists would understand ethnicity, social—especially urban—spaces, and the interactions that shaped them. If epidemiology influenced their methods, public health was among their motivations, and their work shows how the discoveries of bacteriology inflected ideas of cultural transmission and community formation. In turn, those ideas help to explain the ecological vision of community and disease that characterizes the outbreak narrative.

MICROBIAL GEOGRAPHY

It is not surprising that many of the inaugural questions of the new disciplines of both sociology and bacteriology emerged from the effects of the massive immigration and accelerated urbanization in the late nineteenth century. The founding editor of the *American Journal of Sociology* introduced the first issue of the journal with a meditation on the increased conspicuousness of social bonds: "*In our age the fact of human association is more obtrusive and relatively more influential than in any previous epoch,*" he explained. "Men are more definitely and variously aware of each other than ever before. They are also more promiscuously perplexed by each other's presence. . . . Whatever modern men's theory of the social bond, no men have ever had more conclusive evidence that the bond exists."[13] And no evidence was more conclusive than the communicable diseases that attested to often unwitting or unacknowledged social contact. The spread of disease marked the threat of populations in new proximity and people in ever-increasing interactions; the public learned these lessons repeatedly and in detail from the media coverage of bacteriological discoveries in its earliest decades.

Those early discoveries stepped up the alarms that were regularly sounded by public-health officials about the infectious dangers of the tenements. But they also changed the nature of the warnings as well as the practice of public health. Making visible the sources and routes of contagion, bacteriological discoveries altered the understanding and treatment of communicable disease as well as the methods of containment and prevention. In the process, the renovated public-health movement produced a new medicalized political geography. The 1892 quarantines provided an important point of reference and were invoked for a variety of history lessons. Looking back from a distance of three years, for example, Cyrus Edson, whose promotion to New York City's Commissioner of Health resulted partly from his active role in them as the New York City Chief Sanitary Inspector, warned that "we cannot separate the tenement-house district from the portion of the city where the residences of the wealthy stand, and treat this as a separate locality. The disease we find in the tenement-house threatens all alike, for a hundred avenues afford a way by which the contagion may be carried from the tenement to the palace." The vague threat of contagion becomes the specificity of some of those avenues in this piece when Edson tracks "the microbes or their spores" generated in the impoverished quarter, as they inevitably "pass the heavy curtains on the windows of the mansion to find their prey inside."[14]

Entitling the piece "The Microbe as Social Leveller," Edson links a science lesson to a social message. The visual routes of contagion illustrate both the "germ idea of Socialism, that all members of the body politic are theoretically and should be practically joint partners in one great co-operative state" (421) and the "socialistic side of the microbe [which] is to be found ... in the fact that we may only fight diseases in a community by meeting it everywhere" (425). Communicable disease is more than the analog for the interdependence of the body politic that it was for Riis. Edson's microbes not only map but also create the connections: the social bonds that constitute the social body. The microbe was a social leveler because it displayed the artifice of boundaries, because it offered evidence of a common humanity conceived as a common susceptibility, and because it created the communion of bodies as it searched for its prey.

Edson did not advocate socialism, which, after all, he likened in this piece to a communicable disease. Rather, he illustrated why social reform was in the interest of the wealthy. Fear of contagion (or reprisal) was one motivation, but the material evidence of unacknowledged social and biological bonds suggested a moral responsibility as well. And those bonds extended beyond local communities. Tracking microbes from impoverished Russian peasants through the routes of commerce to the United States, he demonstrated the biologized social connections that had not been available to his counterparts in the past. "Disease binds the human race together as with an unbreakable chain," he wrote. "More than this, the industrial development of the world has enlarged this chain until now all nations are embraced within its band" (423). Microbes do not just represent social bonds; they create and enforce them. The physiological devastation that arises from poverty "is the lesson taught by history, which to-day we see by the light of the great discoveries of sanitary science. We might call it the Moral of the Past, as seen through the Microscope" (426). With that microscope, the commissioner of health connected the public-health movement to personal and national health both metaphorically and literally.

While Kay stood at the vanguard of a public-health movement in 1830s England that focused on environmental reform—reformers in the persons of sanitary engineers dedicated to the cleansing of an unhealthy environment—contemporaries of Riis and Edson witnessed the shift to an increasingly medicalized and scientific public-health movement. The bacteriological work that made it possible to understand and track disease transmission with greater accuracy and enabled the identification of healthy human carriers in the first decade of the twentieth century incorporated the insights of the laboratory, with particular focus on the problem of carriers, into reformers' attention to the environment.[15] As a result, microbes and communicable disease became associated with the social dynamics of communities.

"The Microbe as Social Leveller" was a paean to the public-health movement. Disease prevention represented cultural superiority, offering evidence of scientific achievement—the identification of pathogenic microbes that presumably would lead to their control—and effective social control, represented through successful health measures. Edson is sanguine in this piece about the ultimate victory that public-health officials would gain over microbes because of the discoveries of bacteriology. Ignorance of "these little enemies" and the means of transmission of communicable diseases caused their spread in the past. But he assures his readers that they need no longer fear such an outcome. "It would be impossible to-day for the plague to ravage any city in the civilized world as it ravaged London [during the reign of Charles the Second], simply because, although we do not definitely know what the plague was—it is believed to have been typhus fever by many—we are certain it was a disease caused by and developing microbes, we should fight it exactly as we fight any contagious disease, and we should win the same victory. It is owing to the discovery of the laws of hygiene, and their practical application, that we are enabled to check disease when it appears, to seize it and say it shall not spread" (423–24). That word is evidently law, which he goes on to illustrate both with direct reference to the 1892 cholera outbreak that was allegedly thwarted by excellent research and stern measures—in which he played a role—and with the indirect allusion (through the inserted reference to typhus) to the earlier and less successfully managed, because less quickly enacted, typhus quarantine of the same year. Drawing on the past, he creates an outbreak narrative out of an imaginary future outbreak that will assuredly be contained by empowered and well-equipped public-health officials under his leadership.

While the quarantines drew boundaries around social spaces that were associated with particular populations, the public-health movement of the future would have the advantage of tools and methods that promised increasing specificity. The last years of the 1880s, the end of what Victoria A. Harden calls "a heroic decade of bacteriological discovery," witnessed the growth of state and the emergence of public and municipal laboratories in the United States.[16] In 1887 the federal government allocated a small amount of money and one room in Staten Island's Marine Hospital for a bacteriology laboratory that would eventually come to be known as the Hygienic Laboratory. The establishment of this laboratory attested to the changing strategies of public health, and Harden points to its centrality to the federal government's evolving role in public-health regulation. The language of quarantine emphasized the need to safeguard national boundaries against the penetration of communicable diseases conceived as foreign imports carried in by sailors, travelers, and especially immigrants. But quarantines could not address the problem of the healthy carrier already within the borders and the microbes that were everywhere. The identification of "Typhoid Mary," and the publicity around carriers it generated, further strengthened the idea that state-run laboratories were necessary to the effective identification of both.

The discoveries that came out of those laboratories made clear that safeguarding borders and documenting immigrants were not sufficient measures to forestall the transmission of disease. New and improved conveyances that made travel faster, cheaper, and easier created a more mobile population, and with mobility came new exposures and interactions. Trains enabled the growth of the nation, and they represented progress and new possibilities for democracy. Cities could not exist without transportation, of which trains were "the principal vehicle," linking "the world together, abolish[ing] at once national boundaries and national prejudices" and poised to "produce universal brotherhood if anything can."[17] But railway corruption could also ruin the economy of cities and towns along its routes, creating spaces where "labor toils in great prison-pens, and lodges in tenements reeking with disease; [where] . . . enemies of society gather, and in the midst of filth and hunger plant seeds of anarchy; [where] poverty breeds crime, and crime poverty."[18]

Railroads also literally carried the danger of communicable disease. Microbes commingled with mobility, as they suffused the language of social contact, social danger, and social regulation, with railroads in particular becoming the focus of microbial attention. Nothing better emblematized the increasing interconnectedness than the tracks that crisscrossed the nation. And nothing more conspicuously altered the social landscape and political economy. Objections to these transformations routinely found expression in microbial terms; in the mainstream media, discussions of the health risks posed by railroads considerably outweighed other expressions of social concern involving the railroads. A pamphlet circulated in 1910 compiled excerpts from publications as well as addresses that professors of hygiene and sanitary engineers had given at professional conferences where they warned their colleagues of the microbial dangers (specifically, from typhoid) of rail travel. The pamphlet, *A New Idea in Sanitation: The Great Menace to Public Health that Covers Every Mile of Railroad Track in the United States and Other Countries*, called attention to such "unappreciated source[s] of typhoid infection" as "the railway water-closet."[19] Graphic descriptions of "droppings of diseased germs" deposited along the tracks accompanied injunctions to "think of drinking water that contains material from an old rectal abscess, cancer of the stomach, or rectum, tubercular sputum, urine or feces,—typhoid urine and feces."[20]

Communicable diseases transformed people as well as communities. Readers of the *Literary Digest* learned how "our railways carry from place to place some deadly disease-breeding passengers" from the excerpted speech that a medical professional employed by the railroad delivered to the American Association of Railway Surgeons in 1912.[21] Transmission was the result not only of accidental contact but also of the changed behavior of the afflicted. H. Taylor Cronk, a medical doctor and former assistant bacteriologist in New York City's Department of Health, noted that diseased people "are always traveling on our railroads, going from place to place seeking relief. These are the people," he explains, "who must frequently use the toilets. Usually the healthy traveling public are constipated while en route, but quite contrary with the diseased,—traveling seems to increase their desire to use the toilets."[22]

Eventually published as *The Relationship of Railway Corporations to Public Hygiene*, Cronk's speech became one of the numerous pamphlets circulating at this time to sound the alarm about the many disease carriers—human, animal, and insect—traveling by rail, turning rail carriers into disease carriers by association. And more than a decade later, periodicals continued to warn their readership of, as one *Literary Digest* headline proclaimed, "The Transfer of Disease by Travel." The breakdown of geographical boundaries accomplished by improved travel was turning everyone into potential carriers as it reconfigured traditional communities. The danger of imported disease, as the article explained, applied "not so much to the foreign immigrant as to the ceaseless to-and-fro motion of our own citizens, who will not stop moving even when they are ill."[23] The obvious presence of deadly microbes in "the constant daily, hourly pollution of road-beds of railways with human feces and urine" marked the nature and the dangers of the changing relationships and spaces produced by the transformations that railroads fostered.[24]

IMMUNOLOGY AND THE NATIONAL BODY

The gradual acceptance of the dangers of microbes and healthy carriers as facts of life altered their representational significance. To be human was, in some sense, to be a carrier, as Simon Flexner, of the prestigious Rockefeller Institute for Medical Research, explained to readers of *Popular Science Monthly*: "We carry on our skin surfaces constantly the germs of suppuration; on the mucous membranes of the nose and throat the germs of pneumonia, and sometimes those of diphtheria, tuberculosis and meningitis. The intestinal mucous membrane supports a rich and varied bacterial flora among which are several potentially harmful species and sometimes, even under conditions of health, the bacilli of typhoid fever, of dysentery, and in regions in which cholera is endemic, or during its epidemics, of cholera bacilli."[25] Communal life was unavoidable, and even if it were not, "withdrawal absolutely from other human beings and from all human habitations" (7) would still not result in the successful evasion of germs.

These discoveries not only stimulated the growth of public laboratories but also fueled the rise of the field of preventive medicine and its complement, the new science of immunology, which formed important meeting grounds for medical science and public health. Since detection alone failed to offer sufficient protection from apparently healthy carriers, efforts to address their newly recognized role in the spread of disease as an important health problem required more than better-financed laboratories. Even the most socially responsible individuals could not fully police their interactions with others. It was important to understand not only how disease was transmitted but also how it was resisted at the levels of both the individual and the group. Flexner first delivered his *Popular Science Monthly* piece as a public-health lecture at Columbia University in the spring of 1909, and with it he helped to shape a new direction in medical research. He explained that "proper clothing, wholesome food, good hygienic surroundings, avoidance of over fatigue and of depressing psychic impressions" (13) could all contribute to individuals' successful efforts to maintain their health. But the main point of the piece was to explore how the "normal body possesses a mean resistance to bacterial invasion and to bacterial poisoning" (7) and how susceptibility to disease differed among species and races as well as individuals.

Resistance was a key concept not only for the science of immunology but also for the public-health practice of epidemiology, which shifted attention both from the individual and from disease microbes to the group conceived simultaneously as a social *community* and a biological *population*. Disease susceptibility and resistance marked the biological underpinnings of social groups. Flexner pushed that point in a talk delivered in London three years after his Columbia talk and subsequently published in *Science*. The question he posed was of particular interest to an audience that had just lived through a polio epidemic. What, he asked, had prompted the polio virus, which had long been endemic to northern Europe, to start a "unique, and as yet unexplained, movement that has carried it around the globe"?[26] The answer, he insisted, lay as much in the susceptibility of populations as in the nature of the disease. Public health and medical science needed to make that susceptibility a central concern. He made it an important feature of his life's work.

A decade later, he introduced a collection of essays entitled *Experimental Epidemiology* with the observation that "the remarkably wide or pandemic outbreaks of which the recent American epidemics form part all originated in the old world and were communicated, usually after a lapse of time, to the new world, where, in some instances, as in the notable one of the 1916 wave of poliomyelitis, they found a soil so fertile and circumstances of spread so favorable as to reach a height of destructiveness previously unknown."[27] The essays in the collection reported the results of a series of experiments on mice and contagion, but the species made no difference to Flexner who explained that while "the 'carrier' among the old mice . . . provides the 'seed' for the next following epidemic outbursts, it is the highly susceptible individuals among the new which furnish the living 'culture' medium enabling rapid increase and wide dissemination of the bacilli to be effected, just as it is the succumbing and non-reactible mice which check the growth and multiplication that tend to arrest the epidemic spread" (13). The spread of a disease depended on the inextricability of social and biological aspects of an environment, and its prevention required that it be addressed at the level of community. Flexner attributed the decline of epidemics of enteric (intestinal) disease to "general or communal, as opposed to individualistic measures of prevention" (13) and the continuing prevalence, even increase, in epidemics of respiratory infection to the lack of communal means for their prevention and "the rise of multitudinous cities, industrialism, rapid transport, etc., the effects of which are to increase the number and intensity of personal contact associations, and thus to combine, confuse, and distribute quickly and widely the respiratory secretions of unnumbered persons" (14).

Such epidemiological insights reinvigorated the representational connections between contagion and community. If, as Edson argued, disease could "bind human beings together as with an unbreakable chain," the concept of group resistance vividly attested to the biological aspects of that chain. "Considered in its broadest sense," Assistant Surgeon General W. C. Rucker told his colleagues at a meeting of the American Public Health Association (APHA) in 1916, "the ultimate reason for cities is public health. Every other reason for which mankind collects itself into more or less permanent aggregations is subsidiary to the basic idea of community protection and betterment of every sort. This protection is external, against the outside world, and internal, each individual against the entire collection of individuals. Since every action which produces a betterment of the conditions under which the community lives and works gives a definite reaction in increased health, it is at once seen that a public-health program for cities is in reality nothing more or less than a complete plan for communal existence."[28] Health-protective measures would rationalize the community, he explained. To illustrate his point, he posited an optimal biological concentration of people beyond which "there is increased opportunity for promiscuity with a coincident intercommunication of disease and reduction of the acreage ration below the biological limit" (225). Medicine could not address this sociobiological problem alone, hence the need for public health, which he defined as "more than the mere absence of disease. It is the physiological functionation of the community" (226).

Herd immunity represented a biological transformation of a collection of people as they mutually adjusted to each other's germs. The concept reached the public in the 1920s in such forms as a 1923 *New York Times* article entitled "Doctor Says Steady Contact with Germs Makes City Dwellers Immune to Disease." The New York City Department of Health's director of laboratories, William H. Park (Mary Mallon's "Typhoid William Park"), contended that New Yorkers' constant contact with germs was making them immune to disease (as polio researchers would subsequently learn). "Subway travelers breathe in so many germs their systems become used to them," the article explained, "and the germs in traveling about from home to home lose some of their virulence. . . . [I]n the subways, . . . the air is full of millions of germs which would produce terrible epidemics if the human body had not learned to assimilate them."[29] Herd immunity represented the protection afforded to a community when a sufficient number of them had immunity to a disease, which therefore prevented it from spreading. The science of immunology revealed how the social interactions that were the source of the problem could also be the source of the solution. But there would always be new germs. And there would always be individuals to introduce them.

Inevitably, this research contributed to medicalized nativism despite Flexner's intentions. It reinforced in microbial terms the particular danger posed by the (unassimilated) stranger to a susceptible (immunologically naïve) population, increasingly conceptualized with respect to national borders. Public-health discussions from the 1920s witnessed a renewed emphasis on the danger of foreign-born as opposed to domestically mobile carriers. Typical were two papers that were read before the Public Health Administration Section of the APHA in the fall of 1921 and subsequently published in the *American Journal of Public Health*. Both called for the strengthening of public-health departments and the improvement of quarantine measures. Royal S. Copeland, the New York City Commissioner of Health, noted dramatically that if he could have his way, he "would declare Ellis Island an infected port, and . . . not let anyone come to New York from that port."[30] Urging the APHA to arise "in its might" (204) and put pressure on Congress, he warned that "until Congress recognizes the absolute necessity of spending money to protect the nation, the menace of disease from abroad will ever threaten New York City and the country at large" (203). William Park concurred. He underscored the difference between the danger posed by a few undetected native-born carriers of typhoid or diphtheria, who did not introduce a "new kind of infection," and the threat of an overlooked immigrant carrier, who enabled "a spirillum which did not otherwise occur in this country" to "gain entrance."[31] The immigrant carrier embodied a medicalized threat that was difficult to diagnose, and Park therefore called for the addition of personnel "trained in both medicine and laboratory technic" (205) at the quarantine stations.

At the same time, Park, Copeland, and other pragmatic public-health officials recognized the untenable financial burden that quarantine imposed. Accordingly, they sought less expensive methods of addressing the problem. Park advocated the recruitment and training of people with superior visual skills, people who knew how to look. The lesson of the laboratory was not that microbes were invisible—just the opposite—but their identification required a new relationship to perception and to the visual. Microscopes were one way of identifying disease-causing microbes, but surely, he argued, there were other ways of making pathology visible. Public-health officials needed to classify signs of pathology. For Copeland, the danger of "immigrant [or import] disease" justified the expense of tracking and supervising immigrants, but the lack of sufficient funds required other stopgap measures.[32] In the absence of better resources and facilities, he argued, immigrants should be taught better hygienic habits in the interest of national health.[33]

Characteristic in all of these papers are the allegations concerning the nature of immigrants' (unfamiliar) microbes, their mobility, the squalor in which they lived and their irresponsible habits, all of which, as the story of Typhoid Mary demonstrates, contributed to new theories about social responsibility, social interactions, and social spaces. The bacteriological discoveries of microbes and healthy carriers made the study of groups and social interaction as important for medicine and public health as for sociology, and the new theories were articulated through the methods bacteriologists and epidemiologists developed to track the spread of communicable disease and the new means fashioned by students of culture, notably Robert Park and his colleagues, to study the formation of communities. The interanimation of biological and social conceptions of "community" characterized the work of all three areas. As signaled by the prevalence, and overlapping meanings, of terms such as *communication* and *communicable*, communicability in all of its incarnations lay at the heart of the emerging science of society.

A SCIENCE OF SOCIETY

The role that Park and his colleagues imagined for themselves in this work differed from the activism of social reformers like Riis or the famous Chicago settlement worker Jane Addams. Also affiliated with the University of Chicago, Addams and her associates at Hull House certainly had an impact on the work of the sociologists.[34] Yet where Addams offered her primary allegiance to her tenement constituency, the work of the sociologists took place mainly in the classroom and on the page. As academics—and self-proclaimed social scientists—they set out more specifically to study than to reform society. Real change came, they believed, through structural transformations rather than social reforms, and the impetus for change was generally effected by the circumstances of a changing world. The sociologists differed from many traditional academics, however, by nonetheless insisting on the practical implications of their work. Such was the legacy of Albion Small, the founder of the University of Chicago's sociology and anthropology department, who had trained as a Baptist minister and who maintained a reformist impulse throughout his career at Chicago. Religious training and journalism were not unusual backgrounds for the earliest sociologists. Many, including Park, who had himself begun as a reform-minded journalist, believed that the role of the sociologist was to describe, not to intervene. Yet the reformist impulse was hard to resist. Their work often manifests a faith that understanding social processes would lead to better control over them, which, in turn, would help policymakers and social reformers ultimately to alleviate social problems and build a more equitable and healthier society.[35]

Calling the "social system of control . . . a dark jungle harboring warring bands of guerrillas," E. A. Ross, Small's former classmate, articulated the widely held conviction that "when investigators with the scientific method have fully occupied this region the disorder and dacoity ought to cease."[36] The knowledge could be dangerous in the wrong hands, but the identification of social principles by the well-trained sociologist should help "the control of society over its members . . . to become more conscious and effective . . . , and the dismal see-sawing between change and reaction . . . to disappear."[37]

There is probably no better way to establish and define a field than to write a textbook. With the *Introduction to the Science of Sociology,* the so-called Green Bible, Park and Ernest W. Burgess, his more junior colleague, offered their vision of the new discipline. Through the essays they collected, and in many cases authored, as chapters, they sketched a genealogy, approach, methodology, and set of inquiries, which they announced as the "*science* of sociology." Proclaiming "social control . . . the central fact and central problem of society," they described sociology "so far as it can be regarded as a fundamental science and not mere congeries of social-welfare programs and practices, . . . as the science of collective behavior."[38] With the microscope and the laboratory serving as frequent metaphors in the work of the early sociologists, they sought to elevate social observation to a science by discovering the principles that governed human interactions and made communication and, through it, collective behavior, possible. If history offered "the concrete records of that human nature and experience"

(43), the task of sociology was to explain them: to fashion a theory of history and humanity based on the "natural history" (a term that appears frequently in the work of the early sociologists) of institutions, groups, and spaces.

The city was a logical site of inquiry for the earliest U.S. sociologists. From their German predecessors and, in many cases, teachers—notably Georg Simmel and Oswald Spengler—they inherited a view of the city as the site of new social formations with implications for the future of humankind. For Spengler, the changes signaled the inevitable decline of a civilization that, "growing from primitive barter-center to Culture-city and at last to world-city, . . . sacrifices first the blood and soul of its creators to the needs of its majestic evolution, and then the last flower of that growth to the spirit of Civilization—and so, doomed, moves on to final self-destruction."[39] Simmel was more sanguine; the city for him staged the most intriguing and important drama of the nineteenth century: the struggle between two forms of individualism. Its stimulation and anonymity at once liberated individuals from prior social conventions and inaugurated a free fall, forcing them to seek new means of distinction and self-definition.[40]

Calling the city a "laboratory or clinic in which human nature and social processes may be conveniently and profitably studied," Park found the assemblies of people and disintegration of traditional units such as the family or village indispensable to the study of collective behavior—the breakdown and reformation of groups—that formed the cornerstone of his inquiry.[41] While he and his colleagues believed that urbanization entailed the transition from the homogeneities of folk culture to the heterogeneities of a more disjointed existence, they also held that the transition would throw into relief the principles of social cohesion, making them easier to describe, to study, and to reinforce.

Following his graduate work with German sociologists, Park had taken a circuitous route to his academic position and had not been in Chicago long when he wrote "The City." The essay reflects not only his sociological training but also the interests and perspective shaped by years of work as a journalist, a publicist, and a writer first for the Congo Reform Association (under the direction of the psychologist and educator G. Stanley Hall) and later for Booker T. Washington's Tuskegee Institute. Coauthoring studies with Washington, Park was in effect practicing sociology when he met the prominent Chicago sociologist William I. Thomas, who, christening Park his "Dear Brother in Christ," engineered his move to Chicago.[42] Having brought his academic training to his practical work, Park now brought his work experience to his sociological writing.

His varied career as an observer helped him to recognize how "the city acquires an organization which is neither designed nor controlled," yet which manifests a logic that a careful investigator can discern.[43] Such was the lesson that he had learned from epidemiologists and criminologists. And inscribed in their maps was an activist impulse, an effort to solve a mystery: the cause of an illness, the perpetrator of a crime. From the lessons of his early career, Park inherited an understanding of social investigation that, try as he might, he could never fully dissociate from that activism.[44] As he sought to uncover the mystery of social control, to make visible the intrinsic and external codes that governed human behavior, he allowed the image not only of the map but also of the laboratory to shape both his methods and the objects of his study. "Sociological research is at present," he would write in 1921, "in about the situation in which psychology was before the introduction of laboratory methods, in which medicine was before Pasteur and the germ theory of disease."[45] In its collection of data and in its goals, sociology had to become scientific. When he emphasized the importance of the diphtheria epidemic to his method, Park deliberately claimed a specific expertise. In their newly equipped laboratories, bacteriologists were making visible—and thereby redefining—what had long been assumed to be the invisible agents of contagion. Their authority inhered in the expertise that enabled them to do so. Claiming the ability likewise to identify and track the invisible transmission of ideas and attitudes, Park, too, could harness that authority as he redefined the material of culture.

FROM THE GERMS OF COMMUNITY TO THE WEB OF LIFE

The material of culture and the means of its transmission were what Park sought to identify in "The City" with the term *social contagion*. The term registered the coevolution of a variety of theories and methods derived from sociological, bacteriological, and epidemiological research. And it marked an emerging conception of community formation that would be at once shaped and haunted by the multiple meanings of *contagion*.

As in Durkheim's and Freud's usage, the term *contagion* suggested a connective and transformative force and was commonly used to describe how an individual got caught up in the spirit and actions of a group, surrendering personal agency and even rational thought to the collective will. The

French man of letters Gustave Le Bon used it in his popular and influential work, *The Crowd: A Study of the Popular Mind*. Published first in France in 1885, it was translated into English in 1896 and circulated widely in the United States, where it heralded a moment of radical transformation attendant on the breakdown of traditional beliefs and affiliations and the "creation of entirely new conditions of existence and thought as the result of modern scientific and industrial discoveries."[46] Le Bon christened the impending epoch "the ERA OF CROWDS" (xv), which resulted, he believed, from a new model of social transformation: the "destinies of nations are elaborated at present in the heart of the masses, and no longer in the councils of princes" (xv). His volume anatomized crowds, which he likened to "those microbes which hasten the dissolution of enfeebled or dead bodies" because of "the purely destructive nature of their power." Nothing more clearly manifested that power, he maintained, than the role of the masses in bringing down "the structure of a [rotten] civilisation" (xix). Leaving open the question of the fate of the current civilization, he enjoined his readers to resign themselves "to the reign of the masses" (xix) and proposed to offer "insight into the psychology of crowds" (xx).

The concepts of contagion and suggestibility are at the center of that insight, as Le Bon enumerates "the creation of new characteristics" (9) that make the crowd more than the sum of its individual parts: "In a crowd every sentiment and act is contagious, and contagious to such a degree that an individual readily sacrifices his personal interest to the collective interest. This is an aptitude very contrary to his nature, and of which a man is scarcely capable, except when he makes part of a crowd" (10). This contagion is an effect of suggestibility, which is what enables crowds to emerge irrationally and without forethought. They are dangerous in their characteristic loss of all but the most rudimentary ability to reason and their susceptibility to the hallucinations of an individual: "As the result of contagion the perversions are of the same kind," he observes, "and take the same shape in the case of all the assembled individuals. The first perversion of the truth effected by one of the individuals of the gathering is the starting-point of the contagious suggestion" (23). Contagion suggests the power and the pathology of crowds and the importance of an index case.

For Le Bon's contemporary and countryman Gabriel Tarde, contagion expressed the transmissions that constitute not only a *crowd* but also—and more significantly—the more metaphysical *public*. The crowd, he argues in his 1901 *L'Opinion et la foule*, "presents something animalistic. . . . Is it not a bundle of psychical contagions essentially produced by physical contact?"[47]

But what really interests Tarde is how the (contagious) transmission of assumptions transcends physical contact. Nearly three quarters of a century before Anderson's *Imagined Communities*, Tarde puts the daily newspaper at the center of the formation of community. "The strange thing," he notes, "is that the men who are thus involved, who mutually suggest or rather transmit among themselves the suggestion from on high, do not come into contact with each other, neither do they see or hear one another: they sit, each one in his home, reading the same newspaper and dispersed over a vast territory. What is the tie therefore that exists among them? This tie is, with the simultaneity of their conviction or their passion, the sense that each of them has that this idea or this desire is shared at the same moment by a large number of other men."[48] That phenomenon he labels "this invisible contagion of the public," "the contagion without contact," and it explains "the simple prestige of the here and now."[49] Repeatedly summoning *contagion* to express a kind of contact acting *as though* it is physical —acting, that is, on the body but without actual contact—Tarde uses the term to describe the social organism as it is connected through media (the public) as well as physical proximity (the crowd).

Park included Tarde (although not Le Bon) in the genealogy of social theorists that he chronicles in the introductory chapter of *Introduction to the Science of Sociology.*[50] The lineage begins with August Comte and Herbert Spencer and moves to the more contemporary leading voices of Franklin Giddings, Tarde, and Durkheim, with particular attention to the way each attempts to understand the "fundamental problem . . . of social control. How does a mere collection of individuals," he asks, "succeed in acting in a corporate and consistent way? How . . . does the group control its individual members; the whole dominate its parts?"[51]

Yet none of the leading voices of this genealogy finally gets quite at the exact essences either of the social organism or of the material of culture (and the process of its transmission) as Park understands them. For that he turns to his former teacher, the prominent theorist of education and philosopher John Dewey, an associate of Small who taught briefly at the University of Chicago before moving to Columbia. Park had studied extensively with Dewey as an undergraduate at the University of Michigan, and communication was one of the concepts that most interested Dewey. "Communication," Park contends, "is a process by which we 'transmit' an experience from an individual to another but it is also a process by which these same individuals get a common experience."[52] Distinguishing Dewey's term from "what Tarde calls 'inter-stimulation,'" Park emphasizes that "communication" not only involves "the creation, out of experiences that are individual and private," of "an experience that is common and public but such a common experience becomes the basis for a common and public existence in which every individual, to greater or less extent, participates and is himself a part" (14–15). Ethnologists, he explains, call this existence "culture," and it produces an emergent organism called a "community."

The idea of this emergent organism extended a concept that Park had introduced in "The City" when he outlined the "special importance" that the tenements hold for sociologists because of "social contagion."[53] If Spengler's worst portents about the consequences of urbanism were realized in the tenements, and if they posed the greatest challenge to the beneficent forces that Ross cataloged in his work on social control, the "social contagion" in the tenements also threw into relief the processes of communication that constitute groups. The sociophysical bond that Park would subsequently label the "common and public existence" represented not only social interaction but also a new entity: not a social body, which he understood as individuals' acting jointly, but a new organism (as in Le Bon's formulation) that transformed as it "collected" these individuals.

Where Le Bon saw only the crowd as emergent, Park imagined all communities as such. Bacteriologists could trace the routes of unrecognized intimacies through microbes. For Park they made visible the routes of cultural transmission as well, but media broadened the area of influence: culture was even more widely and easily transmissible than disease. And just as microbes helped to show how individuals were transformed as they were incorporated into larger entities (biotic populations), cultural transmission was similarly transformative. *Contagion* effectively captured that transformation, as it inflected his use of the term *communication*. Thus, in 1915, he had fashioned his methodology for the study of the city, "a mechanism—a psychophysical mechanism—in and through which private and political interests find corporate expression"; of communication, the "suggestions" that "may be given and responded to on the instinctive, senso-motor, or ideo-motor levels"; and of social control, which, he argued, "arises for the most part spontaneously, in direct response to personal influences and public sentiment. It is the result of a personal accommodation rather than the formulation of a rational and abstract principle."[54] As in herd immunity, individuals newly in contact gradually adapt to each other in a process of mutual transformation. *Contagion* named the danger as well as the power of the transformation. It picked up on the health threats presumably posed by the tenements and implied the need for a response modeled on that of the bacteriologists: diagnosis and treatment. Through his inquiry into the workings of those processes, Park the sociologist sought to identify the principles that governed it, and Park the reluctant activist hoped ultimately to understand how to channel the processes of pathological associations into a healthy social control: to transform an unhealthy contagion into a generative and transformative communication.

The ambition required a new vocabulary. *Contagion* was powerful, but it lacked the specificity of the concept Park and his colleagues were trying to name. *Social contagion* was distinctive, and Park and Burgess carefully established a genealogy for it in *Introduction to the Science of Sociology*. They rejected Tarde's use of the term to name "the fundamental social phenomenon" of imitation, as in fashion, finding it too superficial.[55] More compelling to them was the phenomenon described by a German historian of medicine and pioneer in the field of "historical pathology" in the early nineteenth century. In *The Black Death and Dancing Mania* Justus Friedrich Karl Hecker had studied the "strange delusion" that swept through parts of Europe, causing people to hallucinate vividly and dance uncontrollably to exhaustion.[56] Hecker was intrigued by the dancing mania, which spread as undeniably as, and in the wake of, the bubonic plague. Park and Burgess were drawn to his description of it as a "social epidemic . . . a form of social contagion" (875), speculating that "it was perhaps [the] similarity in the manner in which they spread—the one by physical and the other by psychical infection—that led [Hecker] to speak of the spread of a popular delusion in terms of a physical science" (875). Excerpting the passage in *Introduction to the Science of Sociology*, they claimed it as the genealogy of their use of the term. The approach appealed to them because, by tracing the hysteria "to the prevailing conditions of the time," Hecker thereby "put the manifestations in the world of intelligible and controllable phenomena, where they could be investigated" (875).

The vocabulary fashioned from Hecker's juxtapositions (more than from his own analysis) helped them describe the interaction of the biological and sociological features of the "social organism" with nuances that Park had sought in "The City": "It is this notion, then, that unrest which manifests itself in social epidemics is an indication of pathological social conditions, and the further, the more general, conception that unrest does not become social and hence contagious except when there are contributing causes in the environment—it is this that gives its special significance to the term and the facts. Unrest in the social organism with the social ferments that it induces is like fever in the individual organism, a highly important diagnostic symptom" (875–76). Unrest is the sign of a disturbed environment, communicable pathology, and an emergent social organism.

In *Introduction to the Science of Sociology* Park and Burgess distinguished between *nominalists,* such as Tarde and Giddings, who viewed "society" as the name given to a collection of individuals who were (or could be) *"like-minded,"* and *realists,* including Small and Simmel, who believed society was *"real,* and not the name of a mere collection of individuals" (36). Park and Burgess aligned as realists. With Dewey, they believed that " 'society not only continues to exist *by* transmission, *by* communication, but it may fairly be said to exist *in* transmission, *in* communication. There is more than a verbal tie between the words common, community and communication' " (36).[57] The notion of interdependence, so important to their vision of society, involved "social contacts and social forces . . . of a subtler sort but not less real than physical" (36). Communication produced a common experience that could eventually shape a community. It could be disorganized and degenerative or productive and integrative.

Park and Burgess were not alone in their attraction to the terms of bacteriology as they reached for words to describe the emergence of a community. They agreed, for example, with W. von Bechterew's observation that "in society that bacillus for which one has found the name 'suggestion' appears certainly as a leveling element, and, accordingly, whether the individual stands higher or lower than his environment, whether he becomes worse or better under its influence, he always loses or gains something from the contact with others" (419).[58] The bacillus and its attributes offered the most palpable images of the material of culture. "Each individual," wrote Dewey, "is the carrier of the life-experience of his group," and "society exists through a process of transmission, quite as much as biological life" (185).

These are the germs of the ecological perspective that Park would develop further in his later writing. The bacillus was such a powerful concept for cultural transmission because communicable disease was palpable evidence of often unperceived social interactions. The metaphor therefore shaded into proof of the relationship between the biotic and social community that Park had been working to formulate in "The City." In the work of plant and animal ecologists, such as J. Arthur Thomson, whose books *The System of Animate Nature* and *Darwinism and Human Life* were especially important to him, Park found useful the Darwinian concept of "the web of life," which named the biological interconnections that bind all living things together. Park's vocabulary shows the strain of his effort to articulate the relationship of social, biotic, and cultural expressions of community as he sought to reimagine the basic terms of human association. He asserts, for example, that "society, from the ecological point of view is, like the natural as opposed to the institutional family, a symbiotic rather than a social unit."[59] Society ceases to be a "*social* unit" because Park is redefining the conventional usage of the term to incorporate the multiple levels of interaction.

Social contagion had heralded this model: ideas and attitudes spread like germs because of individual proximity and interdependence. Although Park continually outlined the differences between "the 'web of life' which binds living creatures all over the world in a vital nexus" and "the web of communication which man has spread over the earth," he could not fully sustain the distinctions, since communication depended on travel (even newspaper and telegraph offices had to be maintained), which was the primary source for increased interconnection.[60] The web of communication was enabled by and, in turn, contributed to the web of life: "The fact seems to be," he elaborated in "Human Ecology," "that human society, as distinguished from plant and animal society, is organized on two levels, the biotic and the cultural. There is a symbiotic society based on competition and a cultural society based on communication and consensus. As a matter of fact the two societies are merely different aspects of one society, which, in the vicissitudes and changes to which they are subject remain, nevertheless, in some sort of mutual dependence each upon the other. The cultural superstructure rests on the basis of the symbiotic substructure, and the emergent energies that manifest themselves on the biotic level in movements and actions reveal themselves on the higher social level in more subtle and sublimated forms" (13). Three years later, he would define ecology as "concerned with communities rather than societies," but would immediately concede the difficulty of distinguishing between them and declare ecology "in the way of becoming a social, without ceasing to be a biological science" and suggest that "the realm of the social is coterminous with the active interaction of living organisms in what Darwin described as 'the web of life.'"[61] Park was gratified to note a change in the sciences of animal and plant ecology, in which researchers were beginning to acknowledge a social dimension, albeit rudimentary, in animal and even plant communities.

The web of life became the governing principle of his sociological vision, with microbial infection and war as its twin (and dangerous) manifestations: "Meanwhile the area within which a world wide struggle for existence is operative is steadily expanding and, seeing that microbes travel by the same means as men, the dangers of disease and the dangers of war tend to grow *pari passu* with increased use of every form of transportation, including the most recent, the airplane. Thus the web of life which holds within its meshes all living organisms is visibly tightening, and there is in every part of the world obviously a growing interdependence of all living creatures; a vital interdependence that is more extensive and intimate today than at any other period in the course of the long historical process."[62] Increasingly, the social and the biological became conceptually interwoven, with microbes as the interlacing term. *Seeing* is an important word in this passage. Although Park uses it in its colloquial sense of "considering," microbes are material and, under the proper circumstances, *visible*. Because of those properties, they can display the literal contacts (the visible tightening) and consequences of a globalizing world. Through microbes, in other words, Park the sociologist envisions—makes visible as he imagines—the bonds of communication and community that are the material of social transformation and sociological inquiry.

SPATIALIZING SOCIAL INTERACTIONS: THE BIOLOGY OF COMMUNITY

Park injects the discussion of microbial travel and the web of life into a discussion of nonhuman ecology. It reads as something of a disjunction, not closely connected to the observations about the similarities between human and nonhuman ecology that follow it. The logic of the disruption emerges, however, when Park appears to have moved entirely beyond it into a description of the uniqueness of plant communities, which "do not, of course, act collectively as animals do, but the associations they form, partly by a natural selection of species and partly by adaptation and accommodation of individuals—as in the case of the vine and the fig tree—do, by diminishing competition within and by resisting invasion from without, make more secure the life of the community and of the individuals of which it is composed."[63] The passage sounds a subtle warning, and the botanical world offers a lesson that Park hoped would work in the human world. In plant communities disease often followed the "invasion" (chance or deliberate introduction) of a new species that produced competition for space, food, and other necessities. One or more species might fail to thrive or they may adapt, accommodate, and form a new ecosystem. Disease and war were the "natural" expressions of "a growing interdependence." Park hoped that a similar "adaptation and accommodation" was in the human future, and he believed they could be facilitated as well as studied by the prescient sociologist.

This model of ecosystemic transformation had particular urgency when

Park published it in 1939, just as the Second World War was beginning in Europe. But it corresponded to an earlier model that readers familiar with the work of Park and his associates could not have missed. Competition, conflict, accommodation, and assimilation, all chapter headings of the *Introduction to the Science of Sociology*, named the stages of Park's controversial mapping of the immigrant experience.[64] Throughout the previous three decades, Americanization had been a much-debated topic and sociologists had played a key and very public role in the debates. Studies financed federally, locally, and privately yielded numerous treatises across disciplines and media on the topic of immigrant spaces, disease, and Americanization. The immigrant problem depicted in the media was complicated. On one hand, unintegrated immigrant neighborhoods represented the threat of balkanization, which would compromise the integrity of the nation; on the other hand, absorption of these foreigners, many argued, would make "America" unrecognizable to itself. Those who favored the restriction of immigration used that paradox to support their position, but their opponents pointed out the incompatibility of restriction with the founding ideals of the nation. The countless arguments that were framed in terms of a health threat reinforced the vocabulary through which students of immigration and the city shaped their ideas about communication and social existence. The understanding of assimilation that Park and his associates fashioned at once registered those ideas and manifested an effort to negotiate the anxieties that had surfaced in the immigration debates. They recognized the particular challenge posed by the massive influx of immigrants, who dangerously swelled the ranks of the tenements and who typified "the conditions imposed by city life," as Park identified them in "The City," "in which individuals and groups of individuals, widely removed in sympathy and understanding, live together under conditions of interdependence, if not of intimacy" and in which "the conditions of social control are greatly altered and the difficulties increased."[65]

Few of the Chicago sociologists, unlike some of their prominent colleagues elsewhere, including Ross and Henry Pratt Fairchild, advocated restricting immigration. Rather, they typically concentrated on the importance of assimilation and, taking their cue from Simmel, were interested in the insights that strangers could yield into social processes as they clashed with and learned to conform to invisible social dictates. In their textbook, Park and Burgess described assimilation as "a process of interpenetration and fusion in which persons and groups acquire the memories, sentiments, and attitudes of other persons or groups, and, by sharing their experience and history, are incorporated with them in a common cultural life."[66] That process, which was at once mental and physical, represented a moment of crisis and change for all involved. Writing that same year in "Sociology and the Social Sciences: The Group Concept and Social Research," Park described immigrant groups as lacking in the control that family and group tradition exerts and "for that very reason . . . all the more open to the influence of the traditions and customs of their adopted country" (177). Because of that lack, however, and the danger of "demoralization," a word that evoked a loss of both morals and morale, Americanization required the expertise of the sociologist. Conversely, their openness to the influence made the immigrant groups a sociological ideal. The urban sociologists could not only test their theories, they could also study—and perhaps learn to facilitate—the nature of that influence. For Park, the processes of cultural transmission and the contours of Americanism were nowhere more visible than in that metamorphosis. They revealed the communicability of culture, which, in the context of the Americanization debates (and, therefore, on a national scale), became a communicable Americanism.

As the ecological model evolved in Park's work, it increasingly shaped his understanding of the mechanisms of Americanization, and it imparted a biological inflection to his understanding of urban spaces. Sociologists who wanted to study, and perhaps facilitate, the Americanization of the foreign-born had to understand the relationship of space to social interactions and practices. For, Park argued, it was "only as social and psychical facts [could] be reduced to, or correlated with, spatial facts that they [could] be measured at all."[67] In "The City" he had begun to explore how the experience of a place emerged from shared ideas about it and in turn reinforced communal affiliations and a shared culture. He built on Simmel's observation in a well-known chapter from his *Sociologie* entitled "The Stranger," which Park and Burgess translated and included in the Green Bible, that "wandering . . . discloses . . . the fact that relations to space are only, on the one hand, the condition, and, on the other hand, the symbol of relations to men."[68] Social space emerged from the communication of ideas and attitudes, a geographical fiction that was, however, no less material for the circumstances of its origin. Understanding that process allowed sociologists to exert an important social influence: to shape the communication that constituted the experience of a place and thereby to create more salubrious social spaces.

The work of Park's students and younger colleagues reflected his fascination with social spaces, and no corner of urban America, especially where immigrants had settled, was beyond the scope of their inquiry. They measured the degree (or absence) of commingling through the idea of "social distance" between social groups.[69] Geographic erosion named the processes of group transformation that resulted from the geographic proximity of social groups. Changing spaces showed that communities—the spatial expression of social groups—were always in flux.

No spaces more readily illustrated both this process and the potential for sociological intervention than the urban neighborhoods where immigrants settled. In "The City" Park had christened places where people congregate because of special interests and temperaments ranging from criminal activities to artistic endeavors "moral regions," and he argued, following Freud, that these spaces allowed for the collective expression of impulses suppressed by social conventions. The denizens of the moral regions, in other words, came together as an outlet for what mainstream society excluded. While Park was writing "The City," William I. Thomas and his informant and coauthor, Florian Znaniecki, were researching and writing their five-volume study of the Polish peasant in Europe and the United States. Both their immigrant neighborhoods and Park's moral regions demonstrated what Park describes as the "social manifestations that we call social unrest" that signal "social change" and that take the form of "social and individual disorganization," including some combination of "accelerated mobility, unrest, disease, and crime."[70] But the difference between them was central to the development of the sociological project. Witnessing a group in the process of its formation better enabled sociologists to witness the processes of disintegration and reintegration—the breakdown and emergence of a community—and facilitated their ability to manage what they believed were ongoing, or at least repetitive, social events. Park argued in "The City" that the "moral regions" were "in a sense, at least, a part of the natural, if not the normal, life of a city" (612), but no particular "moral region" was permanent. Thomas and Znaniecki's Polish-American ghetto and Park's "moral regions" dovetailed in their depictions of a spatial expression of a transitory (and often transitional) community, simultaneously apart from and a part of mainstream U.S. society, rich for sociological study and potentially susceptible to sociological activism. Yet Thomas and Znaniecki's immigrant neighborhoods, in which the Polish peasants incorporated U.S. conventions into a Polish social structure (thereby becoming "Polish-Americans"), were also the converse of moral regions. Representing susceptibility to outside influence rather than reaction against it, the immigrant communities were moving toward rather than away from the mainstream.

Thomas and Znaniecki's work was widely influential both for its content and for its methodology. For Park in particular, the ethnic enclaves they described could offer an antidote to the social degeneration of the tenements. With the sociologist's task in mind, Park and his associates marked and formalized the distinction between a pathological social contagion and a productive and formative communication, as they made it central to understanding and managing the processes of Americanization. The tenements provided the arena where they could witness the processes by which literally and figuratively diseased outsiders became productive bearers of American culture. They sought, in other words, to discover the principles that transformed the pathological processes of cultural transmission into a generative communication, and, as a result, produced a communicable Americanism. Their descriptions characteristically turned tenements into predictably transitional rather than antipathetic communities, and in them the transition followed a prescribed course toward Americanization. Those communities they increasingly termed *ghettos*. The line between describing and influencing processes faded to the point of disappearance when the urban sociologists approached the topic of Americanization, especially in the ghettos.

The story of Typhoid Mary established an important role for sanitary engineers as it informed the concepts of social being and social control with the discoveries of bacteriology. Sociological accounts of "the ghetto" offered a spatial analog to that story, establishing the importance of sociological inquiry to social—and national—health and well-being. The "web of life" further developed the biological features of spatial mappings, which could be articulated on a variety of scales: neighborhoods, cities, regions, even the nation could be conceptualized as ecosystems. Moreover, the model of the ecosystem described the biological relationships not just among individuals within those spaces but also, more dramatically, among the spaces themselves and the groups that inhabited them. Ecosystems depicted biological consolidations, and microbes were their harbingers and facilitators; communicable diseases depicted and could help to shape communal transformation. Immigrant neighborhoods offered the most vivid examples of those metamorphoses; the "ghettos" that were therefore the focus of sociological inquiry turned those spaces into powerful sites in which bacteriological theories informed sociological theories of communication and cultural transmission.

GEOGRAPHIC FICTIONS

The terms *tenement* (or *slum*) and *ghetto* became increasingly distinct in the work of the urban sociologists as they described a transitional geographical space and developmental stage between the tenement and the metropolis. To enforce the distinction, they drew on a depiction of the ghetto that had become one among several—often conflicting—conventions at the turn of the twentieth century: a picturesque community where, for example, the journalist Hutchins Hapgood, writing in 1902, found "charm" and "spirit," the best of the Old World coexisting with the New. Hapgood originally published *The Spirit of the Ghetto* as a series of journalistic essays that he wrote between 1898 and 1902 with the help of the Jewish immigrant journalist and fiction writer Abraham Cahan. In his study of the rich cultural life of Manhattan's Lower East Side, Hapgood at once celebrated folk tradition and bore witness to the processes of Americanization under way in the Jewish ghetto. As a concept, the "ghetto" was at least partly fashioned by the exigencies of Americanization, as the Chicago sociologists understood them.

Fiction, at least as much as social-reform journalism, had already significantly shaped the ghetto in the American imagination by the time the sociologists began their work on it. They were aware of its influence and did not see fiction as antithetical to the project of sociology.[71] Park insisted that people learn more "in the sense of understanding one another and in the ability to communicate from literature and the arts" than "from experience" and that "it is just the function of literature and the arts and of what are described in academic circles as the humanities to give us this intimate personal and inside knowledge of each other which makes social life more aimiable [*sic*] and collective action possible."[72] Literature and the arts represented a special form of communication—"symbolic and expressive" rather than "referential" (as in scientific description)—and he described its transformative power: symbolic and expressive communication "profoundly influences sentiment and attitudes even when it does not make any real contribution to knowledge."[73] Literature and the arts carried and transmitted the material of culture and actually constituted communities. Fictional depictions of social spaces could be formative in a variety of ways: for people who inhabited or visited them, for people who studied them, and for people who lacked any other experience of them. The ghetto of fiction constructed even as it reflected (and reflected on) the lived experience of urban neighborhoods.

Hapgood was not the only analyst of the ghetto who recognized Abraham Cahan as one of the most sophisticated observers (and narrators) of the ghetto. Thomas, too, had been influenced by this labor-movement pioneer, editor, and spokesperson for Yiddish America. Familiar with Cahan's journalism, he recognized the readers' letters Cahan published in the *Jewish*

Daily Forward as an important source of sociological material.[74] And Park attributed the success of the *Forward* to Cahan's skillful management. Years before he revolutionized that journal, Cahan had used his editorial position at the socialist Yiddish *Arbeiter Zeitung* to denounce the biases that led to the 1892 quarantines and other injustices, but nowhere were his powers of observation more acute and his analyses more comprehensive than in his fictional depictions of the ghetto. Preceding the sociological work of Park and his associates by nearly two decades, Cahan's 1896 crossover novella, *Yekl: A Tale of the New York Ghetto*, anatomized the transitional nature of the ghetto that would make it so compelling a topic of inquiry for the urban sociologists. Lincoln Steffens once quipped that "what reporters know and don't report is news—not from the newspapers' point of view, but from the sociologists' and the novelists'."[75] Cahan fashioned *Yekl* out of that journalistic knowledge. His insights make this work powerful not only for the information on ghetto life that it imparts but also for the analysis that it offers. His depiction of life in the fin de siècle Jewish ghetto chronicles how such social spaces were constituted and explains why they were so appealing to sociologists who hoped to understand and influence the processes of Americanization.

In his fiction, as in his journalism, Cahan took every opportunity to bring the squalor of the tenement to the attention of mainstream America. Early in the novel, he describes Yekl's having "to pick and nudge his way through dense swarms of bedraggled half-naked humanity; past garbage barrels rearing their overflowing contents in sickening piles, and lining the streets in malicious suggestion of rows of trees; underneath tiers and tiers of fire escapes, barricaded and festooned with mattresses, pillows, and featherbeds not yet gathered in for the night. The pent-in sultry atmosphere was laden with nausea and pierced with a discordant and, as it were, plaintive buzz. Supper had been despatched in a hurry, and the teeming populations of the cyclopic tenement houses were out in full force 'for fresh air,' as even these people will say in mental quotation marks."[76] The dehumanizing conditions conform to what was already a stereotype. The spaces where immigrants lived, already tainted by the metaphors and dogged by the experience of disease, had come under increased scrutiny by Progressive sociologists and journalists as well as public-health officials by the late nineteenth century. Riis had dubbed the Jewish East Side "the typhus ward," where filth diseases "sprout naturally among the hordes that bring the germs with them from across the sea."[77] Although Jews of course had no monopoly on such medical scapegoating, they had a long history of association with communicable disease dating at least as far back as the Black

Death (bubonic plague epidemic) of the fourteenth century, when they were accused of poisoning their neighbors' wells.[78]

While ghettoization had probably begun as the result of Jews' choice to segregate themselves, it was institutionalized by the sixteenth century and contributed to their portrayal as diseased and dangerous strangers. Histories of the Jews, which appeared in significant numbers in the United States and England at the turn of the twentieth century, documented the language of contagion and the logic of quarantine that is at the core of ghettoization: "As we today remove the victims of a pestilence far away from the inhabited portions of our cities," writes David Philipson in *Old European Jewries*, "so the Jews were cut off by the walls of the ghetto as though stricken with some loathsome disease that might carry misery and death unto others if they lived in close contact with them."[79] In the sixteenth century that contamination would have a heretical cast, while in the late-nineteenth-century United States, the feared corruption was cultural: Jewish practices and customs mingled with and configured as germs were more likely to leak into the polis than religious beliefs. Penning these words in 1893–1894, Philipson may have had in mind the 1892 quarantines, which targeted Eastern European Jews. History was repeating itself for those former denizens of the shtetls.

Yet, as quickly as Cahan's words summon the familiar stereotype in *Yekl*, he complicates it, following the description of filth with an incantatory passage that describes the metamorphosis of Suffolk Street into

> the Ghetto of the American metropolis, and, indeed, the metropolis of the Ghettos of the world. It is one of the most densely populated spots on the face of the earth—a seething human sea fed by streams, streamlets, and rills of immigration flowing from all the Yiddish-speaking centers of Europe. Hardly a block but shelters Jews from every nook and corner of Russia, Poland, Galicia, Hungary, Roumania; Lithuanian Jews, Volhynian Jews, south Russian Jews, Bessarabian Jews; Jews crowded out of the "pale of Jewish settlement"; Russified Jews expelled from Moscow, St. Petersburg, Kieff, or Saratoff; Jewish runaways from justice; Jewish refugees from crying political and economical injustice . . . artisans, merchants, teachers, rabbis, artists, beggars—all come in search of fortune. Nor is there a tenement house but harbors in its bosom specimens of all the whimsical metamorphoses wrought upon the children of Israel of the great modern exodus by the vicissitudes of life in this their Promised Land of today. You will find there Jews born to plenty, whom the new conditions have delivered up to the clutches of penury; Jews reared in the straits of need, who have here risen to prosperity; good people morally degraded in the struggle for success amid an unwonted environment; moral

outcasts lifted from the mire, purified, and imbued with self-respect; educated men and women with their intellectual polish tarnished in the inclement weather of adversity; ignorant sons of toil grown enlightened—in fine, people with all sorts of antecedents, tastes, habits, inclinations, and speaking all sorts of subdialects of the same jargon, pellmell into one social cauldron—a human hodgepodge with its component parts changed but not yet fused into one homogeneous whole. (14)

The "sickening," "malicious," "discordant," "plaintive" streets peel away as the "dense swarms of bedraggled half-naked humanity" metamorphose into "a seething human sea fed by streams, streamlets, and rills of immigration flowing from all the Yiddish-speaking centers of Europe." The Jewish ghetto is a space of transformation, a microcosm of the city itself, its problems a result of overcrowding and economic and social inequity rather than the innate unhealthiness or filth of its denizens.[80]

Cahan stresses the "whimsical metamorphoses," the unpredictable changes in fortune and status, the discontinuities and instabilities that constitute the experience of immigration. Those metamorphoses were the most common experiences of immigration, as the fiction not only of Cahan but of other writers, such as his contemporary Sholom Aleichem, attests. The earliest Jewish immigrants from Eastern Europe were more often the poor Jews from the shtetls, and the reversals of fortunes were of course experienced very differently by those who found themselves worse off than by those who found their status improved.[81] For the more impoverished Jews, who carried with them resentment not only of their Christian oppressors but also of the wealthier Jews, America provided an opportunity to reorganize Eastern European Jewish class structure and, with it, the practice of the religion itself.

Yekl is the prototype of the avid assimilator, and in the model of Americanization he eagerly espouses, immigrants relinquish the specificity of their heritages to blend into an "American" population. Cahan's list of the denizens of the ghetto rhetorically expresses the presumed trajectory of assimilation: the gradual divestiture of the past. Geographical points of origin (Russia, Poland, Galicia) give way to geographical affiliations (Lithuanian Jews, Volhynian Jews) and gradually to individuals' motives for immigrating. In this grammar of assimilation, geographical nouns (Russia) become geographical adjectives (Lithuanian), which are then replaced by the adjective "Jewish," and, in turn, by a diversity of occupations: a gradual disaffiliation and move into individual distinction. Through this grammar, Cahan describes the beginning of the process of social contagion.

The assimilation process, however, gets stalled in Cahan's description of Suffolk Street; the "component parts" of the "human hodgepodge" are "changed but not yet fused into one homogeneous whole" which, conforming to an increasingly conventional metaphor and anticipating the melting pot that Israel Zangwill would subsequently popularize, he calls a "social caldron." The "whimsical metamorphoses" constitute a kind of Americanization, but the experience of the ghetto that Cahan describes is most precisely the experience of a transition that has as its *presumed* end absorption into mainstream American culture. Nothing about the rhetoric or logic of the passage leads to the conclusion that the "homogeneous whole" into which the metamorphosed have not yet fused marks their absorption into that culture. Instead, the logic of Cahan's description leads to a social caldron that is making Jewish Americans out of Russian Jews, Bessarabian Jews, refugees, runaways, rabbis, artists, and beggars.

Cahan's alternative understanding of assimilation and the space of the ghetto anticipates the sociologists' model of breakdown and reformation. The members of this disparate group become Americans by becoming Americanized Jews, just as Thomas and Znaniecki's Polish immigrants would become Polish-Americans in their 1917 study. Immigrants neither fully shed their pasts to become Americans, nor quite preserve their pasts. Following the logic of the rhetoric of Cahan's description, the ghetto implicitly works to link them as Jews—their common experience being their life in the ghetto and the whimsical metamorphoses that mark their changed circumstances—and to "Americanize" them *as Jews*. Cahan's Suffolk Street thereby replaces the specificities of heritage with a generically "Jewish" past.

Cahan anticipates, and perhaps supplies, the logic of the sociologists' studies as he distinguishes between the tenement, the nauseous streets where the immigrants live, which pose a health threat, and the ghetto, which contains that threat. When it becomes the identifiable space of a "ghetto," the malicious, nauseous, discordant, diseased, plaintive street scene (contrary to expectation) turns, as Cahan later notes, unexpectedly "picturesque." The term names the process through which life comes to resemble art. Suffolk Street is picturesque because the observer's perception of the scene has been influenced by its artistic precedents. With the juxtaposition of paragraphs, Cahan conspicuously turns decaying streets into Suffolk Street, "*the Ghetto* of the American metropolis, and, indeed, the metropolis of *the Ghettos* of the world." As "the ghetto," the street scene is already scripted and consequently predictable and therefore contained, assimilable and even paradigmatic. The metamorphosis displays the potential transformation that can be enacted by the machinations of a salutary social control, as with Mary Mallon's recasting as "Typhoid Mary."

Americanization does not just take place in but also actually creates the ghetto. Garbage-strewn streets become Suffolk Street because Jewish immigrants are becoming Americans there, because, that is, it is fulfilling a specific social function. Distinguishing thus between the tenement and the ghetto, Cahan offers the latter as a transitional space of Americanization and implicitly depicts social cohesion (the formation of a group) as the result of a transmissible—a communicable—culture. The juxtaposed descriptions demonstrate how an urban neighborhood becomes a community, the home of a people who become a group by conforming to geographic fictions: by interacting within, and with reference to, the spaces constituted by those fictions.

While Cahan's ghetto is a space of transformation, it nonetheless also conforms to the model of quarantine. His characters never effectively move beyond Suffolk Street, despite the eponymous Yekl's eagerness to become a "reguly Yankee." Preceding his wife and son to the New World, he renames himself Jake and convinces himself that his reluctance to send for his family signals only his resolution to be able to provide a comfortable home before their arrival. But he sends for them only when the death of his father makes it impossible for them to remain in Russia. He is disgusted by his wife, Gitl, when she disembarks. He is troubled by her "uncouth and un-American appearance," which he racializes in accordance with American stereotypes: "She was naturally dark of complexion, and the nine or ten days spent at sea had covered her face with a deep bronze, which combined with her prominent cheek bones, inky little eyes, and, above all, the smooth black wig, to lend her resemblance to a squaw" (34). In this description the immigrant Yekl ironically experiences his own Americanism in comparison to his wife's resemblance to a squaw. When he finally persuades her to shed the wig with which orthodox Jewish women cover their hair for a kerchief, he succeeds only in making her look to him "like an Italian woman of Mulberry Street on Sunday" (34).[82] Gitl is a one-woman melting pot of the identities that he has learned to associate as antithetical to an American identity. Yekl/Jake is ultimately entrapped by his racism and self-hatred. He divorces his wife, and the novella ends with him on his way to marry not an "American," but another Jewish immigrant, Mamie, who has been in New York longer than he and who speaks better English, a more Americanized Jew. He assimilates by divorcing the past and then emulating, but not marrying into, America. It is in fact Yekl's belief that he is becoming a "reguly Yankee" by marrying Mamie that dooms him to the disappointment that Cahan forecasts at the end of the novel; Gitl, by contrast, will enjoy a brighter future because she is content, when she remarries, to stay within the community.

Cahan's insights into the Americanization process depicted a culture continually constituted through social interactions expressed spatially, such as the Chicago sociologists would later describe. The characters who attempt to escape the ghetto—even those who succeed, such as the eponymous protagonist of his 1917 *The Rise of David Levinsky*—end up anguished and alienated. While Cahan focused on the psychological impact of the language and experience of Americanization for immigrants, however, the sociologists concerned themselves almost exclusively with the observation of groups from the perspective of mainstream culture. Thomas addressed the problem of immigrant alienation directly in a 1921 work, *Old World Traits Transplanted*, that he coauthored, with Park and Herbert A. Miller, as one of eleven volumes that comprised a study of Americanization funded by the Carnegie Corporation of New York.[83] They explicitly advocated, in response, an Americanization that would take place through immigrant organizations and in the immigrants' native language. Against those who argued for forced and rapid acculturation, they contended not only that the immigrants were already "becoming Americanized *en masse*, by whole blocks, precisely through their own organizations" (293), but also that they ought to be encouraged to do so. Drawing on Thomas and Znaniecki's observation of "the demoralization of the Poles in America," especially the children of immigrants, in the absence of a "strong social group" with which to identify, they maintained that the "organization of the immigrant community is necessary as a regulative measure" (289). The transformation of the tenement into the "ghetto," such as Cahan depicted, was a fitting spatial analog for the process they advocated; in that space, the inbreeding of "the poor, the vicious, and the delinquent, crushed together in an unhealthful and contagious intimacy" that Park described in "The City" became instead the communicable Americanism of the ghetto: the parts transformed into a coherent but separate whole.[84] *Yekl* explained the appeal of the ghetto as a space for sociologists' inquiry: not only for what they could observe but also for what they could contain. And it dramatized as well how contagion inflected the representation of that space.

THE GHETTO AND THE STRANGER

The influence of this quarantine model is evident in *The Ghetto*, the 1928 landmark study of Louis Wirth, Park's student and subsequently his colleague, for which Park wrote a foreword.[85] Wirth explicitly distinguishes the sociological task from the literary one. "To tell the story of the ghetto in all its uniqueness," he explains, "is the legitimate function of the artist and the historian. But the sociologist sees in the ghetto more than the experiences of a given people in a specific historical setting . . . [M]ore than a chapter in the cultural history of man[, t]he ghetto represents a study in human nature." It offers the sociologist "a rare opportunity . . . of converting history into natural history," of identifying the principles that govern the formation of communities.[86] But Wirth's study makes clear that the process implicitly entails turning those principles (back) into narratives. The sociologists, too, had a story to tell. Wirth's story is the "natural history" of a transformative American space in which the sociological principles of community formation were thrown into relief. It is also a reassuring tale of Americanization that features integration through containment: the preservation of social control through self-imposed quarantine. Where fiction writers depicted the transformative nature of the Jewish ghetto, Wirth showed how it exemplified the principles of social contagion—and the inevitability of transformation—at the heart of community. His conception anticipates that of the germ theorists of history and explains the relationship of disease to the idea of social transformation as well as the mythical features of the stranger-carrier in the outbreak narrative.

Every paradigm needs a history. Wirth begins his account with the derivation of the concept and term *ghetto* from which he constructs an image of the ghetto that supports his quarantine model. "The Italian Jews," he explains, "derived the word which they spelled *gueto* from the Hebrew word *get*, meaning bill of divorce" (1). Drawing on several studies of Jews, particularly Philipson's 1894 *Old European Jewries*, Wirth offers and discards a series of other possible derivations, including the German *gitter* (cage), the Italian *borghetto* (little quarter), the evolution of the Italian *Giudeica* from *Judaicam* (Jewish state) and its subsequent corruption into *ghetto*, before he arrives at his other preferred explanation in the derivation "from the Italian *gietto*, the cannon foundry at Venice near which the first Jewish settlement was located" (2). The argument for *get* rests in the hard "g," or Yiddish, pronunciation of *ghetto*, and for *gietto*, it stems from the specific geography of the allegedly first "ghetto."[87]

These preferences reflect the program of Americanization that the Chicago sociologists favored. Wirth all but dismisses the derivations from spatial descriptions (*borghetto*, for example) that would seem more compatible with his goal of natural history in favor of the specific geographical and historical *gietto*. His choices underscore the importance of language and geography in group formation, which foster the emergence of a common culture. The *get-ghetto* connection implies that a group of people can "divorce" themselves from those among whom they are living and suggests, in the context of twentieth-century immigration debates, a weakening of the ties of nationality (already especially weak in Jewish immigrants) that would enable them more readily to shift their allegiance first to each other and eventually to a new nation, as in Cahan's description. With that emphasis, he stresses a metaphorical consensual relationship, which served the Americanization program of this period: people could divorce their past and (re)marry into their present.[88] And *gietto* establishes that the term "applies to the Jewish quarter of a city" and "is, strictly speaking, a Jewish institution." Wirth certainly acknowledges "forms of ghettos that concern not merely Jews. There are Little Sicilies, Little Polands, Chinatowns, and Black belts in our large cities," he admits, "and there are segregated areas, such as vice areas, that bear a close resemblance to the Jewish ghetto" (6). Yet sociological studies of other ethnic enclaves did not make similar claims to primacy. The focus on the Jewish roots of "the Ghetto" reflected more than Wirth's particular interest in the Jewish ghetto. It was, rather, a feature of the paradigm of assimilation that the sociologists were fashioning.

In his introduction to *The Ghetto* Park superimposes the experience of subsequent ethnic groups on the original experience of the Jews, and Jewish experience becomes, for him as for Wirth, a blueprint of ethnic experience. While acknowledging that " 'Ghetto' . . . has come into use in recent times as . . . a term which applies to any segregated racial or cultural group" (vii–viii), he maintains that "the history of the ghetto is, in large measure, the history, since the dispersion, of the Jewish people" (ix).[89] In the history of the Jews, Park, Wirth, and their colleagues read (and partly wrote) the history of a group that they believed wished to live apart indefinitely. What the German Jewish immigrant Wirth calls the "voluntary ghetto" of the Jews "was an administrative device" that historically facilitated "social control on the part of the community over its members" and made "the supervision that medieval authorities exercised over all strangers and non-citizens [that is, quarantine] possible" (20–21). This quarantine model, for him, offers a mutually beneficial way of incorporating possibly dangerous strangers into a body politic. Cahan's Yekl/Jake, who has renounced his Old World marriage (alliances) for the New World, personifies it. Divorcing and remarrying within the group, Yekl/Jake exemplifies both the fluidity of attachments and their containment within a delineated space.

Wirth describes "a closed community," spatially markable and "perpetuating itself and renewing itself with a minimum of infusion of influences from without, biologically as well as culturally" (226). The denizens are self-policing, surrounding themselves with a "modern invisible ghetto wall . . . no less real than the old, because it is based on the sentiments and prejudices of human beings who are products of distinct cultures, and upon the most fundamental traits of human nature that govern our approach to the familiar and our withdrawal from the strange" (280). Assimilation of individuals was not impossible, but human nature favored segregation, and Jews as a group remained especially identifiable, individuals more often than not returning in some manner to the fold. Wirth's ghetto manifested the general principles of community and of communicable Americanism, as it offered a reassuring image of containment in which the Jews' stereotypical chauvinism ensured that integration into the whole—the professed accommodation that was the end of the process—would be deferred.

The deferral, however, would not be endless, and sociological studies of Americanization and ethnic enclaves included a forecasting of the eventual changes that Americanization would bring for the larger community: first the urban environment and, subsequently, the nation. The anticipated transformations inflected "ghettos" with a sense of instability, which found expression as an uneasy balance between dangerous and productive social contagion. The communication within the ghetto could readily mutate into a dangerous contagion with any threatened blurring or illicit crossing of its boundaries or disruption of its traditions. The language of contagion surfaced in sociological work and especially in the mainstream media to depict any kind of scurrilous outbreak. The experiences of "the ghetto" threatened endlessly to break out into the attributes of "the tenement." Conversely, communicable-disease outbreaks suggested an underlying social violation of the quarantine model that represented a threat to the larger "community" of the city or nation.

Although the instability of the ghetto could mark the failure of quarantine, it offered at the same time an iconic representation of the permanent impermanence of any community. The biotic basis of social existence subjected it to endless metamorphosis, and every breakdown was followed by a new social formation. Reintegration increasingly became the focus of sociological attention as the children of immigrants came of age. By the time Wirth published his study of the ghetto, Park had already begun to turn his attention to an ecological model of social transformation, shifting his focus, in the process, from the urban spaces that had intrigued him to the strangers who moved through them. In his best-known essay, "The Marginal Man," Park drew heavily on Simmel's work to describe this agent of change.

As a group, ghettoized Jews represented assimilation through segregation; as individuals, Jews were, as the German Jewish Simmel explained in his essay "The Sociological Significance of the 'Stranger,'" archetypal strangers, where *stranger* named a relation that was "naturally . . . quite positive . . . , a particular form of interaction."[90] Although mythologized in the image of the Wandering Jew, the stranger was not necessarily a wanderer, but "the *potential* wanderer" who "has not quite overcome the freedom of coming and going" (322). Simmel animates the stranger as a trader, a necessary figure even in a self-sufficient economy as the importer of new ideas, since "trade alone makes possible unlimited combinations, in which intelligence finds ever wider extensions and ever newer accessions" (323). Physically proximate but with the aura of remoteness, the stranger exposes the conventionality of space and the social relationships it expresses.

The figure is troubling, Simmel explains, because that exposure haunts the most intimate experiences and relationships. New lovers reject it when they insist on the uniqueness of their feelings, but the knowledge of contingency hovers "like shadows between men, like a mist gliding before every word's meaning, which must actually congeal into solid corporeality in order to be called rivalry."[91] Simmel names the shadows and mist "estrangement," and the stranger incarnates them, demonstrating "the extent to which common features become general" and therefore "add to the warmth of the relation founded on them, an element of coolness, a feeling of contingency of precisely *this* relation—the connecting forces have lost their specific and centripetal character."[92] Estrangement signals identification with the stranger—not as an outsider, but as a member of the group. It attends the recognition that what members of a group have in common with each other they may also share with others, and it marks the forbidden knowledge and open secret of community: its constitutive mechanisms and its condition of impermanence. The stranger embodies the terror and wonder—and the inevitability—of change. It is, then, no surprise that the stranger is so readily pathologized and mythologized as a possible carrier of communicable disease: literal seeds of destruction and rejuvenation. Estrangement marks the tacit knowledge of impermanence. It is the affect of contagion.

Park reconstituted the figure of the stranger as the marginal man in 1928, the same year Wirth published *The Ghetto*. The concept dominated the work on race and ethnicity that emerged from the University of Chicago and its offshoots in the decades that followed this study, and, as Stow Persons notes, it was stretched beyond recognition when Park's colleagues and students applied it to a broad range of groups and phenomena.[93] For Park, however, "the emancipated Jew" who left the ghetto was the primary example of the eponymous subject of his essay, "historically and typically the marginal man, the first cosmopolite and citizen of the world." He was Simmel's stranger "par excellence" and with "his pre-eminence as a trader and his keen intellectual interest, his sophistication, his idealism and lack of historic sense," he shared his characteristics with "the city man, the man . . . who ranges widely, and lives preferably in a hotel."[94]

Born of the human migrations that characterize modernity, and striving to live in two cultures, the "marginal man"—"who may or may not be a mixed blood"—is "an unstable character."[95] At once liberated and pitiable, "he" represents the experience of change that followed from a clash of cultures. It was the same clash that was being managed in the ghetto, but in the mind of a solitary individual—one who had rejected the community of the ghetto (or tried to)—the "relatively permanent" crisis and turmoil led to a change in temperament and the development of a "personality type" (356). Examples of the type were familiar from novels, where they wondered, with James Weldon Johnson's ex-colored man, whether they had sold their birthrights for a mess of pottage, or rushed headlong, like Cahan's Yekl, into the very situations from which they sought to flee. Park's marginal men were not all Jewish (or, for that matter, male), but Jews were as exemplary of the figure in his work as the Jewish ghetto was for the ethnic neighborhood. The type was of particular interest to the sociologists because, as Park declared, "it is in the mind of the marginal man—where the changes and fusions of culture are going on—that we can best study the processes of civilization and progress" (356).

The promise of change, so distant in the work on the ghetto, was more insistent and immediate in the discussions of strangers. While remaining unintegrated, marginal men—or groups, such as "the Jews"—had a "symbiotic rather than social" (354) relationship to the rest of society. They were essential to the ecology of the group, from the neighborhood to the nation, even as they remained apart from the social community. The biotic community could not fail to influence the social community over the long term; cultural contact would eventually lead to "interbreeding" and mutual assimilation. While Park conceded that the process would be slower when physical characteristics pronounced racial differences between groups, it would transpire nonetheless, and the marginal men of mixed blood forecast the change, challenging the illusion of permanence that was the unspoken premise of identity.[96]

The ecological community was always in flux, with change brought by "invasions" of migrating species; Park believed that the social community evolved according to similar rules. Communicable disease was the harbinger of that invasion for the biotic community. "Steamships and railways have effectually altered the geography of the world," he told the readership of *Survey Graphic* in 1926, "and the barriers which formerly protected the races from one another have been swept away. With the multiplication of modern means of transportation, and with the increased movement and migration of peoples, no part of the world is so remote from one another as to be secure from the invasion of the diseases of which man is the principal carrier."[97] Interbreeding and infection come together in this familiar vision of the interdependence of modernity; both represent the readjustments of the biotic community that precede and foretell the inevitability of consequent social and cultural changes.

The connection between communicable disease and race intermixture continued to appeal to him, as he sought to explain the inevitability of that readjustment and to predict its patterns. "The effects of infections and contagious diseases introduced by foreigners are the more devastating in the first years of intercourse," he noted in "The Nature of Race Relations," an essay written late in his career, when his interests had turned almost exclusively to race relations. "Eventually some sort of biotic equilibrium is achieved, but racial competition on the biotic or ecological level continues, although its consequences are not so obvious."[98] The rhythm of social and cultural communities followed that of their biotic bases: "invasion" found expression in violence. Social accommodation was slower than its biological counterpart. Park recognized that the emphasis on cultural distinctiveness, exemplified in the resurgent nationalisms of his day, arose with increasing insistence as the world became more cosmopolitan and interdependent. He was intrigued by the tremendous reluctance of groups to relinquish the features through which they defined their distinctiveness. It is no wonder, then, that outbreaks and carriers would yield such enormous imaginative power and elicit a complicated array of interconnected anxieties: social and cultural biases as intimately interwoven with the fear of (biological) contagion as social and cultural communities are with their biotic bases.

The lessons of bacteriology turned microbes and carriers into agents of disequilibrium and biotic, social, and cultural transformation. The science of society held out the implicit promise that understanding those changes would lead to their management. The theories and models of the urban sociologists offer insight into the fashioning of modern myths that would become the conceptual underpinning of the outbreak narrative. Communicable-disease outbreaks had to constitute a sufficiently ongoing threat to wield this imaginative power, and the introduction of antibiotics might well have tempered it. But if disease-inflected estrangement showed signs of lessening in the midcentury, the lessons of virology would re-animate it—literally—with a vengeance.

Viral Cultures

4 A magnified photograph of the human immunodeficiency virus (HIV) entering a helper T cell offered the readers of the 3 November 1986 issue of *Time* magazine a visual representation of what scientists and journalists were calling "the disease of the century."[1] Since such images have long been a staple of popular science writing, the photograph does not seem remarkable. The caption explains: "Viruses (blue dots) attack a helper T cell, a crucial part of the immune system. Invading the cell, the virus commandeers its machinery, making it begin producing viruses. This eventually destroys the cell, weakening the immune system."[2] The article is typical of the media coverage of the epidemic, which, especially in its first decade, tended to fall within the science beat.[3] In the 1980s the HIV/AIDS epidemic provided occasion for a range of science lessons for the general public.

The *Time* article is entitled "Viruses," and the subtitle explains that "AIDS research" has spurred "new interest in some ancient enemies." The title and caption interpret the photograph for readers, explaining that what they are witnessing is an invasion. The language is familiar: viruses as enemies and invaders insidiously commandeer the machinery of the cell to reproduce themselves and, in so doing, damage or destroy the host. The article develops the metaphor as the stealthy viral marauder "single-mindedly" eludes "scouts" and "evades . . . rapidly advancing defenders." The virus is a "diminutive foreigner" that, taking "over part of the cellular machinery," directs the cell "to produce more AIDS virus [*sic*]," an "alien product" that eventually overwhelms the entire system (67). This remarkably unremarkable language of the viral foe subtly turns a photograph of macrophages into a story of an invasion; it is the result of conventions that consolidated through a conjunction of science and politics in the 1950s. Inviting the reader to look through the scientist's microscope, the photograph confers the authority of science on the article and on the story of viral invasion.[4]

A microscopic gaze turned with new intensity on human beings in the decade following the Second World War. While viruses first became visible to scientists in the early 1930s, it was not until the 1950s that new technologies of visualization let researchers peer with new eyes into the mysterious workings of viruses, where they marveled at how viruses differed from any entity they had studied before.[5] Unlike their bacterial counterparts, viral microbes existed on—and seemed to define—the border between the living and the nonliving. Viruses showed how the circulation of "information" allowed an organism to function, promising the imminent cracking, as one piece in the *Science News Letter* put it, of the "code for the organization of life from a microscopic egg to a human being."[6] In so doing, they helped to change scientific understanding of the gene—and of life itself. The new insights they provided as well as the media campaign around the mid-century polio epidemics and the widespread trials of a polio vaccine made virology good copy and introduced a general readership to one of science's newest discoveries.

Accounts of viruses frequently shared the page with another topic of particular interest: the allegedly emerging global threat of communism and the politics of the Cold War.[7] The rise of two superpowers competing for world domination and the decolonization movements rippling across continents led to the breakdown of familiar social, economic, and political hierarchies. The inevitable uncertainty attendant on such rapid change fueled the infamous paranoia of Cold War politics. Circulating information animated collective as well as individual organisms, as governments classified "information" on which the integrity and security of the state depended, making its theft a capital crime. Conceptual changes in science and politics commingled, as the possibility of stealing or corrupting information was imagined in the labs of cutting-edge scientists and debated in the highest echelons of government. It was the subject of speculation in the mainstream media and of fascination in popular fiction and film. It generated whispered promises of the creation or preservation of life and terrifying images of "brainwashing" and nuclear devastation, depersonalization escalating into collective annihilation.

In this chapter I document a gradual change in the language through which the media depicted viral contagion and the changing Cold War world that suggests a conceptual exchange between virology and Cold War politics. As viruses became increasingly sinister and wily, sneaking into cells and assuming control of their mechanisms, external agents, such as Communists, became viral, threatening to corrupt the dissemination of information as they infiltrated the nerve center of the state. The exchange crystallized vague and often conflicting anxieties about the changes of the post-war world. The new affiliations that came with political realignments brought the need for new stories of group origins and the triumph of human values shaped in the crucible of possible devastation: the histories and mythologies that accompany profound social change. The insights of virology were central to those stories, as the vocabulary that permeated the newspapers and science journals of the period found extended expression in the plots of novels and films. Those works dramatized the new scientific concepts and, like the media, they acted as a kind of reservoir host—to borrow a metaphor from science—in which scientific and political theories recombined, informing the mythology of the new age.[8] The elusive "diminutive foreigner" that comes from without and assumes control of cellular mechanisms in the *Time* magazine piece is a legacy of the conceptual exchange.

The avant-garde William Burroughs was especially prescient about the conceptual centrality of virology to the fashioning of a midcentury mythology. He followed developments in virology with fascination, finding them useful in his efforts to depict the mechanisms of what he saw as the dangerous mindless conformity of the Cold War world. The "word virus" was a key feature in his witty and arcane novels, in which he offered his own creation story, "a mythology for the space age," to explain and revivify a world he found increasingly devoid of spirit and creativity.[9] Burroughs's critical insights and experimental writing, not surprisingly, earned him a cult following rather than a mass readership, but his analyses elucidate the broader appeal, and the virological features, of a story that would achieve paradigmatic status in Cold War America: Jack Finney's *The Body Snatchers.* Finney's bestselling 1955 novel generated numerous novelistic and cinematic spinoffs and quickly became a reference point in discussions of social and political behavior. His monstrous pod people infused as they embodied the science and politics of their moment, and the many retellings of their story attest to its continuing explanatory power.

Finney's story captured the imagination of a generation that had witnessed the transformation of the promise of atomic energy into a weapon more destructive than most could have imagined and that had heard accounts of the perversion of medical research in the service of torture in the Nazi death camps. Science for them was full of danger as well as promise, and no genre grappled with both in this period more than science-fiction horror. The big screen reveled in monstrous creations resulting from radiation or the encounter with dangerous aliens in the course of space travel and treated audiences to the thrilling horror of an apocalyptic loss of humanity emanating from a variety of sources. Finney's story brought monstrous aliens to medical science and the language of virology into a battle for the survival of the human race. His eerily memorable pod people worked like viruses, stealing the essential information from human beings and producing the mindless conformity that troubled Burroughs, who confessed, in the introduction to his novel *Queer,* that he lived "with the constant threat of possession, and a constant need to escape from possession, from Control."[10]

The Body Snatchers arguably produced a subgenre, epidemiological horror, that depicted the transformative power of disease and groups. With the pod people, Finney captured the horror of a protagonist's dawning awareness that the humanity of his or her closest associates is being drained from them and the terrifying estrangement—as Georg Simmel used the term—that results as they try to maintain their human connections. The terror of their estrangement marks the deferred recognition of commonalities, the uncanny familiarity, that heralds new social configurations.

The monster-alien invasion works of this period have sparked numerous allegorical readings, especially among film critics, who have seen in them anxious depictions of communism, McCarthyism, homosexuality, race, or gender.[11] Those issues represent the pressure points of changing social hierarchies and political realignments worldwide, and the novels and films invite those readings. Yet the underlying concerns of the moment come into sharper focus when the issues are considered together, even (perhaps especially) when they seem contradictory. It is not surprising to find contagion anxieties surfacing with the profound transformations of the moment, and Kirsten Ostherr brings public health into the mix when she argues that the mingling of anti-communism and homophobia with "the imagery and anxieties of world health" manifests their shared concerns with a distrust of appearances, a fear of border crossings, and a lack of faith in the possibilities of detection.[12] Andrew Ross links "the Cold War culture of germophobia" more broadly to "the demonology of the 'alien,' especially in the genre of science fiction film, where a pan-social fear of the other—communism, feminism, and other egalitarianisms foreign to the American social body—is reproduced through images drawn from the popular fringe of biological or genetic engineering gone wrong."[13] But the connection between that pan-social fear and the object of contagion that most intrigued scientific medicine—the virus—allows for more specificity. The microscopic entities that fascinated scientists (atoms and genes as well as viral microbes) threatened potential catastrophe, but they also offered dramatic insights into the nature of life itself. The novels and films reveal a deep concern with the possible loss of humanity conceived as the theft of mind and body, a horrifying metamorphosis that is at once apocalyptic and ecstatic. The power of the viral image came from its simultaneous invocation of disgust and fascination, the mundane and the mystical. It permeated the cultural imagination and imported its power when summoned, consciously or not, by writers and directors. Finney's story offered a winning formula with its viral inflection of the threat of dehumanization and its epidemiological response. Epidemiology, after all, was a science that had not lost its humanitarian promise. William Burroughs urged his readers to keep their eyes open; Finney's story and its offshoots conceded the difficulty, perhaps impossibility, and certainly the urgency of doing so. Yet, ultimately, even at its most hopelessly apocalyptic, it affirmed the worth of humanity and carried the promise of its survival.

The successive versions of *Invasion of the Body Snatchers* illustrate the evolution of the epidemiological horror story and its conventions, notably, in the pod people, the sinister, crafty incarnated virus that could be identified and fought in a mythic battle between Science and Nature, a battle that harnessed apocalyptic energy as an antidote to estrangement and malaise. Philip Kaufman's 1978 film uncannily foreshadowed the early years of the HIV/AIDS epidemic, and epidemiological horror served as a shadow tale, supplying the conventions of horror to the outbreak narrative, as its contours were coming into focus. The pod people forecast and would soon metamorphose into the malevolent, willful viral-human carriers who are featured in the story of disease emergence. Kaufman's 1978 film and its forerunners suggest the importance of the conventions of the epidemiological horror story, and its Cold War roots, to the conceptual landscape in which the epidemic surfaced.

EARLY VIRUSES: THE TWILIGHT ZONE

The earliest treatments of viruses in both the specialty and mainstream press expressed wonder at this unusual life form. Scientists were intrigued to discover viruses' lack of conformity to the traditional definitions of life.

Unable to metabolize or reproduce independently of a host cell, they were not living organisms in the usual sense of the word. Defining them was neither an easy nor an inconsiderable task, as one of the founders of the field, Sylvester E. Luria, attested in *General Virology,* the text he wrote for his virology classes.[14] The textbook helped to define virology as a field of study, which became progressively institutionalized during that decade. Publication of the first issue of the journal *Virology* in 1955 and a growing number of textbooks in the field were accompanied by a noticeable proliferation of journal articles on the topic in both the mainstream and specialty press. The massive and highly publicized trials of Jonas Salk's polio vaccine fueled public interest in this mysterious entity.[15]

Viruses fascinated Luria and his colleagues because they did not simply gain nutrients from host cells, but actually harnessed the cell's apparatus to duplicate themselves. They appeared, explained Luria in *General Virology,* "to depend on the host cells not for a supply of nutritionally required compounds or growth factors, but for the use of the integrated enzymatic machinery of the cell, which provides energy and synthetic machinery for the virus. Indeed, viruses in the free state appear to be completely inert metabolically" (4). These differed from parasites that depended on their hosts for sustenance. They appeared to take their life itself from host cells. In words that were characteristic of the scientific descriptions of viruses in the 1950s and crucial to their conceptual applications in social and political realms, Luria predicted that "we shall see that the relation of true viruses to their host cell is so *intimate* and *integrative* that the hope for cell-free reproduction is about on the same level as the hope for artificially constructed, self-reproducing cells" (4, emphasis added).

By the second edition of *General Virology,* which Luria coedited with James E. Darnell Jr., a biochemist, the question of viral animation mandated a vocabulary lesson. "As usual in cases of this kind," they write, "the difficulties were semantic rather than substantive. Words such as 'organisms' and 'living' have unambiguous meanings only when applied to the objects for which they were originally coined: a frog is an organism, a dog that runs and barks is living. But what is it that makes a frog an organism?"[16] Viruses raised questions that penetrated to the most basic taxonomies and classifications that structured scientific inquiry as well as human experience. Virologists dreamed of synthesizing living viruses compared with which, noted one science writer, "the fission of uranium, the fusion of hydrogen into helium will seem like achievements of secondary importance."[17] For scientists of the early 1950s, viruses represented the possibility of revising the most basic assumptions of human existence.

Their excitement was echoed in the mainstream press. Accounts ranged from abstract science—such as the *New York Times* science writer Waldemar Kaempffert's 1951 description of how "the entry of the virus into a host cell throws a switch which diverts the protein-forming machinery of the cell from the manufacture of normal protein to the synthesis of virus protein"—to more accessible celebrations of medical advances.[18] But in the early years of the decade, pure science and the wonder it generated dominated the mainstream coverage as well as the scientific publications. In September 1952, for example, the *Times* reporter William L. Laurence hailed virological research as "studies on the very frontier of life" which, he proclaimed, "have provided new leads to one of nature's greatest mysteries, the chemical processes employed by living cells and by viruses to duplicate themselves."[19] In what was already a refrain, Laurence paraphrases the formulation of the Nobel Laureate Wendell M. Stanley that viruses are "entities neither living nor dead that belonged to the twilight zone between the living and the nonliving." His language becomes almost biblical as he describes viruses' "ability to create themselves in their own image, in that respect partaking of one of the fundamental attributes of living things."[20]

Through viruses, scientists were peering into the most forbidden knowledge, "the fundamental processes in which living matter in general duplicates itself . . . the very process that makes possible the perpetuation of life through the ages and the transmission of hereditary traits through the infinite variety of living things."[21] A headline on the cusp of the new year reiterated that the news was in these scientific insights rather than their medical applications: "Science Explores Frontier of Life," announced the *New York Times*, as it reported the prominent researcher Barry Commoner's belief that the virus would bring science closer " 'to an effective understanding on [*sic*] this basic sign of life.' "[22]

It is not surprising, then, that religious awe suffuses the language. The study of viruses, as the immunologist and Nobel Laureate Frank Macfarlane Burnet argued in a 1951 *Scientific American* piece, called for more than the traditional approach to disease, which, "as in every important human problem," placed a "more immediate value" on finding "some effective answer than" on having "a clear understanding of the nature of the problem." By contrast, "fundamental research" on viruses rewarded scientists both by opening up "unexpected new approaches" and by "satisf[ying] that almost mystic desire to do something towards seeing the universe 'all of one piece.' "[23] Scientists marveled at the entity that offered insight into questions they hardly dared to ask.

Burnet was especially intrigued by the ecological balance that viruses displayed. In a section of the article labeled "Immunity," he acknowledged his own and the field's tendency to view the virus as an "invader" and the host in a passive role. "Fortunately," he observes, "life is not like that," and he goes on, like Robert Park, to represent this "invasion" as only the first stage in a process of mutual accommodation ending in a new equilibrium: "Whenever a parasite and its host species have lived together for many generations, they will have found a *modus vivendi* whereby the parasite species survives without producing more than minor damage to the host species" (49). Explaining that analogously a virus that wiped out its host species would be eradicating its own means of reproducing and that any dramatic epidemic turns out to be "the result of some new development," he reverses the source of disruption. Rather than viruses, it is the European armies decimated by yellow fever in the West Indies that are "intruders into a virtually stabilized biological equilibrium." This ecological perspective offered insight not only into the processes of life but also into "the practical control of a viral disease," which involved "understanding . . . the means by which the balance between the virus and the host is maintained in nature and how it can be modified in either direction by biological accident or human design" (49).

The focus on "fundamental science" did not preclude the commingling of science and politics. Burnet's example illustrates how contemporary concerns infused scientific inquiry. In the context of the global politics of decolonization in the 1950s, the example of decimated European armies, drawn from the history of conquest and colonization, evokes the spaces of the colonized tropics as intrinsically diseased. That image inhered in the assumptions of tropical medicine, which had its roots in the project of colonization.[24] The equation was increasingly reinforced throughout the 1950s as health became a measure of "civilization" and scientific achievement: one more term in the competition over cultural superiority between the superpowers and a justification for intervention in the "Third World"— a Cold War creation—by both of them.[25] That intervention was at once humanitarian and practical. Disease and violence threatened to spill over insufficiently maintained boundaries.

GERM WARFARE: VIRAL INVADERS

Concern with germ warfare that surfaced in the wake of the Second World War fostered the connection between medicine and politics. It had come in with the decade: on New Year's Day in 1950, the *New York Times* announced that during the previous week "for the first time, one nation accused another of having used BW [bacterial warfare] in World War II."[26] The paper reported on a war-crimes trial in the Soviet Union of twelve Japanese officers accused of operating a unit in Manchuria dedicated to the development of biological weapons. Manchuria was an important symbol of the uncertainty of global politics in the early years of the Cold War. The conclusion of the war ended Japanese colonization in this northeast Chinese region on the Soviet border and turned Manchuria into a battleground between Chinese nationalists and Communists. As the Soviet Union vacillated, unwilling to commit fully to the Communist revolution on its border, Soviet prosecution of the Japanese colonizers displayed their condemnation of a common enemy.[27] The Soviet accusation introduced the threat of biological warfare and aligned it with global instability, resulting from imperialist aggression.

The next few months brought reports of initiatives to enlist the UN in exploring the possibility of international control over biological and chemical warfare, as subsequent accusations quickly shifted to reflect emerging Cold War animosities. By this time, the media had already begun to report Soviet allegations of U.S. experimentation in these areas. In late April the Department of Defense in turn announced its intention to expand its research on germ warfare. This initiative brought military funding for research in both bacteriology and virology, which accelerated developments in the basic science.[28] It contributed as well to public perceptions of the threat of communicable disease and helped to shape the conceptual exchange between contagion and Cold War politics.

Public discussions of germ warfare on all sides intensified during the first year of the new decade. In September the Fourth Congress of Czechoslovak Microbiologists concluded by calling for scientists worldwide to refrain from research on germ warfare. They were joined by scientists from the Soviet Union, China, Poland, Romania, Bulgaria, Hungary, and East Germany.[29] Within a month, Brock Chisholm, director general of the WHO, told Britain's most prominent nuclear scientists that "'biological science had perfected new diseases that were much more powerful weapons of death than the atomic bomb'" and that germ warfare "'could eliminate more than 50 per cent of human life in a continental population against which they were directed.'"[30] Such weapons, he explained, rendered "'the atomic bomb . . . obsolete.'" Although atomic warfare nonetheless remained the more pressing and debated threat, the two threats increasingly intertwined.

A handbook issued by the Civil Defense Administration included information on germ warfare for the first time in December 1950. As *New York Times* readers learned, the manual warned that the "agents" of contagion "could be used by saboteurs as well as by enemy attackers," and it stressed the importance of "prompt and complete reporting of disease to the public health authorities."[31] Further advancing this fusion of military and public-health concerns was the idea that knowing "the nature and the source of the attack" made it amenable to the "principles of epidemiology" (1). Those principles could be employed equally for germ and nuclear warfare, and the manual included instructions for the preparation of population maps and overlays with regular concentric circles to be used for diagnostic purposes in the event of an attack of either kind. The accusations mounted as the Cold War progressed.

In April 1951 *Red Fleet,* the newspaper of the Soviet Navy, accused General Douglas MacArthur of testing biological weapons on Canadian Eskimos, which caused an epidemic of plague in the summer of 1949. The report alleged that in 1946 MacArthur had sent eighteen Japanese scientists to labs and institutes in the United States to conduct germ-warfare research, and that he had established experimental stations throughout Japan that were staffed by Japanese war criminals and heavily guarded by the U.S. military.[32]

The *New York Times* reported the story as Soviet propaganda, but similar accusations about Soviet development of weaponized germs were leveled as well, justifying the U.S. military's refusal to ban germ-warfare research. Spokespeople like Brigadier General William M. Creasy, purportedly the army's "top man in biological warfare research," argued for the necessity of such research for the survival of the nation and its citizens. A *New York Times* piece from October 1951, entitled "Enemy Disease Smog Held a Possibility," included Creasy's assessment "that it would be possible for an enemy to envelop a whole city in a dense smog of disease germs loosed from special bombs or shells."[33] Reassurance tempered the alarm when he called biological warfare "'essentially public health in reverse'" and noted that "'except for novel methods of achieving deliberate dissemination of pathogenic organisms, it is a form of warfare which nature has waged against man for thousands of years and against which modern health practices have produced effective defenses.'" If biological warfare represented a harnessing of nature's weapons, it was also subject to the solutions that had been developed against those weapons. The strange formulation of biological warfare as inverted public health allowed Creasy to configure public health as an aspect of military defense. From there, it was an easy rhetorical step to argue for germ-warfare research as a feature of public-health work.

Even without such explicit links, the connection between disease and warfare was enhanced by their proximity in the media. In one fortuitous juxtaposition, a story about a researcher's effort to use atom-splitting techniques to understand the mechanisms of bacteria and viruses adjoins a photograph of a mushroom cloud with three military personnel in the foreground. The photograph illustrates an account of the role of marines in atomic-warfare testing.[34] More than proximity connects these accounts. The U.S. Atomic Energy Commission funded both the research conducted on the viruses—described conventionally as "halfway between living and nonliving materials"—and the research conducted on the "troopers" in the photograph. The caption explains that it is a photograph of "troopers moving on an 'objective' seconds after explosion during tactical exercises at the Nevada proving grounds northeast of Las Vegas yesterday."[35] The perspective of more than half a century discloses the gruesome appositeness of the juxtaposition, especially when the virology researchers subject the virus to a lethal dose of radiation and "determine that the deadliness of the radiation was independent of the exact spot on the virus that was hit by an accelerated particle from the cyclotron" (10). It would not be long before an analogous discovery about the deadliness of radiation would emerge regarding the "troopers" who, "crouched in foxholes three to four miles from 'ground zero,' the point directly under the explosion, probably were closer to a nuclear blast than any large group in history, with the exception of the Japanese who experienced the World War II atomic attacks" (1).

In the context of this apparently chance apposition and the common funding agency, claims about the insight viruses afford into the definition of life impart an uncanniness that underscores at once their animation and the troops' dehumanization. Adjoining these accounts, the photograph becomes a visual analog for the connections between them: the common funding agency speaks to the promise that science—specifically, atomic energy—will improve all aspects of society, from medical and military to economic and environmental. This juxtaposition illustrates the multiple levels on which virology and Cold War politics inflected one another in the media.

The associations between germs and politics helped to reconfigure the changing spaces of the postwar world. When, for example, Chisholm told the British scientists that germ weapons "could eliminate more than 50 per cent of human life in a continental population against which they were

"Troopers moving on an 'objective' seconds after explosion during tactical exercises at the Nevada proving grounds northeast of Las Vegas yesterday." *New York Times*, 2 May 1952, 10. © 1952 The New York Times Co. Reprinted with permission.

directed," he articulated a geography of disease. The idea of a *continental population* implicitly sets disease in opposition to the geographic entity of a nation. The geopolitics of germs finds literal expression in an October 1953 account of a UN immunization map, the brainchild of Marjorie Farrell, head nurse of the UN's clinic, who had previously worked for the army. Farrell used the WHO's epidemiological updates to chart "the communicable-disease situation in 228 countries, territories and other regions all over the globe" in order to facilitate immunization for travelers engaged in UN business.[36] Colored pins mark outbreaks of different communicable diseases, envisioning global interconnections and the health threat represented by regions in which communicable disease thrived, notably the "developing" world. According to the medical director of the Health Service, Dr. Frank Calderone, the "'chart demonstrates that there are no barriers, no frontiers in disease. . . . Looking at it, you can see for yourself that the world as a whole is really one world. It's a small world when it comes to disease, and this has become particularly true since the advent of rapid air transport, which makes it difficult to keep a disease isolated in one area'" (3). With its multicolored pins, the map implicitly justified—insisted on—the intervention of the United States in the newly decolonized nations. Contagion materialized globalization, demonstrating the persistence of interconnections that defied, as they belied, national frontiers. Humanitarianism as well as the threat represented by the global networks of the Cold War mandated such intervention.

Viral invasion and the history of colonization suffused even the most innocuous metaphors in discussions of virology. "That Old Virus," which appeared in the *Ladies' Home Journal* in April 1953, intended to correct housewives' misconceptions, not turn them into research scientists, and the writer's metaphors illustrate the terms through which the concepts were becoming accessible. The writer begins by distinguishing between bacteria and viruses, explaining that viruses "are much smaller than bacteria and exist in a state somewhere between living and nonliving matter. Unlike germs, viruses cannot grow out of a living plant or animal. They penetrate the cells of living things and take over all functions. Somehow they force the cells to turn out virus parts in a matter of minutes. New viruses are formed to prey on other cells. Literally, the cells are eaten up."[37] The writer's anthropomorphized viruses are penetrating, forceful, and predatory.

They also distinguish between populations. While making the point that cold weather does not cause illness, the writer invokes "Eskimos" who "rarely get colds until white men arrive in the spring and bring their civilized viruses with them" (92). He probably did not have the 1951 *Red Fleet* accusation of MacArthur's alleged testing of biological warfare on Canadian Eskimos in mind when he sketched this scenario. Yet the concept underscores the biological distinction (marked by the viruses) between the "Eskimos" and the "white men" with whom the "civilized" viruses are associated. The awkward *civilized* instead of *endemic* rhetorically replays the deadly scenario of colonization in which the deliberate or unwitting spread of microbial infections to immunologically naïve populations facilitated colonization. By the end of the piece, viruses are a consequence of civilization. There is no "way to avoid viruses altogether," the author explains, unless the reader wants "to go climb Mount Everest and get away from people. Viruses are one of the prices we pay for having neighbors, for being social creatures —for civilization" (95). Yet, those viruses affect populations differently, marking their different levels of medical (and cultural) sophistication. The "civilized viruses" that are a part of daily life are also natural predators with a history of having been harnessed in the all too violent project of "civilization." While "that old virus" gave the unsuspecting Eskimos nothing worse than the sniffles, germ warfare summoned the darker history as it turned the natural predators into potential weapons of mass destruction.

INFILTRATION AND SUBVERSION: VIRAL COMMUNISM

The progression of the decade saw the gradual intensification of military metaphors in discussions of viral reproduction. The change was subtle. The threat of germ warfare was augmented by outbreaks of polio worldwide, which made the "invasive" features of viruses more pressing public concerns than the insights they afforded into human life. Media coverage during the decade witnessed the metamorphosis of the mysterious sojourner in the "no man's land" of partial animation into the devious, infiltrating foreigner and alien invader—with underlying hints of (racialized) violence and anarchy—that posed an ever-present threat to individuals and to the survival of the species. The transformation represented an apparently irresistible attribution of intentionality bordering on human agency that was magnified by both medical and political threats.

The rhetorical difference between a virus's "intrusion" into the host cell and a "life and death struggle . . . waged somewhere within our bodies, between a virus and its antibodies" may register nothing more than authorial variation.[38] But the cumulative evidence shows an amplification in the metaphors of aggression from the mid-1950s on. As early as 1953, William Laurence, whose earlier articles about viruses had reveled in the language of wonder, offered detailed accounts "of viruses attacking and devouring" or "destroying" host cells. Among these viruses "are many of mankind's most serious enemies," and "each virus particle penetrates into one of the tissue cells" to "give[] birth to . . . new particles" that "invade" the neighboring cells" which they "kill."[39]

Laurence's article is about a "new technique that makes it possible for the first time to observe accurately the interrelations between animal cells and animal viruses." The announcement of the discovery in *Science News Letter* the same year had similarly noted that the "battle between body cells and invading disease virus can, it is hoped, be watched and recorded in moving pictures by a new method."[40] The correlation in both pieces between the visual accuracy enabled by the new technique and the violence that Laurence describes suggests that the perception of violence is a function of visual accuracy; now that scientists can see more clearly, they can see how combative the invading virus really is. Yet most of the accounts of viral reproduction in the early 1950s were also of the important discoveries enabled by new visualizing techniques. Increasing representations of viral invasion were more the product of changing attitudes than of the new visual technologies. They coincided with the growing concerns about espionage and brainwashing that characterized the Cold War, and they registered the merging of these two powerful cultural preoccupations.[41]

The acclaimed science writer Paul de Kruif exemplified the trend in virus reporting with a short article he penned for *Today's Health*. Entitling it "Virus Hunters," he intended the 1953 article to be a companion piece to his successful 1926 book *The Microbe Hunters*. De Kruif had vilified bacteria in the earlier work, calling them "small assassins" and "tiny messengers that bring a dozen murderous diseases to mankind," and, following the conventional racist epithet "Asian cholera," dubbing cholera bacilli in particular "puny but terrible little murderers from the Orient."[42] But viruses were "more sinister enemies."[43] Profiling the virus hunters, he describes their foe as "midget microbes" that "sneak" through filters and into victims and even vaccines (referring here to an incident in 1942 when a yellow fever vaccine was tainted with jaundice); they are "crafty" with a tendency to "turn vicious," destroying "plants, animals, men, even other microbes with equal gusto" (32). He intends to show how "[virus] hunters are busy teaching these stupid midgets to kill their own murderous brothers. They tame the killer instinct out of the most vicious viruses. Then they put these reformed assassins into animals and men" (32). But the viruses take over the show, emerging as anything but "stupid," and the drama becomes the fight to identify and vanquish crafty, sneaky foreigners bent on their own reproduction, which involves infiltrating and converting their hosts. In a subsequent issue of the same journal, an article entitled "Virus Facts" similarly describes an entity that is "smaller than bacteria, deadly and elusive as a thief in the night," noting that while researchers "cannot yet agree whether a virus is animate or inanimate[, t]hey do know it is the greatest troublemaker in the medical field today."[44] As descriptions of viruses began to sound more and more like they were penned by Cold Warriors, disease-inflected political threats conformed to the specific mechanisms of viral infection.

Germs were used to depict the Communist threat prior to the virological change in emphasis, but with very different effect, as is evident in a 1931 report to the House of Representatives. Entitled "Investigation of Communist Propaganda," Report 2290 documented Communist Party activities in the United States, ending with a recommendation for minimizing any threat to the nation: "Hungry men are dangerous; but to the man with a home, a family, and a job, communism makes no appeal whatever. Communistic ideals are germs in the body politic, hostile, but harmless so long as that body maintains a healthful condition and reacts normally to human needs. They are dangerous only when the resistance of the body becomes weakened through social or selfish errors. Even then their manifestations are symptoms of something wrong rather than a disease in themselves. Sound therapy indicates an eradication of the disease rather than the symptoms."[45] Here the germs of communism constitute a threat to the national body conceived as an individual. With a strong immune system—a well-managed society—the germs cannot take hold, and the body will remain healthy. According to the report, the "solution of this problem lies in the wisdom of our legislators and in the unselfishness of our industrialists. In proportion as we work out economic justice here in America and so order our social system that labor shall share in the economic life of the Nation as fully and as fairly as it now shares in its social and political life, in just that proportion will radicalism fall of its own inanition and the threat of communism cease to disturb us" (99).

The germ metaphor represents disease from a systemic perspective: just as a strong immune system (a strong constitution) is the best protection against disease, so will economic justice—in particular an attention to labor issues—ensure the health of the nation. Report 2290 led to the creation, in 1938, of the Un-American Activities Committee, also known as the Dies Committee after its chairman, Representative Martin Dies of Texas. Charged with investigating un-American activities, it yielded a standing committee, the notorious House Un-American Activities Committee (HUAC), in 1945. By the mid-fifties, with the Cold War and HUAC in full swing, the conceptions of both social and medical threats had shifted in conformity with Cold War politics and virology.

Immunology and virology, both with roots in the early bacteriology research, evolved as separate disciplines in the postwar period. The fields competed not only for resources but also for conceptual ascendance, as critics who have studied Cold War science and politics have noted. Three such critics, Emily Martin, Cindy Patton, and Darryl Ogden, have in fact argued for the representational power of immunology over virology.[46] While the behavior of microscopic entities concerned virologists, immunology emphasized more "holistic models of health," as Patton puts it: the "idea of a delicately balanced internal ecology" that, in the 1960s, "nicely mirrored the growing perception of the human being precariously perched in a world ecology."[47] Locating the "theoretical breakthrough" of immunology in the 1949 publication of Frank Fenner's and Frank McFarlane Burnet's *The Production of Antibodies*, Ogden finds their rhetoric redolent with "the terms of anti-communist, anti-homosexual political discourses of the post-World War II era . . . a nearly perfect metaphor of how the American body politic, particularly in the McCarthy era, operated as a kind of large-scale human immune system, placing under surveillance and effectively eliminating citizens suspected of foreign sympathies that might weaken internal American resolve to fend off the debilitating disease of communism."[48]

Building on the work of Patton and Martin, Ogden argues for a distinction between virology and immunology that turns on the difference between *hot* and *cold* war.[49] Where "virologists postulated the existence of powerful viruses, dangerous enemies beyond the body's borders, capable of violating those borders under favorable circumstances. . . . immunologists warned healthy and sick Americans alike of formidable enemies within the body that appeared—like Communist sympathizers and homosexuals—to constitute the Self, but were, in fact, the Other. Understood in political terms, virology capitalized on fears of a hot war with America's Communist adversaries whereas immunology was predicated on fear of disloyalty and subversion within the body (politic) itself."[50] The distinction, which underpins all three critics' readings of the HIV/AIDS epidemic, obscures the discovery that most intrigued virologists: the virus's ability to appropriate the mechanisms of the cell for its own reproduction. Ogden's description ignores the scientific and public fascination with the behavior of the virus once it enters the host cell. Politics borrowed from and influenced both fields, but in the early years of the Cold War, the threat was predominantly *foreign*, with agents penetrating from without and converting *susceptible* insiders to their cause. Those agents readily became viral invaders for which prevention was already too late and which therefore required a targeted—and violent—rather than holistic and anticipatory approach. The outbreak narrative registers the legacy of the virological formulation in both medical science and politics.

Contagion, which, when specified, was typically viral, intertwined with the other two types of metaphor that dominated descriptions of the Communist threat: malignancy and mental enslavement, the sinister analog of social control. There was considerable discussion in the period of the viral roots of cancer, and descriptions of viral reproduction shared a conceptual vocabulary with mind control, with the virus's subordinating the cell's mechanisms to its own ends. Moreover, many viruses literally involved the brain and precipitated the loss of mental functions. The self- and non-self distinction that Martin, Patton, and Ogden associate with immunology was equally a feature of virology: the virus "tricked" the cell into "thinking" that it was reproducing itself. There was even speculation that the virus functioned as, or perhaps became part of, the host's DNA. It was therefore easy to imagine the infiltration of Communists and their "conversion" of "normal American citizens" as viral. In turn, those viral agents amplified the sinister agency of viral infection in the popular imagination. Germ warfare contributed to the ascendancy of virology both because it translated into military funding initiatives and because it consolidated the equation between microbes and willful saboteurs.

Following the formation of HUAC, the rhetoric of the threat of secret Communist infiltration became increasingly loud and forceful. Initially, the extreme language was most evident and developed on the reactionary fringes of society. Writing in *American Legion* magazine in 1948, for instance, James F. O'Neil cautioned that "Communists, no matter what their pretenses, are foreign agents in any country in which they are allowed to operate."[51] But the real threat was in their surreptitiousness; their "first step is to disguise, deodorize, and attractively package Moscow's revolutionary products. Next the salesmen and peddlers themselves must be skillfully disguised, deodorized, and glamorized" (16). Borrowing his images from one of the most archetypal discourses of postwar U.S. culture, the sales pitch, O'Neil underscored the danger of the Communist masquerade. Characteristic (and deliberate) carriers, Communists "always appear before the public as 'progressives.' Yesterday they were 'twentieth century Americans,' last week they were 'defenders of all civil liberties,' tonight they may be 'honest, simple trades unionists.' They are 'liberals,' at breakfast, 'defenders of world peace' in the afternoon, and 'the voice of the people' in the evening. These artful dodges and ingenious dissimulations obviously make it difficult for the average trusting citizen to keep up with every new Communist swindle and card game" (16–17). Departing from the logic of Report 2290, which depicted communism as symptomatic of the disease of poor social management, O'Neil insisted "that Communists operating in our midst are in effect a secret battalion of spies and saboteurs parachuted by a foreign foe inside our lives at night and operating as American citizens under a variety of disguises just as the Nazis did in Holland and Belgium" (43).

He assured his readership that there were experts who were trained to see what others could not, who could penetrate the Communist disguise: "Most cities today contain a nucleus of former F.B.I. men, Army or Navy intelligence officers, former Communist Party members who have come over to our side, and other trained or experienced men, many of them Legionnaires" (17). Constituting a kind of anti-Communist cell, this network of experts should be sought out by the would-be resister of communism for purposes of education and information. The danger of trusting "newspapers and other publicity media" was that "many . . . have secret Communists on their staffs who regularly slip in a neat hypodermic needle full of Moscow virus" (42).

Similar language was surfacing more subtly within government organizations. More than a year before the appearance of O'Neil's piece, J. Edgar Hoover had offered testimony before HUAC that similarly emphasized the national threat of Communist infiltration. Labeling "the greatest menace of communism" the sympathizers "who infiltrate and corrupt various spheres of American life," he insisted that the power of the Communist Party is less accurately gauged by its size than by "its influence, its ability to infiltrate."[52] And the consistent focus of all such accounts was the Communists' allegedly concerted effort to "penetrate" systems that involved communication and the dissemination of information—such as education, news media, and the culture industry—and the organizations of the most potentially resentful (hence susceptible) population, the laborers, on whom the daily functioning of the nation relied.

Hoover feared the conditions of tolerance in education and the ministry that would allow Communists to get footholds in those areas, and he feared for the nation "so long as American labor groups are infiltrated, dominated, or saturated with the virus of communism" (43), but he was confident that the identification of Communists (such as Joseph McCarthy would soon seek to perform from the Senate) would save the nation, since "the public will take the first step of quarantining them so they can do no harm" (44). For communism was "a condition akin to disease that spreads like an epidemic and like an epidemic a quarantine is necessary to keep it from infecting the Nation" (120). Increasingly, the message would inundate public media, as sensational trials like those of Alger Hiss and the Rosenbergs and televised hearings of HUAC's most famous investigations became the occasion for massive public commentary as well as the stuff of popular culture; as Communist-Party-members-turned-informants, like Whittaker Chambers and Louis Budenz, wrote editorials, extended magazine pieces, and even books with an alleged insider's authority that made a fair trial in the press or the courts an exceedingly rare phenomenon; and as McCarthy seized the public eye and, however reviled he may have been (even publicly, in the mainstream press), left a legacy of virulent anti-communism as a public litmus test not only for the nation's politicians but for educators and artists, business and labor, the nation's insiders and those most on the margins. Both O'Neil and Hoover use "virus" in its broadest sense of infection, as did National Security Council document 51 (NSC51), which saw in "'revolutionary colonial areas . . . an ideal culture for the breeding of the Communist virus.'"[53] The use of the term prepared for its more specific elaboration. As the anti-Communist hysteria and the understanding of viral mechanisms permeated the mainstream media, the comparison became more detailed and specific, a material analog that exacerbated the well-documented paranoia of the Cold War.

That paranoia cannot be exaggerated. From the press to the movie theater, the classroom to the television screen, Americans, like their Soviet counterparts, were inundated with stories and images of a cunning enemy waiting to infiltrate the deepest recesses of their being. The threat was animated by cinematic depictions of a disturbing loss of humanity. Typical of the many films produced by the Department of Defense (DOD) to alert Americans to the imminent threat to their freedoms, *Red Nightmare* was made and issued by the DOD's Directorate for Armed Forces Information Education and produced by Warner Brothers in 1962. The film opens onto a conventional small American town, rendered uncanny by the presence of armed soldiers, barbed wire and sandbags, and more so when a man in a business suit begins to speak Russian; his companion, in military attire, cautions his "Comrade" to "speak English," advising him to "remember, that is about the only freedom you do not have in this town, this American town."[54]

> "Americans," replies the man in the suit, "they have too many freedoms."
> "That is another thing you must remember, Comrade," replies the soldier. "For one day it will be your mission to destroy those bourgeois, capitalist freedoms."

The host of the film, Jack Webb, best known to the audience as the trustworthy Joe Friday from the popular television show *Dragnet*, steps forward to explain that such towns surely exist "shrouded in secrecy" behind the Iron Curtain. There, he explains, Russians are being trained to learn the habits and fashions of Americans as they prepare to emulate in order to infiltrate the safe and unsuspecting world of small-town USA. The town is a "college town, Communist-style," where students learn "in this strangest of all schools, espionage as a science; propaganda as an art, and sabotage as a business."

The film enacts the "red nightmare" of Jerry Donovan, an all-American dad whose biggest fault is a tendency to skip his meetings (Union, PTA, Reserves) and whose most serious problem is that his oldest daughter wants to marry her eligible but slightly too young all-American boyfriend. The "nightmare" envisioned by the film registers the overwhelming anxiety surrounding infiltration and mind control. Jerry awakens into a profoundly unsettling world in which his family and community have become strangers overnight. The film marks their conversion with the affect of automatism: a vacancy in the eyes and chill in the voices that signals Communist indoctrination and mental enslavement. Jerry's confusion turns to rage when he is pulled into a rally in the town square where an officer who looks and sounds American congratulates the *American* crowd on having moved onto the second phase of their indoctrination. "You will assume control," he tells them. "You will move into every phase of American political and economic life. It will be your responsibility, Comrades, to purge the minds of the reactionary Americans so that they will welcome the enlightened Soviet system and conform without resistance to the dictatorship of the proletariat."

The collapse of Jerry's life turns on the corruption of two institutions, the family and the legal system. His children reject the false values of the bourgeois family, supported by his wife, who admonishes him to adhere to the party line. When he refuses, he ends up in a parody of a court of law, with his wife as one of his three accusers, and is sentenced to death because "as an ugly remnant of a diseased bourgeois class," he "must be eradicated before the contagion can spread." The real contagion, of course, is the converted agents who are being sent off to infect their countrymen. Like a virus, the threat comes from outside and is reproduced by local agents who become alien in the process. "Appearances can be deceptive," intones Jack Webb. Anyone can become a carrier.

The threat of an imperceptible invasion that turns familiars to aliens was the explicit message of all such films, a function of a new kind of warfare. In another DOD film—on the code of conduct for members of the armed forces of the United States—Webb explains that prisoners in camps during the Korean War experienced "something entirely foreign to anything in our experience. For the first time, the enemy tried to subverse, tried to make Communists out of good Americans, tried to make traitors out of American fighting men."[55] The film establishes the hypocrisy of this brainwashing in a scene that features a Korean officer's encouraging U.S. prisoners of war to sign a peace petition. In the background, the shadow of an armed Korean soldier falls across a banner with a dove and the word "PEACE." The image encourages the audience to be alert to the cues that betray the presence of Communist hypocrisy and to be attentive to the enemy's efforts to "convert" (Webb's word) U.S. citizens.

Brainwashing was a new term in the early 1950s, coined by Edward Hunter, a ferociously anti-Communist journalist who worked for the Office of Strategic Services (OSS) and Central Intelligence Agency (CIA). A literal translation of the Chinese *hsi nao*, the term circulated in sensationalistic media reports of a new form of torture, Chinese mind manipulation, among American prisoners of war in Korean camps as well as citizens of China and other Communist regimes. These accounts generated widespread interest among psychiatrists and social psychologists seeking a better understanding of both the human mind and group dynamics. The Columbia University psychiatrist Joost Meerloo, who had served in the Dutch army during the Second World War, drew on his own experience with the Nazis in his influential study, *The Rape of the Mind* (1956), to connect systematic mind control—what, following the UN coinage of *genocide,* he called *menticide*— to totalitarianism in all forms. Meerloo stressed the potential for any society to create a population susceptible to mass mind control and manipulation through communication networks, noting ominously that "he who dictates and formulates the words and phrases we use, he who is master of the press and radio, is master of the mind. . . . Ready-made opinions can be distributed day by day through press, radio, and so on, again and again, till they reach the nerve cell and implant a fixed pattern of thought in the brain."[56]

Meerloo's neurosocial explanation rhetorically resembles Joseph McCarthy's paranoid warnings of Communist infiltration of U.S. society. But the Dutch psychiatrist continually reiterated that such conditioning occurred in all groups and was a function of the act of communication itself. Menticide represented its deliberate application taken to an extreme, but he believed that contemporary trends in even the most democratic societies were producing populations with increased susceptibility to totalitarian practices of mass mental manipulation. Mass communication, aggressive advertising, and public-relations work, and even the "examination mania" (266) that characterized contemporary education in the United States could "take possession" (47) of people, turning them into "opinionated robots" (99). The roots of menticide were located in the quotidian and inevitable processes of "mental contagion," as Meerloo puts it, and overly aggressive social control.

Images of brainwashing in popular media emphasized two threats, both represented in Jerry Donovan's "red nightmare": the idea that the government could be taken over, with the collapse of the justice system as focal, and the image of loved ones turned not only into strangers but into automatons. Cinematic depictions of human robots conveyed the particular horror of the theft of personality that left a loved one without emotion and therefore not fully human.

While communism was not the only threat thus depicted, anti-Communists certainly capitalized on the threat to the government represented by personality theft and subterfuge. The key witness in the Alger Hiss case, Whittaker Chambers, turned his testimony into a tale of intrigue and espionage in the early 1950s, introducing the public to the idea of "a 'sleeper apparatus'" the "first function [of which] is to exist without detection, as any kind of action may expose it. It waits for the future. It is a reserve unit which will be brought into play only when those in control see fit—when events dictate."[57] Spinning an epic tale, Chambers recounts how "between the years 1930 and 1950, some twenty almost-unknown men and women who were Communists and close fellow travelers—working in the United States Government or in some singular unofficial relationship to it, or working in the press—helped to shape the future of every American now alive and indirectly affected the fate of every man now in uniform. . . . [T]heir activities . . . have decisively changed the history of the world" (22). A shared vocabulary—the tendency to speak of Communist "cells" and "nuclei," for example, and the prevalence of the verbs *to infiltrate* and *to colonize* in both virology and Cold War ideology—surely promoted the viral metaphor, but the association between viruses and mind control also turned on the disturbing image of the theft from within.

Viruses graphically conveyed the disgust associated with this theft, as in Herbert Hoover's extended metaphor in a 1954 speech on "The Protection of Freedom," in which he decried the spread of "the Socialist virus and poison gas generated by Karl Marx and Friedrich Engels . . . into every nation on the earth" and the "bloody virus" of communism that was "rotting the souls of two-fifths of all mankind which it has enslaved."[58] The "rank and file of our people are immune from this infection," he hopefully asserted, since the "recruiting grounds for their agents are from our minority of fuzzy-minded intellectuals and labor leaders" (681). Despite that immunity, Hoover advocated an aggressive medical approach, professing "little fear that these Communist agents can destroy the Republic if we continue to ferret them out" (681). But the nation should be most attentive to "the other varieties of the Karl Marx virus" (681), namely, the threat from within, represented by federal agents who "penetrate every part of local government" (680). The danger, for Hoover, came from the infiltration of a centralized authority that sent its message to its agents and, through them, reproduced itself in an ever-expanding sphere of influence.

As communism became increasingly viral, viruses became ever more subversive and invasive. In the spring of 1953, a *Science Digest* report on studies of viral latency noted that " 'increasing evidence indicates the frequency with which viruses can invade hosts from the dawn of post-embryonal and even embryonal life.' "[59] Entitled "Deadly Germs that Play Possum," the piece informed readers that these "masked" (a word virologists preferred to *dormant*) "viruses that we may harbor in our bodies may not be asleep or dead but may have turned to other disguises" (9). A *Scientific American* piece, referring repeatedly to "the invading virus," described how "within the cell the virus's DNA—its reproductive, genetic substance— proceeds to sabotage the bacterium's metabolism, forcing it to produce viral nucleic acid and protein instead of the materials it normally manufactures for its own growth."[60] Even in a specialist journal like *Science*, language such as that in Frank L. Horstall Jr.'s explanation of how "each of the individual DNA transformers can be considered as an independent agent capable of invading, producing a modified bacterial cell, and being reproduced like a virus" was prevalent.[61] The language of viral *agency* and *invasion* became a staple of the scientific literature.

VIRAL INFORMATION

As quickly as viruses seemed to offer new insights into the processes of life, they were themselves subject to revised understanding. By the mid-1950s, biology had narrowed its vision considerably, as one science writer explained in the *Saturday Review,* from "the study of intact creatures" through organs and tissues to cells and finally to "whirling, shifting patterns of chemical molecules within cells."[62] A relatively simple virus, the bacteriophage, was at the center of the new theories, allowing scientists unprecedented access to the mechanisms of cellular reproduction and coming close to parsing "the magnificent chemical poetry that transforms a single small and rather slimy cell, a granular speck of jelly, into a human baby" (46).

The implications of this revision reached the public when a *New York Times* account of a virology conference held in April 1956 announced the production of what seemed to be a synthetic virus and the search for a suitable host that would mean "the creation of life in a test tube." Along with the excitement of this scientific advance, the writer recorded an important shift in imagining viruses, describing how "the chains (genes) of elemental compounds that direct reproduction of a virus do so because they contain information to direct other host cell machinery to replicate the first virus particle."[63] The term "bacterial information" had been proposed in a 1953 letter to the editor of *Nature* by four distinguished researchers in the field (including James Watson) to resolve the "chaotic growth in technical vocabulary" that had followed the burgeoning of the field of bacterial genetics. Concerned that the discussions may become "unintelligible to the non-specialist," they had proposed the term in place of the proliferation of words, including "bacterial 'transformation,' 'induction' and 'transduction' " as well as "infection," used to describe " 'sexual recombination' in bacteria."[64]

Revisions between Luria's 1953 edition of *General Virology* and Luria and Darnell's second edition in 1967 register the conceptual impact of the idea of information: viral reproduction, in the second edition, represented an alteration in the flow of information; viruses are, in effect, information-delivery systems.[65] The years bracketed by these two editions witnessed, in Lily E. Kay's words, "the conceptualization, breaking, and completion of the genetic code, . . . one of the most important and dramatic episodes in twentieth-century science and a manifestation of the stupendous reach of molecular biology."[66] Scientists needed a vocabulary for their discoveries that would, as Kay documents, enable them to communicate their implications, and they drew on the central metaphors of the moment: language, codes, and information. The influence, of course, was mutual. Attention to the circulation of information conjoined the intriguing processes of viral reproduction to the personal and political threats posed by the theft of information.

Information was a term with its own history in the postwar period, independent of virology, genetics, and Cold War ideology, although all three areas were instrumental in the development and circulation of the term.[67] The field of information studies emerged in response to the need for a variety of military applications, such as cryptology and gunnery, and developed in the postwar years, in the areas of communications and cybernetics. One of the founders of the field, Norbert Wiener, offered a popular introduction to the theory of information in *The Human Use of Human Beings: Cybernetics and Society,* first published in 1950 and revised in 1954. "Since the end of World War II," he explains, "I have been working on the many ramifications of the theory of messages. Besides the electrical engineering theory of the transmission of messages, there is a larger field which includes not only the study of language but the study of messages as a means of controlling machinery and society, the development of computing machines and other such automata, certain reflections upon psychology and the nervous system, and a tentative new theory of scientific method."[68] In the words of the biologist Henry Quastler, "information theory" is "based on the concept that information is measurable" and that there are reasons to perform these measurements.[69] He distinguishes between the " 'information' evaluated in Information Theory" and "every-day information": "The 'information in a message, for example, as a type of event, is the measure of the amount of knowledge (intelligence) which a message of this sort ideally can convey through the medium of symbolic representation."[70] A message is an "event," and its information can be measured when it represents a unique choice among possibilities.

In 1948 Wiener named a field, with the publication of his book *Cybernetics*, to which information theory would be central, and it was in "response," he explained, "to a certain demand . . . to make its ideas acceptable to the lay public" that he wrote *The Human Use of Human Beings*.[71] The broadening of the applicability of information theory across a wide range of academic disciplines, and the efforts to make it more accessible to the general public, chiseled away, as Kay notes, at its more specific meaning. But the technical meaning of information remained at the conceptual core even of the most popular usages and helped to produce a conceptual shift in ideas about contagion, communication, and social interaction. The thinking that would eventually lead to an understanding of viruses as "among the most primitive means of *information transfer*" was consistent with that technical meaning, but more mainstream representations of viral information produced the image of the body as a communication system that viruses could hijack, corrupting the information crucial to its healthy functioning.[72]

If the circulation of information explained the essence of life and government, nothing better animated the threat to that essence than the virus. The image invigorated familiar metaphors such as McCarthy's charges, in his 1952 book *McCarthyism: The Fight for America*, that "the systematic infiltration" of the U.S. government was coming primarily through the schools, the "nerve center" of the nation, and the press, its chief means of disseminating information.[73] This image corporealized machines as well as social organisms (the legacy is evident in the idea of a computer virus). The 1950s witnessed a national obsession with information, which was at the heart of national security and the alleged and actual sale of which cost many people their careers, their freedom, and even their lives. The term *classified information* surfaced during this period, and the designation became more frequent as the authority to employ it expanded.[74] Classification helped to create the sense of information as material—the substance of the state—that needed to be safeguarded. More than the state was at stake. The theft of information threatened the life's blood of the nation, for which the individual was both the analog and the most vulnerable unit: threat of the theft of "information" viscerally tied the individual to the nation, and the state was responsible for the security of both.

The circulation of information had to be regulated at the level not only of the message but also of the medium. Anti-Communists argued that Communists had devised alternative means of communicating among themselves, even as they pursued their nefarious purposes by contaminating or controlling the information disseminated through U.S. sources. A 1956 *New York Times* piece, which appeared shortly before the April account of the virology conference, labeled the "Communist Party of Russia . . . a unique instrument for the transmission of information."[75] Detailing the purging of Stalin in the Soviet Union, which took place three years after his death, the writer described the nature of Communist communication: "Word is given out by the party chiefs to lieutenants assembled in Moscow. They carry the message back to cohorts in the sixteen republics. From there it spreads to party units in the cities and towns and villages. Eventually, it reaches every cell in farm and factory across the country that is a Continent" (1E–2E). The viral analog is not lost on the writer, who asks, "Would it not, in the long run, be safer for the Government to smash the Stalin myth itself rather than be infected by the virus of truth from the outside?"(3E). The mode of communication is at once inefficient and insidious, evidence of an antipathy to freedom, an effort of organized social contagion that is simultaneously chilling and, the writer suggests, doomed to failure. While claims of an unrestricted flow of information in the United States allegedly distinguished U.S. democracy from Soviet totalitarianism, "classified information" justified and enabled the regulation of that flow to safeguard the state.[76]

A MYTHOLOGY FOR THE SPACE AGE

No one more insightfully chronicled the anxieties of the age than William S. Burroughs, who was disturbed by the mindless conformity, creeping numbness, and hypocrisy of his native land. A canny observer, Burroughs put viruses at the center of his analysis and of his "mythology for the space age," a wild saga about viral space invaders, designed primarily to challenge his readers to become more critical observers of what he thought of as a deepening cultural pathology that he sought to diagnose and treat in his work. The social contagion that the Chicago sociologists set out to study was, for Burroughs, a sign of a dangerous pathology that was not limited to one side of the Cold War, but was intrinsic to most forms of communication in the postwar world. His barometric writing was an artistic measure of the preoccupations of his moment, into which his status as an expatriate American living in Tangier afforded him a unique perspective.

Like the crowd-psychology theorists, Burroughs understood any communication that produced group thinking as a kind of contagion, and, like them, he meant the term literally. His contagion was explicitly viral, the expression of an invariably corrupting social control, especially pernicious at the level of the state. "The virus power manifests itself in many ways," he told an interviewer in 1964. "In the construction of nuclear weapons, in practically all the existing political systems which are aimed at curtailing inner freedom, that is, at control. It manifests itself in the extreme drabness of everyday life in Western countries. It manifests itself in the ugliness and vulgarity we see on every hand, and of course, it manifests itself in the actual virus illnesses."[77]

The scion whose family name was associated with the late-nineteenth-century invention of the adding machine came of age as a writer against the backdrop of cybernetics, and his work registers the centrality of information to his understanding of all social interactions. Anything that affected that information did not just act *like* a virus, but actually *was* viral and, in his work, involved a sort of genetic alteration. Viral illnesses were no less material, for him, for being metaphors through which social dynamics manifested themselves. Metaphors produced material conditions, and he set out to demonstrate the material consequences of language. As Oliver Harris insightfully puts it, "To say the word is a communicative sickness was not, for Burroughs, metaphoric analysis of poststructuralist platitude but an awareness integral and material to the act of writing, and this is what the toxicity of Burroughs' textual politics insists upon, *ad nauseam.*"[78] The viral, as it develops in his work, is anything that usurps creative agency, from addiction and the corporate interests that sustain the "junk business" to the official policies and customs and habits that enforce unthinking conformity, a species of mind control. In the introduction to his most widely read novel, *Naked Lunch* (1959), Burroughs explains the circumstances of its composition—his own drug addiction—and he offers an analysis that situates addiction in literal as well as metaphorical relationship to capitalism: drugs are "big business."[79] The danger of addiction shades gradually into contagion, beginning with his comparison of addicts, who "can be cured or quarantined," to "typhoid carriers" (xii) and grotesquely exemplified by the especially dedicated narcotics agent-turned-junky, Bradley the Buyer, who literally "assimilates" (liquefies and absorbs) his district supervisor when he attempts to terminate his employment and, as Bradley explains, his "lifeline" (16). Bradley exemplifies the transformative and destructive power not only of addiction but also of bureaucracy and (literally) corporatism. Language was the instrument of the transformation.

Burroughs prided himself on understanding the science he used in his work, and in his novels from the 1960s explanations from virology grew increasingly elaborate. In his 1962 work, *The Ticket That Exploded*, he introduced the concept of "criminal controllers" who "occupy human bodies" but are not visible. " 'Can you see a virus?' " he asks. " 'Well, the criminal controllers operate in very much the same manner as a virus—Now a virus in order to invade, damage and occupy the human organism must have a gimmick to get in—Once in the virus invades damages and occupies a certain area or organ in the body—known as the tissue of predilection—Hepatitis, for example, attacks the liver—Influenza the respiratory tract—Polio and rabies the central nervous system—In the same way a controller invades, damages and occupies some pattern or configuration of the human organism."[80] Burroughs imagines the controllers as space invaders who humorously but distinctly repeat the familiar history of conquest. Specialized, like viruses, in their means of infection, they summon that past through a tangled mythologized history of viral and political invasion and colonization. A controller who operates "through addicts [does so] because he himself is an addict—A heavy metal addict from Uranus—What we call opium or junk is a very much diluted form of heavy metal addiction—Venusians usually operate through sexual practices—In short these controllers brought their vices and diseases from their planet of origin and infected the human hosts very much in the same way that the early colonizers infected so-called 'primitive populations' " (59).

The distinction between mind and body made no sense to Burroughs for understanding addiction, language or physical illness. Daily existence demonstrated the physical impact and consequences, the transformative power, of communication, and viruses explained as they exemplified how such processes became corrupted. As one character observes in *The Ticket That*

Exploded, " 'Anyone who keeps his bloody eyes open doesn't need a Harly St. psychiatrist to tell him that destructive elements enter into so-called normal sex relations: the desire to dominate, to kill, to take over and eat the partner. .these impulses are normally held in check by counter impulses. .what the virus puts out of action is the *regulatory centers in the nervous system*' " (20; ellipses in original). The social analysis is an explicit feature of Burroughs's confrontational aesthetic: he was determined to teach his readers to see the means of infection.

The virus represents communication gone awry: the sources of connection turned into the terms of corruption. In a section of *The Ticket That Exploded* entitled "Operation Rewrite," Burroughs describes the "short step" from "symbiosis to parasitism": "The word is now a virus. The flu virus may once have been a healthy lung cell. It is now a parasitic organism that invades and damages the lungs" (49). The solution, as the title of the section suggests, arises out of the problem. If the word virus not only manifests but is actually generated by the corruption of language, a different approach to words can also supply the antidote: "*Communication must become total and conscious before we can stop it*" (51). In the 1985 introduction to *Queer* (published more than three decades after its composition), he would describe writing itself as "inoculation. As soon as something is written, it loses the power of surprise, just as a virus loses its advantage when a weakened virus has created alerted antibodies. So I achieved some immunity from further perilous ventures along these lines by writing my experience down."[81]

The strategy of inoculation became an explicit aesthetic with a new technique in composition that Burroughs developed with his poet and painter friend Brion Gysin following the publication of *Naked Lunch.* In what became known as his "cut-up" trilogy—*The Soft Machine* (1961–1967), *The Ticket That Exploded* (1962), and *Nova Express* (1964)—he cut, pasted, folded, and patched his own work as well as that of other writers into the middle of works in progress to develop a compositional technique that would disrupt even a loose structure and force readers to focus on the elements of composition and the practice of reading that typically escaped attention. Burroughs shared that goal with other experimental writers; Gertrude Stein, for example, is an acknowledged presence in his work. He was involved in filmmaking while he was writing his trilogy in the early 1960s, and, like Stein, he understood the importance of the visual features of the cultural dynamics that he sought to bring to consciousness. "Most people don't see what's going on around them," he complained. "That's my principal message to writers: for God's sake, keep your *eyes* open."[82] As it did for Stein, cinematography offered him a conceptual analog for the easy manipulation of the perceptual field, and they shared the goal of wanting their readers to become aware of how they are made to see (perceive, understand, and envision) as they do: of how, that is, meaning is produced.

Burroughs specifically evokes Stein and the writing experiments for which she was known—with an allusion to the title of her coauthored *Four Saints in Three Acts*—to mark his move into the cut-up technique in a passage from *The Ticket That Exploded*:

> He had been meaning Sexexcellency Sally Rand cunning Navy pilot Alan B. Weld two acts for three saints in outer space proudly registered in Phoenix was it are you sure that's right infectious night biter Mo. 18 I'm going to answer the doorbell definitely definitely the first time in thirty years Houston's outbreak the first time in who said Atlantic City? I was supposed to have done the sets for it and B. was supposed to acquire the virus from birds yeah then I think they paid a dollar for infectious disease processing the actual film but the disease quietly spread to all West Texas beauty unscheduled in outer space. . 'You mean you did it yourself you didn't have your assistant do it?.' . 'Nope just spreading epidemic of St Vacine maybe we should.' . 'How long did it take you to process this photo to squirt at anything that flew dyeing and all that it's all part of the city's sudden healthy people infectious beauty disease spreading epidemic of immune humans. (11; ellipses in original)

The passage comes near the beginning of a work in which it is already difficult to distinguish between espionage and moviemaking. It interlaces what appears to be the making of a film and the acquisition of a virus (from birds); it is, for example, impossible to tell whether "they paid a dollar for" an "infectious disease" or for "processing the actual film." The "outbreak"—"disease quietly spread to all West Texas beauty unscheduled in outer space"—attests to the lack of control in both cases. The dissemination of information follows its own course and logic. With the cut-up technique, Burroughs, like Stein, conspicuously displayed his relinquishing of control, which was essential to mental liberation and creativity. Even free association was not sufficient for him—"one's mind can't cover it that way," he once remarked.[83] The cut-ups disrupted conventional reading practices and forced readers to think about plot and composition, about how they received and processed information. Cut-ups, as he explained in an interview in 1965, "make explicit a psycho-sensory process that is going on all the time anyway."[84] His determination to envision that process led to the connections Burroughs perceptively emphasized among viruses, mind control, and information. With the added narrative structure of interplanetary commerce, and the space invasions it engendered, he configured these themes into the critical perspective of his new mythology for the space age. If his artistic technique was unusual, however, this configuration was not.

OF PODS AND PEOPLE

By the time he penned his trilogy, the cultural myths that intrigued Burroughs had already found more popular appeal (albeit with less theoretical self-consciousness) in the hybrid genre of science-fiction horror and its offshoot, epidemiological horror, epitomized by Jack Finney's pod people. Finney originally published the 1955 novel as a serial in *Collier's* in 1954, and the first film version was based on the serial. The film was remade in 1978 (in turn prompting a revised edition of the novel) and again in 1993, and the story continues to be retold in spin-off versions, such as Robin Cook's 1997 *Invasion,* which was also made into a film.[85] Burroughs's critical perspective and thematic choices, the cultural preoccupations that he captured so insightfully, explain the broad appeal of this story, which is evident not only in its many retellings but also in its widespread and continuing use as a cultural point of reference and in the appearance in other stories of its central features: the snatched bodies and the conversion of one's most intimate associates into something other than human.

Interest in a presumed political allegory has dominated critical response to the story, as in Harry M. Benshoff's observation that the "human-looking monsters have been thought to reflect a paranoid fear of both mindless U.S. conformity *and* Communist infiltration, wherein a poisonous ideology spreads through small-town USA like a virus, silently turning one's friends and relatives into monsters."[86] No specific ideology fits the story exactly. Rather, the snatched bodies of an American small town register the uncertainties raised by social and political transformation and scientific and medical discoveries in the postwar world. Benshoff's metaphor picks up on the viral features of the pods that run subtly from Finney's novel through the films, becoming explicit in Cook's version, in which the human beings succumb to an aggressive alien virus implanted in primordial DNA. In all versions, *Body Snatchers* recounts the story of an ecological invasion that turns willful and even malicious with the incarnation of the pod people. The pods' viral features fleshed out the viral agency emerging in the medical literature and mainstream media and helped to develop the conventions of the incarnated virus and the epidemiological struggle over the fate of humanity that characterized the outbreak narrative.

The Body Snatchers offered a mythology for the moment: a story about the uncertain nature of human being conceived as a struggle for the future of humanity. Finney's protagonists experience the terror of utter estrangement when they find themselves suddenly certain that everything is different despite the evidence of their senses, which tells them that nothing has changed. It is a story about carriers, spawning one of the few films of the genre, as Benshoff notes, in which the monsters physically resemble human beings. While Burroughs encourages inspection of the nature of human beings, Finney forestalls any such inquiry. "Humanity," in his novel, is at risk, but never in question and, although it seems precarious, it proves finally indestructible.

The novel chronicles the gradual discovery by the doctor narrator, Miles Bennell, of the source of his patients' disturbing insistence that close relatives are not who they claim to be in the personality theft perpetrated by the intergalactic pods. Of the uncle who raised her, one woman puzzles, " 'He looks, sounds, acts, and remembers exactly like Ira. On the outside. But *inside* he's different. His responses . . . aren't *emotionally* right. . . . [T]here's something *missing.*' "[87] The difficulty of detecting the pod people's subtle loss of humanity makes those who notice it seem delusional. Naturally, the experts consulted in this case assume that they are witnessing a psychological phenomenon, what Miles's psychiatrist friend, Mannie Kaufman, calls "the first contagious neurosis" he has ever seen, "a real epidemic" (23) of an imagined disease, panic spreading "like a contagion" (98).

The problem, of course, turns out not to be in the minds, but in the snatched bodies of the residents. Having isolated Santa Mira from the rest of the world, they are invasive and colonizing: actively determined to spread. Miles and his girlfriend, Becky Driscoll, watch in horror from Miles's office while three farm trucks loaded with pods drive up to the town center and begin to distribute the pods to townspeople with "families or contacts" in surrounding towns (147). They are also transformative, leaving no one "what he had been, or what he seemed still, to the naked eye. The men, women, and children in the street below . . . were something else now," Miles explains, "every last one of them. They were each our enemies, including those with the eyes, faces, gestures, and walks of old friends. There was no help for us here except from each other, and even now the communities around us were being invaded" (149).

Humanity is negatively defined by the pod transformation: they become automatons, lacking passion, compassion, and emotions of any sort. They also lose their uniqueness in the display of a hive mentality. Depictions of mass hypnosis and mental control had long preceded Cold War science fiction. David Seed identifies a gothic tradition that associates a horrifying loss of humanity with the state's aggressive manipulation of its citizens.[88] Through the conventions of horror, the loss of humanity becomes a loss of individuality and is configured through features designed to provoke disgust, such as the decaying body and oozing innards of the zombie. By the 1950s, horror and disgust were implicit in the idea of mind control. Finney's novel conjoined these associations with contemporary technological innovations and scientific theories to dramatize the possibility of a transformational loss of humanity and the threat that imperceptibly changed human beings could in turn pose to the state. While Richard Condon's 1959 novel, *The Manchurian Candidate,* pointedly showed how mind control could turn a human being into an assassin, Finney's novel depicted the disturbing biological mechanisms of mental contagion, and virology supplied the vocabulary through which Finney explained the metamorphosis.

When Miles, Becky, and their friends, Jack and Theodora Belicec, begin to piece together the phenomenon, the pod people become viral. Following an odd clue in a daily newspaper, Jack, an author and attentive reader, has led them to the index case, the former botany professor Bernard Budlong, who explains the pod phenomenon in language that might have been lifted from a virology textbook: the pods are a life-form, although not in a conventional sense, and they have arrived on earth " 'by pure chance, but having arrived, they have a function to perform. . . . The function of all life, everywhere—to survive' " (152). Stressing their lack of malevolence, he concedes that " 'the pods are a parasite on whatever life they encounter. . . . But they are the perfect parasite, capable of far more than clinging to the host. They are completely evolved life; they have the ability to re-form and reconstitute themselves into perfect duplication, cell for living cell, of any life form they may encounter in whatever conditions that life has suited itself for' " (153).

Understanding how the pods work entails coming to terms with a new conception of human being, Budlong explains, as he cautions Miles not to be trapped by his limited assumptions about life. Noting that Miles's grandfather would have been dubious about radio waves, Budlong anticipates that Miles will be similarly skeptical of the insights that the human body " 'contains a pattern' " that " 'is the very foundation of cellular life' " (155), that " 'every cell of [an entire body] emanates waves as individual as fingerprints' " (155), and that " 'during sleep . . . that pattern can be taken from [the sleeper], absorbed like static electricity, from one body to another' "

(155–56), which is precisely what the pods do. This description recasts individuality: every human being is unique, but also predictable, conforming to a pattern. Every individual can be reducible to patterns of "information" and can therefore be "snatched."

Budlong's explanation rehearses the version of information theory that Wiener had popularized in *The Human Use of Human Beings*.[89] Wiener had declared a "pattern . . . the touchstone of our personal identity. Our tissues change as we live: the food we eat and the air we breathe become flesh of our flesh and bone of our bone, and the momentary elements of our flesh and bone pass out of our body every day with our excreta. . . . We are not stuff that abides, but patterns that perpetuate themselves."[90] Noting that a "pattern is a message, and may be transmitted as a message" and drawing, like Budlong, on the patterns of sound and light that make radio and television work, he contemplates "what would happen if we were to transmit the whole pattern of the human body, of the human brain with its memories and cross connections, so that a hypothetical receiving instrument could re-embody these messages in appropriate matter, capable of continuing the processes already in the body and the mind, and of maintaining the integrity needed for this continuation by a process of homeostasis" (96). If Wiener suggests that the human body is information that could conceivably be transmitted (a sort of human fax), *Body Snatchers* represents the potential abuse of that information—the alienability of the human personality. In response, Finney's story insists that humanity consists of something at once intangible and physiological that cannot be reduced to information.

The pods in *The Body Snatchers* do not exactly reproduce the human beings whose information they steal. Like viruses, they replace that alienable information with themselves, something distinctly not human. While their initial introduction into the earth's ecosystem was accidental—an "invasion" in the ecological sense—their mandate to survive turns them into willful carriers: " 'From the moment the first effective changeover occurred, chance was no longer a factor' " (160). Family members and service providers, " 'delivery men, plumbers, carpenters, effected others' " (160). The *effected* changes seem initially passive, brought about with the least sense of conscious agency it is possible to convey. *Effected*, however, invokes the more expected *infected*, which implies the deliberate spread of a disease. When the pods take human shape, they evolve into unmistakably sinister, cunning, and conniving beings, a conspiratorial race of carriers.[91] The concept of an invasion, which was added to the title with the 1956 film, *Invasion of the Body Snatchers*, becomes more pronounced with each version. Like any viral invasion, it comes from without and proceeds to take over the host's bodily functions and mechanisms to reproduce itself. The animation of this viral agent is a stock feature of outbreak narratives, and it shows how and why they readily generate narratives of bioterrorism.

The scale of the danger escalates rapidly to a species-threatening event. Budlong explains that the pods have used up the resources of every planet on which they have landed and will use up the earth's within about five years and then move on. Miles and Becky are not convinced by his justification that human beings similarly have used up many of the earth's resources. "'You're going to spread over the *world?*'" Miles asks in disbelief. And Budlong maps out the conquest of "'this county, then the next ones; and presently northern California, Oregon, Washington, the West Coast, finally; it's an accelerating process, ever faster, always more of us, fewer of you. Presently, fairly quickly, the continent. And then—yes, of course, the world'" (163). Budlong's five-year forecast resembles the Soviet's five-year plan, summoning the predictions made in the United States about the industrializing Soviet state and explaining readers' temptation to read the novel as a simple political allegory, despite Finney's demurrals. The wasted police state that Finney describes offers readers a glimpse into the effects of Communist infiltration on prosperous small-town USA. But the pods are more generally colonizers, and the apocalyptic vision of world conquest and rapidly expended resources expresses colonizing anxieties in environmental terms, linking a global exhaustion of resources to a terrifying loss of humanity; social and political transformation becomes a threat to "humanity" that shades into an ecological catastrophe.

MIMICRY AND HYBRIDITY

The danger of the dehumanized pods—and what distinguishes them from most other 1950s science-fiction monsters—lies in their mimicry. They can spread because their human appearance enables them to mask their conversion and communicate normally with human beings. Among themselves, the emotionless pod people manifest their hive mentality as an alternative means of communication, which replaces constructive information with unhealthy information and reproduces an absorptive collective at the expense of its individual hosts. Despite Budlong's insistence that the pod invasion is accidental and that the pods are exclusively concerned with their survival, their subterfuge eventually metamorphoses into malice. Miles experiences the malice while eavesdropping on one of his patients, Becky's cousin Wilma, as she recounts a conversation she had had with Miles, retracting her initial report of her uncle's strange behavior. Listening at the window of Becky's house, where her relatives are waiting to infect the couple, Miles hears Wilma describe their interchange in a way that, he recalls, "made my hair on the back of my neck prickle and stand erect. 'Oh, Miles,' Wilma suddenly said, in a cruel imitation of her last talk with me—and the venom in her caricature of herself made me shiver—'I've been meaning to stop in and see you about—what happened.' Then she laughed falsely, in a hideous burlesque of embarrassment.'"[92] The laughter that follows forces Miles to acknowledge that those former acquaintances were not only no longer themselves but "were not human beings at all," and he is sickened by the thought of their inhumanity.

In the *Collier's* version and in Siegel's film, the scene dramatizes the protagonists' full appreciation of their danger, as they learn that even their family members have become dangerous hybrids determined to convert them as well. Finney revises and significantly expands on the incident in the novel, however, where it marks his effort to turn the pod invasion into broad social critique. In the novel Miles prefaces his account of Wilma's comment with a memory of an experience that had similarly disturbed him. He had been awakened, he recalls, after having slept off the effects of a party in his car, by a conversation between two men, "Billy, . . . a middle-aged black man [who] had a shoeshine stand," whom Miles describes as "a town character" (118), and one of his friends. Billy had always given Miles "the feeling of being with that rarest of persons, a happy man," someone who "obviously took contentment in one of the simpler occupations of the world" (118), and he can barely recognize the "suddenly strange and altered tone," the "queer and twisted heartiness" (119), with which the disembodied voice mimics his usual pleasantries. Miles remembers that "the voice was Billy's, the words and tone those the town knew with affection, but—parodied, and a shade off key. . . . The pent-up bitterness of years tainted every word and syllable he spoke. . . . and never before in [his] life had [he] heard such ugly, bitter, and vicious contempt in a voice, contempt for the people taken in by his daily antics, but even more for himself, the man who supplied the servility they bought from him" (119). Bill (as his friend calls him) disrupts the performance of his expected role—white America's stereotype—and thereby puts the terms of that performance on display. Miles is horrified to see, and see through, the forced performance of a cultural stereotype. As "Billy," Bill performs servility for white America, while as "Bill" he seethes with a resentment that turns him "bitter," "queer," and "twisted." Hearing this act of mimicry makes Miles aware not only of having been duped by a performance but also of the transformative resentment that is its cost.

Miles's memory establishes the disturbing experience of overhearing an act of verbal mimicry as the connection between Wilma and Bill. "Mimicry," for the postcolonial theorist Homi Bhabha, names the uncanny expression of colonized subjectivity. It inheres in the colonized subject's performance of the terms of colonial identity. Bhabha marks the performance as racialized and racializing, describing the colonized subject as "almost the same, but not quite," which is to say, "almost the same, but not white."[93] Mimicry is disturbing because it exposes the performative dimensions of the colonizer's identity as well as the racialized hierarchies that exclude the colonized from the full terms of personhood. Finney's two mimics, by contrast, deliberately mock their conscious performances of their expected roles. Although they occupy different social positions and stand in different relations to Miles, Wilma and Bill come together for him—and for Finney— because they are similarly unsettling. The disjunctive digression reveals the nature of Miles's discomfort, and the key to the pod people's uncanniness, to be their hybridity.

Finney wrote *The Body Snatchers* against the backdrop of desegregation and decolonization and the breakdown of familiar racialized hierarchies worldwide that they promoted. His story appeared in the wake of the 1954 U.S. Supreme Court desegregation decision of *Brown v. Board of Education* and the numerous essays in mainstream newspapers and periodicals about race relations in the United States that the case had generated. In two consecutive issues in October 1954, roughly a month before the first serialized installment of *The Body Snatchers* appeared, *Collier's* had run a piece by the celebrated South African author Alan Paton entitled "The Negro in America Today." The author of *Cry, the Beloved Country* had journeyed to the United States, heartened by the progress represented by the *Brown* decision that declared segregated schools discriminatory. He hoped to find in the United States lessons that he could bring home to South Africa, and the piece documents both the hopeful signs of progress and the persistent racism—exclusion of black Americans from full and equal citizenship—that he discovered. Everywhere he turned, especially in housing (for which legislation was pending in the Supreme Court) and, most disappointing to him, in the churches, segregation remained a fact of life throughout the country. He quotes the "powerful words" of the Bishop of Raleigh, who believes that " 'the virus of prejudice will not die out of itself;

it has to be killed by being exposed to the light of Faith,' " and, hopeful that "Christians" will eventually "cease thinking in categories of race," he nonetheless echoes the Bishop's conviction that "there are times when the virus has to be *killed*; one does not wait for it to die."[94] The memory of "Billy" was the only significant addition Finney made when he turned the 1954 *Collier's* serial into the novel, and it draws out the implicit racialization of the pod people, who, like Bhabha's mimics (colonial hybrids), register the disturbing exposure of racial hierarchies.

The pod people bring to Finney's story the long history of *hybridity*, beginning in botany and zoology, where it referred to the offspring produced by parents of different species.[95] The term moved quickly to the human species, where, with "mixed-blood," it described the offspring of parents from different races and registered the confusion of social and biological classifications that characterizes racism. The term became increasingly common in the nineteenth century, and fiction as well as science and law from that period document the attraction and repulsion, the fear and fascination of social and sexual intermingling. The legacies of mercantilism and migration, of slavery and colonization, are written in the tragic fates and criminal dispositions of literary depictions of "mixed-blooded" products of sexual unions across "races."

A striking metaphor in one of Freud's most influential essays demonstrates the uncanny power of this figure. In "The Unconscious" Freud defines his theory of the mechanisms of repression and human psychology generally, and he reaches for the figure of the mixed-race hybrid to ground an abstract point: why certain ideas that appear as though they should be admissible to consciousness (and would therefore belong to the system preconscious) have characteristics that make them more appropriately assigned to the system unconscious. Freud compares these ideas "with individuals of mixed race who, taken all round, resemble white men, but who betray their coloured descent by some striking feature or other, and on that account are excluded from society and enjoy none of the privileges of white people."[96] Ideas are refused—cannot come to consciousness—because they represent insights that are too disturbing for an individual to acknowledge. By analogy, the figure of the human hybrid, the result of heterosexual reproduction across racial classifications, evokes similarly disturbing insights.[97]

The exclusion of some individuals from "the privileges of white people" shows that hierarchies of power and prestige are racialized and defined by their exclusions. Human hybridity threatens to undermine the racial logic of those hierarchies. It attests to the permeability of social boundaries and the impermanence of racial classifications; it also puts heterosexual reproduction on display as the mechanism of that intermixture, biology confounding rather than reproducing social categories. Those insights are refused, and the biology of classifications reinforced, when the individuals "betray their coloured descent by some striking feature or other" and are thereby excluded from the privileges of whiteness. The visual processes by which such features are produced as indelible difference (the language of "descent") prioritize the biology of the classifications and obscure their social construction. The figure that Freud invokes to illustrate the workings of consciousness and the mechanisms of repression implies a broad social analysis as well. The betrayal and exclusion to which Freud refers depict both the racialization of power and the potential disruption of racialized power posed by sexuality. Freud's analogy also implies that both racialized power and the challenge posed by sexuality are ideas that are sufficiently disturbing to generate mechanisms of collective repression and are therefore formative for social psychology.[98]

The hybrid was a key figure for Robert Park as well. While Park insisted, following an ecological model, that worldwide interconnections would lead inevitably to the dissolution of cultural boundaries (universal hybridity), he also conceded that the process slowed down when differences between groups found expression in distinctive physical traits. His own hybrid—marginal man—displayed the processes of cultural amalgamation, but Park also underscored the anguish experienced by this involuntary herald as he was sacrificed on the altar of social transformation. The role of the hybrid in nineteenth- and twentieth-century social thought explains its imaginative power as a figure of danger, transformation, and sacrifice.

The (viral) strategies of pod reproduction uncannily disrupt—and thereby highlight—the taxonomies on which humanity relies for its distinction. Unlike black Americans, pod people are colonizers, but Miles links Wilma and Bill in the acts of mimicry through which both disturb the social surface. The word "queer" appears several times in the novel to mark that disturbance. The protagonists were originally alerted to the pod presence because Jack Belicec habitually collected newspaper stories that told of the "queer little happenings . . . that simply don't fit in with the great body of knowledge that the human race has gradually acquired over thousands of years" (72). At the end of the novel, Miles establishes his own account of the pod invasion as one of the "occasional queer little stories, humorously written, tongue-in-cheek, most of the time" (191) that circulate in the media or through rumors. The "queerness" of Jack's cut outs, he explains, alerts the writer to new information that conditioning—Burroughs's "psycho-sensory process"—keeps people from noticing. Miles's "queer little stories," Jack's "queer little happenings," and the "queer, twisted heartiness" of Bill's mimicry all signal a tear in the fabric of received wisdom that catch the attention of Jack, the author—and Miles, the reluctant listener—and lead them, in different ways, to the dark underside of Santa Mira.

"Queer" most obviously has its conventional meaning—"odd" or "unusual"—but in the 1950s it was also already a slang term for "homosexual," as in Burroughs's *Queer*. Anticipating queer theory, Burroughs viewed homosexuality as a disruption of normative institutions, and he linked it to other such disturbances that could lead to a questioning of the blind spots of convention. Anxiety surrounding homosexuality in the period—expressed, for example, in the purging of gay men and lesbians from jobs in the government, the media and education (the "nerve center" of U.S. society)—was evidence for him of the threat alternative sexualities posed to habits of thought. Pod reproduction, a feature on which the films graphically dwelled, called attention to the taxonomies that not only reproduced social hierarchies but also defined humanity itself. Neither Wilma nor Bill reproduces the social relations that Miles expects and on which his understanding of humanity rests. Nothing in the novel suggests that Finney was aware of the history summoned by his human/vegetable hybrids or the insights they engendered, and the resolution of the novel affirms the most conventional definition of humanity and the superficiality of Finney's race critique. Although Miles is on the verge of telling a queer story that could expose the racialized and gendered logic of biological classifications and social hierarchies, that is not finally the story Finney tells. Where Burroughs depicted habits of thought as viral, with racism, homophobia, and other biases as signs of illness, Finney saw the problems themselves as viral. Racism had corrupted and transformed Billy, turning him into Bill. The happy shoeshine boy of Miles's fantasy is, for him, the real (uninfected) person. Despite hearing his interlocutor call him "Bill," Miles continues to refer to him as "Billy." He responds to the conversation by feeling "ashamed of [Bill's unsuspecting patron], of Billy, of [himself], and of the whole human race" (120). Racism, Paton noted, was both viral and un-American. Finney seems to have concurred. Like the virus Wilma hosts, it comes from without and corrupts, creating an enemy within. This externalization of racism deflects Burroughs's more difficult and controversial structural analysis of the viral nature of practices and institutions, including such basic unquestioned institutions as marriage and the family. Finney forecloses on any potentially critical insights with his novel's triumphant conclusion.

Studies of brainwashing in the 1950s continually stressed an inalienable humanity that could be heroically maintained by the strongest and most courageous. Edward Hunter, for example, describes the subject of one case study as having "something in him they [the Communists] couldn't take away without destroying his mind or body."[99] Finney similarly insists on the defiant spirit of humanity that expresses itself in Miles's and Becky's final heroic resistance of the pods. Having escaped from their captors, they head for the freeway, only to confront the hopelessness of their situation: a field of pods with hundreds of pod people waiting to intercept them. Although "it made capture an absolute certainty," they decide "to use [themselves] against the pods" (185). Setting the fields on fire, they are quickly surrounded "by hundreds of advancing figures" who hardly touch them— "there was no anger, no emotion in them" (187)—but are nonetheless too numerous to resist. Almost immediately, however, the crowd stops, and "the great pods" ascend into the sky (187). In the original serial version, the Belicecs appear with the FBI, but the pods are already airborne. Finney omitted that detail from the novel, underscoring the triumphant individualism of Miles's and Becky's heroic decision. "Quite simply," Miles recounts,

> the great pods were leaving a fierce and inhospitable planet. I knew it utterly and a wave of exultation so violent it left me trembling swept through my body; because I knew Becky and I had played our part in what was now happening. We hadn't, and couldn't possibly have been—I saw this now—the only souls who had stumbled and blundered into what had been happening in Santa Mira. There'd been others, of course, individuals, and little groups, who had done what we had—who had simply refused to give up. Many had lost, but some of us who had not been caught and trapped without a chance had fought implacably, and a fragment of a wartime speech moved through my mind: *We shall fight them in the fields, and in the streets, we shall fight in the hills; we shall never surrender.* True then for one people, it was true always for the whole human race, and now I felt that nothing in the whole vast universe could ever defeat us. (188–89)

Miles doubts that the pods *thought* or *knew,* so much as "sensed . . . that this planet, this little race, would never receive them, would never yield" (189).

Against the aliens, "this little race"—the human race—is united, the emotionless Wilma implicitly *replacing* the embittered Bill as a threat. The triumph of the human spirit is a victory for a white America—free from disturbance—that, as signified by Churchill's familiar words, has moved beyond racial and national distinctions and contained the potentially global outbreak. The end of the novel returns to the Allied victory during the Second World War, substituting a hot war for a cold war. The solution to the pod invasion, as to racism, is to confront the *external* threat directly and fight heroically to defeat it. Humanity is preserved through the affirmation of threatened institutions. Miles and Becky, both divorced at the beginning of the novel, get married and raise a family in a town and a nation that they helped to save.

The good doctor defeats the pods because he knows how to fashion the "queer little happenings" into an explanatory narrative that allows him to identify and address the pod problem. The defeat of the pods depends on his ability to tell the right story about them. His most important medical act is therefore the fashioning of the "queer little stories" into this—patriotic— outbreak story in which a man of science does apocalyptic battle with a global threat that emanates not from science or the state, but from a space invasion.

The films rejected Finney's conclusion in favor of increasingly ominous endings. Even Cook, who similarly ends *Invasion* victoriously, substituted the more interesting conclusion of *War of the Worlds* for Finney's deus ex machina. Yet Finney's novel underscores an important feature that is contained in the plot of the story itself and retained even in the more ambiguous endings of the films: the appeal of an epidemiological model that would turn all problems (including racism) into sinister embodied viruses that came from elsewhere and could be seen and at least potentially rooted out. It is a deflection from another story that he might have told and that haunts *The Body Snatchers* and its subsequent incarnations.

VISUALIZING THE CONTAGION OF CONFORMITY

When the independent producer Walter Wanger read Finney's story in *Collier's*, he immediately recognized its cinematic potential, and he contacted the director Don Siegel, with whom he had recently worked. Siegel, in turn, brought in the scriptwriter Daniel Mainwaring, with whom he had also successfully worked on a previous project.[100] Since *The Body Snatchers* was a visual story—a story that connected the deceptiveness of appearances to a horrifying loss of humanity—it was an ideal vehicle for cinematic adaptation. Where *The Body Snatchers* described a mental contagion that turned out to be the result of physical possession, the 1956 film showed what that looked like. *Invasion of the Body Snatchers* promoted the iconic status of the story and helped to develop visual conventions for depicting carriers, outbreaks, and mental possession in the performance of affectlessness and as threats to "humanity."

Critics have disagreed about the politics of the film as well as the allegorical meaning of the pods, reading the hope that the FBI will be able to defeat the pods with which the film ends (departing from Finney's story) as a faith in government institutions that marks a shift either to the Left or to the Right. The confused politics is in the film itself, a result both of the differing politics of the many people involved in its production—from Finney to Mainwaring, Siegel, Wanger, and the studio executives, who insisted that Siegel and Mainwaring change their original ending—and of the pressures placed on everyone involved by HUAC's notorious presence in Hollywood in the 1950s. Siegel sidestepped the question of political allegory by emphasizing the social dimension of a mindless conformity to fashion, especially among his Hollywood colleagues. "Many of my associates are certainly pods," he asserted in an interview. "They have no feelings. They exist, breathe, sleep. To be a pod means that you have no passion, no anger, the spark has left you."[101]

It is one thing to read about the pod conversion and another actually to witness it. Point-of-view shots encourage the viewer's identification with the characters' frustration as they try to draw attention to the changes and with their sense of estrangement as their allies are converted. The pod people are more uncanny than the undead creations that populated the 1950s screen, since their difference is barely perceptible, if at all.

Richard Matheson's 1954 novella, *I Am Legend*, and its 1964 film adaptation, *The Last Man on Earth*, similarly distinguish between the zombie-like "vampires" that weakly threaten the protagonist, the sole human survivor of a bacterial infection, and the hybrids, the intermediate creatures who have found a partial antidote that keeps them from full conversion and who can therefore "pass" as human. While the undead vampires taunt the protagonist, they are not sufficiently organized to present an insurmountable threat; the hybrids, however, plan to build a new society. The film makes their racial inflection particularly apparent in their preternatural pallor. These whiter-than-white beings harbor a particular antipathy for the former society and eagerly purge the last remaining human being. Siegel marks the hybridity of his pod people by their featureless protohumanity as they emerge encased in slime from the giant (womblike, of course) pods. He ensures the disgust factor by showing the crushed and bloody faces of the protagonists' would-be pod incarnations as Miles smashes them with a shovel in his greenhouse.

Pod uncanniness inspires a unique spectatorial experience. While grotesque creatures tempt the viewer to look away from the screen, the pod people compel intense scrutiny. Vivian Sobchack describes how Siegel's direction twists "the secure and familiar . . . into something subtly dangerous and slyly perverted. . . . [T]he subject matter is familiar, ordinary, but one experiences a tension which seems to spring from no readily discernible cause, a distortion of angle so slight as to seem almost nonexistent, but so great as to set the teeth intolerably on edge." The viewer is "seduced by the minimal activity and novelty of what's on the screen into an attentive paranoia which makes us lean forward to scan what seem like the most intentionally and deceitfully flat images for signs of aberrant alien behavior from the most improbable of suspects."[102] That attentive paranoia becomes the experience of an invisible threat.

Where Sobchack distinguishes the pod people by their "*negative* behavior, . . . [their] *not* doing something: a gasp not gasped, a kiss not returned," however, there are also distinct visual and aural cues of commission: an uncanny deadening of the eyes and tone (automatism) that can readily turn into contempt, which is troubling in a stranger but devastating in an intimate.[103] It is the horror that Terry Donovan experiences in his *Red Nightmare* when his family and neighbors are overtaken by the Communist conspiracy. *Invasion of the Body Snatchers* helped to create a visual and aural vocabulary of possession, establishing these cues as signs of a pathological loss of humanity resulting from an infectious mental possession that turned human beings into sinister hybrid automatons.

Siegel complements the subtle distortions to which Sobchack refers with extreme close-up shots of the eyes of the pod people that make perception thematic. The protagonists know they cannot fully trust their senses in this disturbing new world, but the eyes can subtly betray the pod people with a lack of focus that suggests the absence of emotion. The extreme close-ups convey the anguish produced by the experience of looking into eyes that should register recognition, fondness, and love and instead show indifference, disdain, and contempt. If the eyes are indeed the window into the soul, the film depicts what soullessness looks like and seeks to produce what it feels like to inhabit a soulless world.

Indifference proves harder to fathom for the protagonists than malice. Miles's first response on witnessing pod reproduction is to look for a plot.

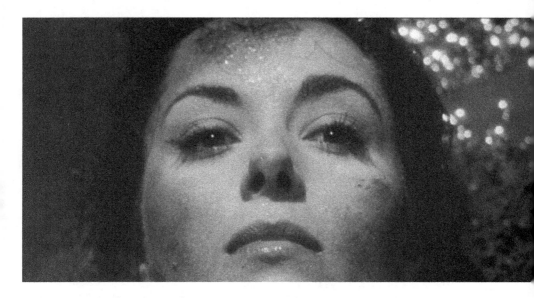

Unable to resist sleep, Becky turns from passionate lover to "inhuman enemy bent on [Miles's] destruction." Her conversion is evident in her eyes. *Invasion of the Body Snatchers* (dir. Don Siegel, 1956).

"Somebody or something wants this duplication to take place," he tells Becky. With a moment of reflection, he begins to think more like a scientist, summoning in the process dominant themes of 1950s science-fiction cinema. "So much has been discovered these past few years," he speculates, "anything's possible. Maybe the results of atomic radiation on plant life or animal life. Some weird alien organism, a mutation of some kind." In the absence of an explanation, he settles on a description that mediates between accident and design. "Whatever it is . . . that it can govern the forming of human flesh and blood out of thin air is fantastically powerful, beyond any comprehension, malignant."[104] When Miles and Becky witness the dissemination of pods in the town square (a scene that visually anticipates the town-square scene in *Red Nightmare*), Miles elaborates on this explanation, calling it "a malignant disease spreading over the whole country."

In science-fiction horror, science frequently proves to be a limiting framework, obscuring a problem until it is too late to solve it. Robert Neville, the protagonist of *I Am Legend*, discovers the bacteria that causes vampirism only after an epidemic turns him into the last surviving human being. He survives because of the immunity he develops after having been bitten by a bat in South America.[105] Matheson's vampires, like Finney's pods, are not the result of atomic fallout or state-sponsored experimentation gone awry, as in much science fiction, or supernatural, as in many horror stories. They are part of the "natural" world, but no less horrifying for their "natural" origins. Not only does "nature" have no special regard for human welfare, but an ecological worldview makes the eventual extinction of human beings a foregone conclusion. Facing execution at the hands of the new hybrid race, Robert Neville accepts that from their perspective the last unevolved human being is indeed an anachronism: extinction is the flip side of evolution.

Finney's (and Siegel's) heroic doctor never concedes that point, and the film, like the novel, ultimately asserts the malice of the pod-human hybrids. *Invasion of the Body Snatchers* draws on the conventions of film noir to depict the sinister shadows that are gradually darkening the sunny northern California town. In an opening voice-over, Miles explains that the town has been "possessed by something evil." When Miles, Becky, and the Belicecs see their first pods, a low-angle shot of Miles suggests the pods' looking back. Although the pod invasion starts out as a chance meeting of alien ecologies, they evolve. Becky's conversion near the end of the film creates, as Miles explains, "an inhuman enemy bent on [his] destruction."

Humanity becomes the unquestioned object of Miles's heroism. "Only when we have to fight to stay human," Miles tells Becky, "do we realize how precious it is." The pod people, in the form of his most trusted friends and colleagues, Mannie Kaufman and Jack Belicec, offer Miles the profound temptation to be "reborn," as Mannie promises, "into an untroubled world." The film insists on the difficulty of Miles's struggle through the temptations of the visual medium itself. Active viewing is stressful. Cultural observers such as Joost Meerloo cautioned against the "hypnotizing, seductive action of any all-penetrating form of communication," especially television; he worried in particular about "the passive peeping contagion of the television screen," which intruded "into family life and cut off the more subtle interfamilial communication" that kept minds alert and alive.[106] *Invasion of the Body Snatchers* reproduces Miles's challenge in the audience's own active viewing experience, which the film depicts as heroic and associated with humanity. Meerloo similarly praises the "heroes of the mind" who bravely "fight their inner battle against rigidity, cowardice, and the wish to surrender conviction for the sake of ease" by "remaining awake when others want to soothe themselves with sleep and oblivion."[107] Burroughs, too, urges his readers to "stay awake," and *Invasion of the Body Snatchers* dramatizes the metaphor, casting the effort to remain awake and alert as a heroic battle for humanity.

Siegel and Mainwaring had intended to end the film with a close up of Miles's anguished face, as he screams, "They're after all of us. Our wives, our children, everybody. They're here already. You're next." Finding that conclusion too bleak, however, the studio insisted on adding the frame story, in which Miles tells his story to a psychiatrist in a hospital emergency room; the psychiatrist assumes he is crazy until external evidence persuades him of the existence of the pods. The revised film ends with the psychiatrist's frantic command to summon help from national law-enforcement agencies and with restored faith in the authority of experts, from the psychiatrist to the military. The emphatic insistence of the film that emotions should fully replace appearance in defining the terms of humanity suggested the role of these experts in establishing and facilitating access to those terms. The position is consistent with a liberal assimilationist recasting of political protest in psychoanalytic terms that characterized the decade, finding expression in such films as *Rebel Without a Cause* (1955).

Siegel's and Mainwaring's preferred ending challenges viewers to assume responsibility for the preservation of humanity, to respond to Miles's invitation to join his heroic struggle. The studio either missed or dismissed the point of Siegel's and Mainwaring's visual and emotional call to arms. The film nonetheless registers both points of view, simultaneously affirming expertise and advocating personal responsibility and active, engaged viewing in its epidemiological instruction: its visual and narrative lessons about how to recognize a contagious dehumanization and its willful disseminators. The contradiction between personal responsibility and deferral to experts did not diminish—and might even have enhanced—the contribution of the film to the development of the mythic features of Finney's story: the heroic struggle to preserve nothing less than humanity itself against both external threats and the personal inattention that operates unwittingly in their service.

THE MYTH UPDATED

Philip Kaufman chose to remake *Invasion of the Body Snatchers* in the late 1970s, at the height of what Christopher Lasch called "the culture of narcissism" and Tom Wolfe dubbed "the me decade."[108] The generation that came of age in that decade was routinely denounced in the media as self-absorbed and disconnected compared to their socially and politically conscious predecessors of the 1960s, but, as the cultural critic Jonathan Schell noted in his widely read book, *The Time of Illusion,* "If the new generation was absorbed in pleasures of the moment and tended to be uninterested in thought or in culture or in anything else that was meant to endure beyond a single generation, it might well be because they were the first generation to doubt that the human species had a future."[109] The seventies generation lived not only with the possibility of nuclear annihilation but also with the threat to the species posed by environmental devastation on a global scale. A 1969 report from the United Nations Economic and Social Council warned that "for the first time in the history of mankind, there is arising a crisis of world-wide proportions involving developed and developing countries alike,—the crisis of the human environment" and that "if current trends continue, the future of life on earth could be endangered."[110] The threat was collective and (often explicitly) racialized.

People coming of age in the seventies had witnessed the Cold War turn hot repeatedly as the superpowers used the decolonizing world as a battleground. The war in Vietnam catalyzed discontents and ignited a social and cultural revolution domestically, as it galvanized opposition to what Harold R. Isaacs, writing in *Foreign Affairs,* called the "common whitism" of the United States and the Soviet Union. Isaacs wrote of the racial tensions of a new world order in which "the entire cluster of some 70 new states carved out of the old empires since 1945 is made up of nonwhite peoples newly out from under the political, economic and psychological domination of white rulers" and of people "stumbling blindly around trying to discern the new images, the new shapes and perspectives these changes have brought, to adjust to the painful rearrangement of identities and relationships which the new circumstances compel."[111] Official political leadership in the United States had fallen notoriously short, as the televised Watergate hearings made clear in 1973, and faith in government and expertise generally waned.[112] Amid accounts of social, cultural, political, economic, and environmental instability worldwide, the "me generation" of white middle-class Americans produced the culture of "self-help" and "New Age" theology against the alienation of a society that was, paradoxically, increasingly connected and atomized.[113]

That generation could see itself reflected in the 1978 remake of *Invasion of the Body Snatchers.* More than two decades after the pods invaded the idyllic town of Santa Mira, Kaufman's pods found root in the gritty, urbane world of San Francisco. His appropriately transformed cast of characters featured the morphing of the earnest small-town physician Miles Bennell into the ironic San Francisco public-health officer Matthew Benell, and of perky Becky Driscoll into his sophisticated co-worker, Elizabeth. The metamorphoses include Jack Belicec's reincarnation as an unappreciated writer who runs a mud-bath with his New Age wife, Nancy, and Mannie/Dan Kaufman's replacement by Leonard Nimoy's brilliantly executed, bestselling pop psychologist David Kibner. Reviewing this hip, campy, and self-referential film in the *New Yorker,* Pauline Kael proclaimed, "For its undiluted pleasure and excitement, it is . . . the American movie of the year—a new classic," possibly "the best movie of its kind ever made."[114] Commenting on Kaufman's brilliant direction, she describes his capture of a zeitgeist as well as a genre and a style. The success of this late-seventies renovation of the story of the body snatchers updated the mythic features of the apocalyptic battle for the survival of humanity as it incorporated them into the concerns of their moment. Kaufman drew out the medicalization of the pods and the epidemiological features of the story at a time when the WHO's conquest of communicable disease promised to be one successful global initiative in an age of massive transition, unrest, and uncertainty. Audiences who filed into theaters across the country to see Kaufman's renovated pods, however, could not have imagined how much the film forecast another mysterious epidemiological crisis—an invasion of sorts— that would soon hit San Francisco (along with New York and Los Angeles). Kaufman could not have predicted how uncannily his film would illuminate the assumptions that colored early accounts of the HIV/AIDS epidemic.

The opening shots create visual associations among several images, lingering on what Kael calls "diaphanous gelatinous spores" (48) against the backdrop of what emerges as a barren, uninhabited planet. The initial shot combines images of scientific expertise, resembling the view through an electron microscope of macrophages and viruses, which accounts of HIV would soon make all too familiar, and summoning the photographs that documented space exploration. The shot widens to chronicle the cosmic journey of the spores as they are blown from the barren landscape to drift through the universe, with a brief pause on an iconic shot of the earth from space: the blue planet, symbol of global interdependence. Disorienting cuts to the point of view of the spores shot at oblique angles mark their entrance into the earth's atmosphere. Time-lapse nature photography, such as was featured in *National Geographic* television specials, captures the pods' taking root amid the earth's flora. The dizzying cross-cutting between these close-ups of nature scenes and extreme long shots of the San Francisco skyline in this opening sequence establishes the "invasion" of the title in

ecological terms—a chance introduction of alien vegetation into an ecosystem—as it conditions the viewer to attend to subtle visual details. The
immediacy and aggression with which they take root suggests the dangerous hybridity of the intergalactic pods; lovely, pink blossoms emerge
that quickly sprout bright red, thrusting, podlike centers. Despite the visual
invocations of scientific expertise, science will prove useless at best in the
disorienting world of Kaufman's film.

Similarly disorienting cross-cuts and oblique angles show how the human world echoes the cosmic one. While pod conversions turn the warm
relationships of Santa Mira sinister, there is already an ominous quality to
the relationships in Kaufman's San Francisco, making it even harder to
recognize the pod conversions than in Siegel's film. A close-up introduces
Elizabeth as she picks one of the pod flowers; she is in a playground, and her
attention is first drawn to the flowers by a group of schoolchildren whose
teacher encourages them to pick them and take them home to their families. Rapid cuts place Elizabeth in a triangular relationship with the grimac-
ing teacher and a smirking priest on a swing set (Robert Duval in a cameo
appearance). Something has turned these trusted figures sinister, and the
canted shot that slants the houses on Elizabeth's block as she returns home
with the flower depicts a skewed world. Kaufman's direction, like that of his
predecessor, emphasizes a visual vocabulary of paranoia, which is augmented by the dissonant, edgy electronic musical score.[115]

The pods take root in a receptive environment. Elizabeth is intrigued to
discover that the strange plant may be a "grex," a hybrid produced by the
cross-pollination of two different species. Characterized by "rapid and
widespread growth" and often observed in the large war-torn cities of Europe, these adventitious botanical survivors seem to "thrive on devastated
ground."[116] If these hybrids were first observed in the postwar landscape of
Europe, the violence and excessive growth of the vegetative oddities suggest
a war-torn jungle landscape in the 1970s. They are certainly out of place in
San Francisco.

Neither Elizabeth nor her live-in boyfriend Geoffrey is distinctly visible
during the conversation in which she shows him her discovery. The scene is
shot through several doorways, and they appear primarily through the reflection on a French door. Geoffrey barely disguises his lack of interest in
Elizabeth's "grex," as she explains that such plants are often "epilobic, from
the Greek 'epi,' 'upon,' and 'lobos,' 'a pod.' . . . Many of the species are
dangerous weeds and should be avoided." The couple appears habituated to
their disconnection, and it is not surprising that Elizabeth inadvertently
brings the strange plant home—grex are dangerous only in a garden, she

The opening shot of Philip Kaufman's 1978 *Invasion of the Body Snatchers* suggests the view through an electron microscope.

assures Geoffrey—where she produces the conditions that will convert her boorish, disheveled dentist boyfriend into a well-groomed, unemotional pod person who will indeed become dangerous in his hybridity.

The disturbing interactions of the public-health officer Matthew Bennell (Donald Sutherland) complement Elizabeth's alienating domestic relations in their display of urban anomie. Bennell is introduced through a distorting fish lens (a peephole) as he engages in a surprise visit to a high-end restaurant, entering a hostile, duplicitous environment that presages his subsequent interactions in a changed world. The restaurant staff communicate among themselves wordlessly as Matthew argues with the manager about whether an "ingredient" of one of the dishes is a caper or, as Matthew insists, a "rat turd." Matthew returns to find his car window smashed by a wine bottle, and the scene heralds the pod world he will enter, first in the cold and menacing glare of two members of the kitchen staff, and then in a quick cut to a shadier figure watching through a dark window. Human relations are already in crisis in Kaufman's San Francisco.

Kaufman revels in the noir aesthetic, with relentless shots of darkened hallways, stairways, and alleys and cross-hatched shadows supplemented with even more sinister and visually taunting shots of distorted reflections in windows and mirrors and shadows falling at impossible angles. But powerfully informing this sinister world is a sense of exhaustion, which Kaufman conveys through cinematic mania. As Elizabeth and Matthew talk in Matthew's car, her efforts to persuade him that something has changed are punctuated by rapid crosscutting between her memories of the meetings between Geoffrey and strangers that she had witnessed as she followed him throughout the day and the images of people staring out of windows and doorways. The urbanity and wit of Matthew's banter and Kaufman's visual excesses are overlaid by a creepy sense of claustrophobia and conspiracy produced by

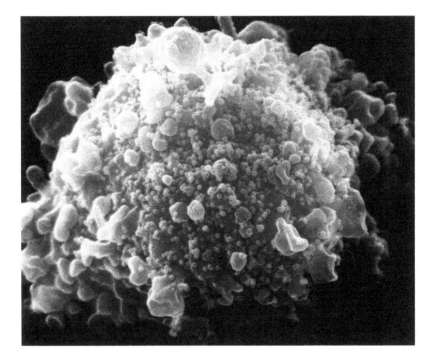

"INFECTED T CELL (a cell of the immune system) produces particles (*small spheres*) of the human immunodeficiency virus (HIV) in this image, made by David Hockley of the National Institute for Biological Standards and Control in England." The image resembles the spores in the opening of Kaufman's *Invasion of the Body Snatchers*. *Scientific American*, October 1988, 100. © NIBSC/Photo Researchers Inc.

tightly framed shots and the film's conspicuous acknowledgment of the iconic status of the story. In his attempt to comfort Elizabeth, Matthew begins to tell her a joke that he has told her before, but he is interrupted by a fleeting shot of Kevin McCarthy, the actor who had played Miles in Siegel's film, screaming the words with which the 1956 film was supposed to have ended: "They're coming! Help! Help! They're coming! Listen to me! Please! You're next! We're in danger! You're next! Please, listen to me! Something terrible—please! You're next! Here they are! They're already here! You're next! They're coming!" Fleeing a crowd like the one that had chased him onto the highway in the earlier film, McCarthy is hit and killed by a car. Shocked by the (non)reaction of the crowd, Matthew is drawn into the pod conspiracy. Later, when he and Elizabeth attempt unsuccessfully to flee San Francisco, Don Siegel is their cabdriver. These references create the sense of enclosed emplotment, of living within an unfolding story that has somehow already been told (like Matthew's joke, which he never finishes retelling).

They are also, however, in-jokes, and the retold, iconic story simultaneously expresses and offers an antidote for exhaustion. The film oscillates between wit and terror, which effectively keeps the audience off balance; it is hard to know if we are in on the joke or the object of it. The shifting perspective involves scientific expertise and cultural authority and turns on the contrast between the quirky Belicecs with their combination of New Age philosophy and conspiracy theories and Nimoy's hyperrational Kibner. Jeff Goldblum plays Jack with his characteristic comic mania, and Veronica Cartwright plays his wife with a charming warmth and earnest compassion, both of which contrast dramatically with Nimoy's emotional deadpan. The man of science's insistence that "people are changing. Becoming less human . . . all around us" deflects attention from the pod invasion. Dismissing any possibility of a literal explanation, he diagnoses the problem as cultural malaise: "People are stepping in and out of relationships too fast," he maintains, "because they don't want the responsibility. That's why marriages are going to hell. The whole family unit is shot to hell." When Elizabeth and others protest that their loved ones really have changed, Kibner diagnoses a "hallucinatory flu" that seems to be going around, and Matthew wonders if it is a public-health problem, asking the question that circulates throughout the film: is it contagious? To a late-1970s audience, an illness that confounded physical and psychological distinctions might invoke such strange ailments as chronic-fatigue syndrome that were similarly and controversially attributed to cultural (and generational) anomie. Again, the audience gets a wink, since Nimoy is best known for his role as Mr. Spock, the emotionless human-alien hybrid of the television drama *Star Trek*.[117] But the Belicecs get the last word—if not the last laugh.

Even the Belicecs are surprised when their over-the-top paranoia turns out to be not nearly paranoid enough. It is Nancy who actually identifies the source of the pod infection when she suggests that it could be the "space flowers" and worries that they "could start getting into our systems and screwing up our genes, like DNA, recombining us, changing us, . . . just the same way those rocket ships landed thousands of years ago so spacemen could mate with monkeys and apes and create the human race." Such is the cosmic joke of evolution.

Kaufman underscores the joke when the creepy Mr. Giannelli, who leaves the pod that almost steals Jack in the mud bath, conspicuously displays a copy of *Worlds in Collision*, a book he tells Nancy he knows she would enjoy. Published by Macmillan in 1950, the book, by Immanuel Velikovsky, a psychiatrist, argued that the repetition of ancient myths across cultures— especially about cosmic invasion—suggested that those myths were in fact repressed memories of catastrophic events that had been obscured by the assumptions of physics and astronomy. Velikovsky's intergalactic ecological analysis found a popular audience in the 1950s, including the "New York literati," concerned about the creeping scientism of their moment.[118] Maybe science did not have all the answers; maybe the urgency of catastrophe needed a fresh perspective. And maybe the almost compulsive retelling of the story of snatched bodies offered new insight into the problems if not the solutions of environmental exhaustion and cultural anomie.

Simultaneously spoofed and respected by the film, New Age Nancy directs the audience to that insight. Only she remains wakeful while the other protagonists sleep and is therefore able to alert Matthew to the process of pod reproduction. And only she is sufficiently attuned to her surroundings to figure out how to move among the pods undetected. Nancy alone remains unconverted at the end of the film when, hailing Matthew, she (and the audience) learns that he, too, has succumbed. The film ends as Nancy adds her human scream to the piercing, inhuman one that identifies Matthew as a pod person. Unlike Miles, Matthew does not hail the viewer, but the film itself does. The pod invasion turns the malaise in the film into an apocalyptic threat, setting the terms of a battle for humanity that, as Nancy resiliently demonstrates, is at least worth waging.[119]

In all of its incarnations, *Body Snatchers* is a story about alienation and dehumanization. By insisting on its epidemiological features, I do not mean to suggest that it is any more "about" viruses than it is "about" Communists or McCarthy conformists—or, as Matthew Bennell quips in Kaufman's version, "Republicans." It is, however, a story about a threat conceived as a public-health concern with medical and/or public-health personnel responsible for solving the mystery: an outbreak in search of a narrative. Epidemiological horror tells the story of that outbreak as the threat of an ecological "invasion" that produces dangerous hybrids and generates an apocalyptic battle for the fate of humanity. That framework, and the simultaneous terror and reaffirmation that it generates, herald the conventions of the outbreak narrative.

More than the San Francisco setting of Kaufman's *Invasion of the Body Snatchers* forecasts the climate of the earliest years of the HIV/AIDS epidemic. Kibner's smug dismissal of the actual threat posed by the pod people echoed the sanguinity of epidemiologists who had already begun to herald the end of communicable disease as a serious problem and turn their attention to social epidemics. With the increasing shift of epidemiology away from the exclusive study of outbreaks of physical ailments and toward widespread behavioral patterns, such as alcoholism and other drug abuse, domestic violence, and teenage suicide, epidemiologists lost their heroic edge; sociology did not make for risky, exciting disease detection.

The mysteries and terrors of the new epidemic would invigorate both the field of epidemiology and the evolving outbreak narrative, inflected by the conventions of epidemiological horror, which *Invasion of the Body Snatchers* helped to produce. The "disease" is spread in the story of *Body Snatchers* in all of its incarnations by carriers who do not appear as such. The storyline stresses simultaneously the lack of intentionality or malice involved in the initial introduction of the pods and the sense that the carriers *become* the infection, which they then transmit willfully. Through these deliberate disseminators, the pod infection becomes an "invasion," which inaugurates a struggle for the fate of humanity. The resonance between the conventions of epidemiological horror and those of scientific and mainstream accounts of the epidemic demonstrate not so much the influence of a particular story, but how the circulation of the conventional features through epidemiological narratives of all kinds shapes the outbreak narrative.[120] The familiarity of the genre of horror could recast the uncertainty of the ending of a movie such as *Invasion of the Body Snatchers* as a mythic struggle for humanity. The grim realities of a devastating communicable disease in the late-twentieth-century United States that genuinely challenged the authority of medical science offered no similar promise. Yet scientists and journalists striving to write the outbreak narrative of this elusive disease drew on the conventions. The social, scientific, and medical consequences of their efforts are an important part of the history of the epidemic and the emergence of the outbreak narrative.

"The Columbus of AIDS"

5 *Invasion of the Body Snatchers* seemed a fitting analog for the science writer Lance Morrow when he chronicled "The Start of a Plague Mentality" for *Time* magazine in 1985. The HIV/AIDS epidemic was growing at a breathtaking rate worldwide when he warned that the "plague mentality is something like the siege mentality, only more paranoid. In a siege, the enemy waits outside the walls. In a plague or epidemic, he lives intimately within. . . . Life slips into science fiction. People begin acting like characters in the first reel of *The Invasion of the Body Snatchers*. They peer intently at one another as if to detect the telltale change, the secret lesion, the sign that someone has crossed over, is not himself anymore, but one of them, alien and lethal."[1] Morrow was one of many cultural observers who worried that the fear generated by the epidemic was more socially disruptive than the virus. Fear of the disease led to paranoid social interactions. Yet his account conveyed more than the effect of that fear. Describing the suspicion as the belief that the infected had become "alien and lethal," he captured the fantasy of the transformative nature of devastating viruses, a fantasy that emerged from the conventions through which viruses were explained to the public. Implicit in those conventions was the monstrosity of the infected and their willful perpetuation of infection.

The human immunodeficiency virus jolted scientific researchers and medical practitioners out of their sanguinity. The new microbe represented a challenge they had not expected to face in the final decades of the twentieth century, when infectious disease was no longer supposed to pose a serious widespread health threat in the developed world. The newly identified retrovirus marked the hubris of contemporary medical science and terrified a public that had grown dependent on promises.[2]

The epidemic dramatically changed the prestige and funding of medical specialties. The belief that communicable disease would cease to threaten the health of the North in the late twentieth century had made it difficult for the area of infectious disease to draw the top researchers. Virology in particular, as Cindy Patton notes, was "considered highly specialized science, incapable of generating wide-ranging explanations for disease processes."[3] Theories of viral sources of cancer had kept some attention focused on the field, but nothing like the explosion of interest that followed the identification of the human immunodeficiency virus within the next decade. HIV/AIDS not only restored but augmented the attention and authority that had characterized virology during the Cold War.

The identification first of a mysterious new syndrome and then of its presumed viral source generated a need for explanatory narratives that could make scientific and social sense of the unexpected events becoming known as "the AIDS epidemic."[4] As Paula Treichler notes, one way of making "sense of a novel cultural phenomenon that is complicated, frightening, and unpredictable . . . involves framing the new phenomenon within familiar narratives, at once investing it with meaning and suggesting the potential for its control."[5] With the renewed interest in virology came its explanatory narratives and other conventions of representation. HIV/AIDS may have been new, but viruses and outbreaks were familiar features of human existence. Morrow drew on those conventions when he dubbed HIV a "bug" with "ambitions." In turn, scientific and mainstream media discussions of the epidemic contributed to the evolution of the narrative.

The ever-prescient William Burroughs seemed almost to have foretold the milieu into which the retrovirus surfaced in his novels from the 1950s, writing, in effect, a pre-biography of HIV/AIDS, not so much a prediction as an analysis of the cultural logic of the outbreak and its accompanying narratives. Having moved away from the virus theme following the trilogy, he returned to it in the introduction he wrote for *Queer*, his novel about a romantic same-sex obsession, when he finally published it in 1985. He had abandoned the book in the 1950s because his would-be publisher wanted him to omit the explicitly queer material, but by the mid-1980s, the literary landscape had radically changed, and his subject no longer shocked. With the HIV/AIDS epidemic, *Queer* had assumed a new dimension—tragic, ironic, heroic—and with the virology theme, Burroughs refashioned it as an AIDS novel. The epidemic reinvigorated Burroughs's insights about the dehumanizing effects of the virus of culture, which, having "gained access . . . uses the host's energy, blood, flesh and bones to make copies of itself."[6]

Neither *Queer* nor Burroughs's virus novels contributed to the pubic fashioning of a narrative of HIV/AIDS, but he became one of the earliest analysts of the epidemic as a cultural phenomenon. Treichler's observation that AIDS is an "epidemic of signification" is in the spirit of Burroughs, as is Douglas Crimp's insistence that "AIDS does not exist apart from the practices that conceptualize it, represent it, and respond to it. We know AIDS only in and through those practices."[7]

By contrast, Randy Shilts's 1987 controversial bestseller *And the Band Played On* brought the story of the early years of the epidemic to a mainstream audience and contributed significantly to an emerging narrative of HIV/AIDS. Shilts intended in his work, which the cover advertised as a "masterpiece of investigative reporting," to offer an analysis of the policies that facilitated the full-fledged epidemic. But the marketing strategies and the reviews make it clear that the popular appeal and much of the controversy of the book stem from his dramatic storytelling. And nowhere are the strategies and consequences of the story he tells more evident than in the story of the French Canadian airline steward Gaetan Dugas incarnated by Shilts, and thereby launched into notoriety, as "Patient Zero." The transformation of Gaetan Dugas into "Patient Zero" represented the animation of the virus, which, like the converted pod people, loosed the specter of a willful scourge.

"Patient Zero" is an "AIDS carrier," a term used in the medical, scientific, and journalistic discussions of HIV/AIDS despite its technical inaccuracy. AIDS is a syndrome, a constellation of opportunistic infections that the medical establishment believes to occur as the result of the human immunodeficiency virus's effect on the immune system. "AIDS," therefore, cannot be "carried" or transmitted. HIV can, and the distinction is more than semantic: it affects the perception and treatment of both the disease and those who test positive for the virus, with and without symptoms. The confusion, manifest in terms such as "AIDS carrier" and "AIDS virus," is evident in even the most reputable scientific and journalistic publications, attesting to Treichler's "epidemic of signification." "Patient Zero" as an "AIDS carrier" illustrates the impact of prior narratives, such as the story of "Typhoid Mary" and *The Invasion of the Body Snatchers*, on the effort to make sense of the experience of HIV/AIDS. The figure silently witnesses the evolution of the narrative; "he" testifies to its extensions and embodies its consequences. If for Geddes Smith the carrier brought contagion into the explanatory realm of the everyday, for Shilts "he" endowed it with the sinister agency of human retribution.

Shilts intended to analyze the factors that had enabled the outbreak to expand past the point of containment, but *And the Band Played On* attests to the strength of his desire, perhaps not entirely conscious, to write a story that would imagine its containment: to turn the outbreak into an outbreak narrative. "Patient Zero" was central to that project. Epidemiologically, the identification of an "AIDS carrier" had established the communicability of the syndrome (or of the microbes that caused it) and brought researchers closer to a solution. The identification of a virus generated a viral narrative: the source of the problem was a foreign agent whose behavior posed a threat to the body politic that required his excision. The story was told not only by Shilts but also in the journalistic and even scientific literature. And it was retold in the popular fiction and film that helped to make "Patient Zero" a mythic figure.

Humanity drains from the gay French Canadian flight attendant during the course of Shilts's story, as he metamorphoses into the familiar human-virus hybrid, haunting San Francisco's gay bathhouses, intent on "converting" as many unsuspecting victims as he can find. Like the virus, he was rapidly Africanized, as is evident in frequent misattributions in the mainstream media. An announcement of Shilts's forthcoming book in the *New York Times*, for example, which was headed "Canadian Said to Have Had Key Role in Spread of AIDS," explains that "in retracing the early spread of AIDS among gay men, the book says scientists suspect Mr. Dugas brought the AIDS virus to this country after having contracted it in Europe through sexual contacts with Africans."[8] Shilts in fact claims only that "Gaetan traveled frequently to France, the western nation where the disease was most widespread before 1980."[9] But the hybridity of "Patient Zero" and the presumed African origins of the disease unleashed narrative conventions of its own, and the story evolved.

With the evolution, however, the outbreak story began to shift away from the HIV/AIDS epidemic. Heroic epidemiologists populate Shilts's book, and following its publication, the mainstream media foretold the impending triumph of science over the virus. But the promised cures and vaccines were not forthcoming. By the 1990s, the disease was considerably more manageable in some parts of the world, but its continuing devastation illuminates social, economic, and political inequities worldwide. Despite considerable progress in the development of treatments, there is no endpoint from which to look back, not even the possibility of a projected closure that is necessary for an outbreak narrative. At the same time, as the epidemic now marks its age in decades rather than years, it is no longer possible to sustain the apocalyptic language that characterized the spread of the disease in its early years. Its long incubation period, moreover, erodes its dramatic potential, making it difficult to chronicle specific and immediate routes of contagion. HIV/AIDS is not well suited to the formula of an outbreak narrative. The legacy of Shilts's depiction of viral agency has not been evident in the considerable artistic output generated by the HIV/AIDS epidemic. AIDS narratives evolved instead into different kinds of stories, recounting, for example, the heroism of afflicted individuals in the face of adversity and the communities that form around them, as in Jonathan Demme's 1993 *Philadelphia* or Paul Monette's 1988 *Borrowed Time*: the tragedy of human suffering and the triumph of the human spirit, rather than the containment of the virus. Or, as in the case of *Rent* (1996) and *Angels in America* (1993, 1994), the drama of the disease may be in the service of broader social commentary, increasingly with a global focus.[10]

Following the heirs of "Patient Zero" actually leads away from the HIV/AIDS epidemic and into accounts of species-threatening outbreaks and even bioterrorism. They are the viral protagonists of popular fiction and film that deflect as they transpose anxieties about HIV/AIDS onto the apocalyptic scenarios of the infections emerging elsewhere, usually in Africa, although increasingly (with the publicity about SARS and avian flu) in Asia. Unlike with HIV/AIDS, when these fictional viruses erupt domestically, rather than just threatening to do so, they are quickly and heroically contained with help from the laboratory and as a result of the brilliant epidemiological detective work that is the cornerstone of the outbreak narrative. As these viruses literally assume human form, they give voice to the viral representations in Shilts's and other journalistic and scientific works, and they enact the story that those works could only imagine: the HIV/AIDS outbreak narrative.

INVENTING AN OUTBREAK:
THE LANGUAGE OF EPIDEMIOLOGY

Accounts of the earliest cases of AIDS feature the epidemiological feat of their identification. The syndrome presented in a variety of symptoms and was notoriously difficult to recognize. Shilts attributes its initial identification to a few conscientious and astute scientists: an alert CDC researcher who noticed an unusual number of requests for a drug to treat a rare form of pneumonia, a few physicians troubled by a strange array of symptoms in their gay male patients. Each new clue made epidemiologists fear that they were seeing "the tip of the iceberg" (a recurring phrase in their accounts) and hope that they were approaching answers that would lead to a cure. Against numbers that rose at an alarming rate, they fashioned stories that would help them to understand the mysterious illnesses and deaths. Written in the language of epidemiology, those stories shaped the cultural as well as scientific narratives of the early years of the epidemic.

The epidemic reinvigorated the field of epidemiology, bringing renewed attention to communicable-disease investigation. In 1985 the CDC announced a new course on applied epidemiology that featured training in how to collect data, recognize patterns, and fashion them into explanatory narratives. The description of that training shows how epidemiological narratives rely on conventions that facilitate the identification of an outbreak, but can also obscure relevant information. It illustrates, moreover, how those narratives can reproduce cultural conventions that influence scientific hypotheses.

Classification is a central part of epidemiological training, and one of the course's thirteen modules teaches participants "to categorize cases according to given definitions and select which categories to include in an analysis of a group of cases by time, place, and person."[11] The "given definitions" emerge from years of careful study of disease and public health; they inevitably reproduce assumptions about populations and social interactions that can be both helpful and restrictive. They register the cultural narratives that mediate experiences: the stories that are told, in a variety of media and forms, about the constitution of the social world and the relations that comprise it. Within the context of such stories, and the biases they perpetuate, Matthew Bennell and his companions must make sense of the events through which they are living in *Invasion of the Body Snatchers*. "Given definitions" help them to see that something is wrong, but also keep them from identifying the source of the problem. The description of the CDC course manifests an awareness of that challenge and includes a promise to train students "to formulate initial and refined definitions of their own." But looking past familiar categories is a difficult task, and the earliest narratives of any new disease will reflect assumptions about the location, population, and circumstances in which it is first identified.

The course description constitutes the epidemiologist as primarily an observer and reporter. The module on "Characterizing the Multiple-Case Outbreak" begins with the assertion that "any patterns that can be observed regarding time of onset of illness, possible exposures and personal features of the cases help to pinpoint an illness's agent, source, and means of transmission," and it promises to teach "participants to organize case data according to variables of time, place, and person so that these patterns can be easily identified and interpreted." The passive voice stresses the act of discovery: the patterns are there in the world to be identified. The grammar downplays both the role of the observer in inventing the patterns and the conventions that can make those patterns misleading. The emphasis on discovery and consequent obscuring of invention explains how the epidemiological construction of an outbreak narrative reproduces conventions that shape perceptions.

The early years of HIV/AIDS illustrate how the construction of a narrative about the outbreak at once facilitated and impeded the diagnosis of the problem. The syndrome first came to researchers' attention when they identified disease patterns in previously healthy young men who identified themselves (or who were identified by their doctors) as "homosexual." The patients' shared sexuality made the patterns more quickly visible to astute doctors and researchers and offered the earliest clues for them to follow. But the early identification of the syndrome as gay-related immunodeficiency (GRID) obscured cases that were surfacing among individuals who did not fit into the category of "homosexual man," which delayed important discoveries about the syndrome, including its transmissibility through sex between men and women and through blood transfusion. It also, of course, pathologized gay men, and, soon thereafter, it constituted HIV/AIDS as primarily transmitted sexually, which has continued to shape its depiction. Even when other populations were (quickly) identified among the afflicted (and also pathologized in the United States), including Haitians, intravenous-drug users, and hemophiliacs, the public and even researchers often found it difficult to abandon the earliest assumptions about the disease. The early years of the epidemic illustrate both the utility and the danger involved in identifying patterns and in incorporating them into an outbreak narrative.

The narrative emerged first in specialty publications and then, more sensationally, in the mainstream media. The CDC's publication *Morbidity and Mortality Weekly Report* (*MMWR*) carried the initial harbinger of the outbreak on 5 June 1981. The report noted a confirmed diagnosis of *Pneumocystis* pneumonia (PCP), typically seen in immune-compromised individuals, in "5 young men, all active homosexuals" between October 1980 and May 1981 at three Los Angeles area hospitals.[12] The men did not know each other, and they had no sexual or casual contacts in common; they shared only their same-sex object choices, their use of inhalant drugs, and the city of Los Angeles. Characteristic of the *MMWR*, the report was descriptive but not speculative, suggesting only "the possibility of a cellular-immune dysfunction related to a common exposure that predisposes individuals to opportunistic infections such as pneumocystosis and candidiasis" (251). It identified gay men as the afflicted population, however, alerting healthcare workers to suspect PCP when "previously healthy homosexual males" presented with certain upper-respiratory symptoms (251).

A month later, in early July, the *MMWR* reported the appearance of Kaposi's sarcoma (KS) and PCP in twenty-six gay men in New York City and California during the previous thirty months. The ten new cases of PCP identified in the article meant "that the 5 previously reported cases were not an isolated phenomenon," and the cluster suggested an outbreak, although the authors of the report declared it too soon to determine "if or how the clustering of KS, pneumocystis, and other serious disease in homosexual men is related."[13] The report was restrained, but it was clear that the authors found the sexuality of the patients too compelling to ignore. While they conceded that it was not certain that only gay men were affected, that group comprised the "vast majority" of reported cases, and the report cautioned physicians to "be alert for Kaposi's sarcoma, Pneumocystis pneumonia, and other opportunistic infections associated with immunosuppression in homosexual men" (307).

The lead author of the July report, the New York dermatologist Alvin E. Friedman-Kien, also published a more detailed account in the *Journal of the American Academy of Dermatology*, where he speculated about what he called the "intriguing" question of the appearance of this particular form of KS "in a highly sexually active segment of the male homosexual subpopulation."[14] The appearance of the disease was surprising because it typically affected elderly men, often of Mediterranean descent, in a less invasive and less aggressive form. Friedman-Kien expressed his reluctance to posit a contagious etiology, noting that "so far only four of forty-one of these KS patients admitted to having had transient, intimate sexual contact with other men in this KS group." But with an immediate "however," he signaled his conviction that gay male sexuality was likely to be involved, since "most of the patients often *indulged* in anonymous sexual activities at gay bathhouses, bars, clubs, and gay resort areas" (469; emphasis added). Less restrained than in the *MMWR* report, he posited "the evolution of a new syndrome of epidemic proportions" and enjoined physicians to "be particularly concerned with their patients' sexual orientation so that they can be better prepared to look for possible immunologic defects, genetic susceptibility and related problems" (469). As he heralded the outbreak, he used the principles of epidemiology to begin to fashion an outbreak narrative. His belief that the common gender and sexuality of the afflicted held the clue to their affliction led him to posit sex as the means of transmission. The embellishments that he added with the word *indulged* and the characterization of the patients' sexual comportment offer insight into how stereotypes and cultural narratives subtly infuse scientific hypotheses.

The coincidences were already too compelling to ignore and generated theories about the strange new syndrome. The three featured articles of the 10 December issue of the *New England Journal of Medicine* later that year reported on the acquired immunodeficiency in male homosexuals and, in one of the pieces, male drug abusers. The population was certainly relevant to theories about the etiology of the syndrome, suggesting to the authors of the first report "that a sexually transmitted infectious agent or exposure to a common environment has a critical role in the pathogenesis of the immunodeficient state. Sexually transmitted infections . . . are highly prevalent in the male homosexual community."[15] The proliferation of reported cases convinced the authors of one of the other articles that their findings were "part of a nationwide epidemic of immunodeficiency among male homosexuals."[16] An account of these three articles comprised the sole mention of the syndrome in the *New York Times* in 1981.

By the spring of the following year, speculation had turned into a pronouncement of a full-blown "epidemic." By that time, the categories were starting to unravel. While the titles of the earliest accounts in the MMWR announced the identification of a pattern of symptoms "among homosexual males," the 11 June 1982 issue offered an "update on Kaposi's sarcoma and opportunistic infections in *previously healthy persons*."[17] Yet, the persistence of the category that seemed to offer the most powerful clue to epidemiologists is evident in the editorial notes of the report explaining that "sexual orientation information was obtained from patients by their physicians, and the accuracy of reporting cannot be determined; therefore, comparisons between KSOI [KS and (other) opportunistic infections] cases made on the basis of sexual orientation must be interpreted cautiously" (301). Similarities among the cases prompted a "laboratory and interview study of heterosexual patients with diagnosed KS, PCP, or other OI . . . to determine whether their cellular immune function, results of virologic studies, medical history, sexual practices, drug use, and life-style are similar to those of homosexual patients" (301). The categories of inquiry continued to be determined by the "population" in whom doctors had first noticed the symptoms. Because it offered the strongest clues about the nature of the infection, that classification was hard for researchers to relinquish.

The tenacity of the classification is evident in the earliest accounts in the mainstream press as well. The 1981 *New York Times* piece that reported on the "cluster of cases in which usually harmless viruses and bacteria can produce illness, *almost exclusively* among homosexual men" cited the cautionary words of Frederick P. Siegal, an immunologist and lead author of one of the *New England Journal of Medicine* pieces from that year, who noted that "it may be premature to say it is a homosexual disease. . . . Whatever the inciting agent is is simply more widely dispersed in that population."[18] Yet the piece also claimed that "studies have shown homosexual men are more susceptible to sexually transmitted disease," and the headline proclaimed, "Homosexuals Found Particularly Liable to Common Viruses."

When the syndrome was next mentioned in the *New York Times*, the following May, the headline announced, "New Homosexual Disorder Worries Health Officials."[19] In this lengthy piece, Lawrence K. Altman explained that researchers have named the disorder "A.I.D., for acquired immunodeficiency disease, or GRID, for gay-related immunodeficiency," but he employed the latter acronym throughout the article. In spelling it out, he dropped the word *disease* (the "d" came from the embedded *deficiency*), as though the immunodeficiency were not the result of an acquired disease, but an outcome of homosexuality itself. The message of the piece is alarm over an epidemic that represents "'just the tip of the iceberg'" (c1), tempered by reassurance that the syndrome "seems to result from an accumulation of risk factors," is not readily contagious, and need not be feared by "the general public" (c6). Nonetheless, the uncertainty about the cause of the syndrome, and the horror of its effects as it shut down the immune system, coupled with words such as *epidemic* and *outbreak*, set the stage for the drama of a major discovery.

THE NON-CALIFORNIAN

The discovery was announced in the 18 June *MMWR*, just one week after the "update" on the immune-system collapse "in previously healthy persons." Earlier accounts had speculated about the infectiousness of the disorder, but always with the disclaimer that the afflicted "had no known contact with each other, had no known sexual partners in common, and had no known contact with patients" suffering from its effects.[20] This account reported on a cluster study of KS and PCP among gay men in southern California (Los Angeles and Orange Counties). The study was precipitated by "an unconfirmed report of possible associations among cases in southern California."[21] Here at last was the break for which epidemiologists had been waiting: the cluster study finally brought an unidentified infectious agent to center stage by demonstrating connections among person, place, and time. Epidemiologists could finally begin to fashion a narrative of the outbreak. "Within 5 years of the onset of symptoms," the report announced, "9 patients (6 with KS and 3 with PCP) had had sexual contact with other patients with KS and PCP" (305). A breakdown of the contacts follows, and with it the significant detail that "2 [patients] from Orange County had had sexual contact with 1 patient who was not a resident of California" (305).

The report established the direct links among nine patients from Los Angeles and Orange counties as "part of an interconnected series of cases that may include 15 additional patients (11 with KS and 4 with PCP) from 8 other cities. The non-Californian with KS mentioned earlier is part of this series" (306). It was the first mention of the figure who would become "Patient Zero." The report remained tentative about the inferences of the data, asserting no more than that "one hypothesis consistent with the observations reported here is that infectious agents are being sexually transmitted among homosexually active males" (306), an assertion that had been advanced from the earliest observations of the disorder. Nonetheless, it marked the beginning of an important change of focus, registered in the altered language of subsequent accounts. The conviction that an infectious agent caused the syndrome intensified the search for the agent and inflected the emerging outbreak narrative. The "non-Californian" was important to the infectious-agent theory, and his transformation into "Patient Zero" would be central to the narrative.

The next day, a *New York Times* headline blazoned, "Clue Found on Homosexual's Precancer Syndrome." The article's author, Lawrence K. Altman, informed readers that epidemiologists had found new evidence to suggest that "the outbreak" of the mysterious syndrome was "linked to an infectious agent." While the CDC epidemiologist Harold Jaffe underscored that the discovery did not imply a solution, he explained that it offered proof that the disorder was "'not occurring as a random event among homosexual men'" and that it had prompted "'scientists at the Atlanta facilities'" to intensify "'laboratory efforts to identify a virus, bacteria or other micro-organism as a possible cause.'"[22] For Cindy Patton, the new emphasis resulted from a change in interpretation and perspective rather than in data, and she located the triumph of virology in "greater financial and scientific [rather than explanatory] power." She argued that "the same AIDS epidemiological studies which immunologists saw as evidence for a social or environmental cause of AIDS" showed virologists "evidence of a sexually transmissible pathogen. . . . [I]n AIDS, etiological agent and immune system breakdown theories were brought into line via the discovery of an agent which 'attacked,' or more accurately, disarmed the immune system."[23] The story could certainly be told in multiple ways, and the narrative choices indeed affected the approach and outcome. Yet, as Patton and Emily Martin both noted, in the decade preceding the identification of HIV/AIDS, immunologists enjoyed more explanatory power and prestige than virologists.[24] The emerging story registered a complex interplay of factors, and the discovery of an infectious agent for AIDS was dramatically transformational. Not since the polio epidemics of the 1950s had an outbreak in North America generated such widespread fear.

The early years of the epidemic illustrate the mutual influence of scientific discoveries, socioeconomic factors, and cultural biases as well as the impact of the narratives they generate. The June announcement of a likely infectious agent in both scientific and mainstream publications unleashed the power of the outbreak narrative and, with it, the triumph of virology that Patton describes. Faced with a terrifying mystery, Altman reassured his readers that the disorder was not random and that a responsible agent would be identified in the laboratory. While the familiar features of an outbreak narrative laid the groundwork for the acceptance of the infectious-disease hypothesis, the contours of that narrative, in turn, were fleshed out by the theory and augmented by the discovery of the virus. Virology henceforth dominated both the research field and the treatment options, and Patton is justified in her lament that "virology's assumption that a virus can simply be eliminated or blocked . . . misdirected research efforts for . . . years, denying thousands of people potential therapies which could have prolonged or improved the quality of their lives."[25] It also imported a vocabulary that would shape perceptions of the disorder and the people it affected.

With the discovery of a virus that attacked the immune system came the renewal of language that had largely gone out of fashion with the Cold War. One of the earliest accounts from 1981, Friedman-Kien's piece in the *Journal of the American Academy of Dermatology*, had described patients' apparently "defective immunologic surveillance mechanisms of defense that render them more susceptible to such infections."[26] The proliferation of scientific and popular accounts of the syndrome in 1983 carried tales of exploding immune systems with detailed descriptions of the consequences of the lowered surveillance. The battle that was AIDS entailed the penetration of the familiarly *wily, crafty, sinister* invader, but this one, with particular cruelty, disabled the very defense mechanisms needed for the fight, leaving the body completely susceptible to all of the other marauders responsible for the physical devastation that constituted the syndrome.

Military metaphors abounded to explain both the psychological and physical experience of AIDS. A 1982 *Newsweek* article cited the early AIDS activist and playwright Larry Kramer's comparison of life as "'a gay man in New York'" at the time to "'living in London during the blitz, when you didn't know when the next bomb would strike.'"[27] It was the ur-virus, the epitome and king of what one writer dubbed "Supergerms: The New Health Menace." Neither the menace, nor the language was new, but it was noteworthy that "after four decades of medical victories, infectious agents [were] striking back with new intensity between human beings and contagious diseases."[28] Military language was familiar to the medical world in the 1980s. Most notably, Richard Nixon's declaration of a "war on cancer" had helped to refocus approaches to and funding for cancer research in the previous decade. But the language that introduced the "mysterious new killers, such as acquired immune deficiency syndrome (AIDS)" and the "elusive killer" lurking in the recesses of the body's defense mechanisms, resurrected the viral foe of the 1950s.[29] The language jumped from virus to host. The viral "suspects" for which the NIH researcher Anthony Fauci described the search were microbial agents, but they readily took human form in the "rumors" of unnamed victims who were "purposely trying to infect as many others as possible."[30]

The incarnation of the threat in gay men was no surprise to those who were familiar with homophobia in the United States. Haitians, intravenous-drug users, and hemophiliacs, designated as belonging to "risk categories" in the summer and fall of 1982, were incorporated into the viral equation, with an accompanying interchange of features for the emerging viral-human hybrid.[31] Those most at risk became perpetrators through vivid descriptions of their interactions, such as the "network" described in the *New Republic* in the summer of 1983, "where thousands of people [were] interacting sexually [which offered] as rich an environment for the dissemination of disease as one could possibly imagine."[32] Promiscuity, the intermingling of bodily fluids of all kinds, created a disease environment that materialized the much-foretold collapse of civilization; "risk groups" were the enemies within.

Stigmatizing is a form of isolating and containing a problem, such as a devastating epidemic. It is also a means of restoring agency—which, as in the rumors of willful infectors, melts into intentionality—in the face of the utter banality of the foe. Nothing better illustrated the strategy or the scientific, medical, and social consequences than the fate of Gaetan Dugas.

"PATIENT 0" AND THE CARRIER DISEASE

The arduous journey that took researchers from the hypothesis of infectivity to the identification of an actual agent was depicted in terms as heroic as Miles's and Becky's last stand against the pods. With mounting hope and desperation, public attention turned to "America's disease detectives, whose special calling it is to track invisible killers, to identify mysterious illnesses that erupt from nowhere to menace life and health," the "elite cadre of . . . experts—pathologists and epidemiologists, assisted by a larger army of lab technicians and doctors—. . . coordinating their skills in an effort to conquer any new threat: Acquired Immune Deficiency Syndrome, the confounding killer known as AIDS."[33] The invisible killer had a name. Soon it would acquire a face and a human form.

A 1984 *American Journal of Medicine* piece represented an important step in the creation of the narrative and the figure of the carrier. It reported the results of a study that pursued the sexual links suggested by the cluster of cases noted in the 18 June 1982 issue of *MMWR* and confirmed the "epidemiologic information suggest[ing] that an infectious agent may cause AIDS." The "non-Californian" figures more prominently in this report, which names him into a new identity as an epidemiological index case with the claim that "AIDS developed in four men in southern California after they had sexual contact with a non-Californian, Patient 0."[34] The numerical discrepancy between this report and the original study can be attributed to the continuing investigations in which epidemiologists had pursued the links of "the non-Californian" and acquired more information.[35] A more significant difference between the reports is the change in the temporality and causality implied by the word *after*. While in the first piece the patients reported having had sex with the non-Californian, the four men in the second piece developed AIDS *after* (and presumably because of) having had sex with him.

The 1984 account begins to confer a specific identity and role in viral transmission on the non-Californian, which the researchers signal by naming him "Patient 0." A diagram that accompanies the article corroborates this transformation. The diagram shows forty linked circles, each representing "an AIDS patient" and identified by place (Los Angeles, New York City, or a state), number, and disease. At the center is a black circle (for KS) marked simply "0." The discussion following the introduction of "Patient 0" explains that he developed lymphadenopathy, a chronic swelling of the lymph nodes usually associated with disease and a characteristic harbinger of AIDS, in December 1979 and was diagnosed with KS the following May. He could name seventy-two of his 750 sexual partners between 1979 and 1981, which enabled investigators to discover that eight of them—four each from New York and Los Angeles—had diagnosable AIDS. "Because Patient 0 appeared to link AIDS patients from southern California and New York City," the researchers "extended [their] investigation beyond the Los Angeles–Orange County metropolitan area. Ultimately, [they] were able to link forty AIDS patients by sexual contact to at least one other reported patient" (489). The diagram represents the linkages, visually placing "Patient 0" at the center of the forty cases. It means only that he is the epidemiological index, the case from whom they tracked other cases; he is central to their tentative conclusions.

Following the initial introduction of "Patient 0," the language of the report highlights the speculative nature of those conclusions: he "*appeared* to link" the Los Angeles and New York cases; he is a "*possible* source" of the disease in several other patients (490; emphasis added). The comments at the end of the report include the observations that AIDS "*may* be caused by an infectious agent that is transmissible from person to person in a manner analogous to hepatitis B virus infection," that the "existence of a cluster of AIDS cases linked by homosexual contact *is consistent with* an infectious-agent hypothesis," that the "cluster *may* represent a group of homosexual men who were brought together by a common interest in sexual relations with many different partners or in specific sexual practices, such as manual-rectal intercourse," and that *if* "the infectious-agent hypothesis is true, Patient 0 *may* be an example of a 'carrier' of such an agent" (490; emphasis added). The account of the study in the *New York Times* introduced him only as "a homosexual man who may have been a carrier of the disease, spreading it across the country without knowing he had it." It included the CDC epidemiologist Bill Darrow's conjecture that the man whom he and his colleagues called "Patient 0 picked up the syndrome from a contact in Los Angeles or New York and carried it across the country to the others."[36] It

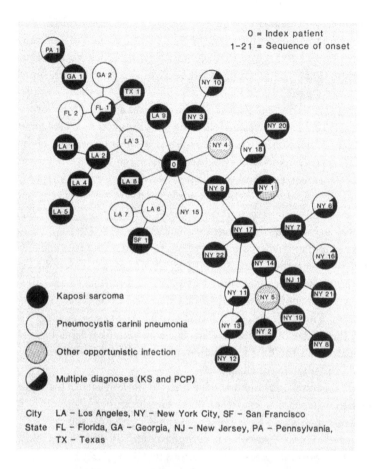

0 = Index patient
1-21 = Sequence of onset

PA 1
GA 1   GA 2
        TX 1
FL 2   FL 1   NY 10
            LA 9   NY 3
                            NY 20
    LA 1   LA 3   NY 4   NY 18
        LA 2   0
    LA 4   LA 8   NY 9   NY 1
LA 5   LA 7   LA 6   NY 15   NY 6
                                NY 7
        SF 1   NY 17
                NY 22   NY 16
                    NY 14
                        NJ 1
        Kaposi sarcoma   NY 11   NY 5   NY 21

        Pneumocystis carinii pneumonia   NY 19
                            NY 13   NY 2
        Other opportunistic infection   NY 8

        Multiple diagnoses (KS and PCP)   NY 12

City   LA – Los Angeles, NY – New York City, SF – San Francisco
State   FL – Florida, GA – Georgia, NJ – New Jersey, PA – Pennsylvania,
        TX – Texas

"Sexual contacts among homosexual men with AIDS. Each circle represents an AIDS patient. Lines connecting the circles represent sexual exposures. Indicated city or state is place of residence of a patient at the time of diagnosis. '0' indicates Patient 0 (described in text)." Reprinted from D. M. Auerbach, W. W. Darrow, H. W. Jaffe, and J. W. Curran, "Cluster of Cases of the Acquired Immune Deficiency Syndrome: Patients Linked by Sexual Contact," *American Journal of Medicine*, vol. 76 (March 1984): 488. © 1984, with permission from Elsevier.

was nonetheless big news, since the definitive existence of these connections—and of a Patient 0—would establish an infectious agent as well as the network of sexual interactions.

Despite the proliferation of qualifications in the medical journal and in the *New York Times*, the initial introduction of "Patient 0," and especially his christening as "Patient 0" and the accompanying diagram, would eventually lead to his depiction as the index case and the cause at least of the forty-person cluster of AIDS cases. In subsequent accounts of this study, "Patient 0" would gradually metamorphose from an epidemiological index case (the source of the study) to the index case and source of "North American AIDS." The transformation lacks scientific validity. The numerous sexual partners reported by many people with AIDS, which had been widely remarked on in the scientific and mainstream media, combined with the lengthy latency period that the evidence increasingly demonstrated, would make it impossible to pinpoint an exact source even for most of the cases recorded on the chart. Even if the onset of AIDS symptoms followed the patient's sexual contact with "Patient 0," it would be difficult to demonstrate direct causality.

The language and images in the study, however, work against its explicit claims, showing how the positing and tracking of a "Patient 0" led to a diagram of and eventually to a narrative about forty ostensibly linked cases of AIDS. Returning to the first study that began to bring the variables of person, place, and time into focus, the study develops the narrative, fleshing out the non-Californian as its main character, simultaneously the epidemiological index case and the archetypal carrier of AIDS. Following the incarnation of "Patient 0" as a carrier in the report, the researchers explain that the "existence of an asymptomatic carrier state of AIDS has been suggested by a report of AIDS-like illness in an infant who had received a platelet transfusion from a man who had no symptoms when he donated blood, but had AIDS eight months later."[37] But if, as they suggest, an infectious agent causes AIDS and the disorder has a long incubation period, then everyone who gets AIDS has presumably been an asymptomatic carrier and then becomes an ailing transmitter. So what distinguishes "Patient 0"?

As illustrated in the diagram, his most distinctive feature is his geographical designation. While every other AIDS case in the diagram is marked by city or state, he is just "0," the absence of place: the non-Californian. The designation prepares him to become the viral incarnation coming in from somewhere else and initiating an outbreak in the United States. Despite the qualifications in the report and the *New York Times*, the lay public, and even many in the scientific and medical communities, failed to distinguish between the epidemiological index and the index case of an epidemic. Randy Shilts was one of them, and with the publication of his journalistic account of the early years of the epidemic, the distinction would be lost. In 1987 the public would learn that "Patient 0" was a French Canadian flight attendant who had traveled to Haiti and who may have brought HIV/AIDS to North America from France. It was in 1987, in other words, that the public would have its flesh-and-blood index case/carrier and its full-fledged carrier—and would-be outbreak—narrative.

The intervening years had witnessed the intensified animation of the newly identified retrovirus in the popular press and a renewed attention to viral mechanisms in the popular media. Announcing the presumed discovery of a viral cause of AIDS by U.S. and French teams, a *Time* magazine piece entitled "Knowing the Face of the Enemy" explained how viruses "infiltrate a host cell and commandeer its reproductive machinery."[38] The piece was accompanied by a diagram of tanks invading a building and taking over its construction. Calling it "the toughest virus of all," another writer deplored "the virus' Machiavellian tactics," by which he meant the rapid mutations of the retrovirus that forestalled the development of an HIV vaccine.[39] The animation amplified the association of the virus with gay men. "Now that the Disease Has Come Out of the Closet," asked another *Time* headline, "How Far Will It Spread?"[40] Readers learned that "the AIDS virus . . . 'turns the T cell off from being a lymphocyte and on to being an AIDS-virus factory'" (42). Citing a study from the journal *Cell*, the author of the article, Claudia Wallis, explained "that the virus has a unique genetic component that allows it to reproduce itself a thousand times as fast as any other kind of virus. . . . It is a peculiar feature of this disease that as it progresses, the helper T cells disappear and so does the virus. By then, however, the patient is invariably beyond recovery" (42). The link established by the title suggested a connection between the rapidly producing and devastating virus, a "'formidable adversary'" (47), and the mainstream (and often scientific) media depictions of the reviled promiscuity of its allegedly suicidal and/or homicidal gay male hosts.

THE FINAL METAMORPHOSIS

The incarnation of the viral-human (gay male) hybrid with sinister intentions was complete when "Patient 0" became "Patient Zero"/Gaetan Dugas.

Shilts intended to show how homophobia, self-interest, personal ambitions, profit motives, and misguided politics prevented the immediate response that could have contained the epidemic and to indict politicians, the mainstream media, academic scientists, and even some gay activist groups for the failure. But his effort to understand—and imagine an endpoint for—HIV/AIDS led to a shift in his account. As "Patient 0" was central to the epidemiologists' effort to argue for an infectious etiology for AIDS, "Patient Zero" was key to the story that Shilts hoped to write.

Shilts recognized in the epidemiological investigation the drama that would make his analysis widely readable. The CDC task force that handled the epidemic comprises some of his most heroic characters in *And the Band Played On*. Their discovery of Gaetan Dugas is a turning point in their investigation. During an interview with an "ailing hairdresser" in Orange County, two members of the task force are interested to hear him invoke an airline steward, named Gaetan Dugas, who gave him hepatitis and to muse, "'I bet he gave me this new disease, too'" (130). Shilts lingers in his story over the meaningful look exchanged by the CDC researchers. "Finally," he writes, "Auerbach and Darrow had a live person telling them he had had sex with this flight attendant. It was, Darrow said later, one of the most significant moments of the epidemic. The ball had dropped on the game show" (130). Darrow looks back in this passage as if from the endpoint of the epidemic, deciding what in retrospect constituted its most significant moments: the identification of Gaetan Dugas as "Patient Zero" is the ball at the end of the game show.

Previews of the book overwhelmingly featured accounts of "Patient Zero," and his exposure as Gaetan Dugas, to advertise the forthcoming work; few reviews of the book failed to mention him and many headlined him. In an interview with a *Washington Post* reporter, when asked about the reaction to his book, Shilts called the attention to Gaetan Dugas "the great irony. Here I've done 630 pages of serious AIDS policy reporting," he complained, "with the premise that this disaster was allowed to happen because the media only focus on the glitzy and sensational aspects of the epidemic. My book breaks, not because of the serious public policy stories, but because of the rather minor story of Patient Zero."[41] It is hard to imagine that Shilts really did not recognize the importance of his character. He weaves him throughout the story, tracking his movements as he depicts his increasing recalcitrance and malevolence. Reviewers singled him out as exemplary of, in Sandra Panem's words, the "sensationalist and seductive devices and gossip, as well as facile writing [that] draw the reader into the book."[42] And a

1995 review of Laurie Garrett's *The Coming Plague* in the *Boston Globe*, which compared Garrett favorably to Shilts, nonetheless noted that her work lacks "the whodunit pizzazz of Patient Zero."[43] The phrase captures both the appeal and the role of the "Patient Zero" story in Shilts's book.

The portrait of "Patient Zero" conforms to the storyline of early carrier narratives. Dubbing Gaetan Dugas "the Québecois version of Typhoid Mary" (157), Shilts explicitly evokes the earlier story, and it is remarkable how much this alleged index case behaviorally resembles his predecessor. Despite being told that he " '*may* be passing [the immunodeficiency] around' " (136; emphasis added), Dugas allegedly refuses to change his behavior. To his doctor's suggestion that he give up sex or at least avoid exchanging bodily fluids, Shilts's Dugas responds in a voice that "betray[s] a fierce edge of bitterness[,] 'Of course, I'm going to have sex. . . . Nobody's proven to me that you can spread cancer' " (138). In Shilts's account the airline steward never fully accepts the reality of the syndrome, insisting that he has cancer (KS) and that cancer is not known to be communicable.

Like "Typhoid Mary," this recalcitrant "carrier" found himself at the center of public-health debates about the conflict of rights: his right to make his own choices and the right of other individuals to be safeguarded. He embodied the dilemma and crystallized the debate. But Shilts demonized Dugas even more than Soper vilified Mary Mallon, and the press responded accordingly. The review of the book for the *Washington Post* observed that "Dugas is a character who would have had to be invented did he not already exist."[44] I am arguing that "Patient Zero" was invented, that the transformation of the Canadian flight attendant with the HIV virus into "Patient Zero" was a necessary component of the effort to write an HIV/AIDS outbreak narrative and that this transformation had scientific and medical as well as social consequences. Describing the motivations of one gay activist, Shilts ventriloquized, "There was a deadly enemy out there. The fucking thing didn't even have a name" (161). Gaetan Dugas gave it a name.

Shilts amplifies the conventional journalistic depictions of the virus in his descriptions of HIV. The virus *invades* and *penetrates*; it is a *killer* (49), a "viral culprit" breeding "international death" (389), a "guilty virus" (451), "the nastiest microbe humanity had encountered in centuries, if not in all of human history" (552), a "horribly cruel and insidious virus" (621). And its human embodiment is vindictive, allegedly telling doctors and friends that he has no obligation to protect others because someone had given it to him. He steps right into the rumors and urban legends (already circulating in the press) as reports began in the Castro of "a strange guy at the Eighth and

Howard bathhouse, a blond with a French accent. He would have sex with you, turn up the lights in the cubicle, and point out his Kaposi's sarcoma lesions. 'I've got gay cancer,' he'd say. 'I'm going to die and so are you' " (165). Selma Dritz, the infectious-disease specialist of San Francisco's public-health department and one of the heroes of Shilts's account, finds the story of Dugas's behavior "one of the most repulsive things [she] had heard in her nearly forty years in public health" (200). Because of these stories he enters the mainstream press as "an avenging angel, deliberately infecting everyone he could find with the disease that was killing him"; he is "an airline steward carrying a disease and a grudge," a "missing link, the human explosive whose promiscuous presence may have triggered an epidemic beyond his imagining," or, as the *National Review* christened him, "the Columbus of AIDS."[45]

With Dugas's introduction near the beginning of the account, Shilts ominously describes how, "when the researchers started referring to Gaetan Dugas simply as Patient Zero, they would retrace the airline steward's travels during that summer, fingering through his fabric-covered address book to try to fathom the bizarre coincidences and the unique role the handsome young steward performed in the coming epidemic" (23). It is hard to know exactly to what "unique role" refers; for in Shilts's narrative Dugas plays more than one: he is—or *may be*—the index case who brought HIV to North America, the unwitting carrier whose sexual practices and occupation (flight attendant) make him an especially efficient vector, the recalcitrant disseminator who embodies the public-health dilemma and the malevolence of the virus itself. With all of these roles, it is difficult not to see Dugas as primarily a narrative device. And Shilts certainly takes poetic license when he imagines Dugas's thoughts, as when the flight attendant contemplates his troubled past while examining himself in a steamy mirror of a San Francisco bathhouse (196).[46] There are no historical records that document exactly what Dugas thought or did in private. And his uncanny conformity to prior narratives of carriers and journalistic descriptions of the virus intimate some of the ways in which Shilts's depiction has been shaped by them.

His status as index case of the AIDS epidemic in the United States is easier to disprove than his motivations. Nothing in the pieces in the 1982 *MMWR* or the 1984 *American Journal of Medicine* actually supports his designation as an index case of the disease, and as Panem points out in her review for *Science*, "Anyone knowledgeable knows that to pin a global epidemic on the actions of a single individual is absurd."[47] It is, in fact, unimaginable that if

HIV entered the United States from without, it did not arrive in multiple hosts. Lack of documentation of the earliest cases and an unpredictable incubation period would make it impossible to pinpoint a single index case. Even Shilts concedes that "whether Gaetan Dugas actually was the person who brought AIDS to North America remains a question of debate and is ultimately unanswerable" (439). Yet he goes on to insist on the details that give "weight to the theory" (439). Clearly, the Québecois-airline-steward-turned-viral-invader serves an important function in the narrative. If the transformation of Gaetan Dugas into "Patient Zero," like that of Mary Mallon into "Typhoid Mary," demonizes the "carrier," it also humanizes the virus; it gives it agency and makes it comprehensible, attributing to it human emotions and responses. The metamorphosis represents the authority of epidemiology and confers that authority on the storyteller. Shilts harnesses the transformative power of medicine and epidemiology and of the disease itself (which, after all, performed the initial transformation) to a narrative that makes sense of that disease. The book and the character captured the imagination of a public very much in need of that sense-making, even if it meant believing in monsters.

"THE GLOBAL-VILLAGE DISEASE"

Shilts casts the emergence of the microbe as the opening scene of a 1950s science-fiction horror movie: "It was November 1, 1980," he writes, "the beginning of a month in which single frames of tragedy in this and that corner of the world would begin to flicker fast enough to reveal the movement of something new and horrible rising slowly from the earth's biological landscape" (41).[48] The description registers key features of the outbreak narrative. The image turns the virus primordial and monstrous and suggests its global reach. It becomes apparent through (metaphoric) visual technologies: single frames flickering fast enough to capture movement and signal emergence. With this image, Shilts evokes the conventions of epidemiological horror to tell the story of the origin of HIV/AIDS, constructing the primordial monster as the ancestor of "Patient Zero."

The new disease readily lent itself to an assortment of origin theories, but none gained as much credibility in the medical communities and media of North America and Western Europe as the African or Haitian origins theories of HIV. The theories became widespread as soon as the *MMWR* called attention to the "Opportunistic Infections and Kaposi's Sarcoma among

Haitians in the United States" in July 1982. Theories of both Haitian and African origins involved epidemiological patterns and, subsequently, the ostensible detection of the virus in samples from African cases that pre-dated the appearance of the disease elsewhere.[49] In a special issue of *Scientific American* devoted to AIDS in October 1988, Robert C. Gallo and Luc Montagnier, credited jointly with the identification of HIV, asked where the virus had been "hiding all those years, and why [we were] only now experiencing an epidemic?" Their answer:

> The virus ha[d] been present in small, isolated groups in central Africa or elsewhere for many years. In such groups the spread of HIV might have been quite limited and the groups themselves may have had little contact with the outside world. As a result the virus could have been contained for decades. That pattern may have been altered when the way of life in Central Africa began to change. People migrating from remote areas to urban centers no doubt brought HIV with them. Sexual mores in the city were different from what they had been in the village, and blood transfusions were commoner. Consequently HIV may have spread freely. Once a pool of infected people had been established, transport networks and the generalized exchange of blood products would have carried it to every corner of the world. What had been remote and rare became global and common.[50]

Their explanation summarizes nearly a decade of speculating about the origins and nicely captures how speculation had quickly become received wisdom, as Shilts's passage attests. The appeal of the theory stemmed at least partly from the familiarity of the story.

Journalistic portraits of AIDS in Africa, as cultural critics have noted, resemble Joseph Conrad's *Heart of Darkness*, "as if HIV were a disease of 'African-ness,'" writes Simon Watney, "the viral embodiment of a long legacy of colonial imagery which naturalizes the devastating economic and social effects of European colonialism in the likeness of starvation."[51] Like others who have written on the subject, Watney describes the racism involved in depictions of "African AIDS," which include a diseased continent, primitive in its cultural, sexual, and medical practices. Richard Preston slides subtly into that familiar depiction in *The Hot Zone* when he describes Tom Geisbert's quest to identify not HIV but the hemorrhagic virus that is killing primates in Reston, Virginia. Peering into his microscope, Geisbert "could see forms and shapes that resembled rivers and streams and oxbow lakes, and he could see specks that might be towns, and he could see belts of forest. It was an aerial view of rain forest. The cell was a world down there, and somewhere in that jungle hid a virus."[52] The story conflates *origin* and *cause*, as Renée Sabatier demonstrates in *Blaming Others: Prejudice, Race and Worldwide AIDS*.[53]

Shilts's Dugas never goes to Africa or has documented contact with Africans. Yet both "Patient Zero" and "African AIDS" are central to the story Shilts tells.[54] Shilts reinforces the African origins thesis, and Dugas, with his easy access to travel, is what network theorists call "a hub," a point of connection who moves the virus rapidly through the global network. The image of the peripatetic Dugas/virus itself traveled insistently through the media, as in the writer and AIDS chronicler Oscar Moore's description in the *Guardian Weekend* of his own and his culture's shock at "the unexpected arrival of new violent and sociopathic illnesses which seemed to have emigrated from distant environments by that most modern of medical transmitters, the aeroplane." Moore thinks of Dugas among the "hundreds, maybe thousands, of sexual tourists" to travel what "the downward plunge in transatlantic fares triggered by Freddie Laker" had made "the gay transatlantic free- (or at least very cheap) way every summer for four years."[55] The "sociopathic illnesses"—willful, malevolent forces unleashed by a continent—are further animated in "Patient Zero," while the sinister decadence of sexual liberation heralds the fall of an empire (recall Garrett's microbial view of Rome in 5 B.C.).

As I noted in chapter 1, the image of the Third World that haunted such accounts was a Cold War legacy. The Cold War politics that turned decolonizing nations into battlegrounds produced not only violence and poverty but also the narrative of struggling nations in need of modernization conceived as emulation of the First World: wild and primitive landscapes plagued by uncontrolled violence and "sociopathic illnesses." The narrative at once justified U.S. intervention in decolonizing nations and registered colonial guilt. Ironically, these Third World landscapes in turn loomed in the U.S. imaginary as harbingers of a potential First World future: a nightmare vision of the post-apocalyptic United States. Just prior to running the three pieces on PCP and acquired immunodeficiency in gay men in the 10 December 1981 issue that helped to announce the outbreak, the *New England Journal of Medicine* issued a special report titled "Medical Problems of Survivors of Nuclear War." The writer offered the stark prediction that "surviving Americans will experience the underdeveloped world as their natural habitat for the first time." Americans would be at a distinct disadvantage in this landscape: "Unlike the inhabitants of impoverished lands, . . . Americans, because of lack of exposure to many organisms, may not have the high natural immunity to a host of dangerous diseases that allows many in the Third World to survive."[56]

Since this image of the Third World arose to depict devastation and the need for modernization, it is not surprising that it would be summoned as a vision of the postnuclear landscape that marked the collapse of the First World. In this context, however, the fantasy registers the anxious reversal of hierarchies conceived in the terms of (inverted) social Darwinism, where the "civilized" are the least fit to survive: previously defeated microbes arise to claim the victims of those whose lack of resistance ironically reflects their technological advances. Like the polio virus, which disproportionately infected the wealthier strata of society, the postnuclear germ landscape mocks scientific and social progress. This medicalized fantasy updates as it absorbs concerns expressed in the 1950s by cultural observers as diverse as Harold Isaacs and William Faulkner about the changing balance of racial power in the decolonizing world.[57]

"African AIDS" realized the vision of a diseased continent as both a Third World present and a First World future. As accounts of African AIDS conformed to familiar narratives, the metaphor of the Third World slid into a threat, and geographical boundaries were recast in temporal terms. The epidemic marked, as columnist George Will put it, the "lethal mixture" of "modernity and primitivism . . . in Africa."[58] Another journalist, writing like Will in the second decade of the epidemic, dubbed "tropical Africa . . . an especially fertile petri dish for pathogens."[59] Hypothesis shifts almost imperceptibly into narrative as the obvious connections among disease, violence, and poverty lead him to posit the origins of the virus "in Africa along the border between Tanzania and Uganda after Idi Amin, the notorious Ugandan dictator, had turned the region into a war zone" where the "volatile mix of refugees, soldiers, prostitutes and the attendant lack of disease surveillance may have given HIV the jump-start it needed to travel the world." HIV is a "clever microbe—a slow, stealthy, incubator" that takes advantage of the mechanisms of globalization for its pathological tourism. Shilts's "Patient Zero" is one of those mechanisms, a confederate converted to the cause. He never had to go to Africa or have sexual relations (directly) with Africans to import African AIDS into the United States. The continent enters his body through the virus, which in turn crosses boundaries through his body.

The slippage between the Third World as metaphor and the Third World as threat is evident in Shilts's depiction of internal agents whose "lifestyles" have made them receptive to the role of "AIDS carrier." The well-known

AIDS activist Michael Callen, for example, had "frequented every sex club and bathhouse between the East River and the Pacific Ocean and had gathered enough venereal and parasitical diseases to make his medical chart look like that of some sixty-five-year-old Equatorial African living in squalor."[60] When they spread those diseases, figures such as Callen and Dugas become agents of Africanization, and the virus, as Watney observes, "threatens to 'Africanize' the entire world."[61] Emerging from a primordial past, HIV is poised to turn that past into a hopeless global future, and the Third World, gay male agents, and the conditions of U.S. inner cities in which the epidemic made early inroads (what Shilts, Garrett, and others call "thirdworldization") constitute the "biological landscape" that would germinate and disseminate it. Shilts's images dovetailed with the emerging evidence of antibiotic-resistant microbes that threatened, as every discussion of "supergerms" warned, to return the United States to the medical primitivism of the pre-antibiotic world. The underdeveloped world that loomed so large in the *future* of the United States marked the failure of science, civilization, and modernity.

Mischaracterizations of Shilts's book in the mainstream media often seem to pick up on some of its unspoken connections. A careless synopsis in Florida's *St. Petersburg Times*, for example, inadvertently conflated two features of the work that offer insight into the anxious vision of globalization through which the disparate elements of Shilts's analysis cohere. The author, Greg Hamilton, told readers that "it's all right to hate the disease. Since July 4, 1976, the nation's 200th birthday and the day Air Canada steward Anton [*sic*] Dugas is believed to have introduced the virus to the United States, AIDS has spread like a prairie fire throughout society."[62] In a spectacular flourish, Hamilton superimposes Gaetan Dugas on the "tall ships," an alternative fantasy of the introduction of HIV into the United States. Shilts begins the first chapter of *And the Band Played On* with an allusion to the tall ships, which were featured in the bicentennial celebration of the nation in New York City. The reference comes from Bill Darrow's interview with a man whose closest circle of friends had all been diagnosed with AIDS; in an effort to determine which summer they had spent together, the man summons the memory of the tall ships. "'The Bicentennial,'" Shilts writes, ventriloquizing Darrow. "'Of course. The Bicentennial. July 4, 1976. An international festival to celebrate America's birthday with ships from fifty-five nations. People had come to New York City from all over the world'" (142). The memory of the tall ships represents a new insight into the disease. Darrow quickly does the math: "'Nothing happened before 1976,' " he thinks, " 'but people had started getting sick in 1978 and 1979. It was clear from the other links in the cluster study that the disease could lie dormant for a long time. People were spreading it all over in 1977 and 1978, which accounted for so many cases spontaneously appearing in so many different regions of the country' " (142).

Ironically, Darrow's theory about the tall ships implicitly refuted the idea of Gaetan Dugas as an index case. If the virus came with the tall ships, then it could not have been brought by Dugas or, in fact, by any single identifiable source, nor, for that matter, was Dugas any more than representative in his capacity as disseminator. But while Dugas and the tall ships are incompatible as theories of the origin of "American AIDS," they are complementary features of its narrative. The tall ships are themselves representative for Darrow, a convenient shorthand for urban cosmopolitanism and New York City in particular as a global destination. Like the "Québecoise Typhoid Mary," they suggest an invasion from without that is enabled by the receptive culture within. "New York City had hosted the greatest party ever known," writes Shilts. "The guests had come from all over the world" (3). And then, somberly: "This was the part the epidemiologists would later note, when they stayed up late at night and the conversation drifted toward where it had started and when. They would remember that glorious night in New York Harbor, all those sailors, and recall: From all over the world they came to New York" (3).

"It" refers to the epidemic, but the grammar of the sentence conflates the virus with the party. The passage immediately segues into an account of Christmas Eve in Zaire in 1976 when a Danish surgeon named Grethe Rask, who ran a clinic in a village in northern Zaire, showed early symptoms of what would be presumptively diagnosed (retroactively) as AIDS. The juxtaposition with Rask's story answers the epidemiologists' question: "it" started in "Africa," where, in words Shilts attributes to Jacques Leibowitch, a French doctor who saw some of the earliest AIDS cases in Europe, "new diseases tended to germinate" (103). Sailors carried it in, and partying spread it. Sexual transmission enabled it, as the CDC's Mary Guinan feared from the outset, "to penetrate far deeper into the nation" (107): Africanization through decadence.

The bicentennial celebration in New York City moves, in Shilts's book, from a man's hazy memory to the Ground Zero of American AIDS. Like "Patient Zero," it is a narrative device that shades into history. It imparts a national frame to the story he is telling about what Jonathan Mann, director of the global AIDS program of the WHO in the late 1980s, called " 'the global-village disease.'"[63] HIV/AIDS does more than illuminate the routes of a global network and the susceptibility of the U.S. population to "foreign" microbes. It also gives epidemiological expression to the dangers of the ideal of democracy.

An analysis implicit in Shilts's book finds explicit articulation in Alex Shoumatoff's 1988 *Vanity Fair* piece about his journey to Africa, "In Search of the Source of AIDS." Shoumatoff ends the piece with his musing, on a 747 en route to New York City, "about the unprecedented merging and mixing and growing together of the world's population in the last few decades, the tremendous release of people from their traditional confines, the enormous flow from the villages to the cities of the Third World to the immediate outskirts of New York, London, Paris, Rome, Cologne, Marseilles" (117). Those interactions make him ponder "how HIV must have become airborne—airplane-borne—moving on slipstreams from continent to continent: tens of thousands of revelers flying down to Rio for Carnaval, for instance" and how "Brazil, one of the world's most mixed societies, [now] faces an epidemic potentially as devastating as Africa's" (117). The crossing of geographic boundaries (the invasion) segues into the breakdown of social ones, as the intermingling of populations leads to (implied) racial mixture (Brazil as "one of the world's most mixed societies").

The spreading virus, however, does not cause that breakdown; HIV, rather, exposes the fiction of containment. The virus cannot be "contained" in "risk groups" because desire cannot be contained by social classifications. HIV indelibly marks a variety of social interactions, some sexual and illicit, and it is not unique in doing so: Shoumatoff imagines "this *archetypal communicable disease* traveling along the mutually manipulative interface of the First and Third Worlds in countless copulations, and like a swallow dye pill illuminating all the *liaisons dangereuses*, the thousands upon thousands of marital, premarital, extramarital, interracial, and homosexual encounters that must have taken place for it to have spread as far as it has" (117; initial emphasis added). HIV makes sex visible; it shows that people's desires are not bound by either the social sanction of marriage or the social classifications of race, gender, and sexuality, and it demonstrates the indifference of those desires, like the virus through which they are manifest, to national boundaries as well.

Shoumatoff Americanizes the global vision when he notes that "among the four hundred passengers winging their way to the great land whose politically admirable but epidemiologically lamentable motto is E Pluribus Unum were Indians and Arabs, Venezuelans, Poles, Africans, Israelis, Italians, Turks and Bulgarians, not to mention Americans of assorted hues and stripes—a rich cross section of the human cornucopia" and "that statistically three people aboard ought to be carrying the virus" (117). The epidemic turns an emblem of national pride, the consequence of new global formations that rhetorically culminate in U.S. nationalism, into a national threat: out of many, one. AIDS is the disease of (too much) democracy; epidemiology exposes the danger of the political ideal as a desire that results in a racialized microbic hybridity.

HIV expresses that hybridity, and it here challenges the reproduction of (white) Americanism just as diseases such as typhoid and tuberculosis carried the threat of "race suicide" in the early twentieth century. Modernity and its chief political institution, the nation, are marked, as Alys Weinbaum argues, by an obsession with race and reproduction.[64] The transmission routes of the virus show why, as they expose the uncontainable force of sexuality. It is not surprising, then, that the Africanization of the United States would be accomplished by the "Third World" immune systems of gay men, inner-city IV-drug users, and (for a time) Haitian "immigrants" (the epithet assigned to those living in Haitian communities in the United States) as well as hemophiliacs, who, without the Factor H that was now "poisoning" their blood, would not as easily have survived and reproduced.[65]

Shilts gestures toward a powerful analysis of the epidemic at the end of *And the Band Plays On* when he notes the divergence of "the story of AIDS in the gay community . . . from the broader story of AIDS in America and in the world" (620). He concedes to one of the gay activists in the book the "romantic" vision of a gay community that survives and learns from the epidemic, which he juxtaposes with "a naturalistic drama with little that could be considered heartening" for inner-city America and "the impoverished masses of the Third World" (620). The distinction turns on the socioeconomic inequities at the heart of the epidemic and the clash not between the primitive and modern, but between the poverty and wealth that characterizes the modern world. But that analysis is undercut by the epidemiological horror story that Shilts has been telling throughout: the transformation of Gaetan Dugas into "Patient Zero," which turns hybridity monstrous and the challenge of democracy mythic. The "cruel and insidious virus" (621) replaces socioeconomic analysis as the link between the divergent stories of HIV/AIDS. He concludes his narrative with a snapshot of African AIDS: a primitive, diseased continent, turning hopefully, in the person of a grieving, desperate Ugandan father, to the United States to save its children. In the process, Shilts recasts the epidemiological challenge to the political ideal as the apocalyptic battle between the monstrous, primordial viral-human hybrids and the heroic scientists and epidemiologists. In the plea of the Ugandan father, he ends his story with an expression of faith in the salvific powers of contemporary science in the United States. It makes sense, in this context, that the most memorable detail of Shilts's work proves to be the dangerous foreign flight attendant who penetrates the protective borders of the nation. "Patient Zero" embodies the message of the book, the story that has emerged and endured: the incarnated sinister virus as national threat.

INTO THE LAB

The October 1988 issue of *Scientific American*, which was devoted to HIV / AIDS, included a review of Shilts's book by William Blattner, chief of the viral epidemiology section of the National Cancer Institute. Calling *And the Band Played On* "*the* AIDS book [that] has been a potent factor in the public perception of the AIDS problem," Blattner is critical of Shilts for choosing sensational storytelling over incisive analysis. "Patient Zero" in particular is "a useful literary device for helping the reader to understand how the AIDS agent spread so rapidly and widely within the gay community," but it is also evidence of Shilts's irresponsibility: his "tendency to personify him leads him astray."[66] It is, of course, not Dugas, a person, whom Shilts personifies, but the HIV virus in what Blattner calls "a novelistic history of the AIDS epidemic" (148). The reviewer's confusion attests to the efficacy of Shilts's characterization of the flight attendant. Blattner is critical as well of Shilts's depiction of maverick scientists, heroic or villainous, such as Robert Gallo, whom he identifies only as "a National Cancer Institute (NCI) researcher whose discovery of the first human retrovirus is passed off as 'a backward scientific affair'" (148). While Blattner defends his NCI colleague from Shilts's indictment of his unprofessional conduct surrounding the identification of the virus, he is more concerned with the "common romantic stereotype" that makes the book readable but inaccurate (148). Shilts spotlights individual scientists, he complains, at the expense of "the accomplishments of the scientific establishment in the seven years since the first cases of AIDS were recognized" (148). Those accomplishments, he argues, "belie Shilts's assertions. It is the scientific establishment, not some romanticized science maverick, that has produced the spectacular and timely current accumulation of scientific knowledge about AIDS" (148). The review offers Blattner a platform from which to laud the "fundamental investment in basic research made over the past 20 years" without which "the discovery of the cause of AIDS might still elude us today" and to hold up that discovery as "stark testimony to the importance of society's investment in the curiosity of scientists" and scientific "instinct" as "crucial to our ability to address this or any other threat to survival" (149).

Blattner believes that Shilts has told a precipitous tale and finds his faith in the promise of science insufficient. The "story of AIDS is still in its early stages; how it will end cannot be described with anything approaching certainty. Yet the positive aspects of the response to AIDS (the agent has been identified, the blood supply protected and promising chemotherapies and immunotherapies have been discovered) are the fruits of the scientific process. If AIDS and other such challenges to our species are to be met successfully this process must be understood and fostered by lay citizens as well as by scientists" (150). It is the duty of "citizens" to understand not the science, but the need to trust the scientific process. And it is the responsibility of scientists and science writers to tell the story properly: "Shilts's position and accomplishments as a journalist who could gain entry both into the gay world and into the world of science and public policy presented a unique opportunity. He could have helped his fellow citizens to share in the effort to cope with AIDS and to understand the tragedy of those afflicted with the disease, so that this challenge and others like it can be surmounted. Perhaps, back in 1987 [this from the perspective of 1988], emotion precluded the writing of such a book. Perhaps another chronicler will find the positive threads in the AIDS story; they are strong enough to produce unity, and therefore hope" (151). The more hopeful story that Shilts could have written, according to Blattner, entailed a shift in focus from epidemiological field work to the laboratory, where the story could be written in the future perfect: an imagined moment when the epidemic will have been contained. That story emerged from the issue of *Scientific American* focused on HIV/AIDS in which Blattner's review appeared. Yet, despite the shift in emphasis, the narrative in the special issue in fact reinforced two important features of Shilts's would-be outbreak narrative: faith in scientific achievement and an injunction to personal responsibility.

Devoted to presenting "What Science Knows about AIDS," the issue features articles pitched to a scientifically literate readership, but generally and broadly accessible. The authors of the introductory essay, Robert Gallo and Luc Montagnier, are presented in the heading as "the investigators who discovered HIV," while the boxed biography at the bottom of the page calls them "the investigators who established the cause of AIDS."[67] The juxtaposition is telling; the issue moves the focus of both the present and future of AIDS further into the laboratory. The equation of the discovery of HIV with the discovery of "the cause of AIDS" witnesses the determined virological thinking that Patton decries, excluding other factors that arguably caused the epidemic. A consistent rhetorical indistinction between HIV and AIDS throughout the issue, moreover, conflates virus and syndrome, turning "the AIDS virus" into a biological entity that is best understood and treated through scientific research rather than socioeconomic analysis. The first paragraph of the introduction rehearses the progress of the science of infectious-disease research as it traces the contours of what was already the familiar narrative of the virus's disruption of its sanguinity:

> As recently as a decade ago it was widely believed that infectious disease was no longer much of a threat in the developed world. The remaining challenges to public health there, it was thought, stemmed from noninfectious conditions such as cancer, heart disease and degenerative diseases. That confidence was shattered in the early 1980s by the advent of AIDS. Here was a devastating disease caused by a class of infectious agents—retroviruses—that had first been found in human beings only a few years before. In spite of the startling nature of the epidemic, science responded quickly. In the two years from mid-1982 to mid-1984 the outlines of the epidemic were clarified, a new virus—the human immunodeficiency virus (HIV)—was isolated and shown to cause the disease, a blood test was formulated and the virus's targets in the body were established. (41)

The monster reared its head, but science has identified and all but contained it. The phrase "science responded quickly" underscores the point of the paragraph, the article, and the issue: the virus has challenged but will not defeat science. Scientific authority is reaffirmed, and modernity and humanity are preserved.

The coauthors of the introduction, and the story they tell, are relevant to that reaffirmation. The previous year, readers of *And the Band Played On* had learned in considerable detail about the bitter disagreement concerning who had actually first identified HIV, which bordered on an international incident but was not covered in such depth in the press at the time. Charges and countercharges flew across the Atlantic, with nationalist undertones and whisperings, as Shilts puts it, of "a scientific scandal of immense proportions" (529). It was publicly resolved, through the help of no less an ambassador than Jonas Salk, with the attribution of "partial credit for various discoveries on the way to isolating" the virus, with the epithet for each "'co-discoverer'" of the virus, and with the christening of the virus not, as Gallo wished, HTLV-III, nor as Montagnier hoped, LAV, but as the compromise HIV (593). Shilts calls the resolution "a pleasant fiction" accomplished "because none of the mainstream press had pursued the controversy in any depth" (593).[68] Gallo's and Montagnier's performance as coauthors of what the journal labels "their first collaborative article" consolidates the story as it seeks to restore to "science" the authority that accounts of the infighting (especially Shilts's) may have challenged.[69] In the introduction the authors recount the role each one played in the search for the virus in an effort (visible to a reader familiar with their story) to restore their own potentially damaged reputations and authority.

Everything about this introduction leads to the laboratory, including the photographs and illustrations, which demonstrate how "science" has made HIV visible (the first step in controlling it), and a chart offering "evidence that HIV causes AIDS." Amid the photographs and charts, they embed, almost as an aside, the theory of the African origins of HIV, which traveled into the global village when a way of life, rather than a virus, underwent important changes. By association, the virus is primitive and will, in the end, prove no match for contemporary science. Gallo and Montagnier confidently advise against panic—most obviously, they chide, because "panic does no good,'" but also because "it now seems unlikely HIV infection will spread as rapidly outside the original high-risk groups in the industrial countries as it has within them" and because "this disease is not beyond the curative power of science" (47). Imagining an endpoint that is not actually in sight, Gallo and Montagnier insist that "although current knowledge is imperfect, it is sufficient to provide confidence that effective therapies and a vaccine will be developed" (47). The cover depicts "a particle of the human immunodeficiency virus (HIV) forming at the outer membrane of an infected cell" (6) that resembles the opening sequence of *Invasion of the Body Snatchers*. This image of scientific expertise illustrates what the issue will argue throughout: that laboratory research offers the most important insight into "What Science Knows about AIDS." The first article, a well-illustrated piece titled "The Molecular Biology of the AIDS Virus," explains the genetics of HIV and concludes with the assertion that "surely this [molecular] description contains the seeds of HIV's eventual defeat."[70]

The subsequent article uses that (genetic) information to posit "The Origins of the AIDS Virus." Scientific research showing that "the AIDS virus is not unique" leads to the reassurance that Nature may participate in the containment of the epidemic, since "studies of related viruses indicate that some have evolved disease-free coexistence with their animal hosts." Science can facilitate that process: "The origin and history of the AIDS viruses themselves may provide the very information that is critical to the prevention and control of AIDS."[71] Epidemiology remains an important part of the battle, and two articles on epidemiology and disease survival on national and international scales follow. But their message that epidemiology eventually leads back to the laboratory is reinforced by the succeeding two companion pieces, entitled "HIV Infection: The Clinical Picture" and "HIV Infection: The Cellular Picture," which underscore the importance of the discovery of the virus that is the theme of the issue.

The importance of the discovery is further dramatized in a full-page photograph that adjoins the first page of "HIV Infection: The Clinical Picture." The photograph depicts a white and obviously middle-class family, the Burks, whose intertwined hands and arms are prominently featured. The caption explains that the photograph is from 1985 when the Burk family "looked like a typical U.S. family."[72] The family, it turns out, both is and is not typical. These typical parents, with their clasping, protective arms, have been unable to protect themselves or their children from the invisible killer. The father, a hemophiliac, contracted HIV from a transfusion and unknowingly passed it on to his wife, and she to their son. Only their daughter is not "infected," yet one look at her painfully sad eyes, as she leans her entire body into her father, shows that she is certainly affected. At the time of the photograph, father and son both had AIDS; by 1988, both had died. The juxtaposition of the photograph with the title of the article suggests dueling pictures, the photographic and the clinical. The photograph represents what can be seen by "typical" people, while the "clinical picture" refers to what scientists can see and the means by which they make that information visible. Oddly, given the size and prominence of the photograph, the Burks are never mentioned in the article, but according to the caption, their "story underscores two important facts. Anyone, regardless of age, sex or sexual orientation, can contract HIV if exposed to it through a known transmission route. And there usually are no symptoms of early infection; many people transmit HIV to others before they know they are ill. For these reasons the authors recommend that anyone who thinks he or she has been exposed to HIV seek an early diagnosis" (91). The caption, like the blood test that enables early detection, exposes what the nonscientists cannot see, and the story of this unwitting carrier illustrates the message of the article: that "the focus should be on the full course of the viral infection, not solely on AIDS" (90). The article ends, like the others, optimistically enjoining "doctors and patients" to "keep in sight the day when medical science will reduce the HIV infection to a curable disease. . . ."

"BURK FAMILY, shown in 1985, looked like a typical
U.S. family." *Scientific American*, October 1988, 91.
© Lynn Johnson/Aurora Photos.

If we persist and are methodical," the authors promise, "we shall unquestionably succeed in curing HIV infection" (98). The subsequent piece, on
the cellular picture, explains how the information researchers have acquired since the discovery of the virus will lead to the therapies and eventually the vaccine that are described in the issue. The two pieces that follow
describe the "AIDS Therapies" and "AIDS Vaccines" that the discovery of
HIV promises: the evidence and hope of scientific success.

Despite the prominence of the laboratory, science alone cannot solve the problem, and the photograph of the Burks also reinforces the message of personal responsibility that runs throughout the issue. From the outset, the Gallo and Montagnier introduction to the issue concedes that while the virus will ultimately not prove resistant to medical knowledge and treatment, as the identification of the virus and the "securing" of the blood supply have shown, "there are parts of the epidemic where" even the long arm of science cannot go and "humanity will be tested. Users of intravenous drugs, for example, are notoriously *resistant* to education campaigns alone."[73] The introduction concludes accordingly with an injunction. While awaiting a scientific resolution, everyone "must accept responsibilities: to learn how HIV is spread, to reduce risky behavior, to raise our voices against acceptance of the drug culture and to avoid stigmatizing victims of the disease. If we can accept such responsibilities, the worst element of nightmare will have been removed from the AIDS epidemic" (48). The point of the issue is to supply the necessary information that could have saved the Burk family. In the story that the issue tells about HIV, the epidemic can be contained by a change in behavior. Those who do not accept the delineated responsibilities are not "victims," but perpetrators, becoming the resistant viral agents and testing humanity. The story shifts responsibility onto individuals when it gets too close to a critique of the social and economic conditions that affect drug use as well as healthcare and contribute to the notorious "resistance" to education campaigns.

The issue moves toward that critique in the final article, "The Social Dimensions of AIDS," in which the (then) dean of the Harvard School of Public Health, Harvey V. Fineberg, explains that the "AIDS epidemic exposes hidden vulnerabilities in the human condition that are both biological and social."[74] Global and local inequities find expression in the "sharp variation in geography, racial and gender composition" (129) that characterizes the epidemic. It "compels a fresh look at the performance of the institutions we depend on and brings society to a crossroads for collective action" (128). The epidemic, however, is not, in his reading, the result of those inequities, but their cause. Blame falls on the virus, which becomes familiarly animated under the social microscope: "HIV is *insidious*. It *corrupts* vital body fluids, turning blood and semen from sources of life into instruments of death. The virus *insinuates* itself into the genetic material of selected cells, where it may remain quiescent for prolonged periods of time. When it is active, the virus gradually *undermines* the body's immune system. . . . HIV infection remains at the present time incurable, a pointed reminder" not of the socioeconomic inequities that find expression in the disproportionate susceptibility to disease, but "of humanity's thrall to the tyranny of nature" (128; emphasis added). The (familiar) threat of a return to the past is evident in the observation that "as if to taunt progress in the life sciences in the twentieth century, HIV not only has caused the disease most feared in America near the end of the century but also has fueled a resurgence of tuberculosis, the disease most feared at the beginning of the century" (133). Against the tyranny of nature and the threat of the past, there is science rather than profound social change.

Fineberg does not entirely retreat into a scientific solution; his analysis of the epidemic includes the "social dimension" that his title promises. Fear and stigmatizing exacerbate the ravages of the virus, and the photographs that accompany his article dramatize his argument. "Fear of contagion" is conveyed, for example, in a juxtaposition of two photographs, one modeling the body suit and face mask worn by French physicians during an outbreak of plague in the early eighteenth century, and the other depicting similar biocontainment suits worn by emergency medical technicians in contemporary (late 1980s) Hong Kong. The caption calls the fear motivating this return to the past "unjustified" in the case of HIV. Other photographs highlight more constructive public-health and social responses: from practical measures urged in a pediatric AIDS ward and a poster from an education campaign to a magnificent display of the AIDS quilt and an AIDS awareness march, both in New York City. The photographs illustrate the components of the response that Fineberg advocates throughout the article: the need for compassion and an aggressive education campaign and scientific response. They are worthy goals, but they depart from the structural and institutional analysis toward which the article initially gestures when it alludes to the potential exposure of hidden vulnerabilities. Instead, the illustrations underscore Fineberg's emphasis on personal responsibility with which Gallo and Montagnier similarly end their introduction. Commendable in its injunction to work for a compassionate and humane response to the epidemic, Fineberg's closing article nonetheless reinforces the message of the whole: social responsibility entails cooperating with public-health officials who through information and education campaigns and the establishment of safety practices based on scientific information will ultimately control the epidemic. The behavioral and scientific solutions that he prioritizes and the animated virus that he indicts as the cause of the epidemic reproduce the features that in their more extreme forms, as in Shilts's narrative, result in the pathologized human-virus hybrids, or "AIDS carriers." He does not pursue the causal dimensions of the "hidden vulnerabilities in the human condition."

Even the advertisements in the issue reinforce the message that individuals

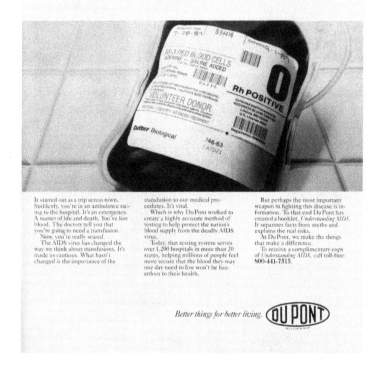

The difference between saving a life and threatening it.

It started out as a trip across town. Suddenly, you're in an ambulance racing to the hospital. It's an emergency. A matter of life and death. You've lost blood. The doctors tell you that you're going to need a transfusion.

Now, you're really scared.

The AIDS virus has changed the way we think about transfusions. It's made us cautious. What hasn't changed is the importance of the

transfusion to our medical procedures. It's vital.

Which is why DuPont worked to create a highly accurate method of testing to help protect the nation's blood supply from the deadly AIDS virus.

Today, that testing system serves over 1,200 hospitals in more than 20 states, helping millions of people feel more secure that the blood they may one day need to live won't be hazardous to their health.

But perhaps the most important weapon in fighting this disease is information. To that end DuPont has created a booklet, *Understanding AIDS.* It separates facts from myths and explains the real risks.

At DuPont, we make the things that make a difference.

To receive a complimentary copy of *Understanding AIDS,* call toll-free: 800-441-7515.

Better things for better living. **DUPONT**

DuPont advertisement in *Scientific American*, October 1988.
Reprinted with permission of DuPont.

can respond to the threat posed by HIV only through responsible behavior, which entails acting on the information that science dispenses. An advertisement for DuPont features a photograph of a bag of transfusion-ready blood and a heading that reads, "The difference between saving life and threatening it" (49). The text below the photograph moves from an accident scenario in which "you" (the reader) need a transfusion through DuPont's "highly accurate method of testing to help protect the nation's blood supply from the deadly AIDS virus" to the assertion that "perhaps the most important weapon in fighting this disease is information" (49). The passage concludes with a number to call in order to receive a complimentary copy of

DuPont's booklet, *Understanding AIDS*. The assumption informing the advertisement, and the issue as a whole, is that readers should have faith that scientific information (the right information) will lead to containment of the virus, but also should cooperate by acting responsibly. The continued spread of the epidemic will signal not the failure of science or the consequences of social and economic inequities, but the pathological behavior of deviant individuals. "Patient Zero" exemplifies the antithesis of the socially responsible citizen.

"THE DENTIST WITH AIDS"

As the epidemic moved into its second decade, the hope of containment, and the outbreak narrative, became more elusive. The laboratory was producing answers, but they were not leading to the promised cure, and AIDS cases were growing exponentially in the United States and abroad. The story of a figure who almost became a "Patient Zero"—he was known at the CDC as "Patient A"—suggests the shift away from signal features of the outbreak narrative in accounts of the HIV/AIDS epidemic, as individuals and the public generally struggled to live with its effects.[75] In 1987 a dentist from Florida named David Acer learned that he had been infected with HIV. In May of that same year, the CDC had announced the first cases of HIV-positive healthcare workers with no other risk factors.[76] Although David Acer was a dentist, he was also bisexual, and sexual transmission was determined to be the most likely route of his infection. The story would have been unremarkable, except that between the fall of 1987 and spring of 1989, Acer was the dentist of a college student named Kimberly Bergalis, who would be instrumental in his metamorphosis into the CDC's "Patient A" and his inscription in history as "the dentist with AIDS."

In 1990 the public learned of a female college student with AIDS whose alleged absence of risk factors made her bisexual dentist the presumed source of her infection. The possibility of this route occurred to Bergalis and her mother because she lacked other risk factors, and they had heard a "rumor" that "he had AIDS."[77] A press conference held in early September introduced Kimberly Bergalis as the college student and the now-deceased David Acer as the dentist.[78] The considerable public attention that this case received registers the fear that it generated; if Acer had infected Bergalis, it meant that healthcare providers not only themselves risked infection from their patients but actually might pose such a threat in return. As the health and privacy needs of people with AIDS made trust in healthcare providers an issue of particular concern, the idea that they could be the source of infection with HIV was especially disturbing; Bergalis was an outspoken and compellingly tragic "victim" who could not have suspected that her dentist might infect her with HIV. The Bergalises wanted someone to take responsibility for Kimberly's infection, and they focused first on David Acer.

The Bergalises were not alone in their efforts. One of Acer's acquaintances suggested that Acer had deliberately infected Bergalis and several other patients, including a grandmother in her sixties, in order to draw more attention to the disease. Here was a "Patient Zero" ready for incarnation, and there were speculative depictions of the homicidal dentist, the murderous monster who sought to take the "innocent" down with him. But they did not catch on and were subordinated to the medical puzzle of the route of transmission in the media accounts of the incident. Acer had stopped practicing dentistry and was close to death by the time Bergalis's infection was tracked back to him. He maintained until his death that he had no idea how (or indeed whether) he had transmitted the virus to his patients, but he assumed responsibility for them when he took out an ad in the local paper announcing his serostatus and advising them to be tested. His culpability was subsequently ascribed to his failure to safeguard his patients: his disturbing but unintentional carelessness. The difference between the fates of David Acer and Gaetan Dugas stem in part from Acer's evident concern for his patients as well as the timing of the discovery of Bergalis's infection (after he was no longer practicing dentistry or circulating in society). But it also suggests that the epidemic had begun to move beyond the reaches of the outbreak narrative and the problems, solutions, and villains it depicted.

The fear the story evoked in the media coverage lay in the banality of the route of transmission: the routine extraction of a college student's wisdom teeth. Media coverage centered on Bergalis's tragedy rather than the criminality of her dentist. When the dying Acer was cast as pitiable rather than monstrous, the Bergalis family sought to turn their personal tragedy into policy by emphasizing the vulnerability of "the general population" and their terrifying dependence on healthcare providers who are themselves, after all, disturbingly ordinary human beings, subject to careless mistakes. The dentist's intentions were not relevant to those goals and became increasingly less important. Indeed, the ordinary and accidental nature of the transmission was much more threatening than if it had been intentional because an accidental infection was more likely to happen again to others.

It therefore would make the Bergalises' plea for mandatory testing more pressing. As the first case of transmission from a healthcare provider, "Patient A" posthumously became the center of policy debates about mandatory testing and disclosure for healthcare providers.

Bergalis's personal struggle with AIDS, her determination to testify at the congressional hearings, and the policy debates made good copy. But the mystery of the story lay in the means of transmission, and the search for answers led to the laboratory. When intensive field epidemiologic investigation failed to turn up any convincing explanation for Bergalis's infection other than Acer, and when five of his other dental patients similarly emerged with him as the presumed source of their infection, the CDC sought answers from a new laboratory technology that could address the question of whether and how Acer had transmitted the disease to his patients. The technique involved performing genetic analyses on the viruses carried by each infected person; the theory was that because of the tendency toward rapid mutation of HIV, strains of the virus in individuals who shared its transmission would show significantly more similarity than those in individuals whose infection was unrelated. For scientists, the new technique meant a more laboratory-based tracking system and a more exact picture of HIV. Ultimately, the studies suggested that Acer and his patients carried the same strain of HIV, but researchers could not definitively establish how—or even whether—Acer had transmitted the virus to them.

While the story of Gaetan Dugas turned "Patient Zero" into the virus incarnate, the account of David Acer attested to its disembodiment. As the shift in the *Scientific American* issue had forecast, the drama of the epidemic and the hope of containment had moved to the laboratory; in the Bergalis-Acer case, the more accurate snapshot of the virus had replaced its animation in human form that was so essential for the epidemiological narratives. Mark Carl Rom points out that at the time of Bergalis's diagnosis, "AIDS was a reportable disease in Florida and all the other states" while "HIV . . . was a reportable disease in less than half of them."[79] It was these policies rather than the federal regulation of health practitioners that the Bergalis family sought that would change.

David Acer was never definitively established as the cause of Bergalis's disease. Reports of the case that the CDC published in *Science* in 1992 were inconclusive, and Rom, who was investigating the CDC's handling of the Acer case for the General Accounting Office, acknowledges that he "began the study expecting to find that the CDC had made major mistakes in its work" (159), but found the incident "a mystery without an ending" (10). In the end, the investigation focused more on the virus than on the man, but the laboratory could not solve the terrifyingly ordinary mystery that was raised by the case, which left the public without a villain and an outbreak narrative. While the Florida dentist with AIDS and the public debate surrounding the testing of healthcare workers received much broader publicity than the handsome stranger with the French accent who was deliberately spreading AIDS in the Castro—and "infected physicians" became, according to a piece in *Newsweek*, "a national obsession"—"Patient A" never rivaled "Patient Zero" for a central place in the story of AIDS.[80]

ZERO'S AFTERLIFE

From his first media appearance into the present, "Patient Zero" has clearly captured the public imagination, summoned each time renewed attention falls on the threat of emerging infections. Like "Typhoid Mary," his status as scapegoat has been noted and lamented, yet it persists. The scapegoating, however, is only part of the problem marked by this persistence. The centrality of "Patient Zero" to the story of the epidemic, like that of "Typhoid Mary," marks a shift in the attribution of blame and a deflection from the structural analysis of the epidemic. A dismayed Shilts wondered why, despite his comprehensive analysis of the institutional and governmental politics that created the conditions of the epidemic, the media focused so heavily on his depiction of "Patient Zero." What he did not seem to consider was the conceptual power of the outbreak narrative, which he helped to evolve, to shift the terms of the analysis.

The scapegoating of "Patient Zero" and the distortion of the story it produced is the subject of the Canadian filmmaker John Greyson's 1993 avant-garde film, *Zero Patience*. Greyson uses the unexpected genre of the musical spoof to indict not only Shilts but also the medical, business, and journalistic forces responsible for the irresponsible story they told about Dugas and HIV/AIDS as well as the unethical practices that the story enabled. Greyson centers his own story on a love affair between the ghost of Zero and Richard Francis Burton, the famed British Victorian adventurer, explorer, man of letters, and sexologist whose "unfortunate encounter with the fountain of youth" has "extended his life indefinitely." The film, which also includes a character named Mary Typhus who calls herself "Typhoid Mary," chronicles the evolving story about the epidemic that follows from the demonization of the French Canadian flight attendant.[81]

From his emergence in the middle of a steam bath in an early scene in the film, the ghost of Zero (visible only to Burton) begs to have his story told; he wants not only to be exonerated of the blame that has consigned him to a living death but also to exist as something other than a caricature. Burton wants to comply at least with the request to tell his story, but it is not initially the story for which Zero asks. When Zero encounters him, Burton is in the process of making a documentary about "Patient Zero" for an exhibit in the Hall of Contagion that he is constructing for the Natural History Museum where he works. The film exposes the conflict between the sensational story Burton wants for his exhibit and the story that Zero and everyone who knew him—from his mother and co-workers to the epidemiologists who first encountered him—tries to tell.

Greyson depicts Burton's gradual awakening to his complicity in perpetuating an irresponsible and inaccurate story of blame as well as his growing dismay as he discovers that he cannot control the story. Greyson filters his didacticism through the campy wit of the film, but the pedagogy is apparent and hard hitting, as in a conversation between Zero and Miss HIV (played by Michael Callen), through which Greyson offers a pointed critique of the faulty assumptions that led to the creation of a "Patient Zero." By the end of the film, Zero accepts that no story will present him as he deserves to be presented, and he persuades Burton to destroy the documentary and let him disappear.

Greyson's "mission is to rewrite gay history," claimed a reviewer for the *Guardian*, "to document legalised and illicit homophobia and, in *Zero Patience*, to call into question fundamental medical and sociological assumptions about Aids."[82] The film is explicitly critical of the institutions—from the medical establishment and pharmaceutical industry to the news and entertainment media—that exploit the epidemic for profit. But, ultimately, Greyson focuses his analysis on how social transformations of the late twentieth century permeate medical theories in the epidemiological story of HIV/AIDS and why the metamorphosis of a gay male French Canadian flight attendant into "Patient Zero" is at the center of that story.

Greyson insightfully performs that analysis through the love story between Burton and Zero. Shilts had called Gaetan Dugas "the man everyone wanted," and Normand Fauteux plays Zero with an enchanting charm.[83] But Shilts's narcissistic Dugas is monstrous in his refusal to abstain from the indiscriminate sexual contacts that define him, and Shilts makes him representative of a "promiscuous" segment of "gay culture" that his book helped to make a characteristic feature in discussions of the epidemic. In contrast,

Greyson's Zero is the boy next door. Burton is drawn to the uncanny famil-iarity of this stranger. Zero's innocence and vulnerability surprises the im-perial Briton, whose attraction to the ghost teaches him the lesson of the epidemic. Through the lens of Greyson's film, their relationship turns the promiscuity that Shilts condemns into a paradigm of the erotics of encoun-ters in a shrinking world: Shoumatoff's *liaisons dangereuses*. *Zero Patience* shows—as Simmel had claimed—that estrangement attests to the disturb-ing familiarity more than the radical difference of the "stranger." The mi-crobe circulates along the circuits of desire in an interconnected world, but governmental indifference and corruption and corporate exploitation turn the outbreaks of disease into a global pandemic (which is where Greyson's and Shilts's analysis converge). When Burton tries to revise his account, he learns the strength of the stigmatizing story that obscures governmental and corporate responsibility. It places blame on the behavior of individuals and "populations" rather than institutions. The tenacity of Shilts's depiction of "Patient Zero" in the mainstream media attests to the aptness of Grey-son's analysis.

Unlike his cinematic avatar in Greyson's film, Shilts's character has not been allowed to disappear. In 1994, the year Preston published *The Hot Zone*, the *Boston Globe* described how, "in horror straight from Jacobean melodrama, [Dugas] took revenge by knowingly pumping the virus to as many partners as he could, reportedly 2,500 men."[84] In the summer of that same year, readers of Glasgow's *Herald* were reminded that "Aids is thought to have been introduced to America by Gaetan Dugas," a "voraciously pro-miscuous homosexual who luxuriated in the spectacular sexual laxity of contemporary San Francisco."[85] Even those who understood the science fell into the narrative, as in Oscar Moore's 1996 description of Dugas as "the infamous Patient Zero who, having become one of the first people to be diagnosed HIV-positive (hence his statistical appellation), then decided to take as many down with him as he could"; he was, Moore observed, "the evil mascot of this era."[86] And Duncan J. Watts summons him in his study of social network theory to illustrate the principle of an epidemiological net-work. "Just as HIV crawled its grisly way down the Kinshasa highway from its birthplace in the jungles," he writes, "and somehow, probably in one of the coastal cities, found Gaetan Dugas—the Canadian flight attendant, better known as *patient zero*—who brought it to the bath houses of San Francisco and introduced AIDS to the Western world, so too could the right chain of events free Ebola from its shackles."[87] Invariably, in the nu-merous accounts of "sexual predators" and "supertransmitters"—people accused of carelessly or knowingly spreading HIV—Gaetan Dugas's name will surface, as well as either his originary status, his alleged revenge motive, or both. He is a stock figure in the history of HIV/AIDS, but, like Mary Mallon, he has also migrated out of a specific pandemic. Separated by a century, Dugas and Mallon are both invoked characteristically in the media, as in the SARS example, in the midst of a new outbreak. Both figures are narrative devices that signal the effort to fashion an outbreak narrative.

Throughout this book, I have shown how novels and films animate the language, images, and storylines of the scientific studies and journalistic portraits of the threat of disease emergence. Figures of speech and images come to life and hypotheses are explored in the extended scenarios that fiction can imagine. Horror stories in particular draw out the anxieties embedded in the chance remarks and illustrations of the scientific, journalistic, and even less fantastical fictional accounts. The infectious zombies of such films as *Resident Evil* (2002) and *28 Days Later* (2002) and especially the more psychologically developed human-virus protagonists of Chuck Hogan's 1998 *The Blood Artists* and Robin Cook's 1997 *Invasion* dramatize the transformative impact of a virus; they are the monstrous fictional prototypes of the metamorphosed carrier, tracing a lineage from "Typhoid Mary" through the body snatchers to "Patient Zero."[88] The contemporary epidemiological horror stories that feature them show how the conventions of horror and myth color the imagined experience of an outbreak at the turn of the twenty-first century, explaining both the fascination elicited by this cultural narrative and its consequences. These stories conspicuously turn the threat of disease emergence into an apocalyptic battle between heroic scientists and the hybrids who embody the threat. Against the backdrop of the uncontrolled spread of the rapidly mutating human immunodeficiency virus, of profound human suffering, and of the failed promise of scientific medicine, they complete the story that Shilts was trying to tell: the outbreak narrative of disease emergence. These stories are doubly reassuring as they depict the containment of viruses that are potentially more devastating than HIV/AIDS and as they restore the promise and authority of science in the heroic service of a threatened "Humanity."[89]

The Blood Artists offers an especially vivid example—reading almost as a blueprint—of the outbreak narrative. An epigraph to the novel explains that "a virus does not want to kill. It does not even want to harm. It wants to change. It wants that part of it that is missing. It wants to become."[90] When the extremely mutable (unstable) retrovirus enters a human host, it quickly enacts that desire. The novel opens with the emergence of a newly identified retrovirus from an illegal uranium mine in the "primordial" jungles of Central African Congo. It is initially devastating to human beings, and the CDC epidemiologists sent to contain it are almost successful, until one, Stephen Pearse, succumbs to his humanity and allows an asymptomatic woman to break quarantine. When the dying woman eventually wanders into the solitary camp of Oren Ridgeway, a botanist working for the environmentalist group Rainforest Ecology Conservation International, she is already part viral and literalizes the viral desire of the epigraph with a passionate kiss that turns Ridgeway into a carrier *par excellence*. The unsuspecting Ridgeway unwittingly produces the initial outbreak in the U.S. in his hometown of Plainville, Massachusetts, which gives the virus its name. But the infection transforms both progenitors (virus and human being), and the evolving hybrid becomes vengeful and calculating, wanting nothing less than the extinction of the human species. Ridgeway/Plainville deliberately infects Pearse, whom "he" blames for "his" infection, and the hybrid commences to seed outbreaks as "he" embarks on an apocalyptic master plan to save the planet by annihilating humanity.

Pearse's infection connects him psychically to Ridgeway/Plainville, whom he and his colleague Peter Maryk call "Patient Zero" or just "Zero," and Maryk keeps Pearse alive to gain insight into their foe. Pearse can therefore narrate the horrifying transformation; the "'character of a virus endowed with human traits,'" he tells Maryk, is "'a being uninhibited by any obligations, social or moral. Combine the worst elements of a serial murderer, a rapist, an impulsive arsonist. Hyperaggressive, hypersexual, homicidal, egocentric, pathological. An unqualified sociopath. The ultimate deviant terrorist mentality. All Zero wants to do is infect, infect, infect'" (249). The synthesis is dramatic: a virus has no social instinct, but when combined with a human being, it develops conscious agency and becomes a sociopath— one of the many charges leveled against Gaetan Dugas—and a bioterrorist.[91]

If human traits make the hybrids vengeful, their viral progenitors bequeath their occult status. The legacy of scientific speculation of viruses' relation to the origins of life continues to prompt scientists to wonder whether viruses may have been the first life form, even the (willful) generators of subsequent organisms. *"What could be a more beautiful supposition,"* asks the virologist Jaap Goudsmit, *"than that viruses no longer saw a future for themselves as independently living organisms and created their own host in order to be able to extend their lives to the end of time?"*[92] In the misty haze of "the RNA world" (156) of this speculative creation myth, viruses are not just primitive, but primordial, holding the secrets of the origin of life and a privileged relation to a pristine Earth. Many of the hybrid protagonists explicitly extend this relation into a righteous indignation for the lack of respect that human beings have shown to their surroundings, which turns them into avenging spirits who speak for a mute Earth. The hybrids' articulation of their position remarkably echoes the language of many of the scientists and science writers that I discussed in chapter 1, as in Maryk's explanation of the "Message" of Plainville/Ridgeway that the " 'Earth is a cell we are infecting. And nature is the Earth's immune system, just now sensing the threat of our encroachment, and arming itself to fight back. Macro versus micro. Viruses are the Earth's white blood cells. We are the Earth's disease' " (224). This characteristic articulation invigorates the mythic status of the hybrids, who become earth demons with apocalyptic intent. The extension of their environmentalism into a program of planned genocide, moreover, undermines the environmental analyses that are central features of discussions of disease emergence.

As embodied (partial) viruses, the hybrid protagonists pose the problem of disease emergence in medical terms. They have a distinctly epidemiological appeal, offering a clear and concentrated solution to the problem of the outbreak. As Hogan explains, the "threat of a mutant virus gifted with human intellect and cunning posed hazards exceeding Maryk's worst imaginings. But all he envisioned was its one great advantage. Epidemic control had never been simpler. Zero was like a tumor Maryk could go in and surgically remove" (240). The hybrids are enemies that can be comprehended, fought and defeated, and they allow medical science and epidemiology to do the work of containment in these epidemiological horror stories, all of which feature a state-of-the art laboratory. The cure for the virus so hopefully promised by Gallo and Montagnier in the co-edited issue of *Scientific American* comes in these versions from the lavishly described laboratories of these accounts. While *Outbreak*'s opening tour of the biocontainment laboratory prepares the audience for the implausible production of an antidote that saves Cedar Creek from annihilation, the hero protagonists in *Invasion* and *The Blood Artists* even more dramatically forestall full-fledged viral apocalypse with the kind of engineering feats anticipated by Gallo and Montagnier. The bioengineered viruses with which the protagonists defeat their viral foes in Cook's and Hogan's novels represent the researchers' deliberate harnessing of microbes. They are feats of science rather than, as in *War of the Worlds*, accidents of the environment. The scientist heroes in these and other fictional accounts renovate Miles's unearned triumph at the end of Finney's novel.[93] Their ingenuity reaffirms scientific authority, and their achievements are successful versions of strategies that contemporary scientists are in fact exploring.

The mythic features of the outbreak narrative complement rather than contradict the authority of scientific medicine. The scientists and epidemiologists who battle the primordial and supernatural hybrids are more than successful in their fight to contain an outbreak; they are triumphant in their archetypal battle against apocalyptic forces of destruction that are not only not new, but that return to the beginning of time and represent an ongoing threat. Lederberg refers to an "eternal competition" between human beings and microbes, and the archetypal nature of the battle turns that competition into a timeless and ritualized story of renewal in which Humanity is reaffirmed as it is redeemed by Science.[94] While the particular microbes described in accounts of "emerging infections" may be "new" to human beings, these novels show how an old story structures the idea of disease emergence. Myths, as Bruce Lincoln explains, characteristically summon "sentiments—above all those of internal affinity (affection, loyalty, mutual attachment, and solidarity) and external estrangement (detachment, alienation and hostility)—[that] constitute the bonds and borders that we reify as society."[95] They can reinforce or break down social borders. The outbreak narrative registers at once the tenacity and the porosity of national boundaries, among other social borders, and thereby manifests—and medicalizes—the tension of the changing spaces and social groupings of global modernity.

Virology supplies a scientific vocabulary for the danger of hybridity. The most dangerous viruses are themselves frequently hybrids: the mutant strains produced when animal and human viruses recombine in animal hosts. In viral terms, hybridity is dangerous because it combines newness and familiarity; in their new incarnations, hybrid viruses can jump the species barrier (be "recognized") and produce outbreaks of especially virulent and untreatable diseases. Viral hybridity is a key term in the vocabulary of disease emergence. Scientific explanations of the concept and the behaviors and practices that enable it abound in discussions of SARS, avian flu, and other "emerging infections." Speculations about activities and conditions that may have led to the barrier crossings show how the concept of viral hybridity slides into characterizations of afflicted people and how the imagined practices and behaviors of those people are racialized and sexualized. Images of perversion are explicit or implied, as in the theory that circulated in the early years of the HIV/AIDS epidemic that the virus jumped species when Africans had sex with monkeys or in the disgust evident in accounts of Asian peasants' sharing their domestic spaces with their animals and in Soper's report of Mary Mallon's alleged fondness for her dog (evidence for him of her lack of hygiene). Deadly diseases mark the danger of "inappropriate" and transformational practices and behaviors; their implicit racialization and sexualization accounts for (white AIDS activist) Michael Callen's "third-world" immune system in *And the Band Played On*.

The monstrous hybrids in the contemporary epidemiological horror stories are not strangers, but transformed familiars—literally, as in body snatchers, the boys (and girls) next door. They embody the dangerously transformative nature of global networks that undergirds the vocabulary of disease emergence. SARS accounts, for example, emphasized the spread of the disease less through strangers than through travelers who brought it home to their families and communities; the superspreaders were characteristically featured in their roles as children, parents, spouses, and doctors. As the spreading disease displays the contours of a contracting world, the estrangement evinced by the monstrous hybrids (as in Georg Simmel's formulation) heralds the deferred but imminent affinities of new social formations and the mutability of human populations. The hybrids show how formatively superspreaders medicalize the breakdown of conventional taxonomies and the social hierarchies they name. They also illustrate how myth infuses this medicalization of global networks.

The mythic frame of the outbreak narrative subtly complements the more explicitly stigmatizing terms through which landscapes and people are portrayed as dangerous, dirty, and diseased. In the introduction to this book, I showed how the depictions of impoverished spaces as "primitive" temporalized the uneven development of global modernity and obscured the socioeconomic conditions of "disease emergence." The mythic temporality of these fictional outbreak narratives works similarly. As the impoverished spaces that amplify outbreaks dissolve into the mythic terrain on which the apocalyptic battle is waged, the landscape becomes not just primitive, but primordial. Associated with *primordial* landscapes and viruses, the inhabitants of these spaces can be implicitly incorporated, collectively *as populations*, into the prehistory of "humanity" and thereby made expendable (always "regrettably" so). Arguing for the priority of containment at all costs, which entails expedited annihilation of the dying village in the Congo, Maryk explains, "'This is Andromeda. . . . The Holocaust paradigm: bombing the rail yards to cut the transport lines, martyring those already in the cattle cars to the millions who would die in the gas chambers. That's what disease control is all about: trading the dead for the living'"

(43). But which dead are invariably exchanged for which living? Sacrificing the citizens of Cedar Creek, California, is unthinkable in *Outbreak*. When, in *The Hot Zone*, the virus hunter Karl Johnson tells Richard Preston that " 'a virus that reduces us by some percentage. By thirty percent. By ninety percent . . . can be useful to a species by thinning it out,' " he speaks with the dispassion of a long-term perspective.[96] The effect on a "species" (or a "population") can only be measured from the perspective of a distant future. When we speak of the effect on "humanity," we are back in the present. A mythologized population—a group that is anachronistic in the present moment—exists precariously in a future past (grammatically, the future perfect). Anachronistic populations can be rhetorically excluded from politics and history, fading into myth where, like Oedipus, they are absorbed (or recuperated) as sacrificial blessings—Nurse Mayinga's life-giving blood, but also "Patient Zero's" epidemiological revelations—in the Land of Science.

The danger, as I have argued throughout this book, lies not in scientific research or epidemiological investigation per se, but in stories, in the conventions of representation that infuse the images, phrases, and narratives through which we make sense of the world. They inflect—and yes, infect— every aspect of the scientific and epidemiological processes from the collection and interpretation of data to the social and medical diagnoses of the problem. In the afterword to *The Tipping Point*, a contemporary study of "epidemics" and social contagion, Malcolm Gladwell recounts the curious rumination of an epidemiologist who had spent his professional life "battling the AIDS epidemic" and who wonders " 'if we would have been better off if we had never discovered the AIDS virus at all?' "[97] Gladwell explains that, after his initial surprise, he realized that what troubled the epidemiologist was the thought that the identification of HIV may have prevented a more effective management of the epidemic. Convinced, he muses that "the AIDS epidemic is a social phenomenon. It spreads because of the beliefs and social structures and poverty and prejudices and personalities of a community, and sometimes getting caught up in the precise biological characteristics of a virus merely serves as a distraction; we might have halted the spread of AIDS far more effectively just by focusing on those beliefs and social structures and poverty and prejudices and personalities" (261–62).

Gladwell shares with Greyson, Shilts, and many other analysts of HIV/ AIDS the conviction that the predominant focus on the virus might have medicalized the approach to the pandemic at the expense of a more comprehensive social analysis. Yet his brief anecdote shows how tempting the medical focus is. The virus is a compelling and easily identified villain for epidemiologists "battling the AIDS epidemic" and also for those asking where "we" went wrong. For the epidemiologist's colleagues, the virus is the source of the pandemic; for him, its identification is the source of the problem. That focus leads him to express regret for a "discovery" that, as Gladwell quickly concedes, led to more reliable diagnoses and blood tests and to significantly more effective treatments. The "distraction" that rightly troubles them both, however, does not come from the identification of HIV; it comes, rather, as Greyson's film makes clear, from the powerful conventions of a mythico-medical story of disease emergence, global networks, and social transformation worldwide through which the identification of HIV and the phenomenon of disease emergence generally are understood. That story—the outbreak narrative—affects which social structures and whose beliefs, poverty, prejudices, and personalities become the focus of analysis, as well as who is included in the "we" who might have been better off had the virus not been identified. By failing to take the story into account, Gladwell and the epidemiologist risk reproducing its terms.

Epilogue

The universe is made of stories, not of atoms.

— MURIEL RUKEYSER, "The Speed of Darkness"

Eyewitness accounts of the plagues of the past stress the equalizing effect of common susceptibility as well as common suffering. Rich and poor, good and evil, cautious and profligate—all alike fall victim to the democratic ravages of disease. The health activist Paul Farmer disagrees. The epidemiological insight that "diseases themselves make a preferential option for the poor" motivates his work in the clinic and on the page.[1] From communicable disease to cancer, disability to drug abuse, health outcomes display the consequences of power and privilege as they register socioeconomic and political inequities worldwide.

In *Pathologies of Power* (2005), Farmer recalls learning that lesson from community health workers in Zanmi Lasante, the medical complex he built in Haiti. When Farmer and his staff came together to discuss why three HIV-negative men in their forties had died of tuberculosis despite undergoing treatment, they discovered "a fairly sharp divide between community health workers, who shared the social conditions of the patients, and the doctors and nurses, who did not."[2] The doctors and nurses attributed the patients' deaths to poor compliance stemming from the patients' belief that their illness was the result of sorcery and therefore would not respond to biomedical treatment. The community health workers disagreed, contending that the patients' superstitions were not the problem since their beliefs about the cause of their illness did not prevent them from taking their medications. Arguing that the exclusive medical focus of the doctors and nurses masked important socioeconomic factors in health outcomes, they offered an alternative account that linked the patients' deaths to their poverty: their already weakened states from malnutrition, overwork, and inadequate living conditions, and their difficulty balancing their treatment regimens with the overwhelming tasks of providing and caring for their families. The remarkable results of a study that included follow-up visits and other kinds of assistance, such as nutritional supplements and home repairs, validated the community health workers' analysis.

The insights he gained from this experience led Farmer to change not only his treatment protocols but also his account of disease emergence. He is critical of the predominant focus on science and medicine in discussions of emerging infections, which, he argues, obscures how global politics create conditions conducive to the amplification of disease outbreaks. Instead, he insists, disease emergence must be narrated in a way that reveals it to be a "socially produced phenomenon" at the global level and an example of "structural violence": an "offense[ ] against human dignity" that is intrinsic to coercive state-sanctioned policies and institutions and adversely affects quality of life for the poor and oppressed.[3]

The epidemic proportions of HIV/AIDS, multi-drug resistant tuberculosis, and other global health problems in the Cange, the impoverished region of Haiti where Farmer built Zanmi Lasante, dramatizes the point. In his biography of Farmer, *Mountains Beyond Mountains,* Tracy Kidder explains how this once fertile region in which farmers could thrive was a casualty of global politics. In the 1950s, the United States had planned and helped to fund and construct the Peligré Dam as " 'a development project.' "[4] The beneficiaries of the dam were the mainly U.S.-owned agribusinesses and the elite Haitians and foreign businesses of Port-au-Prince. The victims were the peasants whose homes and farms were submerged beneath the waters of the dammed river and who were therefore forced to relocate to the mountains, where the considerably less arable land made farms nearly impossible to sustain. Health problems escalated noticeably in the Cange as a result of the impoverishment of its inhabitants; those problems illustrate Thomas Pogge's claim that "desperately poor people, often stunted, illiterate, and heavily preoccupied with the struggle to survive, can do little by way of either resisting or rewarding their rulers, who are therefore likely to rule them oppressively while catering to the interests of other (often foreign) agents more capable of reciprocation."[5] By presenting the lesson he learned from the community health workers of Zanmi Lasante in the form of an anecdote, Farmer shows why attention to storytelling must be part of the analysis of the problem of disease emergence. Changing the story will not, of course, solve the problem, but it is a necessary first step in addressing it. The story that he and his medical staff initially tried to tell—the story he has since replaced with a global analysis of poverty and disease emergence and a vocabulary of responsibility in global terms—demonstrates the impact of the outbreak narrative.

I have shown how the outbreak narrative draws attention to an urgent and important problem. But the conventions that make the story so appealing, which are derived from genres such as myth and horror, also influence the articulation of the global health problem. The "coming plague" heralded by Laurie Garrett offers a good example of how those conventions can deflect the analysis of disease emergence intended by the author. Garrett ends *The Coming Plague* by wistfully recalling the optimism of 12 September 1978—the signing of the *Declaration of Alma-Ata*—when the year 2000, a scant twenty-two years away, seemed a reasonable deadline for the abolition of the threat of communicable disease. "All of humanity was supposed to be immunized against most infectious diseases," she muses, "basic health care was to be available to every man, woman, and child regardless of their economic class, race, religion, or place of birth."⁶ On that mid-September day, delegates from 134 nations assembled in Alma-Ata (now Almaty), Kazakhstan's largest city, for a conference sponsored by the WHO and UNICEF. The *Declaration of Alma-Ata* represented a formal, multinational agreement to understand health as a "state of complete physical, mental and social well being, and not merely the absence of disease or infirmity" and as "a fundamental human right,'" and it recognized a commitment to the idea "that the attainment of the highest possible level of health is a most important world-wide social goal whose realization requires the action of many other social and economic sectors in addition to the health sector."⁷ Locating responsibility for the health of populations mainly in the state, the declaration called on nations worldwide to recognize their responsibility for global health.

The conference was inspired by programs in seven countries—including China, Tanzania, Venezuela, and the Sudan—devoted to providing access to "primary health care" (a term that came from those initiatives) for impoverished rural communities within their borders. These programs for comprehensive access to primary health care were revolutionary in both scope and conception, as they acknowledged the need to address the social, political, and economic conditions affecting the health of individuals and populations, in part through community empowerment. While the declaration registered the considerable compromises required to get diverse endorsement, it also manifested an effort to fashion a new story of global health as well as to implement new policies. The delegates at Alma-Ata officially acknowledged that disease yielded insight into the worldwide inequities created or exacerbated by globalization and that the impact of globalization on health should be central to discussions of economic development.

The Health for All movement that came out of the Alma-Ata conference fashioned a vocabulary in which health needed to be measured not just in terms of survival but also in the quality of people's lives.[8] Communicable disease was one among many health problems that affected the impoverished disproportionately, and their health needed to become a priority not because their diseases might spread to the wealthy but because human beings had a fundamental right to live in conditions conducive to good health and to have access to health care. Health activists called for structural changes from reform of health care delivery systems to redistribution of resources worldwide. They debated new means of measuring what constituted health, but the *Declaration of Alma-Ata* at least marked widespread agreement that health broadly defined was a basic human entitlement.[9]

In *The Coming Plague,* Garrett invokes Alma-Ata to mark the distance between the goals enumerated in the declaration and the contemporary conditions of the "frantic, angry place" in which human beings are microbial prey (618). Precisely when she wants to emphasize the importance of assuming personal and collective responsibility and of acting for change, she reaches for the familiar language of microbial warfare, concluding with the warning that "our predators . . . will be victorious if we, *Homo sapiens,* do not learn how to live in a rational global village that affords the microbes few opportunities. It's either that or we brace ourselves for the coming plague" (620). The familiar story that she thereby summons—the outbreak narrative—shifts the terms of her analysis of global health. Microbial warfare directs attention to the microbes and thereby presents the threat of disease emergence in predominantly medical terms. Joshua Lederberg is an informing presence in Garrett's discussion, pronouncing the world "'just one village'" and warning that "'our tolerance of disease in any place in the world is at our own peril'" (619). Since "microbes, and their vectors recognize none of the artificial boundaries erected by human beings" (618), they illuminate global networks and act as "rivet[s] in the Global Village airplane" (619). The animated microbes are at once ever present and imperceptible, more numerous and adaptable than their human foes in this dramatization of the microbial dangers of human connections in a borderless world.

Although the impending apocalypse threatens humanity as a species, the microbes have human collaborators who trouble the inclusiveness of the first-person plural pronouns ("we" and "our"). The distinctions between animated microbes and human collaborators blur in the depiction of individuals infected with HIV as "walking immune-deficient Petri dishes" (619) and even in the comparison of microbial activity with "the lunch-hour sidewalk traffic of Tokyo" (618). Such images implicitly pathologize particular human beings ("carriers"), human behaviors, and spaces, as they dramatize the dangers of life in a global hot zone.

"Ultimately," Garrett intones, "humanity will have to change its perspective on its place in Earth's ecology if the species hopes to stave off or survive the next plague" (618). Yet, in place of the global analysis of poverty and expanded definition of health offered in the *Declaration of Alma-Ata,* instead of the vocabulary of human entitlement and global responsibility and the accompanying policy recommendations that would implement structural change locally and globally, Garrett offers predatory, border-crossing microbes. The appeal of the image is clear. The widespread problems of global health she identifies and the (unspecified) transformations for which she calls seem dauntingly inevitable and insurmountable. Global health analysts do not agree on the nature of those problems, much less on the solutions, nor even on the definitions of social justice and global poverty. Dangerous microbes, by contrast, offer a focused problem that medical science and epidemiology can address. The epidemiological threat of a coming plague has an urgency that captures attention.

The mythic features of the narrative, in turn, temper the urgency with an implicit promise not only of survival but also of renewal. Even as the species war threatens apocalypse, the conventionality of the story anticipates the triumph of science and epidemiology and affirms the worth of humanity. As it thus sanctions the status quo, the familiar story occludes not only the problem of communicable disease outbreaks worldwide but also the troubling questions and unrealized hopes of social responsibility conceived on a global scale. While Garrett passionately advocates a new worldview in *The Coming Plague,* namely, a change of perspective on the place of humanity in "Earth's ecology," the language of the outbreak narrative promotes a sanguine reliance on science, a fundamental belief that humanity will survive "the coming plague" intact, and even a tacit assurance that global transformations will not (and should not) significantly reconfigure social existence.

As I conclude this book, the threat of avian flu is hovering on the epidemiological horizon. Jeffery Taubenberger's genetic reconstruction of the 1918 flu virus in 2005, which identified it as a bird flu with a distant genetic relation to the bird flu that has infected human beings in recent years, has inflamed the public imagination and intensified the predictive accounts. While many researchers, epidemiologists, and journalists summon the lessons of the past both to argue for the importance of preparing for a possible pandemic and to warn of the danger of panic, anticipation of an avian flu outbreak has already taken a spectacular turn in science, journalism, fiction, and film, putting a narrative frame in place. "Patients Zero" and "Typhoid Marys" of avian flu have surfaced in various incarnations. The microbe is, according to one author, *The Monster at Our Door,* and the *Washington Post* reports that it "is making the world a global village—or, more precisely, a global barnyard." *Newsweek* deplores "The Flimsy Wall of China" and describes an Asian "hot zone"; in *USA Today* the CDC director Julie Gerberding calls "Asia today . . . the perfect incubator" for such a disease. The *New Yorker* writer Michael Specter dubs avian flu "Nature's Bioterrorist" and concludes his piece with the observation of a Thai health official that if you "'take a plane ride to Paris . . . you may be taking an epidemic along with you.'"[10] Flying geese visually metamorphose into missiles in the opening shots of "Fatal Contact: Bird Flu in America," an ABC made-for-television movie that aired on 9 May 2006. Anxiety mounts with every monstrous microbe that emerges from the contagious spaces of a primitive hot zone to bring terror and destruction to the vulnerable, civilized world. Anticipated scenarios of the ravages of avian flu stress the question of survival, turning the undercurrent of fear to an undertow of panic and making it ever more difficult to ask how we want to live.

These images also correspond to medical and epidemiological approaches to this "coming plague." While efforts to prepare for a possible pandemic reflect a variety of strategies, media accounts suggest the predominance of those generated by microbial (vaccine and drug development) and spatial (national border patrols and quarantine) conceptualizations of the threat. Those initiatives far outweigh the urgency of reforming health care delivery systems worldwide in ways that would prioritize the suffering—and the humanity—of those who will be disproportionately affected by the spread of a virulent communicable disease. The goals of Alma-Ata appear to be incompatible with the urgency of the medical threat. Over the din of the call to battle, it is hard to hear the voices of global health analysts, such as Farmer and Amartya Sen, who maintain both that global health care reform is not incompatible with those other initiatives and that a more encompassing approach to global health is not only more just but also medically and epidemiologically effective.

Disease emergence ineluctably evinces human interconnections on a global scale, but the stories of disease emergence fashion the terms in which those connections make sense. It is possible to revise the outbreak narrative, to tell the story of disease emergence and human connection in the language of social justice rather than of susceptibility.[11] In place of the fearful scenario in which monstrous microbes from elsewhere threaten to turn "us" into "them" ("thirdworldification"), the revised story shows "thirdworldification" to be a product of uneven development and exploitation. Disease emergence, in this account, is an urgent problem in the North not only, or even primarily, because disease may spread from the South to the North, but because of the role of the North in perpetuating the conditions of thirdworldification worldwide. The inequities expressed by disease emergence make it imperative to address the conditions of poverty not chiefly because of the fear of contagion but because no human beings should have to live in the impoverished conditions that fuel the spread of disease. Communicable diseases are a part of life; they will continue to emerge and circulate, and people will suffer and die. Yet suffering and death should not be accepted as inevitable in one place and unthinkable in another. Amid the uncertainties about the forecasted pandemic, there is no doubt that it, or any pandemic, will affect the world's populations inequitably. The emerging stories can exacerbate or begin to address the inequities. They can make a difference. It is not only possible but time to change the stories and the world they imagine.

Notes

INTRODUCTION

1. Marilynn Marchione, "Anatomy of an Epidemic," *Milwaukee Journal Sentinel*, 4 May 2003, A1.

2. Marchione, "Anatomy of an Epidemic," A1. My conclusions about SARS coverage are based on my reading of roughly 120 articles from a variety of newspapers and magazines worldwide, including the *New York Times, Newsweek,* the *New Yorker, Time,* the *South China Morning Post,* the *Ottawa Citizen,* the *Toronto Star,* the *Independent* (London), the *Irish Times,* the *Atlanta Journal-Constitution,* the *Washington Post,* the *New Straits Times* (Malaysia), the *Milwaukee Journal Sentinel,* the *Australian,* the *Plain Dealer* (Cleveland), the *Boston Globe,* the *Pittsburgh Post-Gazette,* the *Straits Times* (Singapore), the *Age* (Melbourne), *Rocky Mountain News* (Denver), *Harper's,* and the *Philadelphia Inquirer.*

3. Richard M. Krause sounded the warning in his 1981 book, *The Restless Tide: The Persistent Challenge of the Microbial World,* and the phenomenon was named with a conference at the end of the decade. See chapter 1 herein for a more extended discussion of these events. Not all "emerging infections" are communicable via the routes of human transmission, but the ones featured in the outbreak narratives typically are, and they are the topic of this book.

4. *The Coming Plague* is the title of Laurie Garrett's 1994 nonfiction bestseller that helped to bring the threat of disease emergence to the attention of the public.

5. Although researchers eventually determined that SARS did not spread as easily as had first been feared and that many people developed antibodies without becoming sick, the anxiety generated by the disease never fully dissipated. That anxiety, as I will argue in this book, registers the powerful conventions of the story of disease emergence and containment. On the fear generated by the epidemic, see Karl Taro Greenfield, *China Syndrome: The Killer Virus that Crashed the Middle Kingdom* (New York: HarperCollins, 2006).

6. In thinking about the properties of emergent narratives, I have found especially useful N. Katherine Hayles, *My Mother Was a Computer: Digital Subjects and Literary Texts* (Chicago: University of Chicago Press, 2005), especially chap. 8, and Alex Argyro, *A Blessed Rage for Order: Deconstruction, Evolution, and Chaos* (Ann Arbor: University of Michigan Press, 1991). Over the years, my thinking about narrative has been shaped especially by Fredric Jameson, *The Political Unconscious: Narrative as a Socially Symbolic Act* (Ithaca: Cornell University Press, 1981), and Hayden White, "The Value of Narrativity in the Representation of Reality," in *On Narrative*, ed. W. J. T. Mitchell (Chicago: University of Chicago Press, 1981), 1–23. On the treatment of science in popular fiction, see also José van Dijk, *Imagenation: Popular Images of Genetics* (New York: New York University Press, 1998), and the introduction to Susan Merrill Squier, *Liminal Lives: Imaging the Human at the Frontiers of Biomedicine* (Durham: Duke University Press, 2004).

7. Donald G. McNeil Jr. and Lawrence K. Altman, "How One Person Can Fuel an Epidemic," *New York Times*, Science, Medicine, and Technology, 15 April 2003, A1.

8. Ibid.

9. Nicholas Thompson, "The Myth of the Superspreader: Why the SARS Epidemic Can't Be Blamed on Highly Toxic Individuals," *Boston Globe*, 4 May 2003, H1.

10. McNeil and Altman, "How One Person Can Fuel an Epidemic," A1.

11. "Scientists' Worldwide Race against Virus," *Straits Times*, 10 April 2003, 14.

12. Jeremy Laurance, "Victim Who Infected 133 Will Remain in Quarantine Exile," *Independent*, 11 April 2003, 16. All of the victims were named in the media, despite the repeated protests of the brother of the Singaporean flight attendant, who expressed his dismay at the continuing stigmatization of his sister. I have chosen here to honor his request and not name her or the other victims.

13. Greenfield, *China Syndrome*, 231. As editor of *Time Asia*, Greenfield was stationed in Hong Kong, which gave him front-row seats to the epidemic. While he offers in *China Syndrome* a rich and responsible analysis of the worldwide efforts to identify and contain the sources of the SARS outbreak, his use of the title of a popular 1979 film about a cover-up of a crisis in a nuclear power plant and his acceptance of vocabulary such as *superspreader* and *killer virus* exemplify the sensationalist rhetoric through which the outbreak narrative shapes the experience of a communicable disease, from the perception of spaces of contagion (the geography of disease) to the depiction of individuals and populations. See *China Syndrome*, directed by James Bridges (Columbia Pictures, 1979).

14. Alex Lo, "A Shrinking World Raises the Risk for Global Epidemics," *South China Morning Post*, 14 March 2003, 4, and Abraham Verghese, "The Way We Live Now," *New York Times*, 20 April 2003, 15. Verghese is among those who argue that the threats of global pandemics and emerging infections justify the loss of civil liberties.

15. Claudia Kalb, "The Mystery of SARS," *Newsweek*, 5 May 2003, 28–29.

16. The term *global village* was put into circulation by the well-known theorist of media and interdependence Marshall McLuhan in a book that he co-authored with Quentin Fiore, *The Medium Is the Massage* (New York: Random House, 1967), but he had already introduced the concept in two previous works, *The Gutenberg Galaxy* (Toronto: University of Toronto Press, 1962) and especially *Understanding Media* (New York: McGraw-Hill, 1964).

17. Geoffrey Cowley, "How Progress Makes Us Sick," *Newsweek*, 5 May 2003, 35.

18. Cowley, "How Progress Makes Us Sick," 33, 35.

19. Fintan O'Toole, "Panic Attack," *Irish Times*, 2 May 2003, 50, and Charles Pierce, "Epidemic of Fear," *Boston Globe*, 1 June 2003, 10.

20. Alan M. Kraut, *Silent Travelers: Germs, Genes, and the "Immigrant Menace"* (Baltimore: Johns Hopkins University Press, 1994), 3. On anti-Asian racism and fear of disease in particular, see Nayan Shah, *Contagious Divides: Epidemics and Race in San Francisco's Chinatown* (Berkeley: University of California Press, 2001); John Higham, *Strangers in the Land: Patterns of American Nativism, 1860–1925*, 2d ed. (New Brunswick, N.J.: Rutgers University Press, 1988); and Warwick Anderson, *The Cultivation of Whiteness: Science, Health, and Racial Destiny in Australia* (New York: Basic Books, 2003). In his fourth chapter, "The Making of the Tropical White Man," Anderson explains how social biases became medicalized through images of the racial "other" as a carrier; he identifies a progression from Asians, Africans, and indigenes as "dirty" and therefore health hazards to actual germ disseminators, and he explains that this process can apply to those at the margins domestically or internationally.

Specific cultural anxieties of course intermingle with the disease threats, and media accounts of SARS resonated with the numerous discussions of China's rapid economic growth. On the particular stigma associated with SARS, see Arthur Kleinman and Sing Lee, "SARS and the Problem of Social Stigma," in *SARS in China: Prelude to Pandemic*, ed. Arthur Kleinman and James L. Watson (Stanford, Calif.: Stanford University Press, 2006), 173–95.

21. Kalb, "The Mystery of SARS," 29; Cowley, "How Progress Makes Us Sick," 35.

22. Cowley, "How Progress Makes Us Sick," 35.

23. Thompson, "The Myth of the Superspreader," H1. Thompson refers here explicitly to sexual superspreaders, and he is paraphrasing Albert-Laszlo Barabasi, author of *Linked*, who notes that "'when it comes to viruses and epidemics, hubs make a deadly difference.'" See Albert-Laszlo Barabasi, *Linked* (Cambridge, Mass.: Perseus Books, 2002); Duncan J. Watts makes similar claims in *Six Degrees: The Science of a Connected Age* (New York: W. W. Norton, 2003). Barabasi and Watts use many of the same events and examples to illustrate their claims about social-network theory, which suggests an emerging story. Epidemiology is one area that most obviously applies and has shaped social-network theory, and emergence is one of its key concepts.

24. Globalization explained the spread of disease, but it also attested to the possibilities afforded by new contacts: the new social relationships that enabled worldwide collaboration in response to the outbreak. Indeed, the one thing more frightening than human contact was its absence, as is evident in a disturbing photograph from the 5 May 2003 issue of *Newsweek*, which showed a solitary masked individual in Taiwan's deserted Chiang Kai-shek International airport (Kalb, "The Mystery of SARS," 32). Similarly, the images of suffering and illness in the many fictional depictions of disease outbreaks, while horrifying, nonetheless lack the chill of the deserted urban landscape to which the protagonists awaken in such disease horror films as *28 Days Later* and *Resident Evil*. The haunted landscapes in these films come to life in the viral zombies and vampires that populate them. Richard Matheson first explored that scenario in his 1954 novella, *I Am Legend*, in which a bacterial epidemic turns all but one man into vampires; the novella spawned two films, *The Last Man on Earth* (1964) and *Omega Man* (1971). See chapter 4.

25. O'Toole, "Panic Attack," 50.

26. Mircea Eliade, *Myths, Dreams, and Mysteries: The Encounter between Contemporary Faiths and Archaic Realities*, trans. Philip Mairet (New York: Harper and Row, 1960), 34. Claude Lévi-Strauss, *Structural Anthropology*, trans. Claire Jacobson and Brooke Grundfest Schoepf (New York: Basic Books, 1963–1976).

27. Bruce Lincoln, *Discourse and the Construction of Society: Comparative Studies of Myth, Ritual, and Classification* (New York: Oxford University Press, 1989), 24–25. Joseph Mali, *Mythistory: The Making of Modern Historiography* (Chicago: University of Chicago Press, 2003), 8. "Mythistory" is the term Mali uses to describe "the mythical compulsions that motivate all historical actions and creations" (xi). Myth, for him, is "a story that has passed into and become history" and he sees "these stories as inevitable, and ultimately valuable, histories of personal and communal identity" (Preface, *Mythistory*, xi, xii).

For my understanding of myths, I have found the following works especially useful: Bruce Lincoln, *Theorizing Myth: Narrative, Ideology, and Scholarship* (Chicago: University of Chicago Press, 1999); Talal Asad, *Formations of the Secular: Christianity, Islam, Modernity* (Stanford, Calif.: Stanford University Press, 2003); Robert Segal, *Theorizing about Myth* (Amherst: University of Massachusetts Press, 1999); Claude Lévi-Strauss, *The Raw and the Cooked*, trans. John Weightman and Doreen Weightman (New York: Harper and Row, 1969); Jacques Waardenburg, "Symbolic Aspects of Myth," in *Myth, Symbol, and Reality*, ed. Alan M. Olson (Notre Dame, Ind.: University of Notre Dame Press, 1980), 41–68; Mary Gerhart and Allan Melvin Russell, "Myth and Public Science," in *Thinking through Myths: Philosophical Perspectives*, ed. Kevin Schilbrack (London: Routledge, 2002), 191–206; Christopher Flood, "Myth and Ideology," in *Thinking through Myths*, ed. Schilbrack, 174–90; Wendy Doniger, *The Implied Spider: Politics and Theology in Myth* (New York: Columbia University Press, 1998); and René Girard, *Violence and the Sacred*, trans. Patrick Gregory (Baltimore: Johns Hopkins University Press, 1977).

28. Mali, *Mythistory*, 6.

29. Pierce, "Epidemic of Fear," 10.

30. Disease is only one among the plagues that afflict Oedipus's community; *plague* is used here as it is used in Exodus, to connote a widespread communal affliction.

31. George Rosen, *A History of Public Health*, expanded edition (Baltimore: Johns Hopkins University Press, 1993), 5.

32. Rosen notes the importance of the Hippocratic work *Airs, Waters and Places*, which has offered a model for epidemiological investigation and for the theoretical understanding of epidemics—as well as endemic disease—for more than two millennia.

33. Giovanni Boccaccio, *The Decameron*, trans. G. H. McWilliam (New York: Penguin Books, 1972), 56

34. Daniel Defoe, *A Journal of the Plague Year* (New York: Heritage Press, 1968), 127. The text is from the original 1722 edition, but with changes in punctuation for clarity and correction of typographical errors.

35. Mary Shelley, *The Last Man*, ed. Morton D. Paley (Oxford: Oxford University Press, 1994), 233.

36. Mary Douglas, *Purity and Danger: An Analysis of the Concepts of Pollution and Taboo* (London: Routledge and Kegan Paul, 1966), 35.

37. Louis Pasteur (France) and Robert Koch (Germany) are widely recognized as having laid the foundations of the science of bacteriology. Typical is the trajectory charted at the beginning of Hubert A. Lechevalier and Morris Solotorovsky's classic, *Three Centuries of Microbiology*, which begins with a quick survey "From Fracastoro to Pasteur" and includes chapters on Pasteur and Koch before moving into the discussion of the science (New York: McGraw-Hill, 1974).

38. Émile Durkheim, *The Elementary Forms of Religious Life*, trans. Joseph Ward Swain (New York: Free Press, 1965), 365.

39. Sigmund Freud, *Totem and Taboo and Other Works*, vol. 13 of *The Standard Edition of the Complete Psychological Works of Sigmund Freud*, trans. and ed. James Strachey in collaboration with Anna Freud, assisted by Alix Strachey and Alan Tyson (1955; repr., London: Hogarth Press and the Institute of Psycho-Analysis, 1986), 132.

40. The German words for *primitive* and *primal* that Freud uses are, respectively, *Urzustand* ("Dieser Versuch knüpft an eine Hypothese von Ch. Darwin über den sozialen Urzustand des Menschen an") and *Urhorde* ("Die Darwinsche Urhorde . . ."). In both English and German, the terms are in fact used almost interchangeably. Sigmund Freud, *Totem und Tabu: Einige Übereinstimmungen im Seelenleben der Wilden und der Neurotiker* (Leipzig: Hugo Heller, 1913), 116, 131.

41. Since many readers of my work have suggested that the healthy carrier

exemplifies what the philosopher Giorgio Agamben calls "bare life" and embodies in *homo sacer*, an archaic figure from ancient Roman law, it is worth explicitly distinguishing between them. *Homo sacer* refers to an individual who has been banned by order of the sovereign and may be killed but not sacrificed; the figure represents the "exception" that constitutes the power of the sovereign, the inclusion of the exclusion: "*The sovereign sphere is the sphere in which it is permitted to kill without committing homicide and without celebrating a sacrifice, and sacred life—that is, life that may be killed but not sacrificed—is the life that has been captured in this sphere.*" By contrast, the healthy human carrier may be compelled to surrender individual rights for the safety of the group, and in that sense may be "sacrificed," but not killed. The human carrier embodies the concept of "social being," which, as I will discuss in chapter 2, entails an ecological understanding of the interconnections among human beings. The carrier is the figure of contagion. While *homo sacer* represents the absolute power of the sovereign, the legal battles and public debates that have surrounded the figure of the human carrier attest to the carrier's more complex and even disturbing relation to the state. The human carrier generates an ongoing clash of rights. The similarity between the human carrier and *homo sacer* is that both, like many other figures at the center of legal debates, represent the contingent—conspicuously social—nature of any definition of human beings or human rights. See Giorgio Agamben, *Homo Sacer: Sovereign Power and Bare Life*, trans. Daniel Heller-Roazen (Stanford, Calif.: Stanford University Press, 1998), 83.

42. For René Girard, the myth of Oedipus is paradigmatic of the sacrificial nature and communal logic of the scapegoat. He argues that in the scapegoat, the community finds a "surrogate victim" to express and resolve its conflicts (and the threat of violence) and restore its (violent) unanimity. "The plague is what remains of the sacrificial crisis when it has been emptied of all violence" (*Violence and the Sacred*, 77). Myth and ritual, in his argument, promote this dynamic as it is crystallized in the (sacrificial) figure of the scapegoat, and their "function is to perpetuate or renew the effects of this mechanism . . . [in order] to keep violence *outside* the community" (92). In his reading of *Totem and Taboo*, which is central to his argument, he draws out Freud's theories of the scapegoat as, in Girard's words, "a surrogate victim" linked to the idea of prohibition. I have found Girard's formulations useful in my understanding of the figure of the carrier.

43. Nancy Tomes, *The Gospel of Germs: Men, Women, and the Microbe in American Life* (Cambridge: Harvard University Press, 1998), 7–8. See also Nancy Tomes, "The Making of a Germ Panic, Then and Now," *American Journal of Public Health* 90.2 (February 2000): 191–98; and Nancy Tomes, "Epidemic Entertainments: Disease and Popular Culture in Early-Twentieth-Century American," in "Contagion and Culture," ed. Priscilla Wald, Nancy Tomes, and Lisa Lynch, special issue of *American Literary History* 14.4 (winter 2002): 686–719.

44. George Rosen, *A History of Public Health*, 215, 47.

45. See George Rosen, *A History of Public Health*, 137–38; George Rosen, "Cameralism and the Concept of the Medical Police," *Bulletin of the History of Medicine* 27 (1953): 21–42; and Michel Foucault, "The Birth of Social Medicine," in *Power*, ed. James D. Faubion, trans. Robert Hurley et al., vol. 3 of *Essential Works of Foucault 1954–1984*, series ed. Paul Rabinow (New York: New Press, 2000), 139–42.

46. Foucault, "The Birth of Social Medicine," 151.

47. Michel Foucault, "The Birth of Biopolitics," in *Ethics, Subjectivity and Truth*, ed. Paul Rabinow, trans. Robert Hurley et al., vol. 1 of *Essential Works of Foucault 1954–1984*, series ed. Paul Rabinow (New York: New Press, 1997), 73. Ellipses in original.

The centrality of Rosen's work to the development of these ideas has been generally overlooked in contemporary discussions of biopolitics and biopower.

As he worked out his theory, Foucault moved away from the primary focus on the state that interested Rosen. His analysis of power as diffuse and located in practices, institutions, and relationships resonates intriguingly with the sociological concept of social control that I discuss in chapter 3, although I have found no evidence of his familiarity with the work of the sociologists who developed the concept in the early twentieth century. It would be interesting—and very much in the spirit of Foucault—to do a genealogical study of Foucault and the early-twentieth-century theorists of social control.

48. See especially Foucault, "The Birth of Social Medicine," "The Birth of Biopolitics," "Governmentality," and "The Politics of Health in the Eighteenth Century," in *Power*; *The History of Sexuality*, vol. 1: *An Introduction*, trans. Robert Hurley (New York: Pantheon Books, 1978), 90–105; and *"Society Must Be Defended": Lectures at the Collège de France 1975–1976*, ed. Mauro Bertani and Alessandro Fontana, trans. David Macey (New York: Picador, 2003).

Rosen focused his argument on the formative role of epidemics on the state. See George Rosen, *A History of Public Health*, especially 85–87; and "Cameralism and the Concept of the Medical Police."

49. Gerald M. Oppenheimer points out that "epidemiology . . . has a strong social dimension in that it explicitly incorporates perceptions of a population's social relations, behavioral patterns, and experiences into its explanations of disease processes." See "In the Eye of the Storm: The Epidemiological Construction of AIDS," in *AIDS: The Burdens of History*, ed. Elizabeth Fee and Daniel M. Fox (Berkeley: University of California Press, 1988), 267–68. See also Charles E. Rosenberg, *Explaining Epidemics and Other Studies in the History of Medicine* (Cambridge: Cambridge University Press, 1992).

50. Thomas C. Timmreck, *An Introduction to Epidemiology*, 2nd ed. (Sudbury, Mass.: Jones and Bartlett, 1998), 17.

51. Quoted in Jaap Goudsmit, *Viral Fitness: The Next SARS and West Nile in the Making* (New York: Oxford University Press, 2004), 148.

52. Heather Schell, "The Sexist Gene: Science Fiction and the Germ Theory of History," in "Contagion and Culture," ed. Priscilla Wald, Nancy Tomes, and Lisa Lynch, special issue, *American Literary History* 14.4 (winter 2002): 809.

53. Geddes Smith, *Plague On Us* (New York: Commonwealth Fund, 1941), n.p. The quotation is from the jacket copy of the first edition of the book.

54. On Smith and the creation of the concept of the "disease detective," see Paul Greenough, "What Is a Medical Detective?" in *Epidemic! The World of Infectious Disease*, ed. Rob DeSalle (New York: New Press, 1999), 119–23. Greenough's essay also sent me to Alexander Langmuir and the Epidemiological Investigation Service, to the concept of disease detectives as it was introduced in popular periodicals in the 1950s, and to the work of the *New Yorker* writer Berton Roueché, all of which I discuss in this introduction. See also Elizabeth W. Etheridge, *Sentinel for Health: A History of the Centers for Disease Control* (Berkeley: University of California Press, 1992), especially chapter 3, "Disease Detectives," 36–48.

55. Contemporary medical usage distinguishes between *contagious* diseases that are directly and easily transmissible between people and *infectious* diseases that can spread without direct contact. Colloquial usage does not strictly adhere to these distinctions. *Communicable* is broadly synonymous with both.

56. Smith's quip that the healthy carrier "would have had to be invented if he had not existed" anticipates Bruno Latour's insight that the microbe was invented rather than discovered. That insight emphasizes the conceptual underpinnings that precede scientific "discoveries" and insists that discoveries are always culturally determined theories: one cannot "see" what one has not first imagined. That insight does not preclude the materiality of the discovery, which in turn affects future concepts in a dialectical relationship. My formulation of "the outbreak narrative" presumes that dialectic. See Bruno Latour, *The Pasteurization of France*, trans. Alan Sheridan and John Law (Cambridge: Harvard University Press, 1988).

57. On Langmuir's formative role in both epidemiology and the CDC, see especially Etheridge, *Sentinel for Health*; William H. Foege, "Alexander D. Langmuir: His Impact on Public Health," *American Journal of Epidemiology* 144.8 (15 October 1996), supplement ("A Tribute to Alexander D. Langmuir"): S11–S15; and William Schaffner and F. Marc LaForce, "Training Field Epidemiologists: Alexander D. Langmuir and the Epidemic Intelligence Service," in "A Tribute to Alexander D. Langmuir," supplement, *American Journal of Epidemiology* 144.8 (15 October 1996) : S16–S22.

58. According to Paul Greenough, it was Roueché "more than anyone else, who brought depth, moral purpose, and above all intellectual excitement to the image of the medical detective" ("What Is a Medical Detective?" 121). Perhaps nothing attests more to Roueché's ongoing appeal than the fact that the first episode of the NBC series *Medical Investigation* was an updated version of "Eleven Blue Men," which served as the title chapter for Roueché's 1953 collection, *Eleven Blue Men and Other Medical Mysteries,* and was republished in numerous subsequent col-

lections. The story originally appeared in the *New Yorker* as "The Case of the Eleven Blue Men" on 5 June 1948.

59. Berton Roueché, preface to *Annals of Epidemiology* (Boston: Little, Brown, 1967), x. Roueché repeated the importance of this influence in a 1985 interview with Greenough (see Greenough, "What Is a Medical Detective?" 122). Alexander D. Langmuir, introduction to *Annals of Epidemiology,* xiii.

60. Natalie Davis Spingarn, "Meet Our Medical FBI: They Are the Sleuths from Atlanta Who Fight Epidemics from Coast to Coast," *Parents' Magazine,* October 1963, 78.

61. J. D. Ratcliff, "Medicine's FBI," *Reader's Digest,* May 1959, 21.

62. Van Dijk describes an "anticipatory effect of imagination" that "is not created *in* fiction or *in* science, but is produced in culture at large, as it structures both factual and fictional stories of science" (*Imagenation,* 13).

63. "Disease Detectives," *Newsweek,* 19 January 1953, 62.

64. Kirsten Ostherr, *Cinematic Prophylaxis: Globalization and Contagion in the Discourse of World Health* (Durham: Duke University Press, 2005).

1. IMAGINED IMMUNITIES

1. *Outbreak,* directed by Wolfgang Petersen (Warner Brothers, 1995).

2. See Donald A. Henderson, "Surveillance Systems and Intergovernmental Cooperation," in *Emerging Viruses,* ed. Stephen S. Morse (New York: Oxford University Press, 1993), 283.

3. Since that time, the warning has become commonplace. In addition to the works I discuss in this chapter, see, for example, Barry Zimmerman and David J. Zimmerman, *Killer Germs: Microbes and Diseases that Threaten Humanity* (Chicago: Contemporary Books, 1996); Ed Regis, *Virus Ground Zero: Stalking the Killer Viruses with the Centers for Disease Control* (New York: Pocket Books, 1996); Frank Ryan, *Virus X: Tracking the New Killer Plagues out of the Present and into the Future* (Boston: Little, Brown, 1997); Joseph B. McCormick and Susan Fisher-Hoch, with Leslie Alan Horvitz, *Virus Hunters of the CDC* (Atlanta: Turner Publishing, 1996); Peter Radetsky, *The Invisible Invaders: Viruses and the Scientists Who Pursue Them* (Boston: Little, Brown, 1991); Philip M. Tierno Jr., *The Secret Life of Germs: Observations and Lessons from a Microbe Hunter* (New York: Pocket Books, 2001); and Arno Karlen, *Man and His Microbes* (London: Quantum Research Associates, 1995).

4. See, for example, Hans Kohn, *Nationalism: Its Meaning and History* (New York: Van Nostrand, 1965); Frantz Fanon, *The Wretched of the Earth,* trans. Constance Farrington (New York: Grove Press, 1963); J. A. Armstrong, *Nations before Nationalism* (Chapel Hill: University of North Carolina Press, 1982); Ernest Gellner, *Nations and Nationalism* (Oxford: Oxford University Press, 1983); Benedict

Anderson, *Imagined Communities: Reflections on the Origin and Spread of Nationalism*, rev. ed. (1983; repr., London: Verso, 1991); George L. Mosse, *Nationalism and Sexuality: Respectability and Abnormal Sexuality in Modern Europe* (Madison: University of Wisconsin Press, 1985); Anthony D. Smith, *The Ethnic Origins of Nations* (Oxford: Blackwell, 1986); Anthony D. Smith, *National Identity* (Reno: University of Nevada Press, 1991); E. J. Hobsbawm, *Nations and Nationalism since 1780: Programme, Myth, Reality* (Cambridge: Cambridge University Press, 1990); Homi K. Bhabha, *Nations and Narration* (London: Routledge, 1990); Etienne Balibar and Immanuel Wallerstein, *Race, Nation, Class: Ambiguous Identities*, trans. of Etienne Balibar by Chris Turner (London: Verso, 1991); Andrew Parker et al., eds., *Nationalisms and Sexualities* (New York: Routledge, 1991); Liah Greenfeld, *Nationalism: Five Roads to Modernity* (Cambridge: Harvard University Press, 1992).

5. The miniseries version of *The Stand* was based on the 1978 book by Stephen King, and *Carriers* was made into a television movie (dir. Alan Metzger, 1998).

6. Henderson, "Surveillance Systems and Intergovernmental Cooperation," 283.

7. Lederberg and Henderson were among the participants of the May 1989 "Emerging Viruses" conference that I discuss below, and both contributed essays to the Morse volume, *Emerging Viruses*, that came out of the conference. The question of how to alert the public—and especially policymakers—to the threat was a refrain throughout the conference. On the conversation between Preston and Lederberg that led to *The Hot Zone*, as well as on Lederberg's role in Preston's subsequent bioterror novel, *The Cobra Event*, see Judith Miller, Stephen Engelberg, and William Broad, *Germs: Biological Weapons and America's Secret War* (New York: Simon and Schuster, 2001).

8. The microbes in the film are in fact extraterrestrial.

9. Laurie Garrett, *The Coming Plague: Newly Emerging Diseases in a World Out of Balance* (1994; repr., New York: Penguin Books, 1995), 6.

10. Laurie Garrett, "Amplification," in *Epidemic! The World of Infectious Disease*, ed. Rob DeSalle (New York: New Press, 1999), 193. The volume was published by the American Museum of Natural History and developed in conjunction with a traveling exhibition of the same title that began at the museum.

11. Richard M. Krause, foreword to *Emerging Viruses*, ed. Stephen S. Morse (New York: Oxford University Press, 1993), xvii.

12. Joshua Lederberg, Robert E. Shope, and Stanley C. Oaks Jr., eds. *Emerging Infections: Microbial Threats to Health in the United States* (Washington: National Academy Press, 1992), v.

13. Richard Preston, *The Hot Zone* (New York: Doubleday, 1994), 18.

14. Stephen Morse coined the phrase "viral traffic" to designate viral transmission from one species to another or one group of people to another. His explanations for those transmissions center on the movements and migrations of people, and they foster the stereotype of disease movement from the jungles—and over-

crowded cities—of developing nations (most frequently, Africa) to the North. The scientific concepts of species jumping and other forms of viral transmission shade imperceptibly into the social activities of commerce and travel. Subsequent uses, including the Institute of Medicine report *Emerging Infections*, substituted the more encompassing "microbial traffic." See Morse's account in his "Examining the Origins of Emerging Viruses," in *Emerging Viruses*, ed. Stephen S. Morse (New York: Oxford University Press, 1993), 17.

15. Robert E. Shope and Alfred S. Evans describe HIV "and its devastating clinical result, AIDS," as "the most striking example" of a newly identified disease that had gotten out into the population, and "probably a major motivation for [the 1989] conference" in which they participated. Robert E. Shope and Alfred S. Evans, "Assessing Geographic and Transport Factors, and Recognition of New Viruses," in *Emerging Viruses*, ed. Stephen S. Morse (New York: Oxford University Press, 1993), 112. And in a 1990 piece for *Science* the science journalist Barbara Culliton reported Lederberg's and Morse's sense that the "emergence of AIDS should be sufficient warning to mount an effort to track other 'emerging' viruses worldwide." She identifies them as members of "a small band of scientists who worry about what they regard as 'complacency' about infectious diseases." Barbara Culliton, "Emerging Viruses, Emerging Threat," *Science*, 19 January 1990, 279. See also Jaap Goudsmit, *Viral Sex: The Nature of AIDS* (New York: Oxford University Press, 1997).

16. The CDC has gone through several name changes since the 1950s while retaining the acronym.

17. Preston, *The Hot Zone*, 4. It is important to note that the origins of HIV were in fact uncertain when Preston wrote these words, and they have still not been definitively identified. I will return to this point in my last chapter.

18. Biosafety Level 2 refers to the level of the laboratory in which researchers work with a particular disease. There are four levels, and the rating is determined by the degree of infectivity and severity of the disease and the availablity of effective treatment. Research on hemorrhagic viruses is conducted in BL4 laboratories.

19. Karl M. Johnson, "Emerging Viruses in Context: An Overview of Viral Hemorrhagic Fevers," in *Emerging Viruses*, ed. Stephen S. Morse (New York: Oxford University Press, 1993), 56.

20. See Lederberg, Shope, and Oaks, *Emerging Infections*, 32–33.

21. On visual technologies and contagion in *Outbreak*, see especially Kirsten Ostherr, *Cinematic Prophylaxis: Globalization and Contagion in the Discourse of World Health* (Durham: Duke University Press, 2005).

22. Patrick Lynch, *Carriers* (New York: Villard, 1995), 351.

23. Garrett, *The Coming Plague*, 618.

24. Most episodes of the NBC television series *Medical Investigation*, which premiered in September 2004 and ran through March 2005, began with such a shot.

25. Joshua Lederberg, "Viruses and Humankind: Intracellular Symbiosis and

Evolutionary Competition," in *Emerging Viruses*, ed. Stephen S. Morse (New York: Oxford University Press, 1993), 8.

26. William H. McNeill, "Patterns of Disease Emergence in History," in *Emerging Viruses*, ed. Stephen S. Morse (New York: Oxford University Press, 1993), 31.

27. Lederberg, "Viruses and Humankind," 8.

28. Heather Schell makes a similar point in "Outburst! A Chilling True Story about Emerging-Virus Narratives and Pandemic Social Change," *Configurations* 5.1 (winter 1997): 93–133, especially 108–9.

29. Garrett, "Amplification," 193. The phrase "natural disaster" is itself misleading. Earthquakes and tidal waves, although not subject to human control, are also connected to other ecological events that are, and their impact on human lives is at least in part a result of human behavior: where and how human beings live, for example, is an expression of their socioeconomic position.

30. Tony McMichaels, *Human Frontiers, Environments and Disease: Past Patterns, Uncertain Futures* (Cambridge: Cambridge University Press, 2001), 19, and Richard M. Krause, *The Restless Tide: The Persistent Challenge of the Microbial World* (Washington: National Foundation for Infectious Diseases, 1981), 50, 55.

31. Lederberg, "Viruses and Humankind," 26.

32. Garrett, *The Coming Plague*, 618.

33. Lynch, *Carriers*, 71. The passage displays marked confusion about disease theories and history, as Lynch maps the example (from primatology) of an immigrant who is susceptible to the germs of the host culture onto a historically inaccurate account of Euro-American contact. As all of the histories point out, with the possible exception of syphilis, disease transmission was characteristically one-way in the European conquest of the Americas. The passage does illustrate, however, the power of the concept of an ecosystem, in which disease indeed accompanies first contact.

34. Richard M. Krause, "The Origin of Plagues: Old and New," *Science*, 21 August 21, 1073.

35. Ibid., 1075. Earlier, in *The Restless Tide*, Krause had remarked that "no one had anticipated the microbe guerilla actions that were to break out from enclaves in the rear, as the medical research enterprise regrouped for a frontal assault on chronic and degenerative diseases that deployed the best and brightest for the attack" (11). Combat is a common metaphor for diseases of all kinds—witness Nixon's declared "war on cancer"—but it is especially prevalent in these accounts.

36. Garrett, *The Coming Plague*, 618. The reference to predators is Garrett's paraphrase of a 1994 speech that Lederberg delivered to an audience of investment bankers. It is a common comparison in the scientific literature as well as in the journalism and fiction.

37. Preston, *The Hot Zone*, 85.

38. Ibid.

39. Culliton, "Emerging Viruses, Emerging Threat," 279.

40. Heather Schell notes this trend in "The Sexist Gene: Science Fiction and the Germ Theory of History," in *Contagion and Culture,* ed. Priscilla Wald, Nancy Tomes, and Lisa Lynch, special issue, *American Literary History* 14.4 (winter 2002): 805–27.

41. Preston, *The Hot Zone,* 122.

42. Ibid., 197.

43. Ibid.

44. Garrett, *The Coming Plague,* 619.

45. Culliton, "Emerging Viruses, Emerging Threat," 279.

46. The other two depict "global per capita earnings" and "key gay communities and centers of injecting drug use, 1980s."

47. See especially Paul Farmer, *Infections and Inequalities* and *Power and Pathologies.*

48. Among the many useful discussions of this story, I am particularly indebted to Stephen Dougherty, "The Biopolitics of the Killer Virus Novel," *Cultural Criticism* 48 (spring 2001): 1–29; Lisa Lynch, "The Neo/Bio/Colonial Hot Zone: African Viruses, American Fairytales," *International Journal of Cultural Studies* 1.2 (1998): 233–52; Ruth Mayer, *Artificial Africas: Colonial Images in the Times of Globalization* (Hanover, N.H.: University Press of New England, 2002), especially chap. 7, "Don't Touch! Africa Is a Virus," 256–91; and Heather Schell, "Outburst!" and "The Sexist Gene."

49. The concept of "uneven development" is rooted in a Marxist analysis of the obscured relationships among worldwide concentrations of wealth and capital and of poverty and oppression. For the application of the concept to the socioeconomics and spaces of contemporary globalization, see especially Neil Smith, *Uneven Development: Nature, Capital and the Production of Space* (Oxford: Basil Blackwell, 1991).

50. Johnson, "Emerging Viruses in Context," 55.

51. Lynch, *Carriers,* 366.

52. I will discuss the significance of the Cold War with regard to conventions of viral representation in chapter 4.

53. Laurie Garrett, *Betrayal of Trust: The Collapse of Global Public Health* (New York: Hyperion, 2000).

54. William H. McNeill, *Plagues and Peoples* (New York: Doubleday, 1976), 5.

55. Schell, "The Sexist Gene," 806–7.

56. McNeill, *Plagues and Peoples,* 226.

57. On the origin of the term, see N. T. Begg and N. J. Gay, "Theory of Infectious Disease Transmission and Herd Immunity," in *Bacterial Infections,* ed. William J. Hausler Jr. and Max Sussman, vol. 3 of *Topley and Wilson's Microbiology and Microbial Infections,* series ed. Leslie Collier, Albert Balows, and Max Sussman, 9th ed. (London: Hodder Arnold, 1998), 148.

58. McNeill, *Plagues and Peoples,* 130.

59. Christopher Wills, *Yellow Fever, Black Goddess: The Coevolution of People and Plagues* (Reading, Mass.: Addison-Wesley, 1996), 290.

60. On that connection, see Warwick Anderson, "Going through the Motions: American Public Health and Colonial 'Mimicry,'" in "Contagion and Culture," ed. Priscilla Wald, Nancy Tomes, and Lisa Lynch, special issue, *American Literary History* 14.4 (winter 2002): 686–719; and Susan Lederer, "'Porto Ricochet': Joking about Germs, Cancer, and Race Extermination in the 1930s," in "Contagion and Culture," ed. Priscilla Wald, Nancy Tomes, and Lisa Lynch, special issue, *American Literary History* 14.4 (winter 2002): 720–46.

61. Nancy Tomes, *The Gospel of Germs: Men, Women, and the Microbe in American Life* (Cambridge: Harvard University Press, 1998), 92.

62. Jared Diamond, *Guns, Germs and Steel: The Fates of Human Societies* (New York: W. W. Norton, 1997), 206.

63. Llewellyn J. Legters, Linda H. Brink, and Ernest T. Takafuji, "Are We Prepared for a Viral Epidemic Emergency?" in *Emerging Viruses*, ed. Stephen S. Morse (New York: Oxford University Press, 1993), 277.

64. Lederberg, "Viruses and Humankind," 23.

65. Benedict Anderson, *Imagined Communities*, 6. Nancy Tomes and Warwick Anderson make similar use of Benedict Anderson. See Tomes's *The Gospel of Germs* and Warwick Anderson's *The Cultivation of Whiteness: Science, Health, and Racial Destiny in Australia* (New York: Basic Books, 2003).

66. Etienne Balibar, "The Nation Form: History and Ideology," trans. Chris Turner, in *Race, Nation, Class: Ambiguous Identities*, Etienne Balibar and Immanuel Wallerstein (London: Verso, 1991): 93.

67. Stephen King, *The Stand* (1978; repr., New York: Signet, 1991), 67.

68. One section of the exhibit Epidemic! The World of Infectious Disease, featured at New York City's American Museum of Natural History in 1999, was aptly entitled "It's a Small World." This exhibit, and its accompanying lecture series and film festival, again attests to the popular fascination with this material.

69. Building on the work of Thongchai Winichakul, Benedict Anderson offers maps as visual markers of territorial sovereignty; the epidemiological map, by contrast, displays the evidence of people in physical contact: microbial communion.

70. Robin Cook, *Invasion* (New York: Berkley Publishing, 1997), 238.

71. Quotations are from the film version of *The Stand*.

72. Bruno Latour, *The Pasteurization of France*, trans. Alan Sheridan and John Law (Cambridge: Harvard University Press, 1988).

73. Wills, *Yellow Fever, Black Goddess*, 23.

74. Benedict Anderson, *Imagined Communities*, 5.

75. Ibid., 163.

76. The legacy of the national disenchantment of which Calley and My Lai were a part is evident in the subsequent popularity, in fiction and especially film, of the maverick hero whose disobedience is a form of patriotism.

77. See Arjun Appadurai, *Modernity at Large: Cultural Dimensions of Globalization* (Minneapolis: University of Minnesota Press, 1996).

78. One of them, on hearing Ford and McClintock speaking, exclaims, "You're Americans. Please, get me out of this shit hole." Ironically, it is his blood, which McClintock extracts, that becomes the basis for the antidote that Ford and McClintock go on to develop and that allows them to convert Motaba into a biological weapon.

79. Cook, *Invasion*, 282.

80. *War of the Worlds* is another story that has been retold numerous times. Between the novel and the 1953 film (dir. George Pal), Orson Welles produced a radio broadcast in 1938 that famously caused mass panic when people joining the program late believed they were under extraterrestrial attack. The film was remade in 2005 (dir. Steven Spielberg).

81. Lynch, *Carriers*, 422.

82. The phonetic resonances among Lynch's Muaratebo, *Outbreak*'s Motaba, and Mobutu, president of Zaire from 1965–1997 (during Ebola outbreaks) are striking, perhaps suggesting a political undertone in the naming of the fictional viruses.

83. By the time Billy Ford decides surreptitiously to disobey McClintock's orders, a different strain of the virus has been unleashed in Cedar Creek (the host had been carrying both strains), and the antidote is ineffective. The movie glosses over the fact that the first two people who succumb to the disease in Cedar Creek were infected with the second strain, so it would have been too late even if McClintock had given the go-ahead at the first sign of the California outbreak, but scientific accuracy is not a priority in the film; McClintock's vilification is clearly a crucial feature of the narrative of the film.

84. In a 1995 story about the role of Donna Cline, whom Mary Roach dubs "Hollywood's top medical advisor," in the making of *Outbreak*, Roach explains that Cline consulted with experts in the field who used "a loophole in the plot" to figure out "a longshot scenario in which a new antibody could be made in three days." See Mary Roach, "Virus the Movie," *Health* 9.3 (May–June 1995): 81.

2. THE HEALTHY CARRIER

1. George A. Soper, "The Work of a Chronic Typhoid Germ Distributor," *Journal of the American Medical Association* 48 (June 1907): 2022.

2. The demonstration of healthy carriers required both epidemiological investigation of human contacts and the development of laboratory technologies that could confirm the presence of microbes in healthy human beings. The earliest cases thus investigated in Europe and the United States were diphtheria cases, but none was investigated to the extent of Mary Mallon, and no case received the kind

of publicity to which she was subjected. See especially George Rosen, *A History of Public Health*, expanded ed. (Baltimore: Johns Hopkins University Press, 1993), 295–96.

I base my conclusions about public accounts of carriers, typhoid, venereal disease, and bacteriology in this period on my reading of more than 400 articles from mainstream newspapers and magazines as well as medical journals between 1888 and 1932, including the *New York Times*, the *New York American*, *National Geographic*, *McClure's*, *Current Literature*, *Good Housekeeping*, *Harper's*, *Hygeia*, *Journal of Home Economics*, the *Literary Digest*, *Outlook*, *American Review of Reviews*, *Scientific American*, *World's Work*, *Survey*, the *Nation*, *American City*, *Science News*, *Nature*, *Science*, *Journal of the American Medical Association*, the *Lancet*, *Journal of Infectious Diseases*, *Public Health Reports*, *Medicolegal*, *Journal of Laboratory and Clinical Medicine*, *American Journal of Public Health*, *Journal of the Maine Medical Association*, *British Medical Journal*, *Colorado Medicine*, *Boston Medical and Surgical Journal*, *Journal of the Royal Army Medical Corps*, *Journal of the Iowa State Medical Society*, *Johns Hopkins Hospital Bulletin*, *Science and Discovery*, *American Journal of Hygiene*, *Journal of the Medical Association of Georgia*, *Journal of Preventive Medicine*, *Texas State Medical Journal*, *Northwest Medicine*, *Ohio State Medical Journal*, *Yale Journal of Biology and Medicine*, *Proceedings of the Institute of Medicine (Chicago)*, *Southern Medical Journal*, *Journal of the Medical Society of New Jersey*, *Transactions of the Association of American Physicians*, *Transactions of the International Congress on Hygiene and Demography*, *Journal of the Royal Sanitary Institute*, *Military Surgeon*, *Pennsylvania Medical Journal*, *Public Health Reports*, and *Journal of Bacteriology*. I am especially grateful to Elizabeth Klimasmith for her extraordinary research skills and hard work in helping to track down this material.

3. The idea of epidemiologists as disease detectives emerged with the field's rise to prominence. In 1919, for example, F. M. Meader, director of the Division of Communicable Diseases for the New York State Department of Health, described the epidemiologist as "a detective whose duty it is to discover the hidden lair and paths leading thereto, for the infectious agents of communicable disease." F. M. Meader, "Detection of Typhoid Carriers," *Modern Medicine* 2.3 (1919): 244. Berton Roueché, of course, made both the profession and the idea of disease detectives widely popular with his *New Yorker* pieces starting in the 1950s.

4. George A. Soper, "The Curious Career of Typhoid Mary," *Bulletin of the New York Academy of Medicine* 15 (June 1939): 705.

5. S. Josephine Baker, *Fighting for Life* (New York: Macmillan, 1939), 83; George A. Soper, "Typhoid Mary," *Military Surgeon* 45 (July 1919): 7.

6. S. Josephine Baker, *Fighting for Life*, 75.

7. "Enteric Fever Carriers," *Nature* 85.2144 (December 1910): 145.

8. This shift arguably updates an Enlightenment distinction between civil and natural liberty, representing a renewed emphasis on the former in the United States following an evolving discourse of individualism in the nineteenth century.

9. Samuel Hopkins Adams, "Tuberculosis: The Real Race Suicide," *McClure's* 24 (January 1905): 234.

10. Edward Alsworth Ross, *Social Control: A Survey of the Foundations of Order* (New York: Macmillan, 1901), viii. The book appeared originally as a series of essays in the *American Journal of Sociology.*

11. John W. Ritchie, *Primer of Sanitation: Being a Simple Work on Disease Order* (Yonkers-on-Hudson, N.Y.: World Book, 1910), 6.

12. Charles V. Chapin, *The Sources and Modes of Infection* (New York: John Wiley, 1910), 27–28.

13. S. Josephine Baker, *Fighting for Life,* 83.

14. Ferdinand Hueppe, *The Principles of Bacteriology,* trans. E. O. Jordan (Chicago: Open Court, 1899), vi.

15. The discovery of the healthy human carrier was widely believed to be, in the words of the director of a hygiene laboratory, "probably the most important discovery in preventative medicine since the demonstration of the bacterial origin of disease." Arthur Lederer, "The 'Carrier' Problem," *West Virginia Medical Journal* 13 (1918–19): 127.

16. Carl Snyder, "The Reservoirs of Contagion," *Harper's Monthly* 125 (1912): 838.

17. F. M. Meader, "Treatment of the Typhoid Carrier," *New York State Journal of Medicine* 12 (1912): 355.

18. Henry J. Nichols, *Carriers in Infectious Diseases: A Manual on the Importance, Pathology, Diagnosis, and Treatment of Human Carriers* (Baltimore: Wilkins and Wilkins, 1922), 13.

19. Judith Walzer Leavitt, *Typhoid Mary: Captive to the Public's Health* (Boston: Beacon, 1996), 81.

20. J. Andrew Mendelsohn, "'Typhoid Mary' Strikes Again: The Social and the Scientific in the Making of Modern Public Health," *Isis* 86 (1995): 269.

21. Chapin, *The Sources and Modes of Infection,* 280–81.

22. "Typhoid: A National Disgrace," *Survey,* 27 May 1916, 223.

23. William T. Sedgwick, "Typhoid Fever: A Disease of Defective Civilization," introduction to *Typhoid Fever: Its Causation, Transmission, and Prevention,* by George C. Whipple (New York: John Wiley, 1908), xxiii–xxxvi.

24. Allen W. Freeman, "The Present Status of Our Knowledge Regarding the Transmission of Typhoid Fever," *Public Health Reports* 28 (1913): 65.

25. Samuel Hopkins Adams, "Typhoid: An Unnecessary Evil," *McClure's* 25 (June 1905): 145.

26. Havelock Ellis, *The Nationalisation of Health* (London: T. Fisher Unwin, 1892), 248. "Asiatic cholera" was widely used to designate the disease in North America and Europe.

27. John Bessner Huber, "Fighting American Typhoid," *American Review of Reviews* 43 (1911): 348.

28. Alton G. Grinnell, "Our Army Versus a Bacillus," *National Geographic,* October 1913, 1148.

29. Adams, "Typhoid," 146.

30. Soper, "Typhoid Mary," 7.

31. Soper, "The Curious Career of Typhoid Mary," 704–5.

32. See especially Allan Brandt, *No Magic Bullet: A Social History of Venereal Disease in the United States Since 1880* (New York: Oxford University Press, 1985).

33. For my discussion of female sexuality, the fallen woman, and the New Woman, I am especially indebted to the following sources: Joanne J. Meyerowitz, *Women Adrift: Independent Wage Earners in Chicago, 1880–1930* (Chicago: University of Chicago Press, 1988); Carroll Smith-Rosenberg, *Disorderly Conduct: Visions of Gender in Victorian America* (New York: Oxford University Press, 1986); Ruth Rosen, *The Lost Sisterhood: Prostitution in America, 1900–1918* (Baltimore: Johns Hopkins University Press, 1982); Regina G. Kunzel, *Fallen Women, Problem Girls: Unmarried Mothers and the Professionalization of Social Work, 1890–1945* (New Haven: Yale University Press, 1993); Mary E. Odem, *Delinquent Daughters: Protecting and Policing Adolescent Female Sexuality in the United States, 1885– 1920* (Chapel Hill: University of North Carolina Press, 1995); Margit Stange, *Personal Property: Wives, White Slaves, and the Market in Woman* (Baltimore: Johns Hopkins University Press, 1998); Susan A. Glenn, *Female Spectacle: The Theatrical Roots of Modern Feminism* (Cambridge: Harvard University Press, 2000); Lois Rudnick, "The New Woman," in *1915: The Cultural Moment: The New Politics, the New Woman, the New Psychology, the New Art and the New Theatre in America*, ed. Adele Heller and Lois Rudnick (New Brunswick, N.J.: Rutgers University Press, 1991), 69–81; Elizabeth Ammons, "The New Woman as Cultural Symbol and Social Reality: Six Women Writers' Perspectives," in *1915: The Cultural Moment: The New Politics, the New Woman, the New Psychology, the New Art and the New Theatre in America*, ed. Adele Heller and Lois Rudnick (New Brunswick, N.J.: Rutgers University Press, 1991), 82–97; Ellen Kay Trimberger, "The New Woman and the New Sexuality: Conflict and Contradiction in the Writings and Lives of Mabel Dodge and Neith Boyce," in *1915: The Cultural Moment: The New Politics, the New Woman, the New Psychology, the New Art and the New Theatre in America*, ed. Adele Heller and Lois Rudnick (New Brunswick, N.J.: Rutgers University Press, 1991), 98–115; and, for discussions of corresponding issues in England during this period, Judith R. Walkowitz, *Prostitution and Victorian Society: Women, Class, and the State* (Cambridge: Cambridge University Press, 1980); and Vivien Gardner and Susan Rutherford, eds., *The New Woman and Her Sisters: Feminism and Theatre, 1850–1914* (Ann Arbor: University of Michigan Press, 1992).

34. Ruth Rosen, *The Lost Sisterhood*, xi.

35. William Lee Howard, "The Protection of the Innocent," *Journal of the American Medical Association* 47.23 (8 December 1906): 1893.

36. The phrase is from Bayard Holmes, "The Physical and Evolutionary Basis of Marriage," *Journal of the American Medical Association* 47.23 (8 December 1906): 1,886.

37. Albert H. Burr, "The Guarantee of Safety in the Marriage Contract," *Journal of the American Medical Association* 47.23 (8 December 1906): 1,887.

38. Prince Albert Morrow, *The Social Diseases of Marriage: Social Prophylaxis* (New York: Lea Brothers, 1904), 22.

39. Prince A. Morrow, "The Relations of Social Diseases to the Family," *American Journal of Sociology* 14.5 (March 1909): 622.

40. A. B. Wolfe, discussion following Morrow in *American Journal of Sociology* 14.5 (March 1909): 636.

41. I will chronicle the development and evolution of this idea in the work of Robert Park and other members of the University of Chicago sociology department in the next chapter.

42. Wolfe, discussion following Morrow, 635, 636.

43. Anxieties about female mobility and sexuality in the context of unsupervised urban space also took the form of the narratives of white slavery that circulated at the beginning of the twentieth century. These tales depict innocent white girls who are "sold" into a life of prostitution, frequently by unscrupulous relatives; the difference between these accounts (in journalism and reform literature as well as fiction) and other prostitution stories is the emphasis placed on the lack of agency of the girls. See especially Margit Stange, *Personal Property*, and Joanne J. Meyerowitz, *Women Adrift.*

44. W. I. Thomas, "The Adventitious Character of Woman," *American Journal of Sociology* 12.1 (July 1906): 32.The essay also appeared the following year as a chapter in Thomas's *Sex and Society: Studies in the Social Psychology of Sex* (Chicago: University of Chicago Press, 1907).

45. I am following the Library of America edition of Dreiser's works when I set the sales at fewer than five hundred copies. Other sources have set it higher, but none as high as six hundred. Frank Doubleday had been reluctant to publish the novel, which had been accepted by his colleague, Walter Page, while Doubleday was in Europe, and although Dreiser held him to the original promise, Doubleday did not promote the novel.

46. Students of the period have indeed noted working-class counterparts of the New Woman. Notably, Kathy Peiss uses the term in *Cheap Amusements: Working Women and Leisure in Turn-of-the-Century New York* (Philadelphia: Temple University Press, 1986), a book I have found very useful for this study. But while there are, as I have suggested, correspondences between the unattached woman and the New Woman, again I stress the important distinctions that have typically been overlooked. Joanne Meyerowitz's "women adrift" names the same phenomenon that Thomas is documenting, the swelling population of single women living and working in the cities, but Thomas gives his term a more negative connotation—it implies her amorality—and "she" is typically working class with a tendency to disappear and reappear (with the implication of sexual activity) without consequences.

47. Ruth Rosen, *The Lost Sisterhood*, xii.

48. Ludwig Weiss, "The Prostitution Problem in Its Relation to Law and Medicine," *Journal of the American Medical Association* 47.25 (December 1906): 2073.

49. William H. Park, "Typhoid Bacilli Carriers," *Journal of the American Medical Association* 51.12 (September 1908): 982.

50. Ibid., 981.

51. Soper, "The Curious Career of Typhoid Mary," 707.

52. Private correspondence from file W R - M 258, "In the Matter of the Application for a Writ of Habeas Corpus for the Production of Mary Mallon," New York Supreme Court, Special Term, pt. 2, 1909, Hall of Records of the New York County Clerk, New York, New York.

53. W. H. Hamer, "Typhoid Carriers and Contact Infection: Some Difficulties Suggested by Study of Recent Investigations Carried Out on 'Living Lines,'" *Proceedings of the Royal Science of Medicine* 4 (March 1911): 117.

54. S. Josephine Baker, *Fighting for Life*, 75.

55. Ibid., 57, 70.

56. Edward Alsworth Ross, "The Causes of Race Superiority," in *Foundations of Sociology*, 5th ed. (London: Macmillan, 1905), 384. Originally presented as the annual address before the American Academy of Political and Social Science, Philadelphia, 12 April 1901.

57. John R. McKivigan and Thomas J. Robertson, "The Irish American Worker in Transition, 1877–1914: New York City as a Test Case," in *The New York Irish*, ed. Ronald H. Bayor and Timothy J. Meagher (Baltimore: Johns Hopkins University Press, 1996), 302

58. Hasia R. Diner, *Erin's Daughters in America: Irish Immigrant Women in the Nineteenth Century* (Baltimore: Johns Hopkins University Press, 1983). According to Diner, "By 1900 women of Irish birth made up . . . 41.2 percent of all white servants" (77) in the United States. With the high number of Irish-descended women living in New York City, the numbers were likely even higher there.

59. Soper, "Typhoid Mary," 4.

60. Leavitt, *Typhoid Mary*, and Alan M. Kraut, *Silent Travelers: Germs, Genes, and the "Immigrant Menace"* (Baltimore: Johns Hopkins University Press, 1994). Kraut places Mary Mallon's story in the context of a discussion about the use of disease to express anti-immigrant sentiments.

61. Soper, "The Curious Career of Typhoid Mary," 698.

62. S. Josephine Baker, *Fighting for Life*, 73.

63. Alan M. Kraut, *Silent Travelers*, 97.

64. William H. Park, "Typhoid Bacilli Carriers," 981. See also Leavitt, *Typhoid Mary*, 127–28. Leavitt points out that Rosenau, and subsequent medical professionals, used the term to protect Mallon's anonymity and that it did not necessarily carry negative connotations. While she may accurately describe Rosenau's intentions, the effect is certainly dehumanizing, and it contributed to the justification of Mallon's incarceration, as I will argue.

65. Ibid., 982.

66. Rosenau quoted in ibid., 982.

67. Private correspondence from file WR-M 258, "in the Matter of the Application for a Writ of Habeas Corpus for the Production of Mary Mallon," New York Supreme Court, Special Term, pt. 2, 1909, Hall of Records of the New York County Clerk, New York, New York. Emphasis added.

68. For a fuller discussion of the legal dimensions of this case than I will be offering here, see Leavitt, *Typhoid Mary*, chaps. 3 and 5.

69. "'Typhoid Mary' Never Ill, Begs Freedom: 'Why Should I Be Banished Like a Leper?'" *New York American*, 30 June 1909, 3.

70. "'Typhoid Mary' Must Stay: Court Rejects her Plea to Quit Riverside Hospital," *New York Times*, 17 July 1909, 5.

71. Leavitt, *Typhoid Mary*, 88.

72. Letter to the editor, *New York Times*, 2 July 1909, 3.

73. "Healthy Disease Spreaders," *New York Times*, 1 July 1909, 8.

74. *New York Times*, 21 February 1910, 18.

75. "'Typhoid Mary' Asks $50,000 from City," *New York Times*, 3 December 1911, 9. The article reports only Mallon's and her lawyer's intention to sue. I have found no legal documentation of this suit, nor any reference to its resolution. Perhaps it was never filed.

76. "A Man without a Country" and "'Typhoid Mary,'" *Outlook*, 7 April 1915, 803–4. Subsequent references in this discussion are to these pieces.

77. "'Typhoid Mary' Has Reappeared," *New York Times*, 4 April 1915, 5, 3.

78. Ibid., 4.

79. Soper, "Typhoid Mary," 13.

80. "'Typhoid Mary' Has Reappeared," 4.

81. Judith Walzer Leavitt, "Gendered Expectations: Women and Early Twentieth-Century Public Health," in *U.S. History as Women's History: New Feminist Essays*, ed. Linda Kerber, Alice Kessler-Harris, and Kathryn Kish Sklar (Chapel Hill: University of North Carolina Press, 1995), 160.

82. Quoted in "'Typhoid Mary' Has Reappeared," 4.

83. See especially Nancy Tomes, "The Domestication of the Germ," chap. 6 in *The Gospel of Germs*, 135–54; Susan A. Glenn, *Daughters of the Shtetl: Life and Labor in the Immigrant Generation* (Ithaca, N.Y.: Cornell University Press, 1990); Suellen Hoy, *Chasing Dirt: The American Pursuit of Cleanliness* (New York: Oxford University Press, 1990); Sarah Stage and Virginia Vincenti, eds., *Rethinking Home Economics: Women and the History of a Profession* (Ithaca, N.Y.: Cornell University Press, 1997); Eleanor Arnold, ed., *Voices of American Homemakers* (Bloomington: Indiana University Press, 1985).

84. Carroll Smith-Rosenberg, "The New Woman as Androgyne: Social Disorder and Gender Crisis, 1870–1936," in her *Disorderly Conduct: Visions of Gender in Victorian America* (New York: Oxford University Press, 1986), 245. The term "New Woman" was coined in the mid-1890s in England in a well-known debate

between the writers Sarah Grand and Ouida. The New Woman was predominantly white, but not exclusively so, as Nella Larsen's and Jesse Fauset's African American, New Women protagonists make clear. For discussions of revisions and critiques of the New Woman in the work of nonwhite women authors, see Ammons, "The New Woman as Cultural Symbol and Social Reality."

85. As Smith-Rosenberg points out, New Women made a variety of choices about their sexuality. Some married; some were sexually active with men whom they did not marry, and others with women. Some remained celibate. But regardless of those choices, New Women (as individuals and as a type) were frequently charged with prostitution or lesbianism to discredit them. Their sexuality became the basis for their condemnation, although their perceived resistance to gender and sexual norms was most at issue.

86. Andrew Macphail, "The American Woman," *Living Age*, 31 October 1908, 298, and 7 November 1908. Reprinted from the *Spectator*. The essay began as a letter to the editor.

87. Andrew Macphail, "The American Woman," in *Essays in Fallacy* (London: Longmans, Green, 1910), 14. This essay expands the letter to the editor.

88. *Living Age*, 27 April 1907, 251.

89. Macphail, *Living Age*, 31 October 1908, 302. The editorial response is on the same page.

90. Theodore Roosevelt, letter to Mrs. Bessie Van Vorst, 18 October 1902, in *Works: Presidential Addresses and State Papers*, vol. 14, part 2, Statesman edition (New York: Review of Reviews, 1904), 510. Bessie Van Vorst was active in the public-health movement, and this sentiment appeared frequently in Roosevelt's speeches.

91. D. Clinton Guthrie, "Race Suicide," *Pennsylvania Medical Journal* 15 (1911): 859.

92. Burr, "The Guarantee of Safety in the Marriage Contract," 1889.

93. "'Typhoid Mary' Has Reappeared," 3.

94. Soper, "The Curious Career of Typhoid Mary," 705.

95. Soper, "Typhoid Mary," 13.

96. Soper, "The Curious Career of Typhoid Mary," 711.

97. Soper, "Typhoid Mary," 12.

98. Amy Fairchild has written brilliantly about how the mandatory medical examination to which immigrants were subjected at Ellis Island did much less to exclude would-be immigrants than to discipline them. See her *Science at the Borders: Immigrant Medical Inspection and the Shaping of the Modern Industrial Labor Force, 1891–1930* (Baltimore: Johns Hopkins University Press, 2003).

3. COMMUNICABLE AMERICANISM

1. Quoted in Charles A. Madison, preface to *How the Other Half Lives: Studies among the Tenements of New York*, by Jacob A. Riis (New York: Dover Publications, 1971), vii. The book first appeared in 1890.

2. Jacob A. Riis, *How the Other Half Lives: Studies Among the Tenements of New York* (1890; repr., New York: Dover Publications, Inc., 1971), 2.

3. Mary Poovey, *Making a Social Body: British Cultural Formation, 1830–1864* (Chicago: University of Chicago Press, 1995), 58.

4. On how a somewhat justifiable concern was blown out of proportion in the quarantines, see especially Alan M. Kraut, *Silent Travelers* (Baltimore: Johns Hopkins University Press, 1994); Nayan Shah, *Contagious Divides* (Berkeley: University of California Press, 2001); and Howard Markel, *Quarantine! East European Jewish Immigrants and the New York City Epidemics of 1892* (Baltimore: Johns Hopkins University Press, 1997).

5. For this chapter, I am basing my conclusions on my reading of the first thirty years of the *American Journal of Sociology* as well as more than 350 articles on public health, immigration and Americanization, railroads, and ghettos from other specialty and mainstream periodicals, newspapers, and medical journals, including *Science, North American Review,* the *New York Medical Journal,* the *New York Times, Outlook, Atlantic Monthly, Charities Review, Charities and the Commons, Survey, New York State Journal of Medicine, Journal of the American Medical Association, Literary Digest, Harper's Monthly Magazine, Ladies' Home Journal, Journal of Infectious Diseases, Political Science Quarterly, North American Review, American Journal of Public Health, Journal of Heredity, Annals of the American Academy of Political and Social Science, Medical Record, Journal of the New England Water Works Association, Forum, Scribner's, Arena, Cosmopolitan, Chautauquan, McClure's, Outing,* the *Independent, New England Magazine,* and *Century.* I am especially grateful to Monique Allewaert for her superb research skills and hard work on tracking down this material.

6. Edward Alsworth Ross, "Social Control," *American Journal of Sociology* 1.5 (March 1896): 518.

7. For popular contemporary applications of this concept, see especially Richard Dawkins's discussion of memes in *The Selfish Gene* (1976; repr., Oxford: Oxford University Press, 1989), and Malcolm Gladwell, *The Tipping Point: How Little Things Can Make a Big Difference* (New York: Little, Brown, 2000).

8. For discussions of the importance of Park's essay to urban studies, see especially Richard Sennett, "An Introduction," in *Classic Essays on the Culture of Cities,* ed. Richard Sennett (Englewood Cliffs, N.J.: Prentice Hall, 1969), 3–19; and Rolf Lindner, *The Reportage of Urban Culture: Robert Park and the Chicago School,* trans. Adrian Morris (Cambridge: Cambridge University Press, 1996).

9. Rolf Lindner calls Riis the "boss reporter of Mulberry Street." See *The Reportage of Urban Culture.*

10. Robert Park, "The City: Suggestions for the Investigation of Human Behavior in the Urban Environment," *American Journal of Sociology* 20.5 (March 1915): 611–12.

11. Robert Ezra Park, "Reflections on Communication and Culture," *American Journal of Sociology* 44.2 (September 1938): 191.

12. Luther Bernard never published the accounts that he received from more than two hundred eminent sociologists, but that of Park and his colleague William I. Thomas subsequently appeared in the *American Journal of Sociology*. See Paul J. Baker, "The Life Histories of W. I. Thomas and Robert E. Park," *American Journal of Sociology* 79.2 (September 1973): 254.

13. Albion Small, "The Era of Sociology," *American Journal of Sociology* 1.1 (July 1895): 1.

14. Cyrus Edson, "The Microbe as Social Leveller," *North American Review* 159.467 (October 1895): 425. On Edson, see Nancy Tomes, *The Gospel of Germs: Men, Women, and the Microbe in American Life* (Cambridge: Harvard University Press, 1998), 127–32.

15. On this social transformation of the public-health movement, see especially Paul Starr, *The Social Transformation of American Medicine: The Rise of a Sovereign Profession and the Making of a Vast Industry* (New York: Basic Books, 1982); George Rosen, *A History of Public Health*, expanded ed. (Baltimore: Johns Hopkins University Press, 1993); John Duffy, *The Sanitarians: A History of Public Health* (Urbana: University of Illinois Press, 1990); Charles E. Rosenberg, *No Other Gods: On Science and American Social Thought*, rev. ed. (Baltimore: Johns Hopkins University Press, 1997); and Charles Rosenberg, *Explaining Epidemics and Other Studies in the History of Medicine* (Cambridge: Cambridge University Press, 1992).

16. Victoria A. Harden, *Inventing the NIH: Federal Biomedical Research Policy, 1887–1937* (Baltimore: Johns Hopkins University Press, 1986), 9.

17. Henry J. Fletcher, "American Railways and American Cities," *Atlantic Monthly* 73 (1894): 803.

18. Ibid., 809.

19. Paul B. Barringer, "An Unappreciated Source of Typhoid Infection," in *A New Idea in Sanitation: The Great Menace to Public Health that Covers Every Mile of Railroad Track in the United States and Other Countries*, comp. J. C. Salter (New York: 1910), 7.

20. H. Taylor Cronk, "What Germs Are, How They Are Disseminated, and the Danger of Them," in *A New Idea in Sanitation: The Great Menace to Public Health that Covers Every Mile of Railroad Track in the United States and Other Countries*, comp. J. C. Salter (New York: 1910), 3–4.

21. "Some Deadly Railway Passengers," *Literary Digest*, 13 July 1912, 57.

22. Cronk, "What Germs Are," 4.

23. "The Transfer of Disease by Travel," *Literary Digest*, 1 November 1924, 29.

24. J. Howell Way, "Remarks on Railway Sanitation, with Special Reference to the Dangers of Present Methods of Disposing of Human Excreta, and Suggestions for Improvement," *Charlotte Medical Journal* 29 (1906): 82.

25. Simon Flexner, "Natural Resistance to Infectious Disease and Its Reinforcement," *Popular Science Monthly*, July 1909, 7.

26. Simon Flexner, "Some Problems in Infection and Its Control," *Science* 36.934 (November 1912): 687.

27. Simon Flexner, "Introductory," in *Experimental Epidemiology* (New York: Laboratories of the Rockefeller Institute for Medical Research, 1922), 9.

28. This speech was published the following year. W. C. Rucker, "A Program of Public Health for Cities," *American Journal of Public Health* 7.3 (March 1917): 225.

29. "Doctor Says Steady Contact with Germs Makes City Dwellers Immune to Disease," *New York Times*, 8 July 1923, 1.

30. Royal S. Copeland, "Import Diseases as They Affect the Work of the New York City Health Department," *American Journal of Public Health* 12 (1922): 203.

31. William H. Park, "Functions of the Public Health Laboratory in Controlling the Import Diseases," *American Journal of Public Health* 12 (1922): 204.

32. Copeland, "Import Diseases," 203.

33. On the socializing (rather than exclusionary) purpose of the medical exam, see Amy Fairchild, *Science at the Borders: Immigrant Medical Inspection and the Shaping of the Modern Industrial Labor Force, 1891–1930* (Baltimore: Johns Hopkins University Press, 2003).

34. The historian Dorothy Ross argues that Addams's 1895 *Hull House Maps and Papers* inaugurated "the urban studies and use of maps for which Chicago sociology later became famous." Ross does not take into account Park's own claim that he was influenced by the maps of the epidemiologists while he was still a journalist. Nonetheless, Addams's influence on the sociologists was certainly important. See Dorothy Ross, *The Origins of American Social Science* (Cambridge: Cambridge University Press, 1991), 226.

35. Park was especially known for insisting that his students go out into the field to test their theories and that they build theoretically from their observations, and he was widely credited with developing an empirical approach to the nascent discipline. On Park's empirical legacy, see especially Ralph H. Turner, "Introduction to *Robert E. Park: On Social Control and Collective Behavior*," in *The Emergence of American Sociology: From the Enlightenment to the Founding Fathers*, vol. 1 of *The Classical Tradition in Sociology: The American Tradition*, ed. Jeffrey Alexander, Raymond Boudon, Mohamed Cherkaoui (London: Sage Publications, 1997), 264–91. For more general discussions of the approach of the Chicago School, see especially Andrew Abbott, *Department and Discipline* (Chicago: University of Chicago Press, 1999), and Martin Bulmer, *The Chicago School of Sociology: Institutionalization, Diversity, and the Rise of Sociological Research* (Chicago: University of Chicago Press, 1984).

36. Edward Alsworth Ross, "Social Control. XIII. The System of Social Control," *American Journal of Sociology* 3.6 (May 1898): 821.

37. Ibid.

38. Robert Ezra Park and Ernest W. Burgess, *Introduction to the Science of Sociology* (Chicago: University of Chicago Press, 1921), 42.

39. Otto Spengler, "The Soul of the City," in *Classic Essays on the Culture of Cities*, ed. Richard Sennett (Englewood Cliffs, N.J.: Prentice Hall, 1969), 85.

40. Georg Simmel, "The Metropolis and Mental Life," in *The Sociology of Georg Simmel*, trans. Kurt H. Wolff (New York: Free Press, 1950), 409–24. The essay is the translation of a lecture, "Die Grossstadte und das Geistesleben" (1902–1903).

41. Robert Park, "The City," 612.

42. See Winifred Raushenbush, *Robert E. Park: Biography of a Sociologist* (Durham: Duke University Press, 1979), 68.

43. Robert Park, "The City," 579.

44. Here I depart somewhat from scholars like Rolf Lindner and Fred H. Matthews, who stress Park's move away from the activism of his predecessors, including Small. See Lindner, *The Reportage of Urban Culture: Park and the Chicago School*; and Matthews, *Quest for an American Sociology: Robert E. Park and the Chicago School* (Montreal: McGill-Queens University Press, 1977).

45. Robert Ezra Park, "Sociology and the Social Sciences: The Group Concept and Social Research," *American Journal of Sociology* 27.2 (September 1921): 170.

46. Gustave Le Bon, *The Crowd: A Study of the Popular Mind*, 4th impression (London: T. F. Unwin, 1903).

47. Gabriel Tarde, *L'Opinion et la foule (Public Opinion and the Crowd)*, 2d ed. (Paris: Ancienne Librairie Germer Bailliere et Cie, 1904), 2. The book was originally published as a series of essays in the 1890s. Since I have done my own translations, I am including the French in the notes: "présente quelque chose d'animal. . . . N'est-elle pas un faisceau de contagions psychiques essentiellement produites par des contacts physiques?"

48. "Chose étrange, les hommes qui s'entrainent ainsi, qui se suggestionnent mutuellement ou plutôt se transmettent les uns aux autres la suggestion d'en haut, ces hommes'là ne se coudoient pas, ne se voient ni ne s'entendent: ils sont assis, chacun chez soi, lisant le même journal et disperses sur un vast territoire. Quel est donc le lien qui existe entre eux? Ce lien, c'est, avec la simultanéité de leur conviction ou de leur passion, la conscience possédée par chacun d'eux que cette idée ou cette volonté est partagée au même moment par un grand nombre d'autres hommes" (3).

49. "Cette invisible contagion du public" (4); "la contagion sans contact" (6); "le simple prestige de l'actualité" (4).

50. I attribute the genealogy to Park because this section was originally published as an *American Journal of Sociology* essay authored by Park, "Sociology and the Social Sciences: The Social Organism and the Collective Mind," in 1921.

51. Robert Ezra Park, "Sociology and the Social Sciences: The Social Organism and the Collective Mind," *American Journal of Sociology* 27.1 (July 1921): 5.

52. Ibid., 14.

53. Robert Park, "The City," 611, 612.

54. Ibid., 578, 598, and 594, respectively. In a revised version of the essay, Park would change the description of the city from a "psychophysical mechanism" to "a

state of mind, a body of customs and traditions, and of the organized attitudes and sentiments that inhere in these customs and are transmitted with this tradition." See Robert Ezra Park, "The City," in *Human Communities: The City and Human Ecology*, vol. 2 of *The Collected Papers of Robert Ezra Park* (Glencoe, Ill.: Free Press, 1950), 13.

55. Park and Burgess, *Introduction to the Science of Sociology*, 875.

56. Originally published as two volumes in 1832, *The Black Death* and *The Dancing Mania*, they were translated into English and published together in 1888. J. F. C. Hecker, *The Black Death and the Dancing Mania*, trans. B. G. Babington (London: Cassell, 1888), 105. Park and Burgess excerpted this work; page references are to their *Introduction to the Science of Society*.

57. The quotation is from Dewey's 1916 *Democracy and Education*, which Park and Burgess excerpt. Page references for Dewey and W. von Bechterew are to excerpts from their work in *Introduction to the Science of Sociology*.

58. Wladimir von Bechterew was a Russian neurologist and professor of psychiatry best known for his work on reflexes and conditioning.

59. Robert Ezra Park, "Succession, an Ecological Concept," *American Sociological Review* 1.2 (April 1936): 178.

60. Robert Ezra Park, "Human Ecology," *American Journal of Sociology* 42.1 (July 1936): 12.

61. Robert Ezra Park, "Symbiosis and Socialization: A Frame of Reference for the Study of Society," *American Journal of Sociology* 45.1 (July 1939): 13, 14, 15. Park had made the same point (in almost the exact words) in "Succession, an Ecological Concept" (1936).

62. Ibid., 15.

63. Ibid., 16.

64. These four stages of mutual adjustment when new individuals or groups came into contact were known collectively as "the assimilation cycle," and it constitutes one of the most influential and lasting models of the urban sociologists. Although Park and Burgess emphasized the cultural nature of the process in their chapter on assimilation (the fourth chapter of a series that explores each aspect of the total cycle), the resonance with the ecological model is unmistakable. For them, it was a process of mutual transformation, although a minority group was likely to undergo a more dramatic metamorphosis than a majority group. Henry Yu observes that Park used different terms to distinguish different kinds of interaction cycles: "When dealing with contact between races, Park called the process the race relations cycle; when dealing with the adjustments of immigrants to America, he called it the assimilation or Americanization cycle" (*Thinking Orientals: Migration, Contact, and Exoticism in Modern America* [New York: Oxford University Press, 2001], 40). That distinction is not always evident, however. In their chapter, for example, Park and Burgess extend the "assimilation" and "Americanization" model to different racial groups. Racial assimilation was an issue Park would consider throughout his career, and although he conceded that racial antip-

athies (and the superficial physiological differences among races) would slow the process down considerably, he nonetheless insisted that racial tensions would ultimately be surmounted by the inevitable processes of mutual change, by which he understood assimilation. See especially "Assimilation," chap. 6 in Robert Ezra Park and Ernest W. Burgess, *Introduction to the Science of Sociology*, 734–84, and the essays collected in Robert Ezra Park, *Race and Culture*, vol. 1 of *The Collected Papers of Robert Ezra Park*, ed. Everett Cherrington Hughes et al. (Glencoe, Ill.: Free Press, 1950). Many recent critiques of the Chicago School in general and Park in particular have overlooked the insistence on the mutuality of the transformation, through which they distinguished themselves from other models of assimilation, such as that of the Columbia sociologist Franklin Giddings. On the importance of Park's definition of assimilation, see also Milton M. Gordon, *Assimilation in American Life: The Role of Race, Religion, and National Origins* (New York: Oxford University Press, 1964).

65. Robert Park, "The City," 597.

66. Park and Burgess, *Introduction to the Science of Sociology*, 735.

67. Robert Ezra Park, "The Urban Community as a Spatial Pattern and a Moral Order," in *Human Communities: The City and Human Ecology*, vol. 2 of *The Collected Papers of Robert Ezra Park* (Glencoe, Ill.: Free Press, 1950), 177. Originally published as "The Concept of Position in Sociology," *Publications of the American Sociological Society* 20 (1925): 1–14.

68. Park and Burgess, *Introduction to the Science of Sociology*, 322.

69. It is interesting to note how much this concept anticipated key features in the work of the French theorist of space Henri Lefebvre and the Marxist and feminist cultural geographers, such as David Harvey, Doreen Massey, and Matthew Sparke, who have built on his work to make space an increasingly important term in the study of culture in recent decades. See Henri Lefebvre, *The Production of Space*, trans. Donald Nicholson-Smith (Cambridge, Mass.: Blackwell, 1991); David Harvey, *Social Justice and the City* (London: Edward Arnold, 1973); David Harvey, *Justice, Nature and the Geography of Difference* (Cambridge, Mass.: Blackwell, 1996); David Harvey, *Spaces of Capital: Towards a Critical Geography* (New York: Routledge, 2001); Doreen Massey, *Space, Place and Gender* (Minneapolis: University of Minnesota Press, 1994); and Matthew Sparke, *In the Space of Theory: Postfoundational Geographies of the Nation-State* (Minneapolis: University of Minnesota Press, 2005).

70. Robert Ezra Park, "Sociology and the Social Sciences: The Group Concept and Social Research," 180–81.

71. On fiction and the Chicago sociologists, see especially Carla Capetti, *Writing Chicago: Modernism, Ethnography, and the Novel* (New York: Columbia University Press, 1993).

72. Robert Ezra Park, "Reflections on Communication and Culture, 203.

73. Ibid., 205.

74. See Rolf Lindner, *The Reportage of Urban Culture*, 23 n. 7.

75. Lincoln Steffens, *The Autobiography of Lincoln Steffens* (New York: Harcourt, Brace, 1931), 223.

76. Abraham Cahan, *Yekl and the Imported Bridegroom and Other Stories of Yiddish New York* (New York: Dover Publications, 1970), 112.

77. Riis, *How the Other Half Lives*, 88.

78. See, for example, David Herlihy, *The Black Death and the Transformation of the West*, ed. Samuel K. Cohn Jr. (Cambridge: Harvard University Press, 1977). On the representation of Jews and disease generally, see especially Sander Gilman, *Difference and Pathology: Stereotypes of Sexuality, Race, and Madness* (Ithaca, N.Y.: Cornell University Press, 1985); Sander Gilman, *Disease and Representation: Images of Illness from Madness to AIDS* (Ithaca, N.Y.: Cornell University Press, 1988); and Sander Gilman, *The Jew's Body* (New York: Routledge, 1991).

79. David Philipson, *Old European Jewries* (Philadelphia: Jewish Publication Society of America, 1894), 21–22. Philipson is aware of the irony, noting the appearance of this metaphor in the work of other scholars: "The Ghetto has been well stigmatized as a 'pest-like isolation,' " he notes, and he cites the observation of a sixteenth-century writer that "stone walls arose in all places wherein Jews dwelt, shutting off their quarters like pesthouses; the Ghetto had become epidemic" (22).

80. Even the spread of disease that the public-health officials used to justify quarantine could actually be summoned to mark the lack of immunity to each other's germs, hence their lack of prior contact—their geographical diversity, or, as Park would put it, "cosmopolitanism," although it is hard to know if Cahan would have been familiar with medical theories that were just in the process of being advanced. It is also interesting to note that Hapgood used such a list to represent the ethnic diversity of the tenements.

81. See especially Arthur Hertzberg, "The Russian Jews Arrive," in *The Jews in America: Four Centuries of an Uneasy Encounter* (New York: Columbia University Press, 1997), 140–64.

82. On Gitl as "squaw," see also Werner Sollors, *Beyond Ethnicity: Consent and Descent in American Culture* (New York: Oxford University Press, 1986).

83. Thomas was the chief author of the volume but was not listed among the coauthors until the 1950s because of a scandal, following his arrest for violation of the Mann Act and related charges in 1918. The case was thrown out of court, but the publicity surrounding it resulted in the termination of Thomas's appointment at the University of Chicago and, presumably, his exclusion from authorial credit for the volume. See Donald R. Young, "Introduction to the Republished Edition," in *Old World Traits Transplanted* (1921), by Robert E. Park, and Herbert A. Miller, and W. I. Thomas, vol. 3 of *Americanization Studies: The Acculturation of Immigrant Groups into American Society*, republished under the editorship of William S. Bernard (Montclair, N.J.: Patterson Smith, 1971): vii–xv. Thomas received top billing in this reprinting. On the scandal, see also Morris Janowitz, *W. I.*

Thomas on Social Organization and Social Personality (Chicago: University of Chicago Press, 1966).

84. Robert Park, "The City," 612.

85. Park read fiction avidly, and he believed that the literary realists in particular had a great deal to teach sociologists. Moreover, the acknowledged influence of Cahan on Hapgood and especially on Thomas makes the familiarity of both Park and Wirth with Cahan's work a likelihood.

86. Louis Wirth, *The Ghetto* (University of Chicago Press, 1928), 8.

87. While Philipson also privileges the geographical explanation (although the term he produces is *gheta*), Wirth departs from him in several particulars. *Borghetto*, for instance, is an equally plausible explanation for Philipson. See Philipson, *Old European Jewries*, 23–25. Here I wish to thank Leonard Tennenhouse for calling my attention to the Yiddish pronunciation of these terms that underlies Wirth's choice.

88. On the language of consent and descent in the Americanization debates, see Sollors, *Beyond Ethnicity*.

89. On Park's legacy for the contemporary study of race relations, see especially Henry Yu, *Thinking Orientals*; Barbara Ballis Lal, *The Romance of Culture in an Urban Civilization: Robert E. Park and Ethnic Relations in Cities* (London: Routledge, 1990); Mary Jo Deegan, *Race, Hull-House, and the University of Chicago: A New Conscience against Ancient Evils* (Westport, Conn.: Praeger, 2002); Stow Persons, *Ethnic Studies at Chicago, 1905–45* (Urbana: University of Illinois Press, 1987); and Stanford Lyman, *Militarism, Imperialism, and Racial Accommodation: An Analysis and Interpretation of the Early Writings of Robert E. Park* (Fayetteville: University of Arkansas Press, 1992).

90. Georg Simmel, "The Sociological Significance of the 'Stranger,'" excerpted in Park and Burgess, *Introduction to the Science of Sociology*, 322.

91. Ibid., 326.

92. Georg Simmel, "The Stranger," in *The Sociology of Georg Simmel*, trans. and ed. Kurt H. Wolff (New York: Free Press, 1950), 406.

93. Persons, *Ethnic Studies at Chicago, 1905–45*.

94. Robert Ezra Park, "Human Migration and Marginal Man," *American Journal of Sociology* 33.6 (May 1928): 892.

95. This quotation is from the abstract preceding Robert Park, "Human Migration and Marginal Man," 881.

96. At the height of their influence, Park and his colleagues and students tended to stress the containment model of the ghetto. That may account for the tendency, in the critical response to Park and the Chicago sociologists, to miss the later emphasis on the mutuality of the influence, which became more pronounced as Park increasingly embraced the ecological model. The mutuality of influence was, however, always a part of their understanding of assimilation. The ecological model was one of inevitability, to a certain extent; Park believed that as the world

became increasingly interdependent, cultural merging was inevitable, but he was also interested in the cultural resistance that made such mergers more difficult in human than plant communities.

97. Robert Ezra Park, "Our Racial Frontier on the Pacific," in *Race and Culture*, vol. 1 of *The Collected Papers of Robert Ezra Park*, ed. Everett Cherrington Hughes et al. (Glencoe, Ill.: Free Press, 1950), 138–51. Originally published in *Survey* 61.3 (May 1926): 192–96.

98. Robert Ezra Park, "The Nature of Race Relations," in *Race and Culture*, vol. 1 of *The Collected Papers of Robert Ezra Park*, ed. Everett Cherrington Hughes et al. (Glencoe, Ill.: Free Press, 1950), 105. Originally published in Robert Park, *Race Relations and the Race Problem*, ed. Edgar T. Thompson (Durham: Duke University Press, 1939), 3–45.

4. VIRAL CULTURES

1. Claudia Wallis, "AIDS: A Growing Threat: Now that the Disease Has Come Out of the Closet, How Far Will It Spread?" *Time*, 12 August 1985, 40.

2. Joe Levine, "Viruses: AIDS Research Spurs New Interest in Some Ancient Enemies," *Time*, 3 November 1986, 66. This image resembles the image from *Scientific American* reproduced in figure-8.

3. See Randy Shilts, *And the Band Played On: Politics, People, and the AIDS Epidemic* (New York: St. Martin's Press, 1987), and Cindy Patton, *Fatal Advice: How Safe-Sex Education Went Wrong* (Durham: Duke University Press, 1996).

4. Cindy Patton, among others, traces the authority of science to "its ability to 'see' what ordinary people cannot" (*Inventing AIDS* [New York: Routledge, 1990], 57).

5. On the importance of visualization technologies in medicine, see especially Lisa Cartwright, *Screening the Body: Tracing Medicine's Visual Culture* (Minneapolis: University of Minnesota Press, 1995), and Kirsten Ostherr, *Cinematic Prophylaxis: Globalization and Contagion in the Discourse of World Health* (Durham: Duke University Press, 2005).

6. *Science News Letter* 69.18 (5 May 1956): 275.

7. My conclusions in this chapter are based on my reading of numerous articles on McCarthy, communism, viruses, and the polio vaccine from the following news and science periodicals between 1949 and 1960: the *New York Times*, the *Ladies' Home Journal*, the *Saturday Evening Post*, *Saturday Review*, *Today's Health*, *Vital Speeches*, *Commonweal*, *Scientific American*, *Science Digest*, *Science News Letter*, *Time*, the *New Republic*, *American Mercury*, *Scholastic*, *Reader's Digest*, *Newsweek*, the *New Yorker*, *Harper*, *Commentary*, the *New Statesman*, *Nature*, *Science*, *Esquire*, *Christian Century*, and *Look*.

8. The reservoir host is the organism in which an infectious agent lies dormant or multiplies; in some cases, the organism can host two infectious agents at once,

allowing them to recombine. Unstable viruses such as influenza are especially susceptible to such processes.

9. Eric Mottram, "Rencontre avec William Burroughs," in *Conversations with William Burroughs*, ed. Allen Hibbard (Jackson: University Press of Mississippi, 1999), p. 11.

10. William S. Burroughs, *Queer* (New York: Viking Press, 1985), xxii.

11. On alien invasion and 1950s science-fiction cinema, see especially Ostherr, *Cinematic Prophylaxis*; Vivian Sobchack, *Screening Space: The American Science Fiction Film*, 2d ed. (New Brunswick, N.J.: Rutgers University Press, 2001); Harry M. Benshoff, *Monsters in the Closet: Homosexuality and the Horror Film* (Manchester, U.K.: Manchester University Press, 1997); Peter Biskind, *Seeing Is Believing: How Hollywood Taught Us to Stop Worrying and Love the Fifties* (New York: Pantheon Books, 1983); Charles Derry, *Dark Dreams: A Psychological History of the Modern Horror Film* (South Brunswick, N.J.: A. S. Barnes, 1977); Cyndy Hendershot, *I Was a Cold War Monster: Horror Films, Eroticism, and the Cold War Imagination* (Bowling Green, Ohio: Bowling Green State University Popular Press, 2001); Nora Sayre, *Running Time: Films of the Cold War* (New York: Dial Press, 1982); David J. Skal, *The Monster Show: A Cultural History of Horror* (New York: W. W. Norton, 1993); Jacqueline Foertsch, *Enemies Within: The Cold War and the AIDS Crisis in Literature, Film and Culture* (Urbana: University of Illinois Press, 2001); Ernesto G. Laura, "Invasion of the Body Snatchers," in *Focus on the Science Fiction Film*, ed. William Johnson (Englewood Cliffs, N.J.: Prentice-Hall, 1972), 71–73; Rick Worland, *The Horror Film: An Introduction* (Malden, Mass.: Blackwell Publishing, 2007), especially chapter 8, " 'Horror in the Age of Anxiety': *Invasion of the Body Snatchers* (1956)," 193–207; and Stuart Samuels, "The Age of Conspiracy and Conformity: 'Invasion of the Body Snatchers,' " in *American History/American Film: Interpreting the Hollywood Image* (New York: Ungar, 1980), 203–17. Foertsch was especially helpful in my thinking about the connections between the Cold War and the HIV/AIDS epidemic, as was Daryl Ogden, who formulates the link in terms of virology and immunology. See Daryl Ogden, "Cold War Science and the Body Politic: An Immuno/Virological Approach to *Angels in America*," *Literature and Medicine* 19.2 (2000): 241–61. Susan Sontag's "The Imagination of Disaster" has been influential on critical thinking about science fiction and Cold War anxieties. See Susan Sontag, "The Imagination of Disaster," in Sontag, *Against Interpretation and Other Essays* (New York: Farrar, Straus, and Giroux, 1966).

12. Ostherr, *Cinematic Prophylaxis*, 139.

13. Andrew Ross, *No Respect: Intellectuals and Popular Culture* (New York: Routledge, 1989), 45.

14. Sylvester E. Luria, *General Virology* (New York: Wiley, 1953). As Luria notes in his preface, he wrote the book because there were no other textbooks that covered this new subject. On the history of virology, see especially Sally Smith

Hughes, *The Virus: A History of the Concept* (London: Heinemann Educational Books, 1977).

15. On the cultural significance of polio before the vaccine, see especially Naomi Rogers, *Dirt and Disease: Polio Before FDR* (New Brunswick, N.J.: Rutgers University Press, 1992).

16. Sylvester Luria and James E. Darnell Jr., *General Virology*, 2d ed. (New York: John Wiley and Sons, 1967), 6.

17. Waldemar Kaempffert, "Reconstruction of Virus in Laboratory Reopens the Question: What Is Life?" *New York Times*, 30 October 1955, 4 (Science in Review), 9.

18. Waldemar Kaempffert, "Radioactive Elements Are Used in a Study of the Nature and Growth of Viruses," *New York Times*, 27 May 1951, E9.

19. William L. Laurence, "New Leads Given by Virus Studies," *New York Times*, 11 September 1952, 29.

20. The description of the virus as an entity in the "twilight zone between the living and the nonliving" caught on quickly. It is not surprising, in the decade that witnessed the rise of science-fiction cinema, to see the virus quickly become, in the words of one headline, "as mysterious as it is mean." See Robert K. Plumb, "Virus X-traordinary: The 'New' and Perversely Fashionable Microbe of the Moment Is as Mysterious as It Is Mean," *New York Times*, 20 April 1952, 34–35.

21. William L. Laurence, "Science Explores Frontier of Life," *New York Times*, 30 December 1952, 16.

22. Ibid.

23. Frank Macfarlane Burnet, "Viruses," *Scientific American*, May 1951, 43. In a 1955 virology symposium, however, Burnett reminded the assembled scientists that they "must still be willing to recognize that there is the need for some social justification for biological research" which, in the case of virology, "is claimed mainly for work on the prevention of virus disease of human beings or organisms important to human beings." Frank Macfarlane Burnet, "General Discussion," *The Nature of Viruses* (CIBA Foundation Symposium), ed. G. E. W. Wolstenholme and Elaine C. P. Millar (Boston: Little, Brown, 1957), 277.

24. On colonialism and tropical medicine, see Warwick Anderson, *The Cultivation of Whiteness: Science, Health, and Racial Destiny in Australia* (New York: Basic Books, 2003); Warwick Anderson, *Colonial Pathologies: American Tropical Medicine, Race, and Hygiene in the Philippines* (Durham: Duke University Press, 2006); and Warwick Anderson, "Going through the Motions: American Public Health and Colonial 'Mimicry,'" in "Contagion and Culture," ed. Priscilla Wald, Nancy Tomes, and Lisa Lynch, special issue, *American Literary History* 14.4 (winter 2002): 686–719.

25. On the use of health in the Cold War creation of the "Third World," see Odd Arne Westad, *The Global Cold War: Third World Interventions and the Making of Our Times* (Cambridge: Cambridge University Press, 2005).

26. "About BW," *New York Times*, 1 January 1950, E76.

27. On biological warfare research in Manchuria, see Sheldon H. Harris, *Factories of Death: Japanese Biological Warfare, 1932–1945, and the American Cover-up*, rev. ed. (New York: Routledge, 2002). On the political importance of Manchuria, see Steven I. Levine, *Anvil of Victory: The Communist Revolution in Manchuria, 1945–1948* (New York: Columbia University Press, 1987).

28. From the mid-1950s through the late 1960s, "approximately half of federally supported academic research" was in the area of biomedical research. See Roger L. Geiger, "Science, Universities, and National Defense, 1945–1970," *Osiris*, 2d series 7 (1992): 26.

29. "Red Bloc Bars Bacterial Warfare," *New York Times*, 29 September 1950, 8.

30. "Germ War Is Termed Deadlier than Atom," *New York Times*, 22 October 1950, 4.

31. Harold B. Hinton, "'Critical Target Areas' Urged to Speed Civil Defense Plans," *New York Times*, 28 December 1950, 1.

32. "Soviet Organ Sees Confusion in U.S.," *New York Times*, 13 April 1951, 6.

33. "Enemy Disease Smog Held a Possibility," *New York Times*, 24 October 1951, 18.

34. Robert K. Plumb, "Atomic Idea Urged in Germ Splitting," *New York Times*, 2 May 1952, 10.

35. Gladwin Hill, "Marines Undergo Atomic Bomb Test," *New York Times*, 2 May 1950, 1, 10.

36. Arthur Gelb, "Diseases of the World Listed on U.N. Map," *New York Times*, 17 October 1953, 3.

37. Earl Ubell, "That Old Virus," *Ladies' Home Journal*, April 1953, 92.

38. "How Virus Attacks Sound Tissue," *New York Times*, 6 September 1953, E7.

39. William Laurence, "Virus Study Aided by New Technique," *New York Times*, 10 September 1953, 35.

40. "New Way to Study Cell-Virus Battle," *Science News Letter* 64.8 (22 August 1953): 116.

41. See Peter Knight, *Conspiracy Culture: From the Kennedy Assassination to the X-Files* (New York: Routledge, 2000).

42. Paul de Kruif, *The Microbe Hunters* (New York: Harcourt Brace, 1926), 126, 143.

43. Paul de Kruif, "Virus Hunters," *Today's Health*, July 1953, 32.

44. Jennie Q. Adatto, "Virus Facts," *Today's Health*, September 1954, 39.

45. John E. Nelson, "Investigation of Communist Propaganda," 71st Cong., 3d sess., 17 January 1931, H. Rep. 2290, in Robert K. Carr, *The House Committee on Un-American Activities 1945–1950* (Ithaca, N.Y.: Cornell University Press, 1952), 99.

46. See Patton, *Inventing AIDS*; Darryl Ogden, "Cold War Science and the Body Politic"; and Emily Martin, *Flexible Bodies: Tracking Immunity in American Culture from the Days of Polio to the Age of AIDS* (Boston: Beacon Press, 1994).

47. Patton, *Inventing AIDS*, 59.

48. Ogden, "Cold War Science and the Body Politic," 245–46.

49. See Patton, *Inventing AIDS*; Patton, *Fatal Advice*; Cindy Patton, *Sex and Germs: The Politics of AIDS* (Boston: South End Press, 1985); and Martin, *Flexible Bodies*.

50. Ogden, "Cold War Science and the Body Politic," 247.

51. James F. O'Neil, "How You Can Fight Communism," *American Legion*, August 1948, 16.

52. J. Edgar Hoover, testimony, House Committee on Un-American Activities, *Hearings on H.R. 1884 and H.R. 2122*, 80th Cong., 1st sess., 26 March 1947, 37.

53. Cited in Westad, *The Global Cold War*, 114.

54. *Red Nightmare*, directed by George Waggner for the U.S. Department of Defense Directorate for Armed Forces Information and Education (Warner Brothers, 1962). This film was also known as *The Commies Are Coming*.

55. *Army Information Film AIF No. 7: Code of Conduct—To Resist* (U.S. Department of Defense, 1950).

56. Joost A. M. Meerloo, *The Rape of the Mind: The Psychology of Thought Control, Menticide, and Brainwashing* (Cleveland: World Publishing, 1956), 47.

57. Whittaker Chambers, "I Was the Witness," *Saturday Evening Post*, 23 February 1952, 55. This piece was the third of a ten-part series published between 9 February and 12 April.

58. Herbert Hoover, "The Protection of Freedom: A Constant Battle against the Abuse of Power," *Vital Speeches of the Day* 20 (1 September 1954): 681.

59. Joseph D. Wassersug, "Deadly Germs That Play Possum," *Science Digest*, May 1953, 8.

60. Joseph L. Melnick, "Viruses within Cells," *Scientific American*, December 1953, 39.

61. Frank L. Horstall Jr., "International Symposium on the Dynamics of Virus Infections," *Science*, 2 April 1954, 428.

62. H. Jack Geiger, "Alphabet of Life," *Saturday Review*, 5 January 1957, 46.

63. Robert K. Plumb, "Scientist Makes Synthetic Virus," *New York Times*, 18 April 1956, 33.

64. Boris Eperuss, V. S. Leopold, J. D. Watson, and J. J. Weigle, "Terminology in Bacterial Genetics," *Nature*, 11 April 1953, 701.

65. "Cellular heredity" in Luria and Darnell "is embodied in informational patterns of two kinds. One kind consists of coded macromolecules of nucleic acids which serve as *templates* to guide the synthesis of new macromolecules. The other kind consists of *priming configurations*, whose presence is required to direct the assembly of molecular species into functional two- and three-dimensional structures" (*General Virology*, 443). The revision represents a more sophisticated and nuanced conception of the process of reproduction that centers on the transmission of information and emphasizes the directions for reproduction rather than materials that are reproduced. The shift is evident, for example, in the change of

emphasis from Luria's claim in the 1953 edition that "all speculation as to virus origin leads to the possible modes of merging two genetic systems into a functioning cell" (361) to Luria and Darnell's revised assertion that "all speculations about the origin of viruses lead to consideration of possible modes of merging two or more genetic elements to make a functioning genetic system" (453). The switch from "genetic systems" to "genetic elements" and from "cell" to "genetic system" registers a shift in researchers' understanding of how viruses worked: viruses, in the second formulation, changed the interactions among the parts of an elaborate system that determine the fates of cells and, therefore, the health of individuals; viral reproduction represented an alteration in the flow of information.

66. Lily E. Kay, *Who Wrote the Book of Life? A History of the Genetic Code* (Stanford, Calif.: Stanford University Press, 2000), 3.

67. On information and the Cold War, see especially (in addition to Kay), Paul N. Edwards, *The Closed World: Computers and the Politics of Discourse in Cold War America* (Cambridge: MIT Press, 1996); N. Katherine Hayles, *How We Became Posthuman: Virtual Bodies in Cybernetics, Literature, and Informatics* (Chicago: University of Chicago Press, 1999); Steven J. Heims, *Constructing a Social Science for Postwar America: The Cybernetics Group, 1946–1953* (Cambridge: MIT Press, 1993); and Robert Mitchell and Phillip Thurtle, "Data Made Flesh: The Material Poesis of Informatics," introduction to *Data Made Flesh: Embodying Information*, ed. Robert Mitchell and Phillip Thurtle (New York: Routledge, 2004), 1–23.

68. Norbert Wiener, *The Human Uses of Human Being: Cybernetics and Society* (1950; repr., Garden City, N.Y.: Doubleday Anchor Books, 1954), 3.

69. Henry Quastler, *A Primer on Information Theory*, reprinted from *Symposium on Information Theory in Biology: Gatlinburg, Tennessee, October 29–31, 1956* (New York: Pergamon Press, 1958), 4–5.

70. Ibid., 5.

71. Wiener, *The Human Uses of Human Being*, 15. See also Norbert Wiener, *Cybernetics: Or Control and Communication in the Animal and the Machine* (New York: Technology Press, John Wiley and Sons, 1948).

72. Jay A. Levy, Heinz Fraenkel-Conrat, and Robert A. Owens, *Virology*, 3d edition (Englewood Cliffs, N.J.: Prentice Hall, 1994), 1.

73. Senator Joseph McCarthy, *McCarthyism: The Fight for America* (New York: Devin-Adair, 1952), 23, 101.

74. "Classified information" means that the access to the data or other information thus classified has been restricted. There was an executive order addressing classification of information as early as 1940, but most of the legislation that established the concept and the regulations surrounding it was in the 1950s. See especially Daniel Patrick Moynihan, *Secrecy: The American Experience* (New Haven, Conn.: Yale University Press, 1998); Ellen Schrecker, *The Age of McCarthyism: A Brief History with Documents* (Boston: Bedford Books/St. Martin's Press, 1994); and James Gannon, *Stealing Secrets, Telling Lies: How Spies and Codebreakers Helped Shape the Twentieth Century* (Washington: Brassey's, 2001).

75. "Purge of Stalin," *New York Times*, 25 March 1956, E1.

76. Beginning in the McCarthy years, for example, gay men and lesbians with access to sensitive information were purged with, and often as, Communists because they were thought to be especially susceptible to blackmail. The targeting of gay men and lesbians suggests the corporealization of (viral) threats to the state. On McCarthy and homosexuality, see especially Jennifer Terry, *An American Obsession: Science, Medicine, and Homosexuality in Modern Society* (Chicago: University of Chicago Press, 1999); Jonathan Ned Katz, *Gay American History: Lesbians and Gay Men in the U.S.A.: A Documentary History*, rev. ed. (New York: Plume Books, 1992); John D'Emilio, "Homophobia and the Course of Post-World War II American Radicalism: The Career of Bayard Rustin," in *The World Turned: Essays on Gay History, Politics, and Culture* (Durham: Duke University Press, 2002): 3–22; John D'Emilio, *Sexual Politics, Sexual Communities: The Making of a Homosexual Minority in the United States 1940–1970*, 2d ed. (Chicago: University of Chicago Press, 1998); Robert Corber, *Homosexuality in Cold War America: Resistance and the Crisis of Masculinity* (Durham: Duke University Press, 1997); Harry M. Benshoff, "Pods, Pederasts and Perverts: (Re)criminalizing the Monster Queer in Cold War Culture," in *Monsters in the Closet: Homosexuality and the Horror Film* (Manchester: Manchester University Press, 1997): 122–72; and Stacy Braukman, " 'Nothing Else Matters but Sex': Cold War Narratives of Deviance and the Search for Lesbian Teachers in Florida, 1959–1963," *Feminist Studies* 27.3 (fall 2001): 553–75.

77. Mottram, "Rencontre avec William Burroughs," 12. The original interview was conducted in 1964 and published in *Les Langues Modernes* (January–February 1965): 79–83.

78. Oliver Harris, "Can You See a Virus? The Queer Cold War of William Burroughs," *Journal of American Studies* 33.2 (1999): 247. Literary critical engagements with Burroughs tend in general to stress the nonmetaphorical nature of his idea of contagion. Robin Lydenberg, for example, expains that the " 'evil virus' . . . travels from one host to another along mathematical lines of extension or along biological circuits of need—it proceeds by literal metonymic juxtaposition and contagion rather than by metaphorical resemblance" (*Word Cultures: Radical Theory and Practice in William S. Burroughs' Fiction* [Urbana: University of Illinois Press, 1987], 13). On the virus imagery in Burroughs, see also Barry Miles, *William Burroughs: El Hombre Invisible*, rev. ed. (London: Virgin Books, 2002).

79. William S. Burroughs, "Deposition: Testimony Concerning a Sickness," in *Naked Lunch: The Restored Text*, ed. James Grauerholz and Barry Miles (1959; repr., New York: Grove Press, 2001), 205.

80. William S. Burroughs, *The Ticket That Exploded* (New York: Grove Press, 1962), 58–59.

81. William S. Burroughs, Introduction, *Queer* (New York: Viking Press, 1985), xiv.

82. Conrad Knickerbocker, "White Junk" (interview with William Burroughs),

in *Burroughs Live: The Collected Interviews of William S. Burroughs 1960–1997*, ed. Sylvere Lotringer (Los Angeles: Semiotext(e) Double Agents Series, 2001), 68.

83. Ibid., 67.

84. Ibid.

85. The 1993 film, which takes place on a military base, is an exception; it did not have a significant following, and I do not discuss it in this chapter. The most recent version, *The Invasion*, directed by Oliver Hirschbiegel (Warner Pictures, 2007), was released too late for inclusion in this book, but it is interesting that the pods in this version are replaced by a virus that is transmitted through direct contact with bodily fluids. The alien invasion is understood and described throughout the film as a spreading epidemic. CDC investigators are among the first infected, and the infection is contained by USAMRIID. The alien virus ultimately proves weak enough to destroy.

86. Benshoff, *Monsters in the Closet*, 128.

87. Jack Finney, *The Body Snatchers* (New York: Dell, 1955), 18–19.

88. David Seed, *Brainwashing: The Fictions of Mind Control: A Study of Novels and Films since World War II* (Kent, Ohio: Kent State University Press, 2004). Seed frames his reading of *Body Snatchers* with a discussion of Hunter and Meerloo. See also his chapter on William Burroughs.

89. The mind control literature focused on the work of the Russian scientist Ivan Petrovich Pavlov, who won a Nobel prize for his research on behavioral conditioning, and Pavlovian conditioning was central to works such as Condon's. Finney's novel, however, was more concerned with the biological features of the human personality that would allow the alienation—or literal theft—of human identity.

90. Wiener, *The Human Uses of Human Being*, 96.

91. On conspiracy theories, see Peter Knight, ed., *Conspiracy Culture, Conspiracy Nation: The Politics of Paranoia in Postwar America* (New York: New York University Press, 2002); and Timothy Melley, *Empire of Conspiracy: The Culture of Paranoia in Postwar America* (Ithaca, N.Y.: Cornell University Press, 2000).

92. Jack Finney, "The Body Snatchers," *Collier's*, 10 December 1954, 121. This piece is the second in a three-part series published between 26 November and 24 December 1954.

93. Homi Bhabha, "Of Mimicry and Man: The Ambivalence of Colonial Discourse," *October* 28 (spring 1984): 126.

94. Alan Paton, "The Negro in America Today," *Collier's*, 15 October 1954, 62. The piece was continued the following week. See Alan Paton, "The Negro in the North," *Collier's*, 22 October 1954, 70–80.

95. Much has been written on hybridity and "mixed-bloodedness" in postcolonial and U.S. race and ethnic theory. For a history of the concept of hybridity, see especially Robert J. C. Young, *Colonial Desire: Hybridity in Culture, Theory, and Race* (London: Routledge, 1995). In addition, see the discussions of hybridity in Homi Bhabha, *The Location of Culture* (London: Routledge, 1994);

Tariq Modood and Pnina Werbner, eds. *Debating Cultural Hybridity* (London: Zed Books, 1997); and especially Lisa Lowe's brilliant essay, "The Intimacies of Four Continents," in *Haunted by Empire: Geographies of Intimacy in North American History*, ed. Ann Laura Stoler (Durham: Duke University Press, 1006), 191–212.

The "intimacies" of Lowe's title are the expression of the multiple contacts of continental interdependence in the early nineteenth century. Lowe shows how Chinese immigrant figures ("the Chinese coolie"; "the Chinese woman")—often associated in the colonial imagination with racially mixed figures—serve as cultural hybrids that help to produce "a hierarchy of racial classifications" (197) that underpins liberal humanism and the political economy of modernity. I find in these figures an intriguing lineage for the carrier.

For a variety of discussions of mixed race in the U.S. context, see Werner Sollors, *Neither Black, nor White, yet Both: Thematic Explorations of Interracial Literature* (New York: Oxford University Press, 1997); Ronald Takaki, *A Different Mirror: A History of Multiculturalism in America* (Bay Back Books, 1993); Eva Saks, "Representing Miscegenation Law," *Raritan* 8.2 (1988): 39–69; Walter Benn Michaels, *Our America: Nativism, Modernism, and Pluralism* (Durham: Duke University Press, 1995); David Palumbo-Liu, *Asian/American: Historical Crossings of a Racial Frontier* (Stanford, Calif.: Stanford University Press, 1999); and Alys Eve Weinbaum, *Wayward Reproductions: Genealogies of Race and Nation in Transatlantic Modern Thought* (Durham: Duke University Press, 2004).

96. Sigmund Freud, "The Unconscious," in *On the History of the Psycho-Analytic Movement, Papers on Metapsychology and Other Works*, vol. 14 of *The Standard Edition of the Complete Psychological Works of Sigmund Freud*, trans. and ed. James Strachey in collaboration with Anna Freud and assisted by Alix Strachey and Alan Tyson (1957; repr., London: Hogarth Press and the Institute of Psycho-Analysis, 1986), 191. Freud wrote "The Unconscious" in 1915.

97. See Robert J. C. Young, *Colonial Desire.*

98. On the interarticulation of race and sexuality (specifically, reproduction) in Freud, see Weinbaum, *Wayward Reproductions.* It is interesting that Freud's strongest justification for group psychology turns on a racial metaphor.

99. Edward Hunter, *Brainwashing: The Story of Men Who Defied It* (New York: Farrar, Straus, and Cudahy, 1956), 65.

100. See Al LaValley, "Invasion of the Body Snatchers: Politics, Psychology, Sociology," in *Invasion of the Body Snatchers: Don Siegel, Director*, ed. Al LaValley (New Brunswick, N.J.: Rutgers University Press, 1989), 3–17. See also Stuart M. Kaminsky, "Pods," in *Don Siegel: Director* (New York: Curtis Books, 1974), 99–108.

101. Stuart M. Kaminsky, "Don Siegel on the Pod Society," in *Invasion of the Body Snatchers: Don Siegel, Director*, ed. Al LaValley (New Brunswick, N.J.: Rutgers University Press, 1989), 154.

102. Sobchack, *Screening Space*, 124.

103. Ibid., 125.

104. *Invasion of the Body Snatchers*, directed by Don Siegel (Allied Artists Pictures, 1956).

105. Matheson's novella spawned two film versions, *The Last Man on Earth* (dir. Ubaldo Ragona, 1964) and *Omega Man* (dir. Boris Sagal, 1971). Neither film retains the bat explanation, and in *Omega Man*, the epidemic is the result of government research.

106. Meerloo, *The Rape of the Mind*, 209.

107. Ibid., 292.

108. Christopher Lasch, *The Culture of Narcissism: American Life in an Age of Diminishing Expectations* (New York: Warner Books, 1979); Tom Wolfe, "The 'Me Decade' and the Third Great Awakening," *New York*, 23 August 1976, 26–40.

109. Jonathan Schell, *The Time of Illusion* (1975; repr., New York: Vintage Books, 1976), 14. Most of the book had appeared in a series of *New Yorker* articles, which were also widely read.

110. "Crisis of Human Environment," United Nations Economic and Social Council, *Problems of the Human Environment: Report of the Secretary General*, 47th Session, Agenda Item 10, 26 May 1969, 4.

111. Harold R. Isaacs, "Color in World Affairs," *Foreign Affairs* 47.2 (January 1969): 235.

112. According to Douglas T. Miller, public trust in the medical profession dropped from 73 percent to 42 percent from the mid-sixties to the mid-seventies, and in 1976, faith in the legal profession had dropped to 12 percent. See Douglas T. Miller, "Sixties Activism in the 'Me Decade,'" in *The Lost Decade: America in the Seventies*, ed. Elsebeth Hurup (Aarhus, Denmark: Aarhus University Press, 1996), 133–43.

113. Douglas T. Miller's "Sixties Activism in the 'Me Decade'" documents both the nostalgia and the social and political activism that, contrary to dominant representation of the decade, was prevalent in the seventies.

114. Pauline Kael, "Pods," *New Yorker*, 25 December 1978, 48, 51.

115. Denny Zeitlin, a jazz musician and practicing psychiatrist, did the musical score for the film.

116. *Invasion of the Body Snatchers*, directed by Philip Kaufman (Metro-Goldwyn-Mayer, 1978).

117. He was also subsequently Martin Dysart, the psychiatrist in a 1977 Broadway production of *Equus*. Kibner's role as family counselor might also coyly invoke Spock's nominal predecessor, Dr. Benjamin Spock, on whose advice parents reared the generation that includes Matthew and Elizabeth.

118. See Carl Sagan, *Broca's Brain* (New York: Random House, 1979). The scientific response to Velikovsky was not favorable.

119. It is interesting that the 1971 film *Omega Man* differs from earlier incarnations of that story in positing a small band of human beings dedicated to the survival of the species.

120. On the shaping of the epidemic through epidemiological narratives, see especially Gerald M. Oppenheimer, "In the Eye of the Storm: The Epidemiological Construction of AIDS," in *AIDS: The Burdens of History*, ed. Elizabeth Fee and Daniel M. Fox (Berkeley: University of California Press, 1988), 267–300.

5. "THE COLUMBUS OF AIDS"

1. Lance Morrow, "The Start of a Plague Mentality," *Time*, 23 September 1985, 92.

2. A retrovirus is an enveloped RNA genome that reproduces contra the central dogma of molecular biology by transcribing its genome from RNA into DNA. Retroviruses are accordingly exceptionally mutable.

3. Cindy Patton, *Inventing AIDS* (New York: Routledge, 1990), 61.

4. The connection between HIV and AIDS was widely assumed before it was scientifically demonstrated. There are still some scientists who dispute the connection, although at this point the vast majority assume that HIV causes the collapse of the immune system, hence the opportunistic infections that comprise AIDS.

I am basing my conclusions about the language and images with which HIV / AIDS was presented to the public as well as about "Patient Zero" on my reading of more than a thousand articles from numerous periodicals and newspapers between 1981 and 1995 (with a concentration on the 1980s), including the *New York Times, Newsweek*, the *London Times*, the *Seattle Post-Intelligencer, Science News, Time, New York, Science*, the *Saturday Evening Post*, the *National Review, U.S. News and World Report, USA Today, Ladies' Home Journal*, the *New Republic, Rolling Stone*, the *Nation, Essence, Publisher's Weekly, Black Enterprise, World Health*, the *Progressive, People Weekly, Reader's Digest, Harpers Bazaar, Maclean's*, the *New York Review of Books*, the *National Review, Manchester Guardian Weekly, Jet, Discover, Mademoiselle, Scientific American, Omni, Life, Ms., McCalls, Consumer*, the *Toronto Star*, the *Washington Post, Financial Times*, the *St. Petersburg Times* (Florida), and *Modern Healthcare*. I am grateful to Eden Osucha for compiling an excellent bibliography of the media coverage. On the media treatment of the epidemic, see especially Cindy Patton, *Fatal Advice: How Safe-Sex Education Went Wrong* (Durham: Duke University Press, 1996); Simon Watney, *Policing Desire: Pornography, AIDS, and the Media* (Minneapolis: University of Minnesota Press, 1996); Alexandra Juhasz, *AIDS TV: Identity, Community, and Alternative Video* (Durham: Duke University Press, 1995); and James Kinsella, *Covering the Plague: AIDS and the American Media* (New Brunswick, N.J.: Rutgers University Press, 1989). On the Bergalis-Acer case, see Katharine Park, "Kimberly Bergalis, AIDS, and the Plague Metaphor," in *Media Spectacles*, ed. Marjorie Garber, Jann Matlock, and Rebecca Walkowitz (New York: Routledge, 1993), 232–53.

5. Paula A. Treichler, *How to Have Theory in an Epidemic: Cultural Chronicles of AIDS* (Durham: Duke University Press, 1999), 5.

6. See James Grauerholz, "A Hard-Boiled Reporter," in *Word Virus: The William Burroughs Reader*, ed. James Grauerholz and Ira Silverberg (New York: Grove Press, 1998), 44. The quotation is from Burroughs's introduction to *Queer*, xxiii.

7. Treichler, *How to Have Theory in an Epidemic*, 11; Douglas Crimp, "AIDS: Cultural Analysis/Cultural Activism," in *AIDS: Cultural Analysis/Cultural Activism*, ed. Douglas Crimp (Cambridge: MIT Press, 1988), 3, originally published as an issue of *October* 43 (winter 1987).

There have been a wealth of excellent cultural studies of the HIV/AIDS epidemic. Among those I have found most helpful for this project, in addition to those already cited in these chapter notes, are Cindy Patton, *Sex and Germs: the Politics of AIDS* (Boston: South End Press, 1985); Cindy Patton, "Queer Peregrinations," in *Acting on AIDS: Sex, Drugs, and Politics*, ed. Joshua Oppenheimer and Helena Reckitt (London: Serpent's Tail, 1997), 235–53; Cindy Patton, *Globalizing AIDS* (Minneapolis: University of Minnesota Press, 2002); Simon Watney, *Practices of Freedom: Selected Writings on HIV/AIDS* (London: Rivers Oram Press, 1994); Simon Watney, "The Political Significance of Statistics in the AIDS Crisis: Epidemiology, Representation and Re-gaying," in *Acting on AIDS: Sex, Drugs, and Politics*, ed. Joshua Oppenheimer and Helena Reckitt (London: Serpent's Tail, 1997), 76–100; Simon Watney, *Imagine Hope: AIDS and Gay Identity* (London: Routledge, 2000); Simon Watney, "The Spectacle of AIDS," in *The Lesbian and Gay Studies Reader*, ed. Henry Abelove, Michele Aina Barale, and David M. Halperin (New York: Routledge, 1993), 71–86; Charles E. Rosenberg, "Disease and Social Order in America: Perceptions and Expectations," in *AIDS: The Burden of History*, ed. Elizabeth Fee and Daniel M. Fox (Berkeley: University of California Press, 1988), 12–32; Guenter B. Risse, "Epidemics and History: Ecological Perspectives and Social Responses," in *AIDS: The Burden of History*, ed. Elizabeth Fee and Daniel M. Fox (Berkeley: University of California Press, 1988), 33–66; Cathy Waldby, *AIDS and the Body Politic: Biomedicine and Sexual Difference* (New York: Routledge, 1996); Sander Gilman, *Disease and Representation: Images of Illness From Madness to AIDS* (Ithaca, N.Y.: Cornell University Press, 1988); Sander Gilman, *Sexuality: An Illustrated History: Representing the Sexual in Medicine and Culture from the Middle Ages to the Age of AIDS* (New York: Wiley, 1989); Sander Gilman, "AIDS and Stigma," in *Acting on AIDS: Sex, Drugs, and Politics*, ed. Joshua Oppenheimer and Helena Reckitt (London: Serpent's Tail, 1997), 101–17; Sander Gilman, "The Beautiful Body and AIDS," *Picturing Health and Illness: Images of Identity and Difference* (Baltimore: Johns Hopkins University Press, 1995), 115–72; Susan Sontag, *AIDS and Its Metaphors* (New York: Farrar, Straus, Giroux, 1988); Dennis Altman, *AIDS in the Mind of America* (Garden City, N.Y.: Anchor/Doubleday, 1986); Dennis Altman, *Global Sex* (Chicago: University of Chicago Press, 2001); Alexander Garcia Duttmann, *At Odds with AIDS: Thinking and Talking about a Virus*, trans. Peter Gilgen and Conrad Scott-Curtis (Stanford, Calif.: Stanford University Press, 1996); Evelynn Hammonds, "Missing Persons:

African American Women, AIDS and the History of Disease," *Radical America* 24.2 (1992): 7–23; Eve Kosofsky Sedgwick, *Tendencies* (Durham: Duke University Press, 1993); Eve Kosofsky Sedgwick, "Gary Fisher in Your Pocket," in *Acting on AIDS: Sex, Drugs, and Politics*, ed. Joshua Oppenheimer and Helena Reckitt (London: Serpent's Tail, 1997), 408–29; Leo Bersani, "Is the Rectum a Grave?" in *AIDS: Cultural Analysis, Cultural Activism*, ed. Douglas Crimp (Cambridge: MIT Press, 1996), 197–222; Douglas Crimp, *AIDS Demo Graphics* (Seattle: Bay Press, 1990); Douglas Crimp, *Melancholia and Moralism: Essays on AIDS and Queer Politics* (Cambridge: MIT Press, 2002); and Steven Epstein, *Impure Science: AIDS, Activism, and the Politics of Knowledge* (Berkeley: University of California Press, 1996).

8. "Canadian Said to Have Had Key Role in Spread of AIDS," *New York Times*, 7 October 1987, B7.

9. Randy Shilts, *And the Band Played On: Politics, People, and the AIDS Epidemic* (New York: St. Martin's Press, 1987), 439.

10. *Angels in America* is especially interesting for my purposes in its depiction of Roy Cohn and its consequent representation of the disease in relation to Cold War ideology. See especially Daryl Ogden, "Cold War Science and the Body Politic: An Immuno/Virological Approach to *Angels in America*," *Literature and Medicine* 19.2 (2000): 241–61.

11. Pamphlet, *The Centers for Disease Control Announce the Course Applied Epidemiology, May 8–17, 1985* (Atlanta: U.S. Department of Health and Human Services, Public Health Service, Centers for Disease Control, 1984). It is a seven-page pamphlet, but there is no pagination. For online access to this pamphlet, see *http://library.unc.edu*.

12. "*Pneumocystis* Pneumonia—Los Angeles," *Morbidity and Mortality Weekly Report* 30.21 (5 June 1981): 250.

13. "Kaposi's Sarcoma and *Pneumocystis* Pneumonia among Homosexual Men —New York City and California," *Morbidity and Mortality Weekly Report* 30.25 (3 July 1981): 306, 307.

14. Alvin E. Friedman-Kien, "Disseminated Kaposi's Sarcoma Syndrome in Young Homosexual Men," *Journal of the American Academy of Dermatology* 5 (1981): 469.

15. M. S. Gottlieb et al., "Pneumocystis Carinii Pneumonia and Mucosal Candidiasis in Previously Healthy Homosexual Men: Evidence of a New Acquired Cellular Immunodeficiency," *New England Journal of Medicine* 305.24 (10 December 1981): 1429.

16. F. P. Siegal et al., "Severe Acquired Immunodeficiency in Male Homosexuals, Manifested by Chronic Perianal Ulcerative Herpes Simplex Lesions," *New England Journal of Medicine* 305.24 (10 December 1981): 1444. The remaining article is H. Masur et al., "An Outbreak of Community-acquired Pneumocystis Carinii Pneumonia: Initial Manifestation of Cellular Immune Dysfunction," *New England Journal of Medicine* 305.24 (10 December 1981): 1431–38.

17. "Update on Kaposi's Sarcoma and Opportunistic Infections in Previously Healthy Persons—United States," *Morbidity and Mortality Weekly Report* 31.22 (11 June 1982): 294; emphasis added.

18. "Homosexuals Found Particularly Liable to Common Viruses," *New York Times*, 10 December 1981, 1.

19. Lawrence K. Altman, "New Homosexual Disorder Worries Health Officials," *New York Times* 11 May 1982, C1, C6.

20. "Diffuse, Undifferentiated Non-Hodgkins Lymphoma among Homosexual Males—United States," *Morbidity and Mortality Weekly Report* 31.21 (4 June 1982): 277–78.

21. "A Cluster of Kaposi's Sarcoma and *Pneumocystis carinii* Pneumonia among Homosexual Male Residents of Los Angeles and Orange Counties, California," *Morbidity and Mortality Weekly Report* 31.23 (18 June 1982): 305.

22. Lawrence K. Altman, "Clue Found on Homosexual's Precancer Syndrome," *New York Times* 18 June 1982, B8.

23. Patton, *Inventing AIDS*, 62.

24. See my previous chapter, "Viral Cultures," for a fuller discussion of this claim.

25. Patton, *Inventing AIDS*, 63.

26. Friedman-Kien, "Disseminated Kaposi's Sarcoma Syndrome," 469.

27. Matt Clark et al. "AIDS: A Lethal Mystery Story," *Newsweek*, 27 December 1982, 63.

28. James Mann, "Supergerms: The New Health Menace," *U.S. News and World Report*, 28 February 1983, 35.

29. Ibid., and Walter Isaacson, "Hunting for the Hidden Killers," *Time*, 4 July 1983, 50.

30. John Leo, "The Real Epidemic: Fear and Despair," *Time*, 4 July 1983, 58.

31. Hemophiliacs were more ambiguous, sometimes excluded as "innocent victims."

32. Robert Bazell, "The History of an Epidemic," *New Republic*, 1 August 1983, 18.

33. Isaacson, "Hunting for the Hidden Killers, 50.

34. David M. Auerbach, William W. Darrow, Harold W. Jaffe, and James W. Curran, "Cluster of Cases of the Acquired Immune Deficiency Syndrome: Patients Linked by Sexual Contact," *American Journal of Medicine* 76 (March 1984): 487, 489. It is interesting that while this piece uses the data and much of the language of the study that first identified the cluster and the "non-Californian," that study is not cited. It is an especially odd omission because most of the other early *MMWR* reports are referenced.

35. In 1982 the CDC publication had reported that "2 [patients] from Orange County had had sexual contact with 1 patient who was not a resident of California" and that "1 patient with KS reported having had sexual contact with 2 friends of

the non-Californian with KS" ("A Cluster of Kaposi's Sarcoma and *Pneumocystis carinii* Pneumonia," 11).

36. "U.S. Medical Study Singles Out a Man Who Carried AIDS," *New York Times*, 27 March 1984, A25.

37. Auerbach et al., "Cluster of Cases of the Acquired Immune Deficiency Syndrome," 490. Ironically, "Patient 0" was in fact not an asymptomatic carrier, as they establish when they document that he had had lymphadenopathy since 1979 and developed KS shortly thereafter.

38. Claudia Wallis, "Knowing the Face of the Enemy," *Time*, 30 April 1984, 66.

39. Joe Levine, "The Toughest Virus of All," *Time*, 3 November 1986, 76, 78.

40. Claudia Wallis, "AIDS: a Growing Threat: Now that the Disease Has Come Out of the Closet, How Far Will It Spread?" *Time*, 12 August 1985, 40, 42. Wallis's pun is an example of how the rhetoric of media accounts promoted the embodiment of the disease in gay men. It is in especially poor taste when one considers how many men were "outed" by getting AIDS, a common theme in popular representations, such as Jonathan Demme's 1993 film, *Philadelphia*.

41. Margaret Engel, "AIDS and Prejudice: One Reporter's Account of the Nation's Response," *Washington Post*, 1 December 1987, 10.

42. Sandra Panem, "A Drama and Questions," *Science*, 26 February 1988, 1039.

43. Richard A. Knox, "A Troubling, Persuasive Study of AIDS and Other Health Crises," *Boston Globe*, 22 January 1995, 45.

44. William Hines, "The AIDS Epidemic: A Report From the Front Lines," *Washington Post*, 11 October 1987, X1.

45. Quotations in this sentence are from the following sources respectively: Hines, "The AIDS Epidemic," X1; "MDs Doubt Claim Canadian Carried AIDS to Continent," *Toronto Star*, 12 December 1987, A2; "Patient Zero (AIDS Patient Gaetan Dugas)," *People*, 28 December 1987, 47; "The Columbus of AIDS," *National Review*, 6 November 1987, 19. Despite the negative depiction in the introduction to an excerpt from Shilts's book in the *Toronto Star*, most of the coverage of "Patient Zero" in that newspaper was distinctly skeptical of Shilts's claims.

46. Steven Miles also criticizes this scene in his review for the *Journal of the American Medical Association* 259.2 (8 January 1988): 288.

47. Panem, "A Drama and Questions," 1040.

48. Alex Shoumatoff even describes a theory that volcanic radiation had caused the original virus to mutate into HIV and another that it was extraterrestrial. See Alex Shoumatoff, "In Search of the Source of AIDS," *Vanity Fair*, July 1988, 114.

49. Evidence for the African origins of the virus continues to be updated and is part of the story as well as the science of the disease. The African origins of civilization were under new investigation by geneticists who were in the process of conducting controversial DNA research into human history using newly developed technologies while Shilts was writing his book. The relationship between religion and science was clearly a subject on the minds of researchers who called

an important figure of their research "African Eve." Africa, the "birthplace of civilization" and of many of the world's major religions, harbors secrets—and microbes—that evidently should not be discovered. HIV both signals and mingles their disturbance.

50. Robert C. Gallo and Luc Montagnier, "AIDS in 1988," *Scientific American,* October 1988, 47.

51. Simon Watney, "Missionary Positions: AIDS, 'Africa,' and Race," in "Life and Death in Sexuality: Reproductive Technologies and AIDS," special issue, *differences* 1.1 (winter 1989): 86. See also Tim Dean, "The Germs of Empires: *Heart of Darkness*, Colonial Trauma, and the Historiography of AIDS," in *The Psychoanalysis of Race*, ed. Christopher Lane (New York: Columbia University Press, 1998): 305–29.

52. Richard Preston, *The Hot Zone* (New York: Doubleday, 1994), 194.

53. In particular, Sabatier notes that "two parts of the developing world, Haiti and Africa, have received widespread publicity as the possible birthplace of AIDS. Haiti, a Caribbean nation whose people are racially of African descent, was singled out first" (*Blaming Others: Prejudice, Race, and Worldwide AIDS* [Philadelphia: New Society Publishers for the Panos Institute, 1988], 44). See also Paul Farmer, *AIDS and Accusation: Haiti and the Geography of Blame* (Berkeley: University of California Press, 1992); Alexander Moore and Ronald D. LeBaron, "The Case For a Haitian Origin of the AIDS Epidemic," in *The Social Dimensions of AIDS: Method and Theory*, ed. Douglas A. Feldman and Thomas M. Johnson (New York: Praeger, 1986), 77–93; Laurent Dubois, "A Spoonful of Blood: Haitians, Racism, and AIDS," *Science as Culture* 6.1 (1996): 6–43; Julia Epstein, "AIDS, Stigma, and Narratives of Containment," *American Imago* 49.3 (1992): 293–310.

54. Numerous references to the work, as well as reviews, however, attribute an African connection to Shilts's leading man, perhaps because of that centrality.

55. Oscar Moore, "Rites of Fatality," *Guardian*, 21 September 1996, 16.

56. Herbert L. Abrams, "Medical Problems of Survivors of Nuclear War: Infection and the Spread of Communicable Disease," *New England Journal of Medicine* 305.20 (12 November 1981): 1228.

57. Cultural observers as far ranging as Harold Isaacs, from a radical and critical perspective, and Faulkner, from an anxious and conservative one, remarked on the race politics of decolonization in which the majority of the world's governments and people were not white. See William Faulkner, "On Fear: Deep South in Labor: Mississippi," in *Essays, Speeches and Public Letters* (New York: Modern Library, 2004), 92–106; and Harold R. Isaacs, "Color in World Affairs," *Foreign Affairs* 47.2 (January 1969): 235–50.

58. George Will, "AIDS Crushes a Continent," *Newsweek*, 10 January 2000, 64.

59. Jeffrey Goldberg, "Peril of African-borne Diseases: With AIDS, Ebola as Examples, World Ignores Fourth Continent at Its Own Risk," *Seattle Post-Intelligencer*, 30 March 1997, F1.

60. Shilts, *And the Band Played On*, 209.

61. Watney, "Missionary Positions," 92.

62. Greg Hamilton, "He Restores Hope to Lepers of Our Society," *St. Petersburg Times*, 21 October 1991, 1.

63. Alex Shoumatoff, "In Search of the Source of AIDS," 117.

64. Alys Eve Weinbaum, *Wayward Reproductions: Genealogies of Race and Nation in Transatlantic Modern Thought* (Durham: Duke University Press, 2004). It is interesting to consider the prominence of surrogacy cases and reproductive technology in the media at this time.

65. In this context, the 1987 amendment to the Immigration and Nationality Act that added HIV to the list of communicable diseases that excluded applicants from the status of legal resident makes particular sense. As Jennifer Brier points out in her excellent essay "The Immigrant Infection: Images of Race, Nation, and Contagion in the Public Debates on AIDS and Immigration," the equation of immigrants with the threat of contagion itself is evident in the change in the section under which the Public Health Service requested the addition of AIDS to the list. While the initial request was justified under section 212(a)(7), which targeted for exclusion diseases or disabilities that might make potential immigrants a (financial) burden to the state, the final proposal sought their exclusion under section 212(a)(6), which marked AIDS as a "dangerous contagious disease" and represented those infected with HIV as a public-health threat. Brier shows how, in the rhetoric of the Congressional debates surrounding the amendment, the marking of HIV-infected potential immigrants as a national threat relied on the invocation of "African AIDS" and contributed to the racialization of the virus. Jennifer Brier, "The Immigrant Infection: Images of Race, Nation, and Contagion in the Public Debates on AIDS and Immigration," in *Modern American Queer History*, ed. Allida M. Black (Philadelphia: Temple University Press, 2001), 253–70.

66. William A. Blattner, "A Novelistic History of the AIDS Epidemic Demeans Both Investigators and Patients," *Scientific American*, October 1988, 149.

67. Gallo and Montagnier, "AIDS in 1988," 41.

68. On the Gallo-Montagnier conflict, see John Crewdson, *Science Fictions: A Scientific Mystery, a Massive Cover-Up, and the Dark Legacy of Robert Gallo* (Boston: Little, Brown, 2002); Hal Hellman, "Gallo Versus Montagnier: The AIDS War," in *Great Feuds in Medicine: Ten of the Liveliest Disputes Ever* (New York: Wiley, 2001), 165–83; Jamie Feldman, "Gallo, Montagnier, and the Debate over HIV: A Narrative Analysis," *Camera Obscura* 28 (1992): 101–32; Steve Connor and Sharon Kingman, *The Search for the Virus: The Scientific Discovery of AIDS and the Quest for a Cure*, rev. ed. (New York: Penguin Books, 1989); and Robert C. Gallo, *Virus Hunting: AIDS, Cancer, and the Human Retrovirus: A Story of Scientific Discovery* (New York: Basic Books, 1991), esp. 205–15.

69. Gallo and Montagnier, "AIDS in 1988," 40.

70. William A. Haseltine and Flossie Wong-Staal, "The Molecular Biology of the AIDS Virus," *Scientific American*, October 1988, 62.

71. Max Essex and Phyllis J. Kanki, "The Origins of the AIDS Virus," *Scientific American*, October 1988, 64, 71. The authors use the inaccurate "AIDS Virus" not only in their title but throughout their essay.

72. Max Essex and Phyllis J. Kanki, "HIV Infection: The Clinical Picture," *Scientific American*, October 1988, 91. Patton also discusses this photograph in *Inventing AIDS* (65); a similar picture of the Burks appeared with the caption "AIDS Family" in Claudia Wallis's 12 August 1985 article from *Time*, "AIDS: A Growing Threat."

73. Gallo and Montagnier, "AIDS in 1988," 48; emphasis added. Note how the grammar of this construction excludes "users of intravenous drugs" from the "humanity" that "will be tested."

74. Harvey V. Fineberg, "The Social Dimensions of AIDS," *Scientific American*, October 1988, 128.

75. The CDC uses letters rather than numbers to designate infected health-care individuals. "Patient A" signified the epidemiological index case of a disease cluster.

76. Mark Carl Rom, *Fatal Extraction: The Story behind the Florida Dentist Accused of Infecting His Patients with HIV and Poisoning Public Health* (San Francisco: Jossey-Bass, 1997), 138. On the media representations of Bergalis and Acer, see Katharine Park, "Kimberly Bergalis, AIDS, and the Plague Metaphor," 232–53.

77. Chris Spolar, "3 AIDS Cases Mystify Scientists," *Washington Post*, 2 October 1990, 27.

78. The press conference was held on 7 September. Acer had died on 3 September, and the open letter he had written to his patients, assuring them that he had no idea how any patient may have contracted HIV from him but urging them to get tested to be sure, appeared posthumously in a local newspaper on September 6 and 7. See Rom, *Fatal Extraction*, 43–44.

79. Ibid., 16.

80. Geoffrey Cowley et al., "A Ruling on Doctors with AIDS," *Newsweek*, 6 May 1991, 64.

81. *Zero Patience*, directed by John Greyson (Zero Patience Productions, 1993).

82. Howard Feinstein, "Back to Base Camp," *Guardian*, 28 July 1994, T10.

83. Shilts, *And the Band Played On*, 21.

84. Kevin Kelly, "Tangled 'Pterodactyls,'" *Boston Globe*, 28 October 1994, 41.

85. Arnold Kemp, "A Prophecy Written in the Dust," *Glasgow Herald*, 23 July 1994), 11.

86. Oscar Moore, "Rites of Fatality," 16.

87. Duncan J. Watts, *Six Degrees: The Science of a Connected Age* (New York: W. W. Norton, 2003), 164.

88. The transformative impact of a virus and the creation of "hybrids" is a

common topic in contemporary science-fiction horror films, such as *28 Days Later* (directed by Danny Boyle, 2002), *Resident Evil* (directed by Paul W. S. Anderson, 2002), and *Aeon Flux* (directed by Karyn Kusama, 2005). I focus on the novels, especially *The Blood Artists* and *Invasion*, because of the clarity with which they delineate the contours of the outbreak narrative.

89. The movie version of Stephen King's *The Stand* offers a good example of this dynamic when the size and placement of two headlines in a close-up of a local newspaper reveals the mysterious superflu as a much more serious threat than HIV.

90. Chuck Hogan, *The Blood Artists* (New York: Avon Books, 1998).

91. In *Invasion* Cook depicts the psychology of his index case similarly. The virus is triggered when aliens who, having infused it into primordial DNA, find human beings to be creatures appropriate for their purposes. Despite the simultaneity of infection throughout the world, there is an "index case" who becomes the center of the alien consciousness and who embodies the sinister, conspiratorial bug with assimilative ambitions and apocalyptic overtones. As an alien, Beau plots to infect others, but his inability to relinquish his human attachments makes him disturbingly vengeful in the process. The film that was based on Cook's novel draws this out in particular details; the converted Beau has a dangerous temper, displayed most dramatically when he kills his closest associate in a fit of temper after learning that his beloved Cassy had escaped from his compound. *Robin Cook's Invasion* (dir. Armand Mastroianni, 1997).

92. Jaap Goudsmit, *Viral Fitness: The Next SARS and West Nile in the Making* (New York: Oxford University Press, 2004), 156.

93. Cook's aliens are avowed environmentalists, with his index case, Beau, remarking on the " 'unbelievable tragedy for human beings to have done the damage they have to this gorgeous planet' " (125), and it is unclear in *The Blood Artists* whether it is the misanthropic environmentalist Ridgeway or his viral incarnation that engineers Plainville's mutations so that the virus will infect only human beings, not flora or fauna, before Zero prepares to unleash it on the world. In one variant on this theme, scientists motivated by environmental concerns become the Earth's avengers, unleashing doomsday viruses on an unresponsive population. The female scientist protagonists of Tom Cool's *Infectress* and Stephen Kyle's *Beyond Recall*, the brilliant scientist couple, Carol and John Brightling, of Tom Clancy's *Rainbow Six*, and Margaret Atwood's mysterious genius, Crake, all engineer devastating viruses in order to thin a population that has grown out of control. Cool's eponymous heroine wants to bring the population down to a " 'healthy level. Healthy for the planet. Healthy for our continued survival. . . . Today,' " she explains, " 'the planet is the patient. People are the infection' " (47–48). And Dr. Rachel Lesage in *Beyond Recall* designs a virus that attacks only women because, as she explains to a horrified colleague, if " 'we don't' " reduce the population " 'the earth will balance itself by wiping out the surplus humans' " (171). The

motives of the anonymous bioterrorist who turns himself into a walking smallpox virus in the docudrama *Smallpox 2002: Silent Weapon* are unknown, but over-population of the Earth is chief among the narrator's speculations. Infectress and Rachel Lesage are foiled by the engineering triumphs of their responsible (male) colleagues. Atwood's *Oryx and Crake* is the exception to the outbreak formula; the narrator is one of the very few human beings to survive the virus.

See Tom Cool, *Infectress* (New York: Baen Publishing Enterprises, 1997); Stephen Kyle, *Beyond Recall* (New York: Warner Books, Inc., 2000); Tom Clancy, *Rainbow Six* (New York: G. P. Putnam's Sons, 1998); Margaret Atwood, *Oryx and Crake* (New York: Anchor Books, 2003); *Smallpox 2002: Silent Weapon* was produced for F/X and aired in May 2002. For other variants on the theme of engineered viruses used for bioterror, see Richard Preston, *The Cobra Event* (New York: Ballantine Books, 1997); John Case, *The First Horseman* (New York: Ballantine Books: 1998); Leonard Goldberg, *Deadly Exposure* (London: Penguin Books, 1998); Patrick Lynch, *Omega* (London: Penguin Books, 1998); John D. Connor, *Contagion* (New York: Diamond Books, 1992); Robin Cook, *Vector* (New York: G. P. Putnam's Sons, 1999); Robin Cook, *Contagion* (New York: G. P. Putnam's Sons, 1995); Ken Follett, *Whiteout* (London: Penguin Books, 2004). Robin Cook's *Outbreak* (New York: G. P. Putnam's Sons, 1987) is an early outbreak narrative about the deliberate (economically motivated) spread of Ebola in the United States.

94. Lederberg as quoted in Laurie Garrett, *The Coming Plague: Newly Emerging Diseases in a World Out of Balance* (1994; repr., New York: Penguin Books, 1995), 619.

95. Bruce Lincoln, *Discourse and the Construction of Society: Comparative Studies of Myth, Ritual, and Classification* (New York: Oxford University Press, 1989), 20.

96. Richard Preston, *The Hot Zone* (New York: Doubleday, 1994), 121.

97. Malcolm Gladwell, *The Tipping Point: How Little Things Can Make a Big Difference* (New York: Little, Brown, 2000), 261.

EPILOGUE

1. Paul Farmer, *Pathologies of Power: Health, Human Rights, and the New War on the Poor* (Berkeley: University of California Press, 2003), 140.

2. Ibid, 148.

3. The first phrase is from Paul Farmer, *Infections and Inequalities: The Modern Plagues* (Berkeley: University of California Press, 1999), 5. Farmer discusses "structural violence" in both *Infections and Inequalities* and *Pathologies of Power*. The phrases "offenses against human dignity" is from the latter work, where he acknowledges his debt to liberation theologists such as Johan Galtung for the concept of "structural violence." See *Pathologies of Power*, 8.

4. Tracy Kidder, *Mountains Beyond Mountains* (New York: Random House, 2003), 37.

5. Thomas W. Pogge, "Human Rights and Human Responsibilities," *Global Responsibilities: Who Must Deliver on Human Rights?* ed. Andrew Kuper (New York: Routledge, 2005), 3.

6. Laurie Garrett, *The Coming Plague: Newly Emerging Diseases in a World Out of Balance* (1994; New York: Penguin Books, 1995), 619.

7. *Declaration of Alma-Ata*, www.who.int/hpr/NPH/docs/declaration_alma ata.pdf.

8. See Amartya Sen, *Development as Freedom* (New York: Alfred Knopf, 1999); Amartya Sen, *Rationality and Freedom* (Cambridge: Harvard University Press, 2002); Amartya Sen, *Identity and Violence: The Illusion of Destiny* (New York: W. W. Norton, 2006); Paul Farmer, *Pathologies of Power*; and Paul Farmer, *Infections and Inequalities*.

9. On the *Declaration of Alma-Ata*, see especially V. Navarro, "A Critique of the Ideological and Political Position of the Brandt Report and the Alma Ata Declaration," *International Journal of Health Services* 14.2 (1984): 159-72; John J. Hall and Richard Taylor, "Health for All beyond 2000: The Demise of the Alma-Ata Declaration and Primary Health Care in Developing Countries," *Medical Journal of Australia* 178 (January 2003): 17-20; David Werner and David Sanders, *Questioning the Solution: The Politics of Primary Health Care and Child Survival* (Palo Alto, Calif.: HealthWrights, 1997), esp. chap. 3, "Alma Ata and the Institutionalization of Primary Health Care"; Debbie Taylor, "The Chance of a Lifetime (History of the Alma-Ata Declaration)," *World Health*, September 1983, 2–4. On the problem of measuring poverty, see Amartya Sen, "Conceptualizing and Measuring Poverty," in *Poverty and Inequality*, ed. David B. Grusky and Ravi Kanbur (Stanford, Calif.: Stanford University Press, 2006): 30–46.

10. Mike Davis, *The Monster at Our Door: The Global Threat of Avian Flu* (New York: New Press, 2005); David Brown, "Teamwork Urged on Bird Flu: Conference Plots Global Strategy," *Washington Post*, 8 November 2005: A16; Melinda Liu, "The Flimsy Wall of China," *Newsweek*, 31 October 2005, 28; Anita Manning, "Asia; The 'Perfect Incubator,'" *USA Today*, 28 February 2005, 6; Michael Specter, "Nature's Bioterrorist: Is There Any Way to Prevent a Deadly Avian-Flu Pandemic?" *New Yorker*, 28 February 2005, 61.

My discussion of the media coverage of avian flu is based on my reading of more than fifty news articles and numerous television reports. Written news sources include the *New Zealand Herald*, the *New York Times*, *Newsweek*, the *Daily News* (New York), the *Ottawa Citizen*, the *South China Morning Post*, *The Pittsburgh Post-Gazette*, the *Guardian* (London), the *Atlanta Journal-Constitution*, the *Los Angeles Times*, the *Washington Post*, the *Toronto Star*, the *Spectator*, the *Seattle Times*, the *San Francisco Chronicle*, the *Farm Journal Media*, the *New Yorker*, *USA Today*, the *Toronto Sun*, the *Daily Telegraph* (London), *Star Tribune* (Minneapolis), and *St. Petersberg Times* (Florida).

11. Sen, Farmer, and others have argued for a model of global health premised on the terms of social justice. The essays in *Dying for Growth: Global Inequality*

and the Health of the Poor, ed. Jim Yong Kim, Joyce V. Millen, Alec Irwin, and John Gershman (Monroe, Maine: Common Courage Press, 2000), and in *Health Impacts of Globalization: Towards Global Governance*, ed. Kelley Lee (New York: Palgrave Macmillan, 2003), as well as Kelley Lee's book-length study, *Globalization and Health: An Introduction* (New York: Palgrave Macmillan, 2003), exemplify the kind of analyses that are produced from that premise. See also the essays in *Global Public Health: A New Era*, ed. Robert Beaglehole (Oxford: Oxford University Press, 2003); Laurie Wermuth, *Global Inequality and Human Needs: Health and Illness in an Increasingly Unequal World* (Boston: Pearson Education, Inc., 2003); and Anthony C. Gatrell, *Geographies of Health: An Introduction* (Oxford: Blackwell Publishers, 2002).

Works Cited

Abbott, Andrew. *Department and Discipline*. Chicago: University of Chicago Press, 1999.

"About BW." *New York Times*, 1 January 1950, 75.

Abrams, Herbert L. "Medical Problems of Survivors of Nuclear War: Infection and the Spread of Communicable Disease." *New England Journal of Medicine* 305.20 (12 November 1981): 1226–32.

Adams, Samuel Hopkins. "Tuberculosis: The Real Race Suicide." *McClure's* 24 (January 1905): 234–49.

——. "Typhoid: An Unnecessary Evil." *McClure's* 25 (June 1905): 145–56.

Adatto, Jennie Q. "Virus Facts." *Today's Health*, September 1954, 39, 63.

Agamben, Giorgio. *Homo Sacer: Sovereign Power and Bare Life*. Trans. Daniel Heller-Roazen. Stanford, Calif.: Stanford University Press, 1998.

Altman, Dennis. *AIDS in the Mind of America*. Garden City, N.Y.: Anchor/ Doubleday, 1986.

——. *Global Sex*. Chicago: University of Chicago Press, 2001.

Altman, Lawrence K. "Clue Found on Homosexual's Precancer Syndrome." *New York Times*, 18 June 1982, B8.

——. "New Homosexual Disorder Worries Health Officials," *New York Times*, 11 May 1982, C1, C6.

Ammons, Elizabeth. "The New Woman as Cultural Symbol and Social Reality: Six Women Writers' Perspectives." In *1915: The Cultural Moment: The New Politics, the New Woman, the New Psychology, the New Art and the New Theatre in America*, ed. Adele Heller and Lois Rudnick. New Brunswick, N.J.: Rutgers University Press, 1991. 82–97.

Anderson, Benedict. *Imagined Communities: Reflections on the Origin and Spread of Nationalism*. Rev. ed. 1983. Reprint, London: Verso, 1991.

Anderson, Warwick. *Colonial Pathologies: American Tropical Medicine, Race, and Hygiene in the Philippines*. Durham: Duke University Press, 2006.

——. *The Cultivation of Whiteness: Science, Health, and Racial Destiny in Australia.* New York: Basic Books, 2003.

——. "Going through the Motions: American Public Health and Colonial 'Mimicry.'" In "Contagion and Culture," ed. Priscilla Wald, Nancy Tomes, and Lisa Lynch. Special issue, *American Literary History* 14.4 (winter 2002): 686–719.

Appadurai, Arjun. *Modernity at Large: Cultural Dimensions of Globalization.* Minneapolis: University of Minnesota Press, 1996.

Argyro, Alex. *A Blessed Rage for Order: Deconstruction, Evolution, and Chaos.* Ann Arbor: University of Michigan Press, 1991.

Armstrong, J. A. *Nations before Nationalism.* Chapel Hill: University of North Carolina Press, 1982.

Arnold, Eleanor, ed. *Voices of American Homemakers.* Bloomington: Indiana University Press, 1985.

Asad, Talal. *Formations of the Secular: Christianity, Islam, Modernity.* Stanford, Calif.: Stanford University Press, 2003.

Atwood, Margaret. *Oryx and Crake.* New York: Anchor Books, 2003.

Auerbach, David M., William W. Darrow, Harold W. Jaffe, and James W. Curran. "Cluster of Cases of the Acquired Immune Deficiency Syndrome: Patients Linked by Sexual Contact." *American Journal of Medicine* 76 (March 1984): 487–92.

Baker, Paul J. "The Life Histories of W. I. Thomas and Robert E. Park." *American Journal of Sociology* 79.2 (September 1973): 243–60.

Baker, S. Josephine. *Fighting for Life.* New York: Macmillan, 1939.

Balibar, Etienne. "The Nation Form: History and Ideology." Trans. Chris Turner. In *Race, Nation, Class: Ambiguous Identities,* Etienne Balibar and Immanuel Wallerstein. London: Verso, 1991. 86–106.

Balibar, Etienne, and Immanuel Wallerstein. *Race, Nation, Class: Ambiguous Identities.* Trans. of Etienne Balibar by Chris Turner. London: Verso, 1991.

Barabasi, Albert-Laszlo. *Linked.* Cambridge, Mass.: Perseus Books, 2002.

Barringer, Paul B. "An Unappreciated Source of Typhoid Infection." In *A New Idea in Sanitation: The Great Menace to Public Health that Covers Every Mile of Railroad Track in the United States and Other Countries,* comp. J. C. Salter. New York: 1910. 7–15.

Bazell, Robert. "The History of an Epidemic." *New Republic,* 1 August 1983, 14–15, 17–18.

Beaglehold, Robert, ed. Global Public Health: *A New Era.* Oxford: Oxford University Press, 2003.

Begg, N. T., and N. J. Gay. "Theory of Infectious Disease Transmission and Herd Immunity." In *Bacterial Infections,* ed. William J. Hausler Jr. and Max Sussman. Vol. 3 of *Topley and Wilson's Microbiology and Microbial Infections.* Series ed. Leslie Collier, Albert Balows, and Max Sussman. 9th ed. London: Hodder Arnold, 1998. 147–65.

Benshoff, Harry M. *Monsters in the Closet: Homosexuality and the Horror Film*. Manchester, U.K.: Manchester University Press, 1997.

———. "Pods, Pederasts and Perverts: (Re)criminalizing the Monster Queer in Cold War Culture." In *Monsters in the Closet: Homosexuality and the Horror Film*. Manchester: Manchester University Press, 1997. 122–72.

Bersani, Leo. "Is the Rectum a Grave?" In *AIDS: Cultural Analysis, Cultural Activism*, ed. Douglas Crimp. Cambridge: MIT Press, 1988. 197–222.

Bhabha, Homi K. *The Location of Culture*. London: Routledge, 1994.

———. *Nations and Narration*. London: Routledge, 1990.

———. "Of Mimicry and Man: The Ambivalence of Colonial Discourse," *October* 28 (spring 1984): 125–33.

Biskind, Peter. *Seeing Is Believing: How Hollywood Taught Us to Stop Worrying and Love the Fifties*. New York: Pantheon Books, 1983.

Blattner, William A. "A Novelistic History of the AIDS Epidemic Demeans Both Investigators and Patients." *Scientific American*, October 1988, 148–51.

Boccaccio, Giovanni. *The Decameron*. Trans G. H. McWilliam. New York: Penguin Books, 1972.

Brandt, Allan. *No Magic Bullet: A Social History of Venereal Disease in the United States Since 1880*. New York: Oxford University Press, 1985.

Braukman, Stacy. "'Nothing Else Matters but Sex': Cold War Narratives of Deviance and the Search for Lesbian Teachers in Florida, 1959–1963." *Feminist Studies* 27.3 (fall 2001): 553–75.

Brier, Jennifer. "The Immigrant Infection: Images of Race, Nation, and Contagion in the Public Debates on AIDS and Immigration." In *Modern American Queer History*, ed. Allida M. Black. Philadelphia: Temple University Press, 2001. 253–70.

Brown, Charles Brockden. *Arthur Mervyn*. 1799. Rev. ed. Kent, Ohio: Kent State University Press, 2002.

Brown, David. "Teamwork Urged on Bird Flu: Conference Plots Global Strategy." *Washington Post*, 8 November 2005, A16.

Bulmer, Martin. *The Chicago School of Sociology: Institutionalization, Diversity, and the Rise of Sociological Research*. Chicago: University of Chicago Press, 1984.

Burnet, Frank Macfarlane. "General Discussion." In *The Nature of Viruses* (CIBA Foundation Symposium), ed. G. E. W. Wolstenholme and Elaine C. P. Millar. Boston: Little, Brown, 1957. 277–86.

———. "Viruses." *Scientific American*, May 1951, 43–51.

Burr, Albert H. "The Guarantee of Safety in the Marriage Contract," *Journal of the American Medical Association* 47.23 (8 December 1906): 1887–89.

Burroughs, William S. "Deposition: Testimony Concerning a Sickness." In *Naked Lunch: The Restored Text*, ed. James Grauerholz and Barry Miles. Original publication 1959. New York: Grove Press, 2001. 199–205.

——. *Naked Lunch: The Restored Text.* Ed. James Grauerholz and Barry Miles. Original publication 1959. New York: Grove Press, 2001.

——. *Nova Express.* 1964. In *Three Novels: The Soft Machine, Nova Express, The Wild Boys.* New York: Grove Press, 1980.

——. *Queer.* New York: Viking Press, 1985.

——. *The Soft Machine.* 1961. In *Three Novels: The Soft Machine, Nova Express, The Wild Boys.* New York: Grove Press, 1980.

——. *The Ticket That Exploded.* New York: Grove Press, 1962.

Cahan, Abraham. *Yekl and the Imported Bridegroom and Other Stories of Yiddish New York.* New York: Dover Publications, 1970.

"Canadian Said to Have Had Key Role in Spread of AIDS." *New York Times,* 7 October 1987, B7.

Capetti, Carla. *Writing Chicago: Modernism, Ethnography, and the Novel.* New York: Columbia University Press, 1993.

Cartwright, Lisa. *Screening the Body: Tracing Medicine's Visual Culture.* Minneapolis: University of Minnesota Press, 1995.

Case, John. *The First Horseman.* New York: Ballantine Books, 1998.

The Centers for Disease Control Announce the Course Applied Epidemiology, May 8–17, 1985. Pamphlet. Atlanta: U.S. Department of Health and Human Services, Public Health Service, Centers for Disease Control, 1984. http://library .unc.edu.

Chambers, Whittaker. "I Was the Witness." *Saturday Evening Post,* 23 February 1952, 22–23, 48–63.

Chapin, Charles V. *The Sources and Modes of Infection.* New York: John Wiley, 1910.

Clancy, Tom. *Rainbow Six.* New York: G. P. Putnam's Sons, 1998.

Clark, Matt, et al. "AIDS: A Lethal Mystery Story." *Newsweek,* 27 December 1982, 63.

"A Cluster of Kaposi's Sarcoma and *Pneumocystis carinii* Pneumonia among Homosexual Male Residents of Los Angeles and Orange Counties, California." *Morbidity and Mortality Weekly Report* 31.23 (18 June 1982): 305–7.

"The Columbus of AIDS," *National Review,* 6 November 1987, 19.

Condon, Richard. *The Manchurian Candidate.* New York: McGraw-Hill, 1959.

Connor, John D. *Contagion.* New York: Diamond Books, 1992.

Connor, Steve, and Sharon Kingman. *The Search for the Virus: The Scientific Discovery of AIDS and the Quest for a Cure.* Rev. ed. New York: Penguin Books, 1989.

Cook, Robin. *Contagion.* New York: G. P. Putnam's Sons, 1995.

——. *Invasion.* New York: Berkley Publishing, 1997.

——. *Outbreak.* New York: G. P. Putnam's Sons, 1987.

——. *Vector.* New York: G. P. Putnam's Sons, 1999.

Cool, Tom. *Infectress.* New York: Baen Publishing, 1997.

Copeland, Royal S. "Import Diseases as They Affect the Work of the New York City Health Department." *American Journal of Public Health* 12 (1922): 202–4.

Corber, Robert. *Homosexuality in Cold War America: Resistance and the Crisis of Masculinity.* Durham: Duke University Press, 1997.

Cowley, Geoffrey. "How Progress Makes Us Sick." *Newsweek*, 5 May 2003, 33–35.

Cowley, Geoffrey, et al. "A Ruling on Doctors with AIDS." *Newsweek*, 6 May 1991, 64.

Crewdson, John. *Science Fictions: A Scientific Mystery, a Massive Cover-Up, and the Dark Legacy of Robert Gallo.* Boston: Little, Brown, 2002.

Crichton, Michael. *The Andromeda Strain.* New York: Knopf, 1969.

Crimp, Douglas. "AIDS: Cultural Analysis/Cultural Activism." In *AIDS: Cultural Analysis/Cultural Activism*, ed. Douglas Crimp. Cambridge: MIT Press, 1988. 3–16.

———. *AIDS Demo Graphics.* Seattle: Bay Press, 1990.

———. *Melancholia and Moralism: Essays on AIDS and Queer Politics.* Cambridge: MIT Press, 2002.

Cronk, H. Taylor. "What Germs Are, How They Are Disseminated, and the Danger of Them." *A New Idea in Sanitation: The Great Menace to Public Health that Covers Every Mile of Railroad Track in the United States and Other Countries*, comp. J. C. Salter. New York: 1910. 1–6.

Culliton, Barbara. "Emerging Viruses, Emerging Threat." *Science*, 19 January 1990, 279–80.

Davis, Mike. *The Monster at Our Door: The Global Threat of Avian Flu.* New York: New Press, 2005.

Dawkins, Richard. *The Selfish Gene.* 1976. Reprint, Oxford: Oxford University Press, 1989.

Dean, Tim. "The Germs of Empires: *Heart of Darkness*, Colonial Trauma, and the Historiography of AIDS." In *The Psychoanalysis of Race*, ed. Christopher Lane. New York: Columbia University Press, 1998. 305–29.

Deegan, Mary Jo. *Race, Hull-House, and the University of Chicago: A New Conscience against Ancient Evils.* Westport, Conn.: Praeger, 2002.

Defoe, Daniel. *A Journal of the Plague Year.* New York: Heritage Press, 1968.

de Kruif, Paul. *The Microbe Hunters.* New York: Harcourt Brace, 1926.

———. "Virus Hunters." *Today's Health*, July 1953, 32–33, 60–62.

D'Emilio, John. "Homophobia and the Course of Post-World War II American Radicalism: The Career of Bayard Rustin." Chapter 1 in *The World Turned: Essays on Gay History, Politics, and Culture.* Durham: Duke University Press, 2002. 3–22.

———. *Sexual Politics, Sexual Communities: The Making of a Homosexual Minority in the United States 1940–1970.* 2d ed. Chicago: University of Chicago Press, 1998.

Derry, Charles. *Dark Dreams: A Psychological History of the Modern Horror Film*. South Brunswick, N.J.: A. S. Barnes, 1977.

Diamond, Jared. *Guns, Germs, and Steel: The Fates of Human Societies*. New York: W. W. Norton, 1997.

"Diffuse, Undifferentiated Non-Hodgkins Lymphoma among Homosexual Males —United States." *Morbidity and Mortality Weekly Report* 31.21 (4 June 1982): 277–79.

Diner, Hasia R. *Erin's Daughters in America: Irish Immigrant Women in the Nineteenth Century*. Baltimore: Johns Hopkins University Press, 1983.

"Disease Detectives." *Newsweek*, 19 January 1953, 60–62.

"Doctor Says Steady Contact with Germs Makes City Dwellers Immune to Disease." *New York Times*, 8 July 1923, 1.

Doniger, Wendy. *The Implied Spider: Politics and Theology in Myth*. New York: Columbia University Press, 1998.

Dougherty, Stephen. "The Biopolitics of the Killer Virus Novel." *Cultural Criticism* 48 (spring 2001): 1–29.

Douglas, Mary. *Purity and Danger: An Analysis of the Concepts of Pollution and Taboo*. London: Routledge and Kegan Paul, 1966.

Dreiser, Theodore. *Sister Carrie*. New York: Doubleday, Page, 1900.

Dubois, Laurent. "A Spoonful of Blood: Haitians, Racism, and AIDS." *Science as Culture* 6.1 (1996): 6–43.

Duffy, John. *The Sanitarians: A History of Public Health*. Urbana: University of Illinois Press, 1990.

Durkheim, Émile. *The Elementary Forms of Religious Life*. 1912. Trans. Joseph Ward Swain. New York: Free Press, 1965.

Duttmann, Alexander Garcia. *At Odds with AIDS: Thinking and Talking about a Virus*. Trans. Peter Gilgen and Conrad Scott-Curtis. Stanford, Calif.: Stanford University Press, 1996.

Edson, Cyrus. "The Microbe as Social Leveller." *North American Review* 161.467 (October 1895): 421–26.

Edwards, Paul N. *The Closed World: Computers and the Politics of Discourse in Cold War America*. Cambridge: MIT Press, 1996.

Eliade, Mircea. *Myths, Dreams, and Mysteries: The Encounter between Contemporary Faiths and Archaic Realities*. Trans. Philiop Mairet. New York: Harper and Row, 1960.

Ellis, Havelock. *The Nationalisation of Health*. London: T. Fisher Unwin, 1892.

"Enemy Disease Smog Held a Possibility." *New York Times*, 24 October 1951, 18.

Engel, Margaret. "AIDS and Prejudice: One Reporter's Account of the Nation's Response." *Washington Post*, 1 December 1987, Z10.

"Enteric Fever Carriers." *Nature*, December 1910, 145.

Eperuss, Boris, V. S. Leopold, J. D. Watson, and J. J. Weigle. "Terminology in Bacterial Genetics." *Nature*, 11 April 1953, 701.

Epstein, Julia. "AIDS, Stigma, and Narratives of Containment." *American Imago* 49.3 (1992): 293–310.

Epstein, Steven. *Impure Science: AIDS, Activism, and the Politics of Knowledge.* Berkeley: University of California Press, 1996.

Essex, Max, and Phyllis J. Kanki. "The Origins of the AIDS Virus." *Scientific American*, October 1988, 64–71.

Etheridge, Elizabeth W. *Sentinel for Health: A History of the Centers for Disease Control.* Berkeley: University of California Press, 1992.

Fairchild, Amy. *Science at the Borders: Immigrant Medical Inspection and the Shaping of the Modern Industrial Labor Force, 1891–1930.* Baltimore: Johns Hopkins University Press, 2003.

Fanon, Frantz. *The Wretched of the Earth.* Trans. Constance Farrington. New York: Grove Press, 1963.

Farmer, Paul. *AIDS and Accusation: Haiti and the Geography of Blame.* Berkeley: University of California Press, 1992.

——. *Infections and Inequalities: The Modern Plagues.* Berkeley: University of California Press, 1999.

——. *Pathologies of Power: Health, Human Rights, and the New War on the Poor.* Berkeley: University of California Press, 2003.

Faulkner, William. "On Fear: Deep South in Labor: Mississippi." In *Essays, Speeches and Public Letters.* New York: Modern Library, 2004. 92–106.

Feinstein, Howard. "Back to Base Camp." *Guardian*, 28 July 1994, T10.

Feldman, Jamie. "Gallo, Montagnier, and the Debate over HIV: A Narrative Analysis." *Camera Obscura* 28 (1992): 101–32.

Fineberg, Harvey V. "The Social Dimensions of AIDS." *Scientific American*, October 1988, 128–47.

Finney, Jack. "The Body Snatchers." *Collier's* 134.11 (26 November 1954): 26, 27, 90–99; 134.12 (10 December 1954): 114–25; and 134.12 (24 December 1954): 62–73.

——. *The Body Snatchers.* New York: Dell, 1955.

Fletcher, Henry J. "American Railways and American Cities." *Atlantic Monthly*, June 1894, 803–11.

Flexner, Simon. "Introductory." In *Experimental Epidemiology.* New York: Laboratories of the Rockefeller Institute for Medical Research, 1922. 9–14.

——. "Natural Resistance to Infectious Disease and Its Reinforcement." *Popular Science Monthly*, July 1909, 5–16.

——. "Some Problems in Infection and Its Control." *Science*, November 1912, 685–702.

Flood, Christopher. "Myth and Ideology." In *Thinking Through Myths: Philosophical Perspectives*, ed. Kevin Schilbrack. London: Routledge, 2002. 174–90.

Foege, William H. "Alexander D. Langmuir: His Impact on Public Health." *American Journal of Epidemiology* 144.8 (15 October 1996), supplement ("A Tribute to Alexander D. Langmuir"): S11–S15.

Foertsch, Jacqueline. *Enemies Within: The Cold War and the AIDS Crisis in Litera-ture, Film and Culture.* Urbana: University of Illinois Press, 2001.

Follett, Ken. *Whiteout.* London: Penguin Books, 2004.

Foucault, Michel. "The Birth of Biopolitics." In *Ethics, Subjectivity and Truth,* ed. Paul Rabinow, trans. Robert Hurley et al. Vol. 1 of *Essential Works of Foucault 1954–1984.* Series ed. Paul Rabinow. New York: New Press, 2000. 73–79.

———. "The Birth of Social Medicine." In *Power,* ed. James D. Faubion, trans. Robert Hurley et al. Vol. 3 of *Essential Works of Foucault 1954–1984.* Series ed. Paul Rabinow. New York: New Press, 2000. 134–56.

———. "Governmentality." In *Power,* ed. James D. Faubion, trans. Robert Hurley et al. Vol. 3 of *Essential Works of Foucault 1954–1984.* Series ed. Paul Rabinow. New York: New Press, 2000. 201–22.

———. *The History of Sexuality.* Vol. 1: *Introduction.* Trans. Robert Hurley. New York: Pantheon Books, 1978.

———. "The Politics of Health in the Eighteenth Century." In *Power,* ed. James D. Faubion, trans. Robert Hurley et al. Vol. 3 of *Essential Works of Foucault 1954– 1984.* Series ed. Paul Rabinow. New York: New Press, 2000. 90–105.

———. *"Society Must Be Defended": Lectures at the Collège de France 1975–1976.* Ed. Mauro Bertani and Alessandro Fontana. Trans. David Macey. New York: Picador, 2003.

Freeman, Allen W. "The Present Status of Our Knowledge Regarding the Trans-mission of Typhoid Fever." *Public Health Reports* 28 (1913): 64–68.

Freud, Sigmund. *Totem and Taboo and Other Works.* Vol. 13 of *The Standard Edition of the Complete Psychological Works of Sigmund Freud.* Ed. and trans. James Strachey in collaboration with Anna Freud, assisted by Alix Strachey and Alan Tyson. 1955. Reprint, London: Hogarth Press and the Institute of Psycho-Analysis, 1986.

———. *Totem und Tabu: Einige Übereinstimmungen im Seelenleben der Wilden und der Neurotiker.* Leipzig: Hugo Heller, 1913.

———. "The Unconscious." In *On the History of the Psycho-Analytic Movement, Papers on Metapsychology and Other Works.* Vol. 14 of *The Standard Edition of the Complete Psychological Works of Sigmund Freud.* Ed. and trans. James Strachey in collaboration with Anna Freud, assisted by Alix Strachey and Alan Tyson. 1957. Reprint, London: Hogarth Press and the Institute of Psycho-Analysis, 1986. 159–22.

Friedman-Kien, Alvin E. "Disseminated Kaposi's Sarcoma Syndrome in Young Homosexual Men." *Journal of the American Academy of Dermatology* 5 (1981): 468–71.

Gallo, Robert C. *Virus Hunting: AIDS, Cancer, and the Human Retrovirus: A Story of Scientific Discovery.* New York: Basic Books, 1991.

Gallo, Robert C., and Luc Montagnier. "AIDS in 1988." *Scientific American,* Octo-ber 1988, 40–48.

Gannon, James. *Stealing Secrets, Telling Lies: How Spies and Codebreakers Helped Shape the Twentieth Century.* Washington: Brassey's, 2001.

Gardner, Vivien, and Susan Rutherford, eds. *The New Woman and Her Sisters: Feminism and Theatre, 1850–1914.* Ann Arbor: University of Michigan Press, 1992.

Garrett, Laurie. "Amplification." In *Epidemic! The World of Infectious Disease*, ed. Rob DeSalle. New York: New Press, 1999. 193–96.

———. *Betrayal of Trust: The Collapse of Global Public Health.* New York: Hyperion, 2000.

———. *The Coming Plague: Newly Emerging Diseases in a World Out of Balance.* 1994. Reprint, New York: Penguin Books, 1995.

Gatrell, Anthony C. *Geographies of Health: An Introduction.* Oxford: Blackwell, 2002.

Geiger, H. Jack. "Alphabet of Life." *Saturday Review*, 5 January 1957, 46–47.

Geiger, Roger L. "Science, Universities, and National Defense, 1945–1970." *Osiris*, 2d series 7 (1992): 26–48.

Gelb, Arthur. "Diseases of the World Listed on U.N. Map." *New York Times*, 17 October 1953, 3.

Gellner, Ernest. *Nations and Nationalism.* Oxford: Oxford University Press, 1983.

Gerhart, Mary, and Allan Melvin Russell. "Myth and Public Science." In *Thinking through Myths: Philosophical Perspectives*, ed. Kevin Schilbrack. London: Routledge, 2002. 191–206.

"Germ War Is Termed Deadlier than Atom." *New York Times*, 22 October 1950, 4.

Gilman, Sander. "AIDS and Stigma." In *Acting on Aids: Sex, Drugs, and Politics*, ed. Joshua Oppenheimer and Helena Reckitt. London: Serpent's Tail, 1997. 101–17.

———. "The Beautiful Body and AIDS." In *Picturing Health and Illness: Images of Identity and Difference.* Baltimore: Johns Hopkins University Press, 1995. 115–72.

———. *Difference and Pathology: Stereotypes of Sexuality, Race, and Madness.* Ithaca, N.Y.: Cornell University Press, 1985.

———. *Disease and Representation: Images of Illness from Madness to AIDS.* Ithaca, N.Y.: Cornell University Press, 1988.

———. *The Jew's Body.* New York: Routledge, 1991.

———. *Sexuality: An Illustrated History: Representing the Sexual in Medicine and Culture from the Middle Ages to the Age of AIDS.* New York: Wiley, 1989.

Girard, René. *Violence and the Sacred.* Trans. Patrick Gregory. Baltimore: Johns Hopkins University Press, 1977.

Gladwell, Malcolm. *The Tipping Point: How Little Things Can Make a Big Difference.* New York: Little, Brown, 2000.

Glenn, Susan A. *Daughters of the Shtetl: Life and Labor in the Immigrant Generation.* Ithaca, N.Y.: Cornell University Press, 1990.

———. *Female Spectacle: The Theatrical Roots of Modern Feminism*. Cambridge: Harvard University Press, 2000.

Goldberg, Jeffrey. "Peril of African-borne Diseases: With AIDS, Ebola as Examples, World Ignores Fourth Continent at Its Own Risk." *Seattle Post-Intelligencer*, 30 March 1997, F1.

Goldberg, Leonard. *Deadly Exposure*. New York: Penguin Books, 1998.

Gordon, Milton M. *Assimilation in American Life: The Role of Race, Religion, and National Origins*. New York: Oxford University Press, 1964.

Gottlieb, M. S., R. Schroff, H. M. Schanker, J. D. Weisman, P. T. Fan, R. A. Wolf, and A. Saxon. "Pneumocystis Carinii Pneumonia and Mucosal Candidiasis in Previously Healthy Homosexual Men: Evidence of a New Acquired Cellular Immunodeficiency." *New England Journal of Medicine* 305.24 (10 December 1981): 1425–31.

Goudsmit, Jaap. *Viral Fitness: The Next SARS and West Nile in the Making*. New York: Oxford University Press, 2004.

———. *Viral Sex: The Nature of AIDS*. New York: Oxford University Press, 1997.

Grauerholz, James. "A Hard-Boiled Reporter." In *Word Virus: The William Burroughs Reader*, ed. James Grauerholz and Ira Silverberg. New York: Grove Press, 1998. 37–46.

Greenfeld, Liah. *Nationalism: Five Roads to Modernity*. Cambridge: Harvard University Press, 1992.

Greenfield, Karl Taro. *China Syndrome: The Killer Virus that Crashed the Middle Kingdom*. New York: HarperCollins, 2006.

Greenough, Paul. "What Is a Medical Detective?" In *Epidemic! The World of Infectious Disease*, ed. Rob DeSalle. New York: New Press, 1999. 119–24.

Grinnell, Alton G. "Our Army Versus a Bacillus." *National Geographic*, October 1913, 1146–52.

Guthrie, D. Clinton. "Race Suicide." *Pennsylvania Medical Journal* 15 (1911): 859.

Hall, John J., and Richard Taylor. "Health for All beyond 2000: The Demise of the Alma-Ata Declaration and Primary Health Care in Developing Countries." *Medical Journal of Australia* 178 (January 2003): 17–20.

Hamer, W. H. "Typhoid Carriers and Contact Infection: Some Difficulties Suggested by Study of Recent Investigations Carried Out on 'Living Lines.'" *Proceedings of the Royal Science of Medicine* 4 (March 1911): 117.

Hamilton, Greg. "He Restores Hope to Lepers of Our Society." *St. Petersburg Times*, 21 October 1991, 1.

Hammonds, Evelynn. "Missing Persons: African American Women, AIDS and the History of Disease." *Radical America* 24.2 (1992): 7–23.

Harden, Victoria A. *Inventing the NIH: Federal Biomedical Research Policy, 1887–1937*. Baltimore: Johns Hopkins University Press, 1986.

Harris, Oliver. "Can You See a Virus? The Queer Cold War of William Burroughs." *Journal of American Studies* 33.2 (1999): 243–66.

Harris, Sheldon H. *Factories of Death: Japanese Biological Warfare, 1932–1945, and the American Cover-up.* Rev. ed. New York: Routledge, 2002.

Harvey, David. *Justice, Nature and the Geography of Difference.* Cambridge, Mass.: Blackwell, 1996.

——. *Social Justice and the City.* London: Edward Arnold, 1973.

——. *Spaces of Capital: Towards a Critical Geography.* New York: Routledge, 2001.

Haseltine, William A., and Flossie Wong-Staal. "The Molecular Biology of the AIDS Virus." *Scientific American,* October 1988, 52–62.

Hayles, N. Katherine. *How We Became Posthuman: Virtual Bodies in Cybernetics, Literature, and Informatics.* Chicago: University of Chicago Press, 1999.

——. *My Mother Was a Computer: Digital Subjects and Literary Texts.* Chicago: University of Chicago Press, 2005.

"Healthy Disease Spreaders." *New York Times,* 1 July 1909, 8.

Health Impacts of Globalization: Towards Global Governance. Ed. Kelley Lee. New York: Palgrave Macmillan, 2003.

Hecker, J. F. C. *The Black Death and the Dancing Mania.* Trans. B. G. Babington. London: Cassell, 1888.

Heims, Steven J. *Constructing a Social Science for Postwar America: The Cybernetics Group, 1946–1953.* Cambridge: MIT Press, 1993.

Hellman, Hal. "Gallo Versus Montagnier: The AIDS War." In *Great Feuds in Medicine: Ten of the Liveliest Disputes Ever.* New York: Wiley, 2001. 165–83.

Hendershot, Cyndy. *I Was a Cold War Monster: Horror Films, Eroticism, and the Cold War Imagination.* Bowling Green, Ohio: Bowling Green State University Popular Press, 2001.

Henderson, Donald A. "Surveillance Systems and Intergovernmental Cooperation." In *Emerging Viruses,* ed. Stephen S. Morse. New York: Oxford University Press, 1993. 283–89.

Herlihy, David. *The Black Death and the Transformation of the West.* Ed. Samuel K. Cohn Jr. Cambridge: Harvard University Press, 1977.

Hertzberg, Arthur. "The Russian Jews Arrive." Chapter 10 in *The Jews in America: Four Centuries of an Uneasy Encounter.* New York: Columbia University Press, 1997. 140–64.

Heyward, William L., and James Curran. "The Epidemiology of AIDS in the U.S." *Scientific American,* October 1988, 52–62.

Higham, John. *Strangers in the Land: Patterns of American Nativism, 1860–1925.* 2d ed. New Brunswick, N.J.: Rutgers University Press, 1988.

Hill, Gladwin. "Marines Undergo Atomic Bomb Test." *New York Times,* 2 May 1950, 1, 10.

Hines, William. "The AIDS Epidemic: A Report From the Front Lines," *Washington Post,* 11 October 1987, X1.

Hinton, Harold B. "'Critical Target Areas' Urged to Speed Civil Defense Plans." *New York Times*, 28 December 1950, 1, 4.

Hobsbawm, E. J. *Nations and Nationalism since 1780: Programme, Myth, Reality*. Cambridge: Cambridge University Press, 1990.

Hogan, Chuck. *The Blood Artists*. New York: Avon Books, 1998.

Holmes, Bayard. "The Physical and Evolutionary Basis of Marriage." *Journal of the American Medical Association* 47.23 (8 December 1906): 1886–87.

"Homosexuals Found Particularly Liable to Common Viruses." *New York Times*, 10 December 1981, 1.

Hoover, Herbert. "The Protection of Freedom: A Constant Battle against the Abuse of Power." *Vital Speeches of the Day* (1 September 1954): 679–82.

Hoover, J. Edgar. Testimony before the House Committee on Un-American Activities. *Hearings on H.R. 1884 and H.R. 2122*. 80th Cong., 1st sess., 26 March 1947. 33–50.

Horstall, Frank L., Jr. "International Symposium on the Dynamics of Virus Infections." *Science*, 2 April 1954, 427–29.

Howard, William Lee. "The Protection of the Innocent." *Journal of the American Medical Association* 47.23 (8 December 1906): 1891–94.

"How Virus Attacks Sound Tissue." *New York Times*, 6 September 1953, E7.

Hoy, Suellen. *Chasing Dirt: The American Pursuit of Cleanliness*. New York: Oxford University Press, 1990.

Huber, John Bessner. "Fighting American Typhoid." *American Review of Reviews* 43 (1911): 344–49.

Hueppe, Ferdinand. *The Principles of Bacteriology*. Trans. E. O. Jordan. Chicago: Open Court, 1899.

Hughes, Sally Smith. *The Virus: A History of the Concept*. London: Heinemann Educational Books, 1977.

Hunter, Edward. *Brainwashing: The Story of Men Who Defied It*. New York: Farrar, Straus, and Cudahy, 1956.

Isaacs, Harold R. "Color in World Affairs." *Foreign Affairs* 47.2 (January 1969): 235–50.

Isaacson, Walter. "Hunting for the Hidden Killers." *Time*, 4 July 1983, 50–55.

Jameson, Fredric. *The Political Unconscious: Narrative as a Socially Symbolic Act*. Ithaca: Cornell University Press, 1981.

Janowitz, Morris. *W. I. Thomas on Social Organization and Social Personality*. Chicago: University of Chicago Press, 1966.

Johnson, Karl M. "Emerging Viruses in Context: An Overview of Viral Hemorrhagic Fevers." In *Emerging Viruses*, ed. Stephen S. Morse. New York: Oxford University Press, 1993. 46–57.

Juhasz, Alexandra. *AIDS TV: Identity, Community, and Alternative Video*. Durham: Duke University Press, 1995.

Kael, Pauline. "Pods." *New Yorker*, 25 December 1978, 48, 50–51.

Kaempffert, Waldemar. "Radioactive Elements Are Used in a Study of the Nature and Growth of Viruses." *New York Times*, 27 May 1951, E9.

———. "Reconstruction of Virus in Laboratory Reopens the Question: What Is Life?" *New York Times*, 30 October 1955, 4 (Science in Review), 9.

Kalb, Claudia. "The Mystery of SARS." *Newsweek*, 5 May 2003, 26–32.

Kaminsky, Stuart M. "Don Siegel on the Pod Society." In *Invasion of the Body Snatchers: Don Siegel, Director*, ed. Al LaValley. New Brunswick, N.J.: Rutgers University Press, 1989. 153–57.

———. "Pods." In *Don Siegel: Director*. New York: Curtis Books, 1974. 99–108.

"Kaposi's Sarcoma and *Pneumocystis* Pneumonia among Homosexual Men—New York City and California." *Morbidity and Mortality Weekly Report* 30.25 (3 July 1981): 305–8.

Karlen, Arno. *Man and His Microbes*. London: Quantum Research Associates, 1995.

Katz, Jonathan Ned. *Gay American History: Lesbians and Gay Men in the U.S.A.: A Documentary History*. Rev ed. New York: Plume Books, 1992.

Kay, Lily E. *Who Wrote the Book of Life? A History of the Genetic Code*. Stanford, Calif.: Stanford University Press, 2000.

Kelly, Kevin. "Tangled 'Pterodactyls,' " *Boston Globe*, 28 October 1994, 41.

Kemp, Arnold. "A Prophecy Written in the Dust." *Glasgow Herald*, 23 July 1994, 11.

Kidder, Tracy. *Mountains Beyond Mountains*. New York: Random House, 2005.

Kim, Jim Yong, Joyce V. Millen, Alec Irwin, and John Gershman, eds. *Dying for Growth: Global Inequality and the Health of the Poor*. Monroe, Maine: Common Courage Press, 2000.

King, Stephen. *The Stand*. 1978. Reprint, New York: Signet, 1991.

Kinsella, James. *Covering the Plague: AIDS and the American Media*. New Brunswick, N.J.: Rutgers University Press, 1989.

Kleinman, Arthur, and Sing Lee. "SARS and the Problem of Social Stigma." In *SARS in China: Prelude to Pandemic?*, ed. Arthur Kleinman and James L. Watson. Stanford, Calif.: Stanford University Press, 2006. 173–95.

Knickerbocker, Conrad. "White Junk." Interview with William Burroughs. In *Burroughs Live: The Collected Interviews of William S. Burroughs 1960–1997*, ed. Sylvere Lotringer. Los Angeles: Semiotext(e) Double Agents Series, 2001. 60–81.

Knight, Peter. *Conspiracy Culture: From the Kennedy Assassination to the X-Files*. New York: Routledge, 2000.

———, ed. *Conspiracy Nation: The Politics of Paranoia in Postwar America*. New York: New York University Press, 2002.

Knox, Richard A. "A Troubling, Persuasive Study of AIDS and Other Health Crises." *Boston Globe*, 22 January 1995, 45.

Kohn, Hans. *Nationalism: Its Meaning and History*. New York: Van Nostrand, 1965.

Krause, Richard M. Foreword to *Emerging Viruses*, ed. Stephen S. Morse. New York: Oxford University Press, 1993. xvii–xix.

———. "The Origin of Plagues: Old and New." *Science*, 21 August 1992, 1073–77.

———. *The Restless Tide: The Persistent Challenge of the Microbial World.* Washington: National Foundation for Infectious Diseases, 1981.

Kraut, Alan M. *Silent Travelers: Germs, Genes, and the "Immigrant Menace."* Baltimore: Johns Hopkins University Press, 1994.

Kunzel, Regina G. *Fallen Women, Problem Girls: Unmarried Mothers and the Professionalization of Social Work, 1890–1945.* New Haven, Conn.: Yale University Press, 1993.

Kyle, Stephen. *Beyond Recall.* New York: Warner Books, 2000.

Lal, Barbara Ballis. *The Romance of Culture in an Urban Civilization: Robert E. Park and Ethnic Relations in Cities.* London: Routledge, 1990.

Lasch, Christopher. *The Culture of Narcissism: American Life in an Age of Diminishing Expectations.* New York: Warner Books, 1979.

Latour, Bruno. *The Pasteurization of France.* Trans. Alan Sheridan and John Law. Cambridge: Harvard University Press, 1988.

Laura, Ernesto G. "Invasion of the Body Snatchers." In *Focus on the Science Fiction Film*, ed. William Johnson. Englewood Cliffs, N.J.: Prentice-Hall, 1972. 71–73.

Laurance, Jeremy. "Victim Who Infected 133 Will Remain in Quarantine Exile." *Independent*, 11 April 2003.

Laurence, William L. "New Leads Given by Virus Studies." *New York Times*, 11 September 1952, 29.

———. "Science Explores Frontier of Life." *New York Times*, 30 December 1952, 16.

———. "Virus Study Aided by New Technique." *New York Times*, 10 September 1953, 35.

LaValley, Al. "Invasion of the Body Snatchers: Politics, Psychology, Sociology." In *Invasion of the Body Snatchers: Don Siegel, Director*, ed. Al LaValley. New Brunswick, N.J.: Rutgers University Press, 1989. 3–17.

Leavitt, Judith Walzer. "Gendered Expectations: Women and Early Twentieth-Century Public Health." In *U.S. History as Women's History: New Feminist Essays*, ed. Linda Kerber, Alice Kessler-Harris, and Kathryn Kish Sklar. Chapel Hill: University of North Carolina Press, 1995. 147–69.

———. *Typhoid Mary: Captive to the Public's Health.* Boston: Beacon, 1996.

Le Bon, Gustave. *The Crowd: A Study of the Popular Mind.* 4th impression. London: T. F. Unwin, 1903.

Lechevalier, Hubert A., and Morris Solotorovsky. *Three Centuries of Microbiology.* New York: McGraw-Hill, 1974.

Lederberg, Joshua. "Viruses and Humankind: Intracellular Symbiosis and Evolutionary Competition." In *Emerging Viruses*, ed. Stephen S. Morse. New York: Oxford University Press, 1993. 3–9.

Lederberg, Joshua, Robert E. Shope, and Stanley C. Oaks Jr., eds. *Emerging Infec-*

tions: Microbial Threats to Health in the United States. Washington: National Academy Press, 1992.

Lederer, Arthur. "The 'Carrier' Problem." *West Virginia Medical Journal* 13 (1918–19): 127–32.

Lederer, Susan. "'Porto Ricochet': Joking about Germs, Cancer, and Race Extermination in the 1930s." In "Contagion and Culture," ed. Priscilla Wald, Nancy Tomes, and Lisa Lynch. Special issue, *American Literary History* 14.4 (winter 2002): 720–46.

Lee, Kelley. *Globalization and Health: An Introduction.* New York: Palgrave Macmillan, 2003.

——, ed. *Health Impacts of Globalization: Towards Global Governance.* New York: Palgrave Macmillan, 2003.

Lefebvre, Henri. *The Production of Space.* Trans. Donald Nicholson-Smith. Cambridge, Mass.: Blackwell, 1991.

Legters, Llewellyn J., Linda H. Brink, and Ernest T. Takafuji. "Are We Prepared for a Viral Epidemic Emergency?" In *Emerging Viruses*, ed. Stephen S. Morse. New York: Oxford University Press, 1993. 269–82.

Leo, John. "The Real Epidemic: Fear and Despair." *Time*, 4 July 1983, 56–58.

Lévi-Strauss, Claude. *The Raw and the Cooked.* Trans. John Weightman and Doreen Weightman. New York: Harper and Row, 1969.

——. *Structural Anthropology.* Trans. Claire Jacobson and Brooke Grundfest Schoepf. New York: Basic Books, 1963–76.

Levine, Joe. "The Toughest Virus of All." *Time*, 3 November 1986, 76–78.

——. "Viruses: AIDS Research Spurs New Interest in Some Ancient Enemies." *Time*, 3 November 1986, 66–70, 73–74.

Levine, Steven I. *Anvil of Victory: The Communist Revolution in Manchuria, 1945–1948.* New York: Columbia University Press, 1987.

Levy, Jay A., Heinz Fraenkel-Conrat, and Robert A. Owens. *Virology.* 3d ed. Englewood Cliffs, N.J.: Prentice Hall, 1994.

Lincoln, Bruce. *Discourse and the Construction of Society: Comparative Studies of Myth, Ritual, and Classification.* New York: Oxford University Press, 1989.

——. *Theorizing Myth: Narrative, Ideology, and Scholarship.* Chicago: University of Chicago Press, 1999.

Lindner, Rolf. *The Reportage of Urban Culture: Robert Park and the Chicago School.* Trans. Adrian Morris. Cambridge: Cambridge University Press, 1996.

Liu, Melinda. "The Flimsy Wall of China: A Health-Care System in Ruins May Be the World's Forward Line of Defense." *Newsweek*, 31 October 2005, 28.

Lo, Alex. "A Shrinking World Raises the Risk for Global Epidemics." *South China Morning Post*, 14 March 2003, 4.

Lowe, Lisa. "The Intimacies of Four Continents." In *Haunted by Empire*, ed. Ann Laura Stoler. Durham: Duke University Press, 2006. 191–212.

Luria, Sylvester E. *General Virology.* New York: Wiley, 1953.

Luria, Sylvester E., and James E. Darnell Jr. *General Virology.* 2d ed. New York: John Wiley and Sons, 1967.

Lydenberg, Robin. *Word Cultures: Radical Theory and Practice in William S. Burroughs' Fiction.* Urbana: University of Illinois Press, 1987.

Lyman, Stanford. *Militarism, Imperialism, and Racial Accommodation: An Analysis and Interpretation of the Early Writings of Robert E. Park.* Fayetteville: University of Arkansas Press, 1992.

Lynch, Lisa. "The Neo/Bio/Colonial Hot Zone: African Viruses, American Fairytales." *International Journal of Cultural Studies* 1.2 (1998): 233–52.

Lynch, Patrick. *Carriers.* New York: Villard, 1995.

——. *Omega.* New York: Penguin, 1998.

Macphail, Andrew. "The American Woman." *The Living Age,* 31 October and 7 November 1908.

——. "The American Woman." In *Essays in Fallacy.* London: Longmans, Green, 1910. 1–54.

Madison, Charles A. Preface to *How the Other Half Lives: Studies among the Tenements of New York,* by Jacob A. Riis. New York: Dover Publications, 1971. v–viii.

Mali, Joseph. *Mythistory: The Making of Modern Historiography.* Chicago: University of Chicago Press, 2003.

Mann, James. "Supergerms: The New Health Menace." *U.S. News and World Report,* 28 February 1983, 35.

Mann, Jonathan M., James Chin, Peter Piot, and Thomas Quinn. "The International Epidemiology of AIDS." *Scientific American,* October 1988, 82–89.

Manning, Anita. "Asia: The 'Perfect Incubator.'" *USA Today,* 28 February 2005, 6.

"A Man without a Country." *Outlook,* April 1915, 803–4.

Marchione, Marilynn. "Anatomy of an Epidemic." *Milwaukee Journal Sentinel,* 4 May 2003, A1.

Markel, Howard. *Quarantine! East European Jewish Immigrants and the New York City Epidemics of 1892.* Baltimore: Johns Hopkins University Press, 1997.

Martin, Emily. *Flexible Bodies: Tracking Immunity in American Culture from the Days of Polio to the Age of AIDS.* Boston: Beacon Press, 1994.

Massey, Doreen. *Space, Place and Gender.* Minneapolis: University of Minnesota Press, 1994.

Masur, H., M. A. Michelis, J. B. Greene, I. Onorato, R. A. Stouwe, R. S. Holzman, G. Wormser, L. Brettman, M. Lange, H. W. Murray, and S. Cunningham-Rundles. "An Outbreak of Community-acquired Pneumocystis Carinii Pneumonia: Initial Manifestation of Cellular Immune Dysfunction." *New England Journal of Medicine* 305.24 (10 December 1981): 1431–38.

Matheson, Richard. *I Am Legend.* New York: Fawcett Publications, 1954.

Matthews, Fred H. *Quest for an American Sociology: Robert E. Park and the Chicago School.* Montreal: McGill-Queens University Press, 1977.

Matthews, Thomas J., and Dani P. Bolognesi. "AIDS Vaccines." *Scientific American*, October 1988, 120–27.

Mayer, Ruth. *Artificial Africas: Colonial Images in the Times of Globalization.* Hanover, N.H.: University Press of New England, 2002.

McCarthy, Joseph. *McCarthyism: The Fight for America.* New York: Devin-Adair, 1952.

McCormick, Joseph B., and Susan Fisher-Hoch, with Leslie Alan Horvitz. *Virus Hunters of the CDC.* Atlanta: Turner Publishing, 1996.

McKivigan, John R. and Thomas J. Robertson. "The Irish American Worker in Transition, 1877–1914: New York City as a Test Case." In *The New York Irish*, ed. Ronald H. Bayor and Timothy J. Meagher. Baltimore: Johns Hopkins University Press, 1996. 301–20.

McLuhan, Marshall. *The Gutenberg Galaxy.* Toronto: University of Toronto Press, 1962.

———. *Understanding Media.* New York: McGraw-Hill, 1964.

McLuhan, Marshall, and Quentin Fiore. *The Medium Is the Massage: An Inventory of Effects.* New York: Random House, 1967.

McMichaels, Tony. *Human Frontiers, Environments and Disease: Past Patterns, Uncertain Futures.* Cambridge: Cambridge University Press, 2001.

McNeil, Donald D., Jr., and Lawrence K. Altman. "How One Person Can Fuel an Epidemic." *New York Times*, Science, Medicine, and Technology, 15 April 2003, A1.

McNeill, William H. "Patterns of Disease Emergence in History." In *Emerging Viruses*, ed. Stephen S. Morse. New York: Oxford University Press, 1993. 29–36.

———. *Plagues and Peoples.* New York: Doubleday, 1976.

"MDs Doubt Claim Canadian Carried AIDS to Continent." *Toronto Star*, 12 December 1987, A2.

Meader, F. M. "Detection of Typhoid Carriers." *Modern Medicine* 2.3 (1919): 244–46.

———. "Treatment of the Typhoid Carrier." *New York State Journal of Medicine* 12 (1912): 355–58.

Melley, Timothy. *Empire of Conspiracy: The Culture of Paranoia in Postwar America.* Ithaca, N.Y.: Cornell University Press, 2000.

Melnick, Joseph L. "Viruses within Cells." *Scientific American*, December 1953, 38–41.

Mendelsohn, Andrew. "'Typhoid Mary' Strikes Again: The Social and the Scientific in the Making of Modern Public Health." *Isis* 86.2 (June 1995): 268–77.

Meerloo, Joost A. M. *The Rape of the Mind: The Psychology of Thought Control, Menticide, and Brainwashing.* Cleveland: World Publishing, 1956.

Meyerowitz, Joanne J. *Women Adrift: Independent Wage Earners in Chicago, 1880–1930.* Chicago: University of Chicago Press, 1988.

Michaels, Walter Benn. *Our America: Nativism, Modernism, and Pluralism.* Durham: Duke University Press, 1995.

Miles, Barry. *William Burroughs: El Hombre Invisible.* Rev. ed. London: Virgin Books, 2002.

Miles, Steven. Review of *And the Band Played On. Journal of the American Medical Association* 259.2 (8 January 1988): 288.

Miller, Douglas T. "Sixties Activism in the 'Me Decade.'" In *The Lost Decade: America in the Seventies,* ed. Elsebeth Hurup. Aarhus, Denmark: Aarhus University Press, 1996. 133–43.

Miller, Judith, Stephen Engelberg, and William Broad. *Germs: Biological Weapons and America's Secret War.* New York: Simon and Schuster, 2001.

Mitchell, Robert, and Phillip Thurtle. "Data Made Flesh: The Material Poesis of Informatics." Introduction to *Data Made Flesh: Embodying Information,* ed. Robert Mitchell and Phillip Thurtle. New York: Routledge, 2004. 1–23.

Modood, Tariq, and Pnina Werbner, eds. *Debating Cultural Hybridity.* London: Zed Books, 1997.

Moore, Alexander, and Ronald D. LeBaron. "The Case for a Haitian Origin of the AIDS Epidemic." In *The Social Dimensions of AIDS: Method and Theory,* ed. Douglas A. Feldman and Thomas M. Johnson. New York: Praeger, 1986. 77–93.

Moore, Oscar. "Rites of Fatality." *Guardian,* 21 September 1996, 16.

Morrow, Lance. "The Start of a Plague Mentality." *Time,* 23 September 1985, 92.

Morrow, Prince Albert. "The Relations of Social Diseases to the Family," *American Journal of Sociology* 14.5 (March 1909): 622–37.

———. *The Social Diseases of Marriage: Social Prophylaxis.* New York: Lea Brothers, 1904.

Morse, Stephen S. "Examining the Origins of Emerging Viruses." In *Emerging Viruses,* ed. Stephen S. Morse. New York: Oxford University Press, 1993. 10–28.

———, ed. *Emerging Viruses.* New York: Oxford University Press, 1993.

Mosse, George L. *Nationalism and Sexuality: Respectability and Abnormal Sexuality in Modern Europe.* Madison: University of Wisconsin Press, 1985.

Mottram, Eric. "Rencontre avec William Burroughs." In *Conversations with William Burroughs,* ed. Allen Hibbard. Jackson: University Press of Mississippi, 1999. 11–15.

Moynihan, Daniel Patrick. *Secrecy: The American Experience.* New Haven, Conn.: Yale University Press, 1998.

Navarro, V. "A Critique of the Ideological and Political Position of the Brandt Report and the Alma Ata Declaration." *International Journal of Health Services* 14.2 (1984): 159–72.

Nelson, John E. "Investigation of Communist Propaganda," 71st Cong., 3d sess., 17 January 1931, H. Rep. 2290. In *The House Community on Un-American*

Activities 1945–1950, by Robert K. Carr. Ithaca, N.Y.: Cornell University Press, 1952. 99.

"New Way to Study Cell-Virus Battle." *Science News Letter* 64.8 (22 August 1953): 116.

Nichols, Henry J. *Carriers in Infectious Diseases: A Manual on the Importance, Pathology, Diagnosis, and Treatment of Human Carriers.* Baltimore: Wilkins and Wilkins, 1922.

Odem, Mary E. *Delinquent Daughters: Protecting and Policing Adolescent Female Sexuality in the United States, 1885–1920.* Chapel Hill: University of North Carolina Press, 1995.

Ogden, Daryl. "Cold War Science and the Body Politic: An Immuno/Virological Approach to *Angels in America." Literature and Medicine* 19.2 (2000): 241–61.

O'Neil, James F. "How You Can Fight Communism." *American Legion,* August 1948, 16–17, 42–44.

Oppenheimer, Gerald M. "In the Eye of the Storm: The Epidemiological Construction of AIDS." In *AIDS: The Burdens of History,* ed. Elizabeth Fee and Daniel M. Fox. Berkeley: University of California Press, 1988. 267–300.

Ostherr, Kirsten. *Cinematic Prophylaxis: Globalization and Contagion in the Discourse of World Health.* Durham: Duke University Press, 2005.

O'Toole, Fintan. "Panic Attack." *Irish Times,* 2 May 2003, 50.

Palumbo-Liu, David. *Asian/American: Historical Crossings of a Racial Frontier.* Stanford, Calif.: Stanford University Press, 1999.

Panem, Sandra. "A Drama and Questions." *Science,* 26 February 1988, 1039–40.

Park, Katharine. "Kimberly Bergalis, AIDS, and the Plague Metaphor." In *Media Spectacles,* ed. Marjorie Garber, Jann Matlock, and Rebecca Walkowitz. New York: Routledge, 1993. 232–53.

Park, Robert Ezra. "The City: Suggestions for the Investigation of Human Behavior in the Urban Environment." *American Journal of Sociology* 20.5 (March 1915): 577–612.

———. "The City." In *Human Communities: The City and Human Ecology.* Vol. 2 of *The Collected Papers of Robert Ezra Park.* Ed. Everett Cherrington Hughes et al. Glencoe, Ill.: Free Press, 1950. 13–51.

———. "The Concept of Position in Sociology." *Publications of the American Sociological Society* 20 (1925): 1–14.

———. "Human Ecology." *American Journal of Sociology* 42.1 (July 1936): 1–15.

———. "Human Migration and the Marginal Man." *American Journal of Sociology* 33.6 (May 1928): 881–93.

———. "The Nature of Race Relations." In *Race Relations and the Race Problem.* Ed. Edgar T. Thompson. Durham, N.C.: Duke University Press, 1939. 3–45.

———. *Race and Culture.* Vol. 1 of *The Collected Papers of Robert Ezra Park.* Ed. Everett Cherrington Hughes et al. Glencoe, Ill.: Free Press, 1950.

——. "Reflections on Communication and Culture." *American Journal of Sociology* 44.2 (September 1938): 187–205.

——. "Sociology and the Social Sciences: The Group Concept and Social Research." *American Journal of Sociology* 27.2 (September 1921): 169–83.

——. "Sociology and the Social Sciences: The Social Organism and the Collective Mind." *American Journal of Sociology* 27.1 (July 1921): 1–21.

——. Succession, an Ecological Concept." *American Sociological Review* 1.2 (April 1936): 171–79.

——. "Symbiosis and Socialization: A Frame of Reference for the Study of Society." *American Journal of Sociology* 45.1 (July 1939): 1–25.

——. "The Urban Community as a Spatial Pattern and a Moral Order." 1925. In *Human Communities: The City and Human Ecology*. Vol. 2 of *The Collected Papers of Robert Ezra Park*. Ed. Everett Cherrington Hughes et al. Glencoe, Ill.: Free Press, 1950. 165–77.

Park, Robert Ezra, and Ernest W. Burgess. *Introduction to the Science of Sociology*. Chicago: University of Chicago Press, 1921.

Park, Robert Ezra, Herbert A. Miller, and W. I. Thomas. *Old World Traits Transplanted*. 1921. Vol. 3 of *Americanization Studies: The Acculturation of Immigrant Groups into American Society*. Ed. William S. Bernard. Montclair, N.J.: Patterson Smith, 1971.

Park, William H. "Functions of the Public Health Laboratory in Controlling the Import Diseases." *American Journal of Public Health* 12 (1922): 204–6.

——. "Typhoid Bacilli Carriers." *Journal of the American Medical Association* 51.12 (September 1908): 981–82.

Parker, Andrew, et al., eds. *Nationalisms and Sexualities*. New York: Routledge, 1991.

"Patient Zero (AIDS Patient Gaetan Dugas)." *People*, 28 December 1987, 47.

Paton, Alan. "The Negro in America Today." *Collier's*, 15 October 1954, 52–66.

——. "The Negro in the North." *Collier's*, 22 October 1954, 70–80.

Patton, Cindy. *Fatal Advice: How Safe-Sex Education Went Wrong*. Durham: Duke University Press, 1996.

——. *Globalizing AIDS*. Minneapolis: University of Minnesota Press, 2002.

——. *Inventing AIDS*. New York: Routledge, 1990.

——. "Queer Peregrinations." In *Acting on AIDS: Sex, Drugs, and Politics*, ed. Joshua Oppenheimer and Helena Reckitt. London: Serpent's Tail, 1997. 235–53.

——. *Sex and Germs: The Politics of AIDS*. Boston: South End Press, 1985.

Peiss, Kathy. *Cheap Amusements: Working Women and Leisure in Turn-of-the-Century New York*. Philadelphia: Temple University Press, 1986.

Persons, Stow. *Ethnic Studies at Chicago, 1905–45*. Urbana: University of Illinois Press, 1987.

Philipson, David. *Old European Jewries*. Philadelphia: Jewish Publication Society of America, 1894.

Pierce, Charles. "Epidemic of Fear." *Boston Globe*, 1 June 2003, 10.

Plumb, Robert K. "Atomic Idea Urged in Germ Splitting." *New York Times*, 2 May 1952, 10.

——. "Scientist Makes Synthetic Virus." *New York Times*, 18 April 1956, 33.

——. "Virus X-traordinary: The 'New' and Perversely Fashionable Microbe of the Moment Is as Mysterious as It Is Mean." *New York Times*, 20 April 1952, 34–35.

"*Pneumocystis* Pneumonia—Los Angeles." *Morbidity and Mortality Weekly Report* 30.21 (5 June 1981): 250–52.

Pogge, Thomas. "Human Rights and Human Responsibilities." In *Global Responsibilities: Who Must Deliver on Human Rights?*, ed. Andrew Kuper. New York: Routledge, 2005.

Poovey, Mary. *Making a Social Body: British Cultural Formation, 1830–1864.* Chicago: University of Chicago Press, 1995.

Preston, Richard. *The Cobra Event.* New York: Ballantine Books, 1997.

——. *The Hot Zone.* New York: Doubleday, 1994.

"Purge of Stalin." *New York Times*, 25 March 1956, E1–E3.

Quastler, Henry. *A Primer on Information Theory*, reprinted from *Symposium on Information Theory in Biology: Gatlinburg, Tennessee, October 29–31, 1956.* New York: Pergamon Press, 1958.

Radetsky, Peter. *The Invisible Invaders: Viruses and the Scientists Who Pursue Them.* Boston: Little, Brown, 1991.

Ratcliff, J. D. "Medicine's FBI." *Reader's Digest*, May 1959, 21–26.

Raushenbush, Winifred. *Robert E. Park: Biography of a Sociologist.* Durham: Duke University Press, 1979.

"Red Bloc Bars Bacterial Warfare." *New York Times*, 29 September 1950, 8, 5.

Redfield, Robert R., and Donald S. Burke. "HIV Infection: The Clinical Picture." *Scientific American*, October 1988, 90–99.

Regis, Ed. *Virus Ground Zero: Stalking the Killer Viruses with the Centers for Disease Control.* New York: Pocket Books, 1996.

Riis, Jacob A. *How the Other Half Lives: Studies Among the Tenements of New York.* 1890. Reprint, New York: Dover Publications, 1971.

Risse, Guenter B. "Epidemics and History: Ecological Perspectives and Social Responses." In *AIDS: The Burden of History*, ed. Elizabeth Fee and Daniel M. Fox. Berkeley: University of California Press, 1988. 33–66.

Ritchie, John W. *Primer of Sanitation: Being a Simple Work on Disease Order.* Yonkers-on-Hudson, N.Y.: World Book, 1910.

Roach, Mary. "Virus the Movie." *Health* 9.3 (May–June 1995): 78–83.

Rogers, Naomi. *Dirt and Disease: Polio Before FDR.* New Brunswick, N.J.: Rutgers University Press, 1992.

Rom, Mark Carl. *Fatal Extraction: The Story behind the Florida Dentist Accused of Infecting His Patients with HIV and Poisoning Public Health.* San Francisco: Jossey-Bass, 1997.

Roosevelt, Theodore. Letter to Mrs. Bessie Van Vorst, 18 October 1902. In *Works: Presidential Addresses and State Papers*, vol. 14, part 2. Statesman ed. New York: Review of Reviews, 1904. 510.

Rosen, George. "Cameralism and the Concept of the Medical Police." *Bulletin of the History of Medicine* 27 (1953): 21–42.

———. *A History of Public Health*. Expanded ed. Baltimore: Johns Hopkins University Press, 1993.

Rosen, Ruth. *The Lost Sisterhood: Prostitution in America, 1900–1918*. Baltimore: Johns Hopkins University Press, 1982.

Rosenberg, Charles E. "Disease and Social Order in America: Perceptions and Expectations." In *AIDS: The Burden of History*, ed. Elizabeth Fee and Daniel M. Fox. Berkeley: University of California Press, 1988. 12–32.

———. *Explaining Epidemics and Other Studies in the History of Medicine*. Cambridge: Cambridge University Press, 1992.

———. *No Other Gods: On Science and American Social Thought*. Revised ed. Baltimore: Johns Hopkins University Press, 1997.

Ross, Andrew. *No Respect: Intellectuals and Popular Culture*. New York: Routledge, 1989.

Ross, Dorothy. *The Origins of American Social Science*. Cambridge: Cambridge University Press, 1991.

Ross, Edward Alsworth. "The Causes of Race Superiority." In *Foundations of Sociology*. 5th ed. London: Macmillan, 1905. 353–85.

———. "Social Control." *American Journal of Sociology* 1.5 (March 1896): 513–35.

———. "Social Control. XIII. The System of Social Control." *American Journal of Sociology* 3.6 (May 1898): 809–28.

———. *Social Control: A Survey of the Foundations of Order*. New York: Macmillan, 1901.

Roueché, Berton. Preface to *Annals of Epidemiology*. Boston: Little, Brown, 1967. ix–x.

———. *Eleven Blue Men and Other Narratives of Medical Detection*. Boston: Little, Brown, 1953.

Rucker, W. C. "A Program of Public Health for Cities." *American Journal of Public Health* 7.3 (March 1917): 225–34.

Rudnick, Lois. "The New Woman." In *1915: The Cultural Moment: The New Politics, the New Woman, the New Psychology, the New Art and the New Theatre in America*, ed. Adele Heller and Lois Rudnick. New Brunswick, N.J.: Rutgers University Press, 1991. 69–81.

Ryan, Frank. *Virus X: Tracking the New Killer Plagues out of the Present and into the Future*. Boston: Little, Brown, 1997.

Sabatier, Renée. *Blaming Others: Prejudice, Race, and Worldwide AIDS*. Philadelphia: New Society Publishers for the Panos Institute, 1988.

Sagan, Carl. *Broca's Brain*. New York: Random House, 1979.

Saks, Eva. "Representing Miscegenation Law." *Raritan* 8.2 (1988): 39–69.

Samuels, Stuart. "The Age of Conspiracy and Conformity: 'Invasion of the Body Snatchers.'" In *American History/American Film: Interpreting the Hollywood Image.* New York: Ungar, 1980. 203–17.

Sayre, Nora. *Running Time: Films of the Cold War.* New York: Dial Press, 1982.

Schaffner, William, and F. Marc LaForce. "Training Field Epidemiologists: Alexander D. Langmuir and the Epidemic Intelligence Service." In "A Tribute to Alexander D. Langmuir." Supplement, *American Journal of Epidemiology* 144.8 (15 October 1996): S16–S22.

Schell, Heather. "Outburst! A Chilling True Story about Emerging-Virus Narratives and Pandemic Social Change." *Configurations* 5.1 (winter 1997): 93–133.

———. "The Sexist Gene: Science Fiction and the Germ Theory of History." In "Contagion and Culture," ed. Priscilla Wald, Nancy Tomes, and Lisa Lynch. Special issue, *American Literary History* 14.4 (winter 2002): 805–27.

Schell, Jonathan. *The Time of Illusion.* 1975. Reprint, New York: Vintage Books, 1976.

Schrecker, Ellen. *The Age of McCarthyism: A Brief History with Documents.* Boston: Bedford Books/St. Martin's Press, 1994.

"Scientists' Worldwide Race against Virus." *Straits Times,* 10 April 2003, 14.

Sedgwick, Eve Kosofsky. "Gary Fisher in Your Pocket." In *Acting on AIDS: Sex, Drugs, and Politics,* ed. Joshua Oppenheimer and Helena Reckitt. London: Serpent's Tail, 1997. 408–29.

———. *Tendencies.* Durham: Duke University Press, 1993.

Sedgwick, William T. "Typhoid Fever: A Disease of Defective Civilization." Introduction to *Typhoid Fever: Its Causation, Transmission, and Prevention,* by George C. Whipple. New York: John Wiley, 1908. xxiii–xxxvi.

Seed, David. *Brainwashing: The Fictions of Mind Control: A Study of Novels and Films since World War II.* Kent, Ohio: Kent State University Press, 2004.

Segal, Robert. *Theorizing about Myth.* Amherst: University of Massachusetts Press, 1999.

Sen, Amartya. "Conceptualizing and Measuring Poverty." In *Poverty and Inequality,* ed. David B. Grusky and Ravi Kanbur. Stanford, Calif.: Stanford University Press, 2006. 30–46.

———. *Development as Freedom.* New York: Alfred Knopf, 1999.

———. *Identity and Violence: The Illusion of Destiny.* New York: W. W. Norton, 2006.

———. *Rationality and Freedom.* Cambridge: Harvard University Press, 2002.

Sennett, Richard. "An Introduction." In *Classic Essays on the Culture of Cities,* ed. Richard Sennett. Englewood Cliffs, N.J.: Prentice Hall, 1969. 3–19.

Shah, Nayan. *Contagious Divides: Epidemics and Race in San Francisco's Chinatown.* Berkeley: University of California Press, 2001.

Shelley, Mary. *The Last Man.* Ed. Morton D. Paley. Oxford: Oxford University Press, 1994.

Shilts, Randy. *And the Band Played On: Politics, People, and the AIDS Epidemic.* New York: St. Martin's Press, 1987.

Shope, Robert E., and Alfred S. Evans. "Assessing Geographic and Transport Factors, and Recognition of New Viruses." In *Emerging Viruses*, ed. Stephen S. Morse. New York: Oxford University Press, 1993. 109–19.

Shoumatoff, Alex. "In Search of the Source of AIDS." *Vanity Fair*, July 1988, 94–105, 112–17.

Siegal, F. P., C. Lopez, G. S. Hammer, A. E. Brown, S. J. Kornfeld, J. Gold, J. Hassett, S. Z. Hirschman, C. Cunningham-Rundles, B. R. Adelsberg et al. "Severe Acquired Immunodeficiency in Male Homosexuals, Manifested by Chronic Perianal Ulcerative Herpes Simplex Lesions." *New England Journal of Medicine* 305.24 (10 December 1981): 1439–44.

Simmel, Georg. "The Metropolis and Mental Life." In *The Sociology of Georg Simmel.* Trans. Kurt H. Wolff. New York: Free Press, 1950. 409–24.

———. "The Sociological Significance of the 'Stranger.'" Excerpted in *Introduction to the Science of Sociology*, by Robert Ezra Park and Ernest W. Burgess. Chicago: University of Chicago Press, 1921. 322–27.

———. "The Stranger." In *The Sociology of Georg Simmel.* Ed. and trans. Kurt H. Wolff. New York: Free Press, 1950. 402–8.

Skal, David J. *The Monster Show: A Cultural History of Horror.* New York: W. W. Norton, 1993.

Small, Albion. "The Era of Sociology." *American Journal of Sociology* 1.1 (July 1895): 1–15.

Smith, Anthony D. *The Ethnic Origins of Nations.* Oxford: Blackwell, 1986.

———. *National Identity.* Reno: University of Nevada Press, 1991.

Smith, Geddes. *Plague On Us.* New York: Commonwealth Fund, 1941.

Smith, Neil. *Uneven Development: Nature, Capital and the Production of Space.* Oxford: Blackwell, 1991.

Smith-Rosenberg, Carroll. *Disorderly Conduct: Visions of Gender in Victorian America.* New York: Oxford University Press, 1986.

———. "The New Woman as Androgyne: Social Disorder and Gender Crisis, 1870–1936." In *Disorderly Conduct: Visions of Gender in Victorian America*, ed. Carroll Smith-Rosenberg. New York: Oxford University Press, 1986. 245–96.

Snyder, Carl. "The Reservoirs of Contagion." *Harper's Monthly* 125 (1912): 832–38.

Sobchack, Vivian. *Screening Space: The American Science Fiction Film.* 2d ed. New Brunswick, N.J.: Rutgers University Press, 2001.

Sollors, Werner. *Beyond Ethnicity: Consent and Descent in American Culture.* New York: Oxford University Press, 1986.

———. *Neither Black, nor White, yet Both: Thematic Explorations of Interracial Literature.* New York: Oxford University Press, 1997.

"Some Deadly Railway Passengers." *Literary Digest*, 13 July 1912, 57.

Sontag, Susan. *AIDS and Its Metaphors.* New York: Farrar, Straus, Giroux, 1988.

———. "The Imagination of Disaster." In *Against Interpretation and Other Essays*. New York: Farrar Straus and Giroux, 1966. 209–25.

Soper, George A. "The Curious Career of Typhoid Mary." *Bulletin of the New York Academy of Medicine* 15 (June 1939): 698–717.

———. "Typhoid Mary." *Military Surgeon* 45 (July 1919): 1–15.

———. "The Work of a Chronic Typhoid Germ Distributor." *Journal of the American Medical Association* 48 (June 1907): 2019–22.

Sparke, Matthew. *In the Space of Theory: Postfoundational Geographies of the Nation-State*. Minneapolis: University of Minnesota Press, 2005.

Specter, Michael. "Nature's Bioterrorist: Is There Any Way to Prevent a Deadly Avian-Flu Pandemic?" *New Yorker*, 28 February 2005, 50–61.

Spengler, Otto. "The Soul of the City." In *Classic Essays on the Culture of Cities*, ed. Richard Sennett. Englewood Cliffs, N.J.: Prentice Hall, 1969. 61–88.

Spingarn, Natalie Davis. "Meet Our Medical FBI: They Are the Sleuths from Atlanta Who Fight Epidemics from Coast to Coast." *Parents*, October 1963, 73–79, 184–85.

Spolar, Chris. "3 AIDS Cases Mystify Scientists." *Washington Post*, 2 October 1990, 27.

Squier, Susan Merrill. *Liminal Lives: Imaging the Human at the Frontiers of Biomedicine*. Durham: Duke University Press, 2004.

Stage, Sarah, and Virginia Vincenti, eds. *Rethinking Home Economics: Women and the History of a Profession*. Ithaca, N.Y.: Cornell University Press, 1997.

Stange, Margit. *Personal Property: Wives, White Slaves, and the Market in Woman*. Baltimore: Johns Hopkins University Press, 1998.

Starr, Paul. *The Social Transformation of American Medicine: The Rise of a Sovereign Profession and the Making of a Vast Industry*. New York: Basic Books, 1982.

Steffens, Lincoln. *The Autobiography of Lincoln Steffens*. New York: Harcourt, Brace, 1931.

Takaki, Ronald. *A Different Mirror: A History of Multiculturalism in America*. Boston: Bay Back Books, 1993.

———. *Strangers from a Different Shore: A History of Asian Americans*. Rev. ed. Boston: Little, Brown, 1998.

Tarde, Gabriel. *L'Opinion et la foule (Public Opinion and the Crowd)*. 2d ed. Paris: Ancienne Librairie Germer Bailliere et Cie, 1904.

Taylor, Debbie. "The Chance of a Lifetime (History of the Alma-Ata Declaration)." *World Health*, September 1983, 2–4.

Terry, Jennifer. *An American Obsession: Science, Medicine, and Homosexuality in Modern Society*. Chicago: University of Chicago Press, 1999.

Thomas, W. I. "The Adventitious Character of Woman." *American Journal of Sociology* 12.1 (July 1906): 32–44.

———. *Sex and Society: Studies in the Social Psychology of Sex*. Chicago: University of Chicago Press, 1907.

Thompson, Nicholas. "The Myth of the Superspreader: Why the SARS Epidemic Can't Be Blamed on Highly Toxic Individuals." *Boston Globe*, 4 May 2003, H1.

Tierno, Philip M., Jr. *The Secret Life of Germs: Observations and Lessons from a Microbe Hunter*. New York: Pocket Books, 2001.

Timmreck, Thomas C. *An Introduction to Epidemiology*. 2nd ed. Sudbury, Mass.: Jones and Bartlett Publishers, 1998.

Tomes, Nancy. "Epidemic Entertainments: Disease and Popular Culture in Early-Twentieth-Century America." In "Contagion and Culture," ed. Priscilla Wald, Nancy Tomes, and Lisa Lynch. Special issue, *American Literary History* 14.4 (winter 2002): 625–52.

———. *The Gospel of Germs: Men, Women, and the Microbe in American Life*. Cambridge: Harvard University Press, 1998.

———. "The Making of a Germ Panic, Then and Now." *American Journal of Public Health* 90.2 (February 2000): 191–98.

"The Transfer of Disease by Travel." *Literary Digest*, 1 November 1924, 29.

Treichler, Paula A. *How to Have Theory in an Epidemic: Cultural Chronicles of AIDS*. Durham: Duke University Press, 1999.

Trimberger, Ellen Kay. "The New Woman and the New Sexuality: Conflict and Contradiction in the Writings and Lives of Mabel Dodge and Neith Boyce." In *1915: The Cultural Moment: The New Politics, the New Woman, the New Psychology, the New Art and the New Theatre in America*, ed. Adele Heller and Lois Rudnick. New Brunswick, N.J.: Rutgers University Press, 1991. 98–115.

Turner, Ralph H. "Introduction to *Robert E. Park: On Social Control and Collective Behavior*." In *The Emergence of American Sociology: From the Enlightenment to the Founding Fathers*. Vol. 1 of *The Classical Tradition in Sociology: The American Tradition*. Ed. Jeffrey Alexander, Raymond Boudon, and Mohamed Cherkaoui. London: Sage Publications, 1997. 264–91.

"Typhoid: A National Disgrace." *Survey*, 27 May 1916, 223.

"'Typhoid Mary.'" *Outlook*, April 1915, 803–4.

"'Typhoid Mary' Asks $50,000 from City." *New York Times*, 3 December 1911, 9.

"'Typhoid Mary' Has Reappeared." *New York Times*, 4 April 1915, sec. 5, 3.

"'Typhoid Mary' Must Stay: Court Rejects her Plea to Quit Riverside Hospital." *New York Times*, 17 July 1909, 5.

"'Typhoid Mary' Never Ill, Begs Freedom: 'Why Should I Be Banished Like a Leper?'" *New York American*, 30 June 1909, 3.

Ubell, Earl. "That Old Virus." *Ladies' Home Journal*, April 1953, 57, 92–93, 95.

"Update on Kaposi's Sarcoma and Opportunistic Infections in Previously Healthy Persons—United States." *Morbidity and Mortality Weekly Report* 31.22 (11 June 1982): 294–301.

"U.S. Medical Study Singles Out a Man Who Carried AIDS." *New York Times*, 27 March 1984, A25.

Van Dijk, José. *Imagenation: Popular Images of Genetics*. New York: New York University Press, 1998.

Verghese, Abraham. "The Way We Live Now." *New York Times*, 20 April 2003, 15.

Waardenburg, Jacques. "Symbolic Aspects of Myth." In *Myth, Symbol, and Reality*, ed. Alan M. Olson. Notre Dame, Ind.: University of Notre Dame Press, 1980. 41–68.

Waldby, Cathy. *AIDS and the Body Politic: Biomedicine and Sexual Difference.* New York: Routledge, 1996.

Walkowitz, Judith R. *Prostitution and Victorian Society: Women, Class, and the State.* Cambridge: Cambridge University Press, 1980.

Wallis, Claudia. "AIDS: A Growing Threat: Now that the Disease Has Come Out of the Closet, How Far Will It Spread?" *Time*, 12 August 1985, 40–45, 47.

———. "Knowing the Face of the Enemy." *Time*, 30 April 1984, 66–67.

Wassersug, Joseph D. "Deadly Germs that Play Possum." *Science Digest*, May 1953, 6–9.

Watney, Simon. *Imagine Hope: AIDS and Gay Identity.* London: Routledge, 2000.

———. "Missionary Positions: AIDS, 'Africa,' and Race." In "Life and Death in Sexuality: Reproductive Technologies and AIDS." Special issue, *differences* 1.1 (winter 1989): 83–100.

———. *Policing Desire: Pornography, AIDS, and the Media.* Minneapolis: University of Minnesota Press, 1996.

———. "The Political Significance of Statistics in the AIDS Crisis: Epidemiology, Representation and Re-gaying." In *Acting on AIDS: Sex, Drugs, and Politics,* ed. Joshua Oppenheimer and Helena Reckitt. London: Serpent's Tail, 1997. 76–100.

———. *Practices of Freedom: Selected Writings on HIV/AIDS.* London: Rivers Oram Press, 1994.

———. "The Spectacle of AIDS." In *The Lesbian and Gay Studies Reader,* ed. Henry Abelove, Michele Aina Barale, and David M. Halperin. New York: Routledge, 1993. 71–86.

Watts, Duncan J. *Six Degrees: The Science of a Connected Age.* New York: W. W. Norton, 2003.

Way, J. Howell. "Remarks on Railway Sanitation, with Special Reference to the Dangers of Present Methods of Disposing of Human Excreta, and Suggestions for Improvement." *Charlotte Medical Journal* 29 (1906): 80–84.

Weber, Jonathan N. and Robin A. Weiss. "HIV Infection: The Cellular Picture." *Scientific American*, October 1988, 100–109.

Weinbaum, Alys Eve. *Wayward Reproductions: Genealogies of Race and Nation in Transatlantic Modern Thought.* Durham: Duke University Press, 2004.

Weiss, Ludwig. "The Prostitution Problem in Its Relation to Law and Medicine." *Journal of the American Medical Association* 47.25 (December 1906): 2071–75.

Wermuth, Laurie. *Global Inequality and Human Needs: Health and Illness in an Increasingly Unequal World.* Boston: Pearson Education, 2003.

Werner, David, and David Sanders. *Questioning the Solution: The Politics of Primary Health Care and Child Survival.* Palo Alto, Calif.: HealthWrights, 1997.

Westad, Odd Arne. *The Global Cold War: Third World Interventions and the Making of Our Times*. Cambridge: Cambridge University Press, 2005.

Whipple, George C. *Typhoid Fever: Its Causation, Transmigration, and Prevention*. New York: John Wiley, 1908.

White, Hayden. "The Value of Narrativity in the Representation of Reality." In *On Narrative*, ed. W. J. T. Mitchell. Chicago: University of Chicago Press, 1981. 1–23.

Wiener, Norbert. *Cybernetics: Or Control and Communication in the Animal and the Machine*. New York: Technology Press, John Wiley and Sons, 1948.

———. *The Human Uses of Human Being: Cybernetics and Society*. 1950. Reprint, Garden City, N.Y.: Doubleday Anchor Books, 1954.

Will, George. "AIDS Crushes a Continent." *Newsweek*, 10 January 2000, 64.

Wills, Christopher. *Yellow Fever, Black Goddess: The Coevolution of People and Plagues*. Reading, Mass.: Addison-Wesley, 1996.

Wirth, Louis. *The Ghetto*. Chicago: University of Chicago Press, 1928.

Wolfe, Tom. "The 'Me Decade' and the Third Great Awakening." *New York*, 23 August 1976, 26–40.

Worland, Rick. *The Horror Film: An Introduction*. Malden, Mass.: Blackwell, 2007.

Yarchoan, Robert, Hiroaki Mitsuya, and Samuel Broder. " AIDS Therapies." *Scientific American*, October 1988, 110–19.

Young, Donald R. "Introduction to the Republished Edition." In *Old World Traits Transplanted* (1921), by Robert E. Park, Herbert A. Miller, and W. I. Thomas. Vol. 3 of *Americanization Studies: The Acculturation of Immigrant Groups into American Society*. Ed. William S. Bernard. Montclair, N.J.: Patterson Smith, 1971. vii–xv.

Young, Robert J. C. *Colonial Desire: Hybridity in Culture, Theory, and Race*. London: Routledge, 1995.

Yu, Henry. *Thinking Orientals: Migration, Contact, and Exoticism in Modern America*. New York: Oxford University Press, 2001.

Zimmerman, Barry, and David J. Zimmerman. *Killer Germs: Microbes and Diseases that Threaten Humanity*. Chicago: Contemporary Books, 1996.

FILMS AND TELEVISION

Aeon Flux. Directed by Karyn Kusama. Paramount Pictures, 2005.

The Andromeda Strain. Directed by Robert Wise. Universal Pictures, 1971.

And the Band Played On. Directed by Roger Spottiswoode. Home Box Office, 1993.

Army Information Film AIF No. 7: Code of Conduct—To Resist. No director. U.S. Department of Defense, 1950.

Carriers. Directed by Alan Metzger. Paris Video, 1998.

China Syndrome. Directed by James Bridges. Columbia Pictures, 1979.

The Invasion. Directed by Oliver Hirschbiegel. Warner Brothers Pictures, 2007.

Invasion of the Body Snatchers. Directed by Don Siegel. Allied Artists Pictures, 1956.

Invasion of the Body Snatchers. Directed by Philip Kaufman. Metro-Goldwyn-Mayer, 1978.

The Last Man on Earth. Directed by Ubaldo Ragona. American International Pictures, 1964.

Omega Man. Directed by Boris Sagal. Warner Brothers, 1971.

Outbreak. Directed by Wolfgang Petersen. Warner Brothers, 1995.

Philadelphia. Directed by Jonathan Demme. Tristar Pictures, 1993.

Red Nightmare. Directed by George Waggner for the U.S. Department of Defense Directorate for Armed Forces Information and Education. Warner Brothers, 1962.

Resident Evil. Directed by Paul W. S. Anderson. Columbia Pictures, 2002.

Robin Cook's Invasion. Directed by Armand Mastroianni. Von Zerneck Sertner Films, 1997.

Smallpox 2002: Silent Weapon. Directed by Daniel Percival. Docudrama. fX Network, 2002.

The Stand. Directed by Mike Garris. Miniseries. American Broadcasting Corporation, 1994.

Twelve Monkeys. Directed by Terry Gilliam. Universal Pictures, 1995.

28 Days Later. Directed by Danny Boyle. Twentieth Century Fox, 2002.

Zero Patience. Directed by John Greyson. Zero Patience Productions, 1993.

Index

Americanism (*cont.*)
and, 176–80; ghettoization and, 147–49, 152–56; motherhood and home metaphors in, 110–11; in *Outbreak*, 58–67; social contagion and urban spaces and concepts of, 114–56; "Typhoid Mary" narratives and motif of, 96–104

American Journal of Medicine, 226–30, 233–34, 314n.34

American Journal of Public Health, 75

American Journal of Sociology, 87–89, 116, 119, 293n.5

American Legion magazine, 174–75

American Medical Association, Hygiene and Sanitary Science Section of, 86

American Public Health Association (APHA), immunology research and, 126–28

American Review of Reviews, 81

American Society for Sanitary and Moral Prophylaxis, 87

"American Woman, The," 108–10

Amin, Idi, 237

Anderson, Benedict, 33, 51–53, 57–58, 133, 284n.69

Anderson, Warwick, 273n.8

Andromeda Strain, The, 31–33, 42, 261, 280n.8

And the Band Played On, 215–16., 231–34, 238–42, 244, 261, 315n.45

Angels in America, 217, 312n.10

antibiotics, legacy of, 29

anti-Semitism: epidemics and growth of, 115; ghettoization and, 144–49, 152–56

Appadurai, Arjun, 60

Arthur Mervyn, 11

assimilation cycle: ghettoization and, 146–49, 152–56; mutuality of influence and, 155–56, 300n.96; Park's

mapping of immigrant experience and, 139, 297n.64

Atwood, Margaret, 319n.93

avian flu outbreaks, global health policies and, 268–70

bacteriology: communicable disease and emergence of, 13–15, 275n.37; contagion theory and, 116; epidemiology and, 19–20; healthy carrier and theories of, 73–79; influence on Freud of, 15–16, 18; social contagion theory influenced by, 136–38; typhoid epidemiology and, 79–84

bacteriophage research, emergence of, 180–81

Baker, Sara Josephine, 69, 74–75, 95–97

Balibar, Etienne, 52–53

Barabasi, Albert-Laszlo, 273n.23

belonging: emerging infections and theories of, 30–33; healthy carrier model and theories of, 76–79

Bergalis, Kimberly, 251–54

Bernard, Luther, 118, 293n.12

Betrayal of Trust: The Collapse of Global Health, 46–47

Beyond Recall, 319n.93

Bhabha, Homi, 192–99, 225–26

biological warfare: emerging disease research and concern over, 51; in fictional narratives, 159–61; politics and science of, 27; public anxiety concerning, 24, 42. *See also* germ warfare, virology research and

biology of community, Park's theories on, 138–42

biopolitics: Foucault's discussion of, 18, 277n.47; in outbreak narratives, 58–67, 259–63, 319n.93; "third-worldification" bias in emerging disease research and, 45–47; typhoid epidemiology and, 80–81

Biosafety Levels, viral transmission research and, 35–36, 281n.18

bisexuality, AIDS risk and, 251–54

Black Death and Dancing Mania, The, 135

Blattner, William, 242

Blood Artists, The, 31, 56, 257–63, 318n.88, 319n.93

Boccaccio, Giovanni, 11–12

Body Snatchers, The, 27, 63; brain-washing imagery in, 189–92, 198–99, 308n.89; Cold War politics and, 159–61; mimicry and hybridity in, 192–99; racial identity and, 194–99; virus imagery in, 188–92

Bolivian hemorrhagic fever, 36

Borrowed Time, 217

Boston Globe, 9–10, 256

brainwashing: images in *Body Snatchers* of, 189–92, 198–99, 308n.89; media images of, 178–80

Broca's Brain, 310n.118

Brown, Charles Brockden, 11

Brown v. Board of Education, 194

Budenz, Louis, 175

Burgess, Ernest W., 129–30, 135–36, 139, 297n.64

Burk family, AIDS and victimization of, 247–48, 317n.72

Burnet, Frank Macfarlane, 163–64, 173, 303n.23

Burr, Albert H., 86

Burroughs, William: Cold War politics and work of, 159–61, 183–88, 197, 203–4, 307n.78; HIV/AIDS epidemic foreshadowed by, 197, 214–15

Burton, Richard Francis, 254–56

Cahan, Abraham, 143–49, 151, 154, 299n.80, 300n.85

Calderone, Frank, 169

Callen, Michael, 238, 255, 261

Calley, William (lieutenant), 59, 284n.76

capitalism, biopolitics and, 64–67

Carnegie Corporation of New York, 149

carriers: in AIDS outbreak narratives, 230–34; bacteriology and concept of, 16, 275n.41; healthy carrier model, 68–113; history of epidemiology and, 26–28; immunology research and acceptance of, 124–28; media portrayal of, 9; myths concerning, 9–10; "Patient Zero" narratives and image of, 4, 215–17, 226–34, 236–42, 254–57, 316n.54 (*see also* "Patient Zero"); popular images of, 21–23, 278n.55; role in AIDS/HIV outbreak narrative of, 215–63; role in outbreak narrative of, 56–57; stranger/carrier motif, 56–57; surveillance and containment of, 112–13; transportation networks and impact of, 123–24. *See also* healthy carrier; super-spreader of disease

Carriers, 31, 37, 280n.5, 282n.33; biopolitics in, 63–66; distortion of science in, 41–42; stranger/carrier figure in, 56; vengeful microbe motif in, 46

causality, healthy carrier and role of, 70, 106

Cell (journal), 230

Centers for Disease Control (CDC), 25, 281n.16; Acer AIDS case and, 251–53; AIDS epidemic and, 219–20; epidemiology training course at, 218–22; hemorrhagic fevers management and, 34, 36

Chambers, Whittaker, 175, 179

Chapin, Charles V., 73–74

Cheap Amusements: Working Women and Leisure in Turn-of-the-Century New York, 289n.46

Chicago, University of. *See* University of Chicago

China, brainwashing stereotypes about, 178

China Syndrome: The Killer Virus that Crashed the Middle Kingdom, 271n.5, 272n.13

Chinese immigrants, epidemics and bias against, 115

Chisholm, Brock, 165, 167–68

"City: Suggestions for the Investigation of Human Behavior in the Urban Environment, The," 116–17, 130–38, 296n.54, 410–142

Civil Defense Administration, 166

civil rights: epidemics and role of, 59–67; healthy carriers and role of, 70–113; "Typhoid Mary" narratives and role of, 98–104

Clancy, Tom, 319n.93

classified information, concepts of, 183, 306n.74

class politics: communicable disease and, 114–15; female mobility and, 87–94, 289n.43, 289n.46; ghettoization and, 146–49; typhoid epidemiology and, 80–84; "Typhoid Mary" story and, 84–94, 96–104, 106–11

Cobra Event, The, 280n.7

Cohen, Nathan, 104–5

Cohn, Roy, 312n.10

Cold War politics: AIDS epidemic narratives and, 236–42; emerging disease concepts and, 46–47; germ warfare and, 165–70; HIV/AIDS epidemic and, 312n.10; outbreak narratives and, 63–67; seventies

generation and, 205; viruses and virology and, 157–212

collective identity, outbreak narratives and, 26

Collier's magazine, 188, 193–95, 199

colonization. *See* decolonization

Coming Plague, The, 31–33, 44, 232, 266–68, 271n.2

Commoner, Barry, 163

communicable disease: biological transformation through, 53–67; germ theories of history and, 49–53; healthy carriers and, 68–113; historical and literary narratives of, 12–23; laboratory research and, 122–24; religious associations with, 13–15, 21–22; social connectedness and, 115; typhoid epidemiology as, 79–84. *See also* contagion; contagious disease; infectious disease

Communicable Disease Center (CDC), 23–28. *See also* Centers for Disease Control (CDC)

communication and communicability: in Burroughs's fiction, 184–86; historical theories about, 12–13; of ideas and sensations, 88, 289n.41; Park's theories on, 134–38; social contagion as, 117–19

communism: information management and, 183; virology research politics and, 159–61, 165–80. *See also* Cold War politics

community: contagious disease and formation of, 18–19, 22–23; epidemics as threat to, 59–67; ghetto model of, 150–56; herd immunity theory and, 53–67; Park's theories on, 134–38; social interaction and biology of, 138–42

Comte, Auguste, 133

Conan Doyle, Arthur, 24

Condon, Richard, 190, 308n.89
Congo Reform Association, 130
Conrad, Joseph, 235
contagion: bacteriology and theories
   of, 116; cultural concepts of, 2–9;
   healthy carrier model and, 70–113;
   historical definitions of, 10–13,
   131–38; imagined communities and
   networks of, 54–67; immigrant
   threat of, 97–104; "menticide" concept of, 178–79; microbial traffic
   concept of, 37–39; mystical powers
   of, 54–55; social interconnectedness
   through, 12–13; sociological context of, 88–94, 110–13; typhoid epidemiology and theories of, 82–84;
   virology research and role of, 173–
   80. *See also* social contagion theory
Contagion, 31
contagious disease, definitions of, 21,
   278n.56
containment strategies: AIDS narratives and fiction of, 240–42, 253–
   54; ghetto model of, 155–56,
   300n.96; "Patient Zero" metaphor
   and, 216; in public health policy,
   113, 148, 292n.96
continental population concepts,
   germ warfare and role of, 168–70
Cook, Robin, 31, 54, 59–60, 63, 188,
   199, 257, 318n.91, 319n.93
Cool, Tom, 319n.93
Copeland, Royal S., 127–28
coronavirus, SARS etiology and, 1
Crane, Stephen, 116
Creasy, William M., 166
Crichton, Michael, 31–33
Crimp, Douglas, 215
"Crisis in the Hot Zone," 31
Cronk, H. Taylor, 123
*Crowd: A Study of the Popular Mind,
   The*, 132–38

crowd psychology, social contagion
   theory and, 132–38, 184
Cry, The Beloved Country, 194
Culliton, Barbara, 42–44, 280n.15
cultural frameworks: for AIDS epidemic narratives, 213–17, 224–26;
   AIDS origin theses and, 235–42,
   316n.57; Cold War politics and,
   175–80; disease prevention as social
   control, 121–24; for epidemics,
   214–15; female mobility and, 87–
   94; geographic fictions and, 142–
   49; group interactions and social
   ties and, 14; historical accounts of
   plagues and, 11–20; immigrant
   assimilation cycle and, 139–42,
   297n.64; origin theories on AIDS
   and, 235–42; SARS outbreak analysis and, 3–9, 273n.20; scientific
   discoveries in context of, 21–23,
   278n.55; for seventies generation,
   204–12; social contagion theory
   and, 132–38; social space and, 140–
   42, 298n.69; sociology research on,
   128–32; species interdependence
   theories and, 50–53; stranger/
   carrier motif in outbreak narratives
   and, 57; "thirdworldification" bias
   and, 45–47; typhoid epidemiology
   and, 79–84; "Typhoid Mary" narratives and, 101–4
Cybernetics, 182

Darnell, James E. Jr., 162, 181, 305n.65
Darrow, Bill, 227–28, 231, 238–39
Darwin, Charles, 15; healthy carrier
   model and theories of, 76; social
   contagion theory and, 136–37
Darwinism and Human Life, 136–37
"Deadly Germs that Play Possum," 180
Decameron, The, 11–12, 18
Declaration of Alma-Ata, 266–70

decolonization: AIDS origin theses and stereotypes and, 235–42, 316n.57; *Body Snatchers* and backdrop of, 194–95; emerging disease research and role of, 45–53; virology research and impact of, 168–70

Defoe, Daniel, 11–12

De Kruif, Paul, 20, 171

Demme, Jonathan, 217, 314n.40

dentists, AIDS infection in, 251–54

desegregation, *Body Snatchers* and backdrop of, 194–95

Destruction of Gotham, The, 115

developing nations: emerging disease research and role of, 44–47; viral traffic concept and, 280n.14

Dewey, John, 133, 136

Diamond, Jared, 31, 47–48, 51

Dies, Martin, 172

Diner, Hasia R., 97, 290n.58

dirt: class and ethnicity politics and role of, 96–97; as symbol of disease, 13–14

disease detectives: in AIDS epidemic narratives, 217–22; healthy carrier motif and, 68, 286n.3; historical concepts of, 20–28, 277n.54; sensationalization of, in outbreak narratives, 36–39

disease emergence: in *Blood Artists,* 259–63; contemporary narratives of, 1–2, 271nn.3–4; ecological theories concerning, 39–53; evolution of concept of, 25–28; germ warfare and, 166–70; historical accounts of, 10–20; media coverage of, 25–28; modern evolution of, 30; mythical aspects of, 43–47; one-way microbial traffic concept and, 34, 280n.14; socioeconomic conditions and, 261–63. *See also* emerging diseases

disease transmission: healthy carrier

motif and, 79–113; microbial traffic concept of, 34, 37–39; one-way transmission (European-American), 34, 280n.14, 282n.33; typhoid epidemiology and mechanics of, 79–84

diversity, infectious disease and growth of, 56–57

Doubleday, Frank, 90, 289n.45

Douglas, Mary, 13–14

Dragnet, 176

Dreiser, Theodore, 90–91, 289n.45

Dritz, Selma, 233

drug addiction, corporatism and, 185

Dugas, Gaetan, 4, 215–17, 230–34, 236–42, 254–57, 316n.54. *See also* "Patient Zero"

DuPont Corporation, 249–51

Durkheim, Émile, 14–15, 18, 131, 133

Duval, Robert, 207

Ebola virus: agency metaphor in description of, 43; mythical aspects of, 43–44; outbreak narratives about, 30–33; political analysis of outbreaks of, 46–47; scientific attention on, 34–35

ecological model of contagion: biology of community and, 138–42; development of, 39–53; in fictional outbreak narratives, 257–63, 319n.93; healthy carrier model and, 75, 287n.15; immigrant assimilation cycle and, 297n.64; mimicry and hybridity and, 196–99; mutuality of influence and, 155–56, 300n.96; Park's social contagion theory and, 136–38; species interdependence and, 50–53, 70–79, 217; virology research and, 163–64, 172–80

economic justice: AIDS epidemic and, 216–17, 248–51; disease outbreaks and, 264–65; health linked to, 172

Edson, Cyrus, 119–21, 126
Elementary Forms of Religious Experience, 14
Eliade, Mircea, 9
Ellis, Havelock, 81
Ellis Island, quarantine system on, 127, 292n.96
Emergency Interagency Working Group, 51
emerging diseases. *See* disease emergence
Emerging Infections, 30
Emerging Viruses, 30, 33–34, 36, 280n.7; ecological view of disease in, 41
"Emerging Viruses" conference, 30, 33–34, 36, 280n.7
Epidemic! The World of Infectious Disease, 33, 280n.9
"Epidemic! The World of Infectious Disease" (museum exhibit), 284n.68
Epidemiological Investigation Service, 23–28, 277n.54
epidemiology: decolonization and, 47–53; disease detectives model of, 20–28, 36–39, 68, 286n.3; epidemic disease and role of, 19–20, 277n.49; gender roles in, 106–11; historical accounts of, 11–20; historical theories in, 48–53; immunology research and, 125–28; impact of AIDS epidemic on, 217–22; language of, in outbreak narratives, 217–22
ethnicity: Chicago theories concerning, 153–54; class and, 96–97; immigrant stereotypes of, 96–97; Park's theories concerning, 128–32, 196–99; "Typhoid Mary" story and role of, 96–104
Evans, Alfred S., 280n.15

evolution, communicable disease and, 49–53
Experimental Epidemiology, 125–26

Fairchild, Amy, 292n.96, 295n.33
Fairchild, Henry Pratt, 139–40
fallen-woman narratives, "Typhoid Mary" story as example of, 85–94
Farmer, Paul, 264–65
Farrell, Marjorie, 168–70
Fauci, Anthony, 225
Faulkner, William, 237, 316n.57
fecal contamination, typhoid epidemiology and, 79–84
female mobility, social order threatened by, 87–94, 289n.43, 289n.46
feminist theory, social space and, 298n.69
Fenner, Frank, 173
Ferber, Edna, 107
fictional outbreak narratives: AIDS epidemic and, 254–57, 263, 318n.88; Cold War politics and, 159–61; emerging disease theory and, 31–33; evolution of, 41–42, 282n.33; ghettos depicted in, 143–49; mimicry and hybridity motifs in, 192–99; religious motifs in, 53–67; in science fiction genre, 27, 257–60, 261; tenements described in, 114–15; vengeful microbe motif in, 45–46; virus imagery in, 188–92
film versions of outbreak narratives, 29, 31, 257, 259; AIDS epidemic in, 254–57, 263; Cold War politics and, 159–61, 176–80; HIV/AIDS epidemic and, 217
Fineberg, Harvey V., 248–51
Finney, Jack, 27, 63, 159–61, 188–204, 259
Flexner, Simon, 124–28
Fogarty International Center, 30

Greenough, Paul, 277n.54
Greyson, John, 254–56, 262
Guardian, The, 255
Guinan, Mary, 239
Guns, Germs and Steel: The Fates of Human Societies, 31

Haiti: in Farmer's work, 264–65; origin theory for AIDS epidemic in, 234–42, 315n.53; in Sabatier's work, 236, 315n.23
Hall, G. Stanley, 130
Hamer, W. H., 95–96
Hamilton, Greg, 238
hantavirus, 33
Hapgood, Hutchins, 143, 300n.85
Harden, Victoria A., 122
Harper's magazine, 75
Harris, Oliver, 184
Harvey, David, 298n.69
healthcare professionals: AIDS infection in, 251–54; power structure and, 264–65
Health for All movement, 267–70
healthy carrier: civil rights of, 98–104; cultural acceptance of concept of, 105–11; historical research about, 68, 285n.2; medical controversies concerning, 95–96; surveillance and containment of, 111–13; Typhoid Mary as model of, 68–113
Heart of Darkness, 235
Hecker, Justus Friedrich Karl, 135
hemophiliacs, HIV transmission in, 246–51
hemorrhagic fevers, scientific attention on, 34–35
Henderson, Donald A., 25, 30–31, 280n.7
herd immunity: emerging disease research and, 48–53; evolution of theories about, 126–28

Hippocrates, 11, 275n.32
Hiss, Alger, 175, 179
history, outbreak narratives and, 47–53
Hockley, David, 209
Hoffman, Dustin, 37
Hogan, Chuck, 31, 56, 257, 259
Holmes, Bayard, 86
Home Economics Movement, 107–11
homophobia: in AIDS outbreak narratives, 225–26, 314n.40; Cold War politics and, 160–61; McCarthyism and, 307n.76
homo sacer concept, 275n.41
homosexuality: in AIDS outbreak narratives, 219–22; cultural anxiety concerning, 197–99; McCarthyism and targeting of, 307n.76
Hoover, Herbert, 179
Hoover, J. Edgar, 175–76
Horstall, Frank L. Jr., 180
Hot Zone, The, 31, 43–45 256, 280n.7, 281n.18; biopolitics in, 64, 67; global interconnectedness as theme in, 34–37; mythical aspects of disease in, 43–47, 55–56; racial metaphors in, 235–36; sacrifice motif in, 262
House Un-American Activities Committee (HUAC), 172–80
How the Other Half Lives, 114–15
Hueppe, Ferdinand, 74–75
Hull House, 128–32, 295n.34
human immunodeficiency virus (HIV): AIDS infection distinguished from, 243–51; conflicts over research on, 244–51; connection between AIDS and, 213–14, 310n.4; disease emergence concept and, 27–28; emerging threat of, 30; global interconnectedness and pandemic spread of, 34–39, 280n.15; *Invasion of the Body Snatchers* 1978

human immunodeficiency virus (*cont.*) remake as foreshadowing of, 206–12; laboratory research on, 242–51; media images of, 157; origins of, 35, 240–42, 281n.17; outbreak narratives triggered by, 2, 6, 213–63; Shilts's description of, 232–34; T cell infection, image of, 209

human migration, viral traffic concept and, 280n.14

Human Use of Human Beings: Cybernetics and Society, The, 181–82, 191

human-vector thesis: healthy carriers and, 68; medical debate concerning, 95–96

Hunter, Edward, 178–80, 198

hybridity: in AIDS outbreak narratives, 225–26, 230–34, 241–42, 318n.88; in *Blood Artists*, 258–63; in *Body Snatchers*, 192–99; virology and, 260–63

Hygienic Laboratory, establishment of, 122

I Am Legend, 200–203, 274n.24, 309n.105

Iliad, The, plague narrative in, 11

Imagined Communities, 33, 51–53, 57–67, 133

immigrant groups: AIDS epidemic narratives and, 238–42, 316n.65; class and ethnicity stereotypes concerning, 96–97; ghettos and tenements as transitional space for, 142–43; immunology research and focus on, 127–28; media stigmatization of, 7–9; in outbreak narratives, 97–104, 290n.60; Park's assimilation cycle for, 139–42, 297n.64; as public health risk, 115, 122–24; surveillance and containment of, 112–13, 292n.96; typhoid epidemiology and racism concerning, 80–84

immigrant metaphor, virus descriptions using, 42–43

Immigration and Nationality Act, AIDS epidemic and, 316n.65

immunization programs: in Burroughs's fiction, 186–88; germ warfare policies and, 168–70

immunology research: agency motif in, 45–47; Cold War politics and, 172–73; ecosystem view of, 47–53; evolution of, 124–28; impact of AIDS epidemic on, 222–26; virology and, 163–64, 173–80

index case concept: in AIDS outbreak narratives, 230–34, 238–42, 317n.75; in fictional outbreak narratives, 318n.91, 319n.93; media myths concerning, 3–4, 272n.12

individualism, healthy carriers and role of, 70, 72–79, 113, 286n.8

industrialization: gender roles and, 109–10; typhoid epidemiology and role of, 82–84

infectious disease: accidental nature of, 42; antibiotics and decline of, 29–30; definitions of, 21, 278n.56; immunological effects of, 47–53

Infectress, 319n.93

influenza: global health policies and, 268–70; history of, 161–64; in outbreak narratives, 42–47; transmission of, 35–39

information theory, virology and, 180–83, 305n.65

Institute of Medicine, 30, 34, 36

intentionality: in outbreak narratives, 4; in virology research, 170–80. See also agency

interdependency theories: emerging

disease research and, 50–53;
healthy carriers and, 70–79
Introduction to the Science of Sociology, 129–33, 135–36, 139,
296n.50
Invasion, 54, 59–60, 63–64, 188, 191–92, 199, 257–63, 308n.85, 318n.88,
318n.91, 319n.93
Invasion of the Body Snatchers, The
(1956 film): political themes in,
199–204; viral imagery in, 191–93
Invasion of the Body Snatchers, The
(1978 film), 204–13, 218, 245; HIV/
AIDS epidemic foreshadowed by,
161, 218, 245
"Investigation of Communist Propaganda" (Report 2290), 172
Irish Times, 9–10
Isaacs, Harold R., 205, 237, 316n.57

Jaax, Nancy, 36, 44
Jaffe, Harold, 223
James, William, 13
Jewish Daily Forward, as sociological
resource, 143–44
Johnson, James Weldon, 154
Johnson, Karl M., 36, 43, 45, 65, 262
*Journal of the American Academy of
Dermatology*, 220–22, 224–25
Journal of the American Medical Association (JAMA), 86, 109
Journal of the Plague Year, A, 11–12

Kael, Pauline, 206
Kaempffert, Waldemar, 163
Kaposi's sarcoma (KS), AIDS epidemic and appearance of, 220, 223–26
Kaufman, Philip, 161, 204–12
Kay, James Phillips, 115, 121
Kay, Lily E., 181
King, Stephen, 54–55, 318n.89
Koch, Robert, 75, 275n.37

Kramer, Larry, 225
Krause, Richard M., 30, 33–34, 40–42, 67
Kraut, Alan, 8, 97–98
Kyle, Stephen, 319n.93

laboratory research: AIDS outbreak
narratives and role of, 242–51; evolution of, 122
Ladies' Home Journal, 169–70
Langmuir, Alexander, 24, 277n.54
Lasch, Christopher, 204
Lassa fever, scientific attention to, 34–35
Last Man, The, 11–12
Last Man on Earth, The, 11–12, 200,
309n.105
Latour, Bruno, 56, 278n.55
Laurence, William L., 163, 170–71
Leavitt, Judith Walzer, 77–79, 97, 100,
106, 290n.64
Le Bon, Gustave, 132–38
Lederberg, Joshua, 29, 31, 280n.7,
280n.15; on competition between
humans and microbes, 260; ecological view of disease and, 39–42, 47,
67; on global health policies, 51
Lederle, Ernst J., 102
Lefebvre, Henri, 298n.69
Legters, Llewellyn J., 51
Leibowitch, Jacques, 239
Lévi-Strauss, Claude, 9
Lincoln, Bruce, 10, 260, 274n.27
Lindner, Rolf, 296n.44
Linked, 273n.23
Literary Digest, 75, 123
Living Age (periodical), 109
L'Opinion et la foule, 132–33,
296nn.47–49
Lowe, Lisa, 308n.95
Luria, Sylvester, 162, 181, 302n.14,
305n.65

lymphadenopathy, in AIDS patients, 227, 314n.37
Lynch, Patrick, 31, 37, 41, 46, 63, 282n.33

MacArthur, Douglas, 166, 169
Macphail, Andrew, 108–10
Mainwaring, Daniel, 199–200, 204
Mali, Joseph, 10, 274.n27
Mallon, Mary, 9–10, 22, 26–28, 57; class and sexual politics in accounts of, 84–94; as example of female mobility, 92–94; as healthy carrier model, 68–113; lawsuit filed by, 99–104, 291n.75; media images of, 101–11; surveillance and containment of, 111–13, 148
Manchuria, Cold War conflict in, 165
Manchurian Candidate, The, 190, 308n.89
maps: emerging disease research and role of, 44–45, 58, 284n.69; germ warfare and role of, 167–70; in sociological research, 128–29, 295n.34
Marburg virus, scientific focus on, 34–35
"Marginal Man, The," 153–56
Markel, Howard, 115
marriage, protection of social order through, 86–94
Martin, Emily, 172–74, 224
Marxist theory, social space and, 298n.69
Massey, Doreen, 298n.69
Matheson, Richard, 200–204, 274n.24, 309n.105
Matthews, Fred H., 296n.44
McCarthy, Joseph, 175–76, 178, 182–83
McCarthyism: The Fight for America, 182–83

McClure's magazine, 80
McLuhan, Marshall, 273n.16
McMichael, Tony, 40
McNeill, William H., 40, 47–50
Meader, F. M., 75–76, 286n.3
media role in outbreak narratives: AIDS epidemic coverage, 218–63; AIDS in healthcare workers and, 251–54; avian flu outbreak and, 268–70; And the Band Played On and, 216–17; brainwashing images and, 178–80; Cold War politics and, 175–80; disease detectives imagery and, 23–28; epidemiology language in AIDS narratives, 218–23; emerging-disease outbreaks dramatized by, 31; germ warfare theories and, 165–70; ghetto and tenement depictions by, 142–14; healthy carrier model and, 68, 75–76, 285n.2; immigrant spaces and Americanization and, 139–42; immunology role in AIDS research and, 223–26; origin theories on AIDS and, 234–42; "Patient 0" carrier figure in AIDS narratives, 226–30; popular images of epidemiology and, 20–23, 277n.54; sensationalist coverage of SARS outbreak, 3–9, 272nn.12–13, 273n.16; seventies generation and, 205–12; typhoid epidemiology and, 83–84; "Typhoid Mary" narrative and, 101–11; virology research coverage and, 158–61, 163–68, 170–80. See also science journalism
Medical Investigation, 281n.24
medicalized nativism: in media accounts of disease, 8, 273n.20; in "Typhoid Mary" story, 98–104
medical materialism, bacteriology and emergence of, 13
"medical police," German concept of, 18

memes, social contagion theory and, 293n.7

Mendelsohn, J. Andrew, 77–79

Meerloo, Joost, 178, 203

Meyerowitz, Joanne, 85, 289n.46

"Microbe as Social Leveller, The," 120–21

Microbe Hunters, 20, 171

microbial animation: in AIDS/HIV narratives, 215–17, 218–22; biopolitics discourse and metaphor of, 259–63; in nonfiction outbreak narratives, 42; in Typhoid Mary narrative, 88–94

microbial research: evolution of, 56; healthy carriers and, 69–70, 75–113; microbial geography, 119–24; traffic concept, 34, 37–39

middle-class women, negligent mother stereotype of, 107–8

military metaphors: AIDS epidemic narratives and, 225–26; in typhoid epidemiology, 82–84; virology research politics and, 170–80

Miller, Douglas T., 310nn.112–13

Miller, Herbert A., 149

Miller, Joaquin, 115

mimicry, in *Body Snatchers*, 192–99

Mobutu Sese Seko, 46

Monette, Paul, 217

Monster at Our Door, The, 269

Montagnier, Luc, 235, 243–51, 258–59

Moore, Oscar, 236, 256

moral contagion metaphor: AIDS origin theses and, 237–42; in public health research, 115–17. *See also* social contagion theory

"moral regions," Park's concept of, 141–42

Morbidity and Mortality Weekly Report (MMWR), 219–20, 233–35

Morrow, Lance, 213–14

Morrow, Prince Albert, 87–88

Morse, Stephen, 44, 67, 280nn.14–15

Mortimer, Philip, 19

motherhood, negligence in, as health threat, 107–11

Mountains Beyond Mountains, 265

mutuality of influence concept, ghetto models and, 155–56, 300n.96

My Lai massacre, 59, 284n.76

"mythistory," Mali's concept of, 10, 274n.27

myths and mysticism: in AIDS outbreak narratives, 216–57; definitions of, 9–10, 274n.27; in fiction and film outbreak narratives, 259–63; in outbreak narratives, 43–44, 54–67; scapegoat figures in, 17, 276n.42; in virology research, 159–61, 163–64, 170–80, 183–88, 301n.8, 303n.20

Naked Lunch, 184–86

Nation, The, 108–9

National Geographic, 82

National Institute of Allergy and Infectious Disease, 30

National Review, 233

nation as ecosystem, catastrophic epidemics and, 58–67

nativism: epidemics and growth of, 115; immunology research and, 127; typhoid epidemiology and politics of, 83–84

Naturalization Act of 1906, 83

nature: AIDS origins research and role of, 245–51; disease emergence and role of, 42–47

Nature magazine, 181

network theory: in AIDS outbreak narratives, 225–26; AIDS outbreak narratives and, 256–63; biology of

network theory (*cont.*)
community theory and, 138–42;
disease epidemics and, 9, 12, 17–18,
22–23, 273n.23; imagined communities and, 54–67; nation-building
and, 58–67
New England Journal of Medicine,
221–22, 235–36
*New Idea in Sanitation: The Great
Menace to Public Health that
Covers Every Mile of Railroad Track
in the United States and Other
Countries, A,* 123
New Republic magazine, 225–26
Newsweek magazine: AIDS coverage
in, 225–26; avian flu coverage in,
269; disease detectives coverage in,
23–24; SARS outbreak coverage in,
5–9, 274n.24
New Woman motif, role in public
health research, 108–9, 291n.84,
292n.85
New York American, 100–101
New Yorker magazine, 24–28, 31, 206,
277n.54; avian flu coverage in, 269
New York State Journal of Medicine,
75–76
New York Times: AIDS epidemic coverage in, 216, 221–30; on communism, 183; germ warfare coverage
in, 165–68; herd immunity discussed in, 126–28; SARS outbreak
coverage in, 3–5; "Typhoid Mary"
narratives in, 100–102, 105–7, 111;
virology research coverage in, 163,
180–81
Nichols, Henry J., 76–77, 83
Nimoy, Leonard, 210, 310n.117
Nixon, Richard, 225
nominalist theory, 136
"non-Californian" figure in AIDS narratives, 222–26

noncommunicable diseases, epi-
demiological research on, 25
Nova Express, 186
nuclear testing, germ warfare and,
167–70
Nurse Mayinga, 30–33, 43–44, 262
Oedipal complex, in *Totem and
Taboo,* 15–17
Oedipus Rex, plague narrative in, 11,
16–17, 262, 276n.42
Ogden, Darryl, 172–74
Old European Jewries, 145, 150,
299n.79
Oldstone, Michael B. A., 30, 47
Old World Traits Transplanted, 149
Omega Man, 309n.105, 310n.119
*On Contagion, Contagious Diseases,
and Their Treatment (De con-
tagione, contagiosis morbis et eorum
curatione),* 11
O'Neil, James F., 174–76
Oppenheimer, Gerald M., 277n.49
origin theories, for AIDS epidemic,
234–42, 245–51, 315nn.48–49
Oryx and Crake, 319n.93
Ostherr, Kirsten, 27, 160–61
Ouida (pseud.), 291n.84
Outbreak (film), 29, 31, 41, 43, 46;
biopolitics in, 59, 60–67, 284n.78,
285nn.82–84; disease detectives in,
36–39, 65–67; sacrifice motif in,
262; viral threat images in, 259
outbreak narratives: biopolitics in,
58–67; class and sexual politics in,
84–94, 96–107; Cold War politics
and virology research in, 158–61;
communal belonging ideology in,
47–53; evolution of, 1–3, 23–28;
global nature of emerging disease
and, 33–39, 265–70; healthy carrier
model in, 68–113; historical prece-

dents for, 10–11; of HIV/AIDS epidemic, 2, 6, 213–63; imagined communities concept in, 51–67; immunological ecosystems in, 47–53; institutions of power in, 58–67; laboratory research collaborations in AIDS narratives, 242–51; microbial agency as motif in, 42–43, 282nn.35–36; mythic struggle motif in, 39–47; in popular culture, 29; religious motifs in, 53–67; role of scapegoat in, 17, 276n.42; sacrifice motif in, 55–57; science fiction and role of, 27; stranger/carrier role in, 56–57; typhoid epidemiology and, 79–84; vengeful virus motif in, 45–47; visual technology employed in, 36–39

Outlook magazine, 104–5

Page, Walter, 90, 289n.45
Panem, Sandra, 231–32
Parents' Magazine, 24–25
Park, Robert E., 26–27, 116–17, 289n.41, 293n.12, 295nn.34–35; biology of community theory of, 138–42; containment model of, 300n.96; on fiction as sociology, 143, 300n.85; hybridity concept of, 196–99; race relations cycle concept, 297n.64; social contagion theory and, 116–19, 131–38, 164, 296n.50; sociology research and, 128–32, 196–99, 296n.44; spatial transformation research of, 140–42, 298n.69; urban sociology and, 132–38, 296n.54; Wirth's collaboration with, 150–56
Park, William H., 93–95, 98–99, 126–27
Pasteur, Louis, 75, 275n.37
Pathologies of Power, 264–65

"Patient Zero" (AIDS carrier): AIDS in healthcare professionals and metaphor of, 251–54; AIDS outbreak narrative and, 11, 215–18, 223–42; media focus on, 226–30, 254–63, 314n.34
Paton, Alan, 194, 197–98
Patton, Cindy, 172–74, 224, 244, 301n.4
Pavlov, Ivan Petrovich, 308n.89
Peiss, Kathy, 289n.46
Pennsylvania Medical Journal, 110–11
personal responsibility: AIDS outbreak narratives and role of, 247–51; epidemics and role of, 59–67; healthy carrier model and cult of, 78–113; Home Economics Movement and, 107–11; immunology research and role of, 128; seventies generation and, 205–6, 310n.113; social order and responsibilities of, 86–94
personhood, healthy carrier model and concept of, 78–113
Persons, Stow, 154
Petersen, Wolfgang, 29, 31
Philadelphia, 217, 314n.40
Philipson, David, 145, 150, 299n.79, 300n.87
phorology: healthy carrier model and, 76–77; tyhpoid epidemiology and, 79–84
Plague On Us, 20–23
plagues, historical accounts of, 11–20
Plagues and Peoples, 47–53
Pneumocystis pneumonia (PCP), AIDS epidemic and appearance of, 219–20, 223–26
Pogge, Thomas, 265
polio vaccine, virology research and, 162

political theory: AIDS epidemic and, 216–17; contagion and role of, 27; imagined communities principle and, 52–53; *Invasion of the Body Snatchers* and, 199–204; seventies generation disillusionment and, 205–12

political transformation, emerging infections and, 30–33

Poovey, Mary, 115, 117

Popular Science Monthly, 124

population change: benefits of, 56–57; communicable disease impact on, 49–53

poverty: cultural constructions of, 8–9; disease outbreaks and role of, 264–70; emerging disease research and role of, 44–47

power: biopolitics and, 18, 264–65, 277n.47; epidemics and role of, 58–67; germ theories of history and role of, 50–53

predator metaphor, for infectious disease microbes, 42, 282nn.35–36

Preston, Richard, 31, 34–36, 256, 280n.7, 281n.17; global interconnectedness of disease and, 44–45, 67; on mythical aspects of disease, 43–44, 55–56, 262; predator metaphor used by, 42–43; racial metaphors in work of, 235–36

preventive medicine: healthy carriers and role of, 74–79; immunology research and growth of, 124–28

Primer of Sanitation, 73–74

Production of Antibodies, The, 173

prostitution: female mobility and, 87–94, 289n.43, 289n.46; as motif in "Typhoid Mary" narratives, 85–94

"Protection of Freedom, The," 179

public health movement: class politics of, 24; epidemics and growth of,

17–18, 115–16; gender roles and stereotypes in research on, 108–11; germ warfare and, 166–70; healthy carriers and role of, 16, 26, 69–79, 275n.41; immigrants and, 97–104, 115, 122–24, 127–28; immunology research and, 124–28; microbial geography and, 119–24; social management by, 14; surveillance and containment strategies in, 111–13; "Typhoid Mary" narratives and power of, 99–104; venereal disease education in, 87–88

Punch, 101

quarantines: ghettoization and, 143–56, 299n.80; immunology research and role of, 127–28; microbial geography theory and, 119–24

Quastler, Henry, 182

Queer, 197, 214–15

racial identity: *Body Snatchers* and backdrop of, 194–99; hybridity theory and, 195–99; "marginal man" metaphor and, 154–56; origin theories for AIDS and, 235–42; "Patient Zero" metaphor and, 216; race relations cycle, Park's concept of, 297n.64; race suicide in outbreak narratives, 110–11, 241–42; typhoid epidemiology and bias involving, 80–84; virology and role of, 195–99, 260–63

railroads, as public health risk, 122–24

Rainbow Six, 319n.93

Rape of the Mind, The, 178

Rask, Grethe, 239

Rats, Lice and History, 47

Reader's Digest, 24–25, 27

Rebel Without a Cause, 204

Red Fleet, 166, 169

Red Nightmare, 63, 176, 201–2, 305n.54

religion: communicable disease associations with, 13–15, 21–22; imagined community in outbreak narratives and, 53–67; virology research and, 163–64

Rent, 217

reproductive politics, AIDS narratives and, 316n.64

research funding, outbreak narratives as spur for increases in, 36

Resident Evil, 257, 274n.24, 318n.88

resistance, immunology research and concept of, 125

Restless Tide: The Persistent Challenge of the Microbial World, The, 30, 40–41, 282 n.35

retrovirus research, AIDS epidemic and evolution of, 213–14, 310n.2

Riis, Jacob, 114–18, 120–21, 128, 144

Rise of David Levinsky, The, 149

Roach, Mary, 285n.84

Rockefeller Institute for Medical Research, 124

Rockefeller University, 30

Rom, Mark Carl, 253

Roosevelt, Theodore, 110, 292n.90

Rosen, George, 11, 17–18, 23, 277nn.47–48

Rosen, Ruth, 85, 91

Rosenau, Milton J., 98–99, 290n.64

Rosenberg, Ethel, 175

Rosenberg, Julius, 175

Ross, Andrew, 160–61

Ross, Dorothy, 295n.34

Ross, E. A., 72, 97, 113, 129, 139

Roueché, Berton, 24–25, 277n.54, 278nn.58–59, 286n.3

Rucker, W. C., 126

Sabatier, Renée, 236, 315n.53

sacrifice motif in outbreak narratives, 55–57, 262–63

Sagan, Carl, 310n.118

St. Petersburg Times, 238

Salk, Jonas, 162, 244

sanitation policies: healthy carrier impact on, 72–79; microbial geography theory and, 121–24; "Typhoid Mary" and role of, 142

Saturday Review, 180

Schell, Heather, 19–20

Schell, Jonathan, 205

science: AIDS epidemic and role of, 216–17, 223–26, 242–51; biopolitics and, 64–67; Cold War politics and, 159–64; contagion theory and role of, 27; fictional distortions of, 41–42, 282n.33; mystical metaphors in outbreak narratives about, 55–67; in outbreak narratives, 258–63; professionalization of homemaking as, 107–11; virology and authority of, 158, 301n.4

Science Digest, 180

science fiction: AIDS outbreak narratives and, 256–63, 318n.88; outbreak narratives in, 27, 41–42; virology research and images of, 163, 303n.20

science journalism, outbreak narratives in, 31–33; microbe research and, 13–15, 19–20, 42–43; virology research and, 161–64, 180–88

Science magazine, 42, 75, 180, 253–54

Science News Letter, 158, 170–71

Scientific American, 75, 163–64, 180, 235, 242–44, 253, 259

scientific authority: legal acceptance of, 100–101; reaffirmation of, in AIDS epidemic, 242–51

Seed, David, 190, 308n.88

Sen, Amartya, 259–60

sensationalism in outbreak narratives, 35–39

severe acute respiratory syndrome (SARS): outbreak narratives about, 1, 3–9, 271n.5, 272nn.12–13, 273n.16, 274n.24; "superspreaders" myth concerning, 3–5

sexism, in outbreak narratives, "Typhoid Mary" as example of, 97–104

sexuality: in AIDS outbreak narratives, 219–22, 225–26, 254–63; cleanliness rituals and, 17; race and, 195, 309n.98; role in public health research, 108–9, 292n.85; "Typhoid Mary" story and role of, 84–94, 97–104, 289n.43

Shah, Nayan, 115

Shelley, Mary, 11–12

Shilts, Randy, 215–18, 230–43, 254–56, 315n.45

Shope, Robert E., 280n.15

Shoumatoff, Alex, 240–42, 256, 315n.48

Siegal, Frederick P., 222

Siegel, Don, 199–204, 207

Simmel, Georg, 130, 139–40, 153, 160, 261

Sister Carrie, 90–91, 289n.45

Small, Albion, 129, 133

smallpox: anti-Chinese bias linked to outbreaks of, 115; global eradication of, 25, 29–30

Smallpox 2002: Silent Weapon, 319n.93

Smith, Geddes, 20–23, 49, 51, 58

Smith-Rosenberg, Carroll, 108, 291n.84

Sobchack, Vivian, 201

social contagion theory, 26–27; Burroughs's critique of, 184–88; cultural aspects of, 132–38; emergence of, 111–13, 116; ghettoization and, 144–49, 299n.79; Park's contributions to, 116–19, 131–38

social control/social order: AIDS epidemic as threat to, 216–17; brainwashing as tool for, 178–79; disease prevention as preservation of, 121–24; epidemics as threat to, 58–67; female sexuality as threat to, 85–94; healthy carrier narratives and, 71–79, 111–13; mimicry and hybridity and, 195–99; plagues and collapse of, 11–12; Ross's concept of, 72, 97, 113, 129, 139; sociological research and theories of, 129–32; theories on origins of, 14–17

Social Diseases and Marriage, 87

social-network theory: in AIDS outbreak narratives, 225–26; AIDS outbreak narratives and, 256–63; biology of community theory and, 138–42; disease epidemics and, 9, 12, 17–18, 22–23, 273n.23; imagined communities and, 54–67; nation-building and, 58–67

"Social Significance of the Stranger, The," 154

Sociologie, 140

sociology: AIDS outbreak narratives and role of, 248–51; biopolitics and, 277n.47; communicable disease management and role of, 14; emerging infections and, 30–33; health carrier and, 72–79; HIV/AIDS epidemic impact on, 217, 224–26; microbial geography, 119–24; scientific aspects of, 128–31; social contagion theory and evolution of, 114–19; viral traffic concept and role of, 280n.14. *See also* University of Chicago; urban sociology

"sociopathic illness" metaphor: AIDS epidemic narratives and, 236; in *Blood Artists*, 258–61

Soft Machine, The, 186

I gratefully acknowledge all of the following for permission to reprint previously published work. A version of chapter 1 appeared as "Imagined Immunities" in *Cultural Studies and Political Theory*, edited by Jodi Dean (Cornell University Press, 2000). An earlier version of chapter 2 was published as "Cultures and Carriers: 'Typhoid Mary' and the Science of Social Control," in *Queer Transexions of Race, Nation, and Gender*, a special issue of *Social Text* edited by Phillip Brian Harper, Anne McClintock, José Esteban Muñoz, and Trish Rosen (vols. 52–53, December 1997, Duke University Press). A version of chapter 3 was first published as "Geographics: Writing the Shtetl into the Ghetto" in *Revista Canaria de Estudios Ingleses* (November 1999) and then revised as "Communicable Americanism: Contagion, Geographic Fictions, and the Sociological Legacy of Robert E. Park" for *Culture and Contagion*, a special issue of *American Literary History* edited by Priscilla Wald, Nancy Tomes, and Lisa Lynch (vol. 14.4, 2002, Oxford University Press).

PRISCILLA WALD

is a professor of English at Duke University

and the editor of *American Literature*. She is the author

of *Constituting Americans: Cultural Anxiety and*

Narrative Form (Duke University Press, 1995).

Library of Congress Cataloging-in-Publication Data
Wald, Priscilla.
Contagious : cultures, carriers, and
the outbreak narrative / Priscilla Wald.
p. ; cm.
"A John Hope Franklin Center book."
Includes bibliographical references and index.
ISBN 978-0-8223-4128-4 (cloth : alk. paper)
ISBN 978-0-8223-4153-6 (pbk. : alk. paper)
1. Epidemics—History. 2. Emerging infectious diseases
—History. I. Title. [DNLM: 1. Communicable Diseases,
Emerging—history. 2. Disease Outbreaks—history.
3. Carrier State. 4. Communications Media—history.
5. Disease Transmission—history. 6. Health Knowledge,
Attitudes, Practice. 7. History, 20th Century. 8. History,
21st Century. WA 11.1 W157C 2007]
RA649.W25 2007
614.4—dc22   2007029318

CPSIA information can be obtained
at www.ICGtesting.com
Printed in the USA
BVHW090730220121
598325BV00004B/442